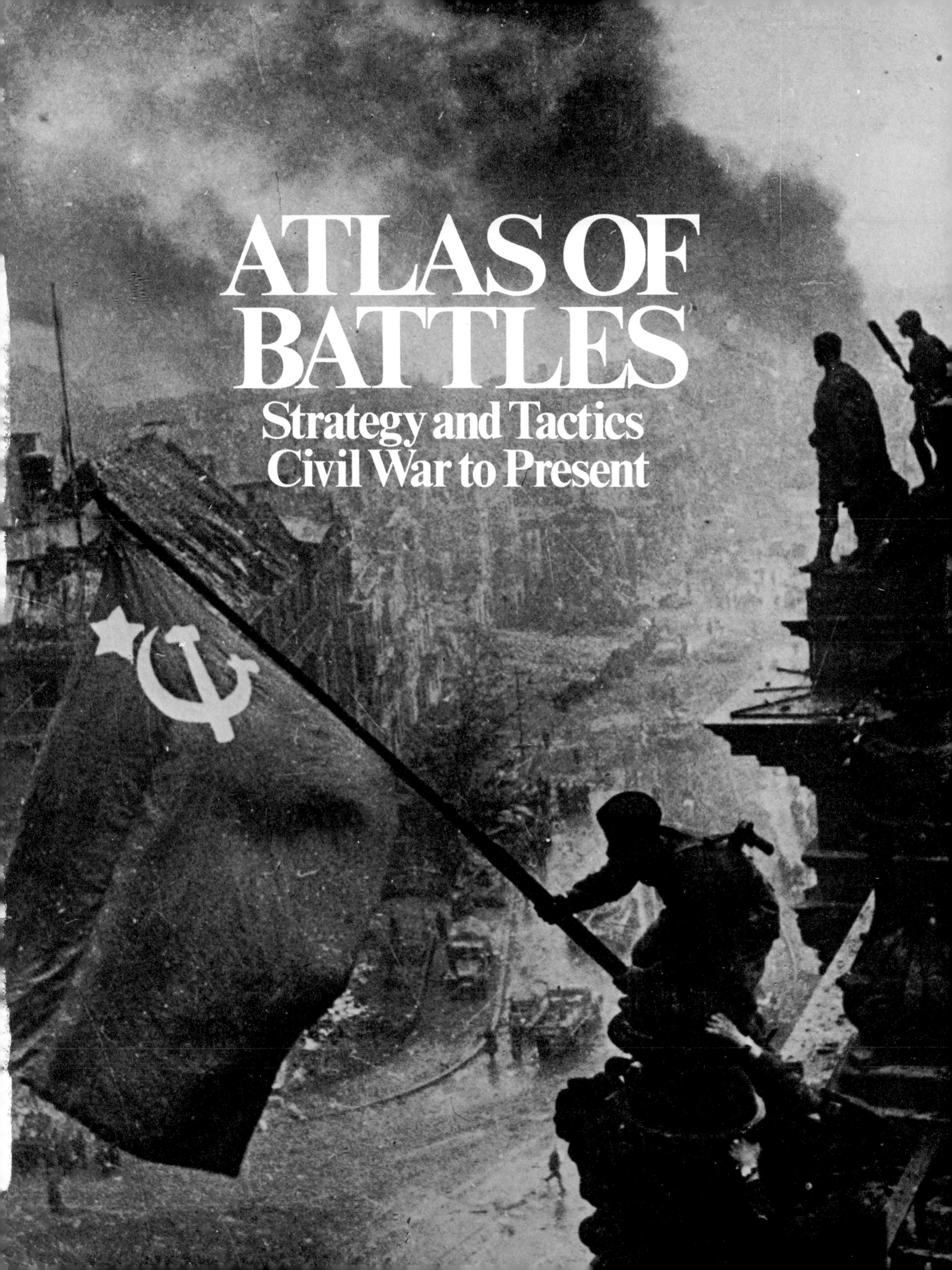

ATLAS OF BATTLES

Strategy and Tactics Civil War to Present

ATLAS OF BATTLES

Strategy and Tactics Civil War to Present

Richard Natkiel

Text by S.L.Mayer & Robin Sommer

THE MILITARY PRESS

Distributed by Crown Publishers Inc.
New York

A Bison Book

Contents

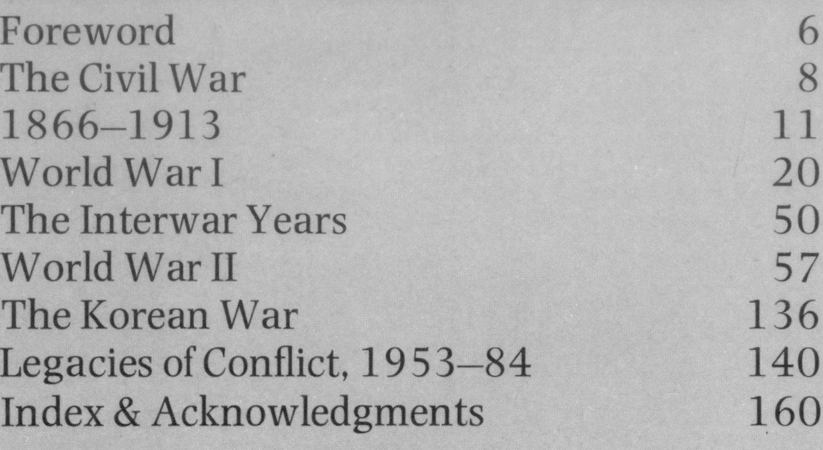

This edition is Published by
The Military Press, distributed by
Crown Publishers Inc.

Produced by
Bison Books Corp
17 Sherwood Place
Greenwich
CT 06830
USA

Printed in Hong Kong

ISBN 0-517-44286-8

Library of Congress Catalog Card Number 84-60738

Page 1 : Soviet soldiers hoist the Victory banner over the Reichstag, 2 May 1945.
Page 2–3 : A devastated area near Ypres in 1918.
This page : An Israeli armored corps of Centurion tanks standing by in the Negev, on the eve of the 1967 War, 20 May 1967.

Foreword by S L Mayer

The period from the American Civil War to the present is scarcely more than a hundred years, yet the character of both war and civilization has altered remarkably. The age of Abraham Lincoln and the Confederacy, of Napoleon III and Bismarck, seems far more than a century away from that of computer technology and space exploration, but in one sense the earlier age gave a foretaste of the world to come – in the way wars were fought. Throughout the 19th century a battle raged at centers of military science from West Point to Sandhurst, from St Cyr to the secret office of Baron Friedrich von Holstein, over the conduct of warfare. Members of the old school, whose students included Robert E Lee and Napoleon III, believed that war was to be fought among and by professionals, mercenaries if possible, and if not, then among long-serving career soldiers at both the officer and NCO levels. Others, like Generals Helmuth von Moltke and Ulysses S Grant, believed in the mass army, composed largely of conscripts, two to three times the size of the adversary's, led by professional officer corps and winning short wars by brute strength, speed and *force majeure*. If war was the ultimate instrument of national policy, they thought, then carry out that policy quickly so as not to sap a nation's strength and, incidentally, save lives on both sides.

The American Civil War was more than a struggle between Lee and Grant and their contending philosophies, of course, but it was neither swift nor bloodless. Lincoln believed that as long as the Confederacy survived, the war must continue; the result was the development of static warfare along the front in Virginia and in other areas, such as Vicksburg, where siege conditions seemed appropriate. The South knew that if it could survive, and not capitulate, the Union would inevitably weary of a no-victory, no-defeat policy and, under pressure from its civilians, accept a compromise that would be tantamount to defeat. The origin of modern warfare can be seen in this titanic struggle, with the Confederacy playing for time with its soldiers' lives and its civilians' homes, while the Union sought to overwhelm it by superior numbers, railroad facilities, industrial might and naval power. The result was inevitable, but the cost was high. More Americans lost their lives in the Civil War than in any conflict before or since. The age of both trench warfare and total warfare, involving whole populations rather than armies alone, had begun.

Helmuth von Moltke, ever prepared for every contingency, saw the fighting at Gettysburg and learned his lessons well. In short wars against Denmark in 1864, Austria in 1866 and France in 1870, he proved that mass armies can prevent static warfare by swift and sudden victory – a lesson not lost on the Afrikaners who fought two wars of national survival, not dissimilar to the role of the American South, in the 1880s and again in the Boer War at the turn of the century. Pitted against the might of the British Empire, the citizen-army of the Orange Free State and Transvaal adopted siege tactics, trench warfare and guerrilla warfare to retain their independence. Although eventually overwhelmed after three years of conflict, they sent an unspoken signal to Europe and the world that went largely unheeded by the generals who planned World War I. Their example showed that weak opponents must be swiftly overwhelmed: if not, long wars involving mass armies and whole populations would be the result. So would huge numbers of casualties.

The Europe of 1914 embarked upon World War I expecting quite another thing, a short war involving merely professional armies. The result was the destruction of three of the six major nations which began the war, Austria-Hungary, Imperial Germany and Imperial Russia, and the loss of tens of millions of lives. A war of movement, which began the conflict, soon slowed to a war of deadly inches, with victories measured by the yard, and thousands of lives paid for each foot of territory won. By 1918 northern France was devastated, the whole world was dragged into the struggle and a durable peace was not achieved. The lessons that should have been learned from the Civil War and the Boer War were dearly bought, and the price in lives and wrecked civilizations was too high for anyone, it was thought, to dream of attempting war again.

This fear of another bloodbath like the First World War helped to create the Second. Those who dreamed of war, like Hitler and Mussolini, thought only in terms of lightning-like attacks, swift enemy capitulations and small casualties – war on the cheap. Those who prayed for peace believed that almost no price was too high, which explains why men like Daladier and Chamberlain were prepared to sacrifice nations like Czechoslovakia to avoid another war – and were praised at the time by their fellow citizens. When war did break out in 1939, it was a halfhearted affair. Hitler overwhelmed Poland in less than a month; then not much of anything happened for another six months, as Germany sought a truce. The Russo-Finnish War lasted four months, the attack on Denmark and Norway a few weeks. The fall of the Low Countries and France took six weeks. After each triumph a formal peace was sought, but Britain was unwilling to acquiesce to a Nazi-dominated Europe. When Germany aided its Italian ally in North Africa, a limited war was sought and achieved, principally due to the terrain, as conflict could take place only along the Mediterranean coast. Only when mass armies were involved for long periods, as in Germany's invasion of Russia in 1941, did the war reach the casualty levels of the Great War. Even then, Hitler hoped for a swift victory, but the Soviet Union could sell space to gain time, and another chapter in the history of total war, involving whole populations and mass armies, was written.

Above: Union and Confederate dead at Gettysburg. The Confederates lost over 30,000 in the battle.
Right: The T-34 'Vladimir Mayakovski' in Berlin in April 1945.

Similarly, in the Pacific, Japan sought a swift and complete victory by surprising the United States at Pearl Harbor in December 1941. Failing to achieve total naval victory at the Coral Sea and Midway, a long, drawn-out slogging match across the Pacific island chains was the result. Another inevitable result of the long war was the utter destruction of the nations which began it in the hope of cheap victory: Germany and Japan. In the end there were no victors save the United States, spared the agony of war on its own territory by its vast ocean moat. The Soviet Union lost over 20 million; Germany lost over 10 percent of its population, its empire, over a third of its territory and its unity. Japan lost its empire, its conquests and colonies, millions of combatants and civilians alike. Its cities were ruined, its economy a shambles, and Japan was occupied by foreign troops for six years. Static war, the pattern from the Civil War through World War I, gave way to sweeping broad-scale conflicts that involved as many civilian deaths as men in the field. The age of total warfare had begun.

The reaction to World War II was not unlike the global reaction to its predecessor, except that this time atomic conflagration was the great fear. Large-scale war was to be avoided at all costs. The result was a series of limited wars involving no more than one super-power, many fought by proxies of the great powers, the USA and the USSR. The Suez War was one example; the Vietnam and Korean Wars two more. No major nation has dared to cross the threshold of all-out war since 1945, for fear of destroying not merely its own population, but that of the world. Limited war meant wars largely of attrition, with siege and guerrilla tactics replacing the sweeping movements of mass armies of previous centuries.

The development of modern warfare, and the strategy and tactics which accompanied these changes, are shown in the unique and brilliant cartography of Richard Natkiel, whose maps are the principal illustrations in this *Atlas of Battles*. Richard Natkiel began his map-making career during World War II. After World War II he joined the staff of *The Economist*, the weekly world newspaper produced in London, where for many years he has been chief cartographer. His dynamic style makes for both clarity and precision. The *Atlas of Battles* which he has produced will prove to be an invaluable tool for the student of history, military strategy and tactics, and all those fascinated by the great cataclysms which have shaped our times.

The Civil War (Vicksburg and Gettysburg)

The American Civil War was fought on five fronts. On the diplomatic front the Confederacy managed to gain tacit support from Britain and France during the first two years of the conflict, which brought them munitions, a French invasion of Mexico, border clashes between the United States and Canada, and financial assistance which proved vital while the military lines of battle remained stationary. On the economic front the Union mobilized its rail network and industrial machine, always far superior to that of the Confederacy. Although slow to organize, it was to play a critical role in the Union victory. On the naval front the small Union Navy attempted a blockade of Southern ports, which was not always successful, and by 1863 Union forces were slowly forging up the Mississippi in order to split the South in two. But the two main fronts, shown on the general map here, were in Virginia, where the conflict was fought to a stalemate throughout most of the war, and in the West, where Union forces under General Ulysses S Grant attempted to drive a wedge between the two halves of the Confederacy by taking the fortress of Vicksburg on the Mississippi.

The culmination of the first and perhaps most dramatic act of the Civil War was at Vicksburg. As Farragut's Navy made its way up the Mississippi, Grant's troops moved down it. Blocking the way was the fortress of Vicksburg, which commanded the river. The South could not be split asunder unless Vicksburg fell into Union hands. No further penetration of the South could ever have been secure with a major fort, held by an enemy army, remaining behind Union lines. Taking the fortress, however, proved a lesson in trench warfare which the military historians of the day were slow to learn. In co-ordination with Admiral Farragut, Grant managed to gain control of the river and from April to mid-May sent his troops down the west bank of the Mississippi, crossing it at Bruinsburg on 30 April. His forces then proceeded under William T Sherman to Jackson, far to the east, and in taking it forced the last Confederate reinforcements northward on 14 May. The Union forces,

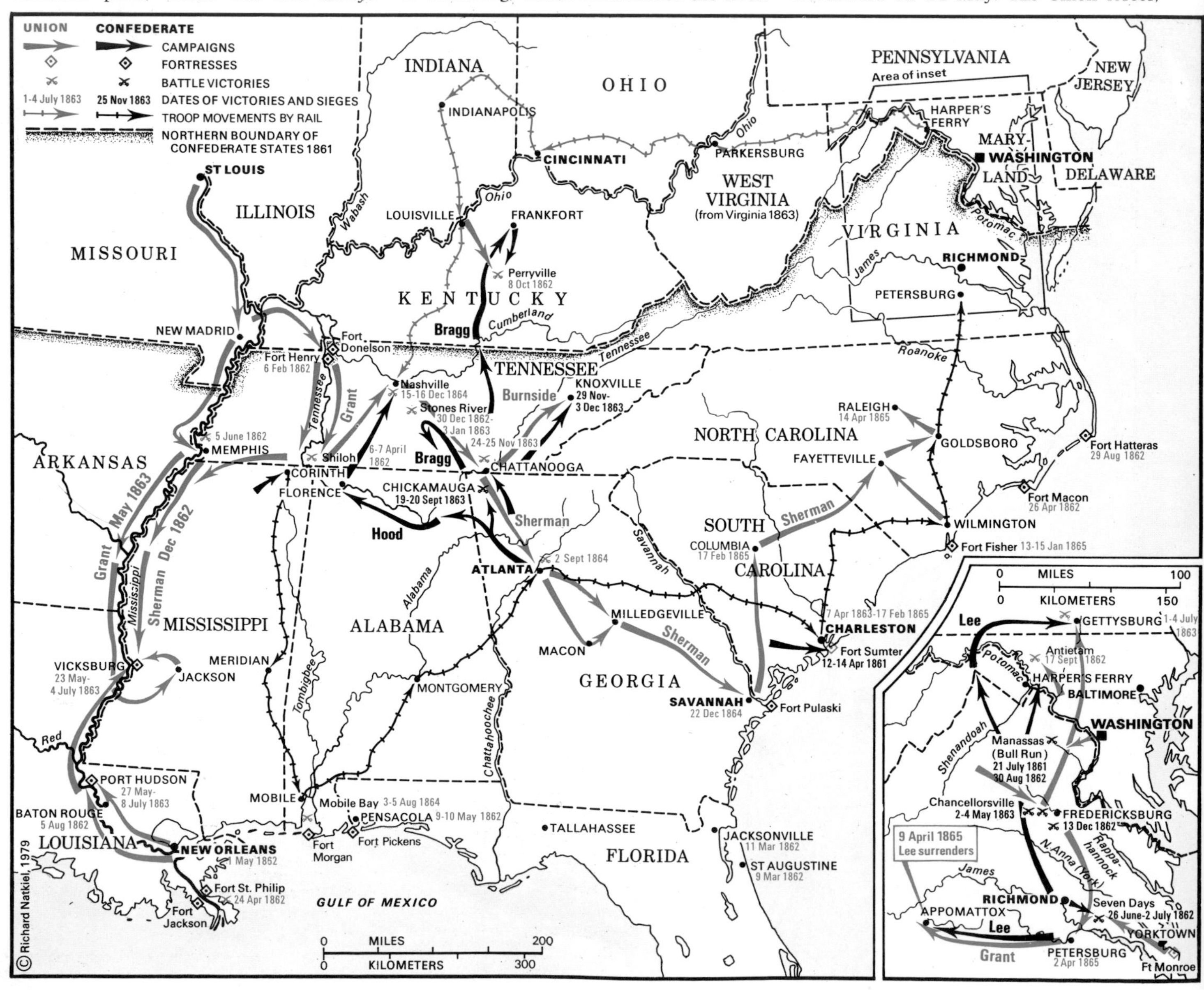

Below left: The major campaigns of the Civil War showing the North's strategy of splitting the Confederacy and the series of battles which held Lee's Army of Northern Virginia away from Washington.
Below: The intricate maneuvers in the siege of Vicksburg.

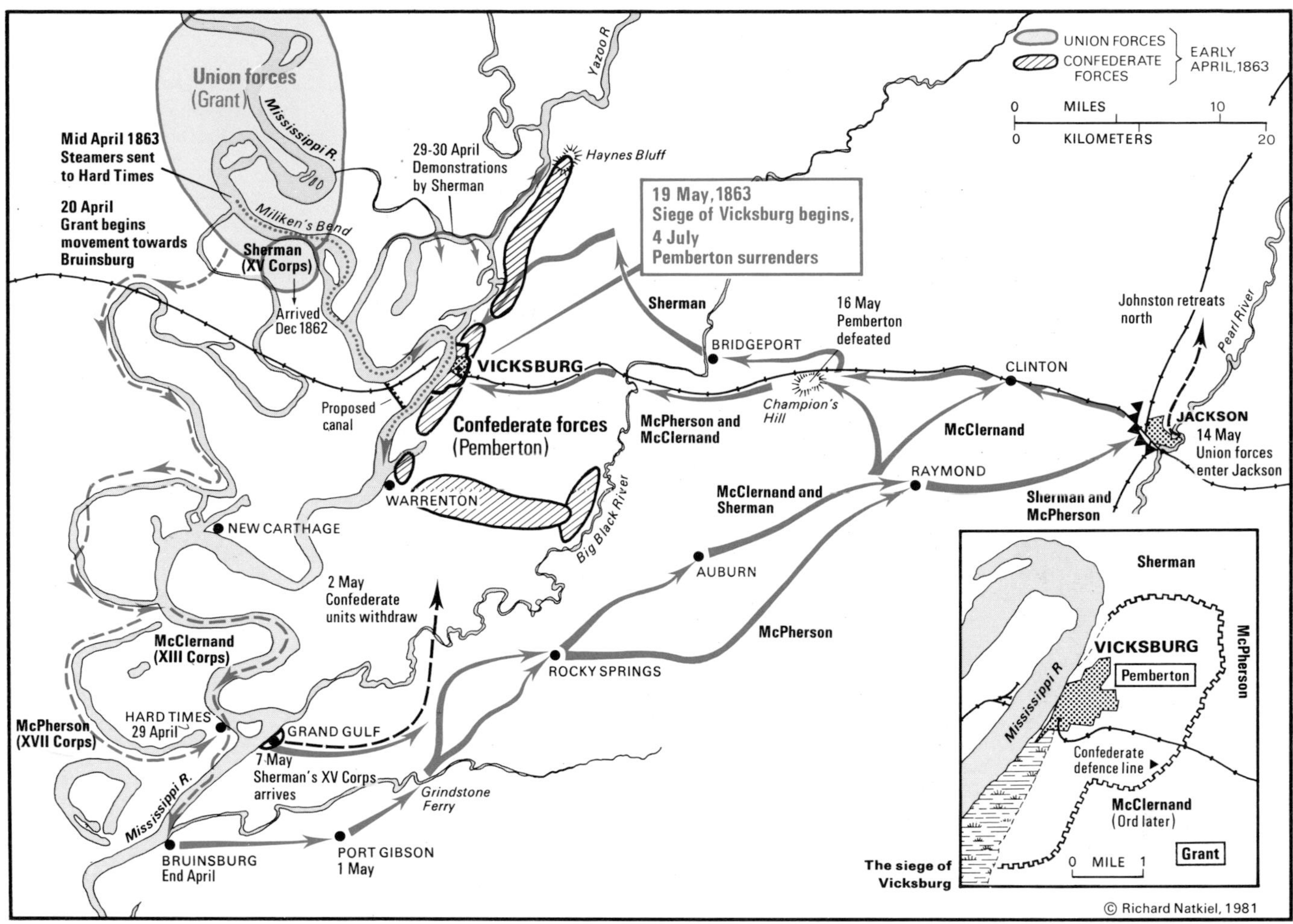

unencumbered by the enemy, moved due west toward Vicksburg and began laying siege to the fortress on 19 May. No hope of relief in sight, the Confederates dug in for a classic siege, which moved inexorably, trench by trench, barrage for barrage, until Grant, Sherman, McClernand and McPherson reached the hills around the fortress. Unable to take it by storm, Lieutenant-General John Pemberton withdrew all his forces from the periphery. Having been stationed at Vicksburg for a year, Pemberton and his chief engineer, Colonel H S Lockett, had cleared the commanding ground around the city of undergrowth and had replaced it with a series of redans, lunettes, redoubts and other field fortifications, connected by rifle pits and trenches. The siege went on for six weeks, the Union soldiers baking under the Southern sun in dusty trenches, dirty, unable to wash, parched with thirst. The situation within Vicksburg was, if anything, worse. Food was scarce. Flour was replaced by ground peas and cornmeal. Roast rat and mule stew became sought-after delicacies. Rebel soldiers soon became so weak they could not do more than stay awake at their posts. Pemberton reluctantly chose the course of surrender on 2 July, and on 4 July 1863 Grant marched into Vicksburg, as 30,000 Rebels surrendered with 172 artillery pieces and 60,000 small arms, many of them recently smuggled in from Britain. These were losses the Confederacy could ill afford. The Union now controlled the entire length of the Mississippi and the South was divided in two. The long march toward Georgia and ultimate victory could now begin.

While the siege of Vicksburg was going on, action on the fifth and perhaps most vital front of the war, the Eastern Front, concentrating on northern Virginia between Washington and Richmond, reached a climax. Rightly described as 'the greatest battle ever fought on the American continent,' it was the one and only successful attempt by the South to cross the Mason-Dixon Line. In May 1863 General Robert E Lee defeated 'Fighting Joe' Hooker at Chancellorsville, a battle in which Lee's ablest lieutenant, 'Stonewall' Jackson, was accidentally killed. Lee's plan to invade the North was a counterpoise to Grant's victories in the Western campaigns. He felt that another defeat at his hands would weaken the Union's resolve to continue the war and would increase the Confederacy's chances of gaining diplomatic recognition by Britain and France. The promise of acquiring much-needed supplies in the North was an added incentive.

Lee moved his outnumbered and outgunned forces northward, followed by the Union troops, who were always careful to place themselves between Lee and Washington, which they were pledged to protect from capture. As the Union troops moved northward, Lincoln replaced Hooker by Major-General George Meade, as Lee's forces moved west of Gettysburg. Meade moved his troops to the heights of Cemetery Ridge

Right: The Battle of Gettysburg.

south of the town on 1 July. In the three days of battle which ensued, Lee's forces under Longstreet attacked Union positions (the most foolhardy and glorious effort was General George Pickett's cavalry charge) in an attempt to break through Union lines on 3 July. Although Lee's troops in the field actually outnumbered Meade's, the Union had reinforcements at the ready, and a long struggle would have spelled the end of the Army of Northern Virginia. Failing to break through the Union lines, and in the face of increasingly heavy artillery barrages, the Rebel leader chose to withdraw on the very day that Vicksburg fell, 4 July 1863. His retreat could have turned into a rout, as his beleaguered and fatigued units moved southward through Maryland, crossing the Potomac north of Washington, but Meade chose not to pursue him. Gettysburg was viewed at the time as a major defeat for the Confederacy. Lee recognized the battle for what it was, an unmitigated disaster, and offered his resignation to Confederate President Jefferson Davis, who wisely refused to accept it.

Not only had the combined losses of Vicksburg and Gettysburg been military defeats in the ordinary sense: they had spelled the beginning of the end of the Civil War. Whatever confidence had been placed overseas in the Confederacy prior to July 1863 quickly melted away. Lee realized that of the five fronts involved, the war had already been lost on the economic and naval fronts. These two battles made certain that on the diplomatic and Western fronts, the war had been effectively lost, too. All that remained was for Lee to hold out in northern Virginia for as long as he could, which, because of Union strategy, including a scorched-earth policy in Georgia, took almost two more years. The Southern strategy should have been to hold out against the Union as long as possible in the hope that the Northern will to fight would flag. As a result of these two battles, the Union will to continue the war strengthened. Before Vicksburg and Gettysburg the Confederacy stood a reasonable chance to win the war simply by remaining in the field. After July 1863 all chances had been dissipated. In early July the war came to Gettysburg because all the roads led there. After the battle, all roads led to Appomattox.

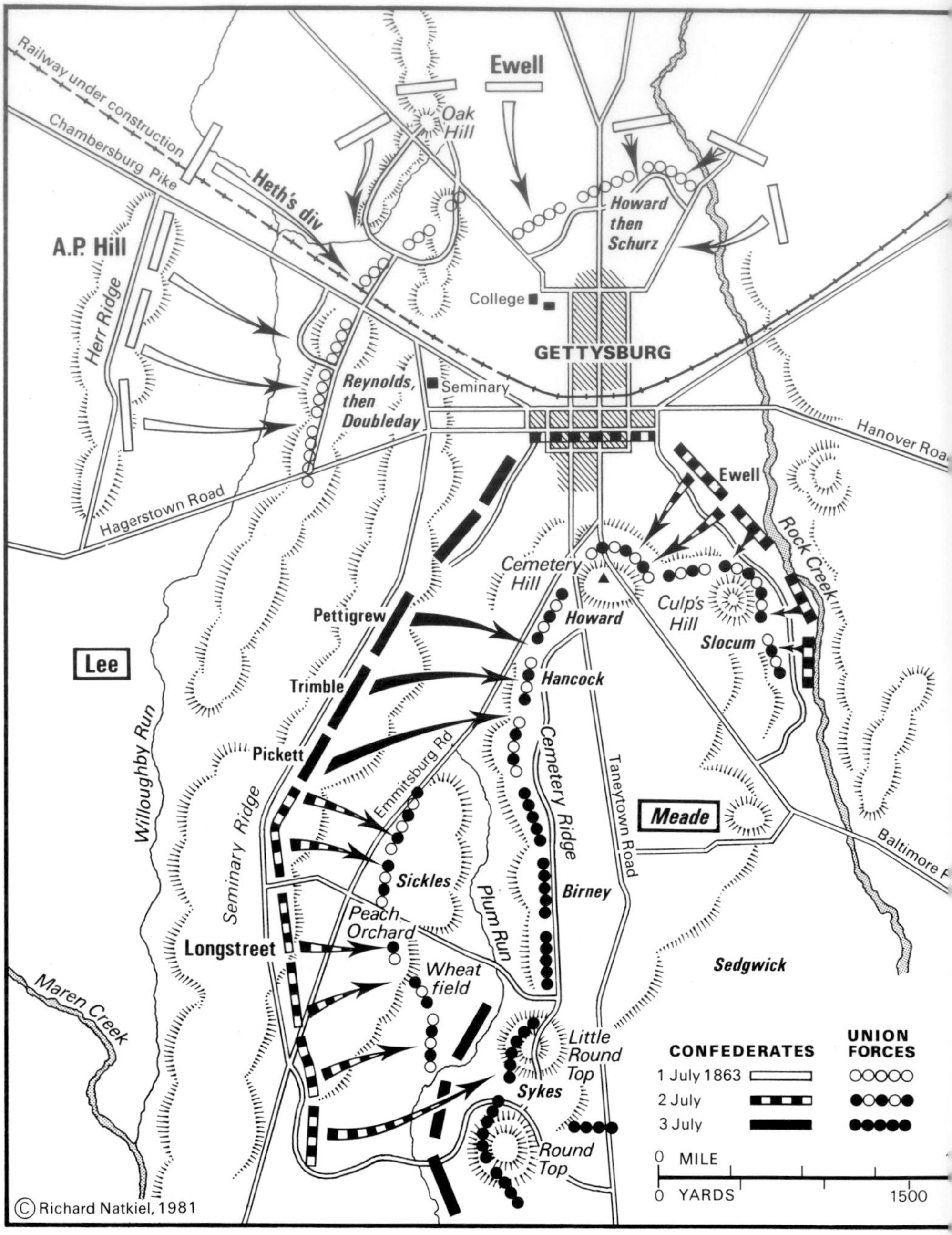

Königgrätz

The battle of Königgrätz was, in one sense, a triumph of the theory of the mass army over the smaller, professional army. Ever since Napoleon it had been thought that conscript troops, because of their lack of professionalism, could not be trusted. Most of the European armies opted for the cheaper, more comfortable formula. When Count Otto von Bismarck became Chancellor of Prussia in 1862, he set upon his grand design to unify Germany. First on his list was Schleswig-Holstein, which his forces seized from Denmark in 1864 in a short war. But control of southern Germany, largely Catholic and supportive of Austria's Hapsburg monarchy, was to be a more difficult matter. The Hapsburg monarch, Franz Josef, was head of the German Confederation, the post-1815 reconstruct of the Holy Roman Empire which the Hapsburg had also led, a ramshackle group of states in which Prussia was a junior partner. Bismarck hoped to destroy the Confederation, placing all the German-speaking states apart from Austria under Prussian leadership. Austria faced a dual problem, as Lombardy and Venetia were under her control, but were sought by an expanding Italian state which hoped to bring all Italian-speaking people under its flag. When Austria began her mobilization in April 1866, Prussia took no action until the third week in May, by which time Austria was able to mobilize some 320,000 men. But one-third of these had to be placed on the Italian front to protect the southern provinces. Helmuth von Moltke, Chief of Staff of the Prussian Army, mobilized 350,000 men rapidly, all of whom could be placed against Austrian forces.

King Wilhelm I of Prussia lacked confidence in von Moltke, who was forced to rush his troops to battle by train in early June. Austria's allies, Hanover and Hesse, were quickly overrun, and the Prussians invaded Saxony. The Saxon Army fell back into Bohemia to join the Austrian force, led by Feldzeugmeister Ludwig August von Benedek. As the Prussians moved forward Benedek realized that his forces could not be effectively concentrated quickly enough, and asked the Austrian Emperor to sue for peace at all costs. This request was ignored, and Benedek felt he could defend in the hills around Königgrätz: the Prussian First Army faced his defenses across the River Bistritz. He was unaware that the Second Army was crossing the Elbe to his rear. On 3 July the two armies surrounded the Austrians and attacked. By that afternoon the Austrian position was hopeless and the remnants of Benedek's army were allowed to retreat. The conscripts, employing the breech-loading 'needle' gun, proved courageous and steady. The Prussians lost only 9000 casualties, of whom less than 2000 were killed. The Austrians lost almost 43,000, of whom almost 6000 were killed. There were additional Saxon casualties. Bismarck quickly sued for peace, and Austria agreed to the dissolution of the German Confederation. A North German Confederation was formed under Prussian leadership. The second step in Bismarck's grand strategy for the unification of Germany had been completed.

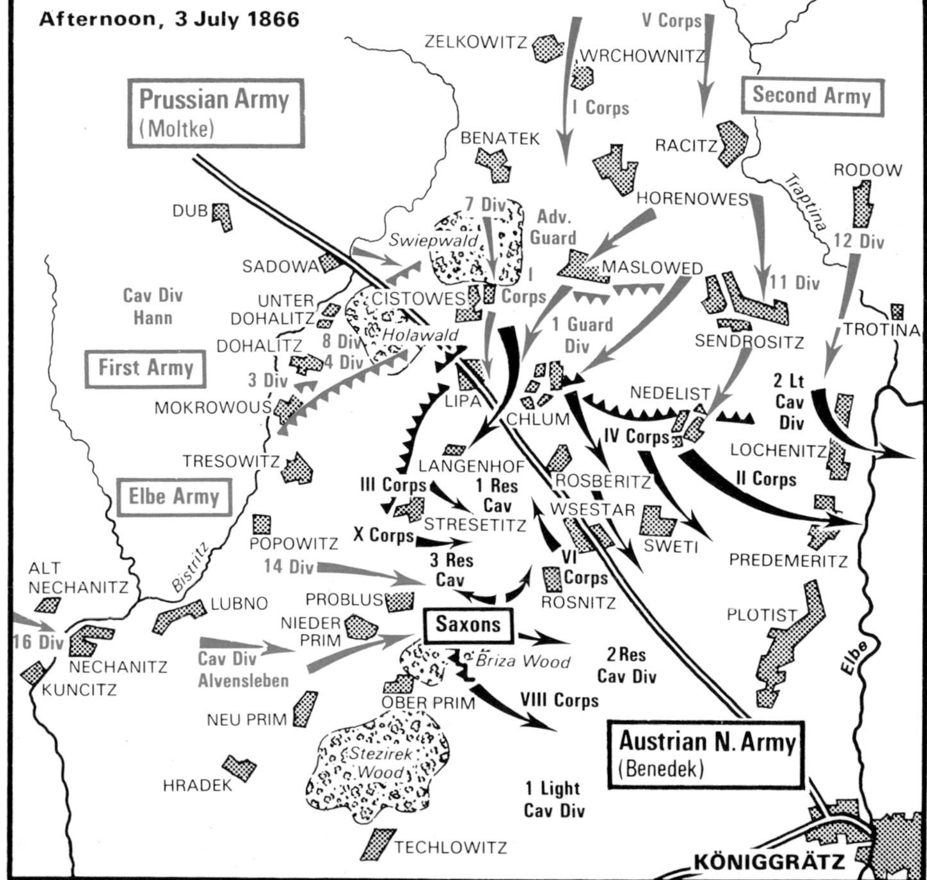

Right: The Battle of Königgrätz was one of the first in which railroad movement had been used to decisive effect, in the deployment of the Prussian forces.
Below: Fierce fighting during the Battle of Gettysburg. Union casualties were about 23,000 while the Confederates lost about 28,000.

Sedan

If the Prussian victory at Königgrätz was a shock to the Austrians, it was no less a surprise to the French, who now found a powerful and threatening neighbor to the north. The French, like the Austrians, had believed in the principle of a small, professional army, and in 1868 Marshal Niel proposed a series of military reforms to change the comparatively weak French position. The reforms which were adopted fell far short of his expectations, and conscription was never universal or fair. It was relatively simple to buy one's way out of military service. But French foreign policy did not reflect this weak position. On, the contrary, French troops were placed in Mexico, Indo-China, Algeria and elsewhere, and under the leadership of Napoleon III, the nephew of the great general, dash and initiative proved poor substitutes for massive strength, economic power and a rail network geared for war – all of which the Prussians had. French artillery was poor and organization weak compared to Prussian. Above all, in Marshals Bazaine and MacMahon, as well as the Emperor himself, the French lacked the impressive political and military expertise of Bismarck and von Moltke.

In a clever move by Bismarck that forced the vain Napoleon III to declare war against Prussia despite his unreadiness – the Ems Dispatch – French mobilization went particularly badly. Food and munitions were scarce and indiscipline was rife. MacMahon, in Alsace, called for reinforcements and was forced to retreat by the Prussian Third Army. By mid-August Bazaine was encircled in the fortress of Metz in Lorraine, and the Prussian Second Army crossed the Meuse below Verdun. French forces were trapped in a pocket, and von Moltke ordered his armies to move northward to engage the remainder of the French troops, the Army of Châlons, under the command of MacMahon and the Emperor himself. Moltke ordered the Army of the Meuse to advance on Sedan from the east, while the Third Army attacked from the south, cutting the French lines of retreat. By the evening of 31 August 1870, the French were surrounded. As one of their generals, Ducrot, remarked: *'Nous sommes dans un pot de chambre et nous y serons emmerdes'* (We are in a chamber pot and we are about to be covered in shit). In the early hours of 1 September the Prussians and Bavarians attacked. MacMahon was woun-

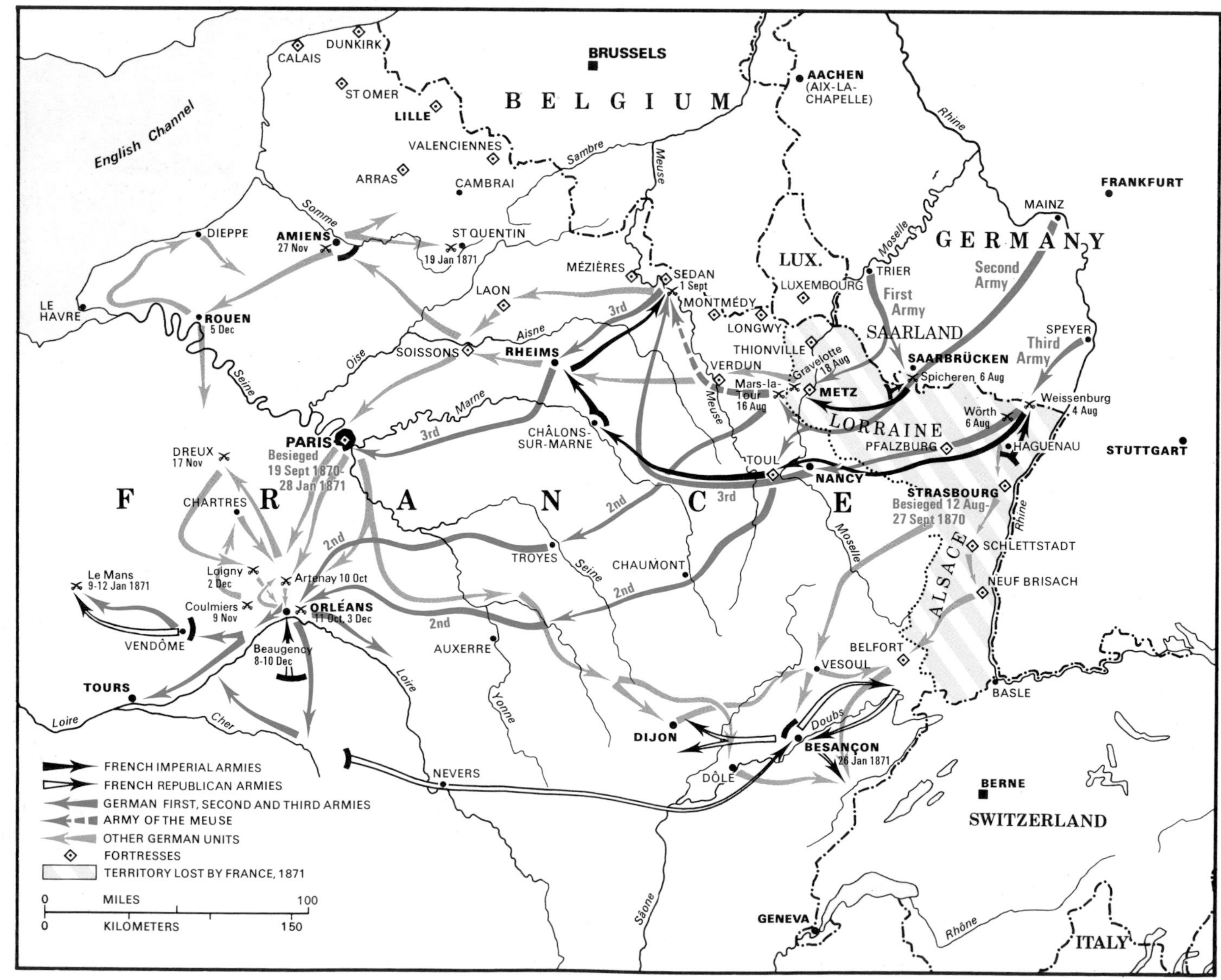

Below left: The course of the Franco-Prussian War. The French greatly underestimated the number of men that Germany would be able to mobilize.
Below: The final stages of the German encirclement of Sedan.

ded and was replaced by Ducrot, and then General Wimpffen arrived to turn chaos into disaster. He ordered that no retreat was possible, saying, 'We need a victory, not a retreat!'

Unfortunately for him, a retreat was virtually impossible at this juncture, and a defeat unavoidable. German artillery fire caused heavy casualties among the French, and Wimpffen attempted a breakout, which was a dismal and bloody failure, due to the chaotic conditions within his defensive perimeter. Napoleon himself spent the day riding about within the perimeter in a state of fatalistic resignation, looking for death. One of his staff was cut in half riding beside him, but death eluded the Emperor. However, 17,000 casualties were suffered by the French, while 21,000 prisoners were taken. The white flag was raised later in the afternoon, and Napoleon tried to arrange a meeting with Wilhelm I of Prussia to discuss truce terms. The meeting never took place, and Napoleon's sword was placed in the hands of the King.

The capitulation took place the next day, 2 September 1870, when Wimpffen and Castelnau met with Moltke and Bismarck. Castelnau killed all hopes of a moderate peace by announcing that the loss of the battle, the armies and the Emperor did not signify a surrender by France. The entire army became prisoners-of-war, giving the Germans 83,000 more men to look after. German casualties numbered only 9000, indicating the importance of Prussian artillery in the battle. As Napoleon was driven off into captivity in Bismarck's black carriage, a revolution took place in Paris, bringing a left-wing government into control. German armies surrounded Paris and besieged the city for months. The Paris Commune fell and was replaced by the Third Republic, eventually presided over by the unfortunate MacMahon. In the peace negotiations, which concluded in May 1871, France lost Alsace-Lorraine, the German Empire was proclaimed at the Palace of Versailles, and German unification was complete. France had fallen to the second rank among world powers and Germany was propelled into the first. The Battle of Sedan was the most significant and vainglorious battle to be fought in Europe between Waterloo and World War I.

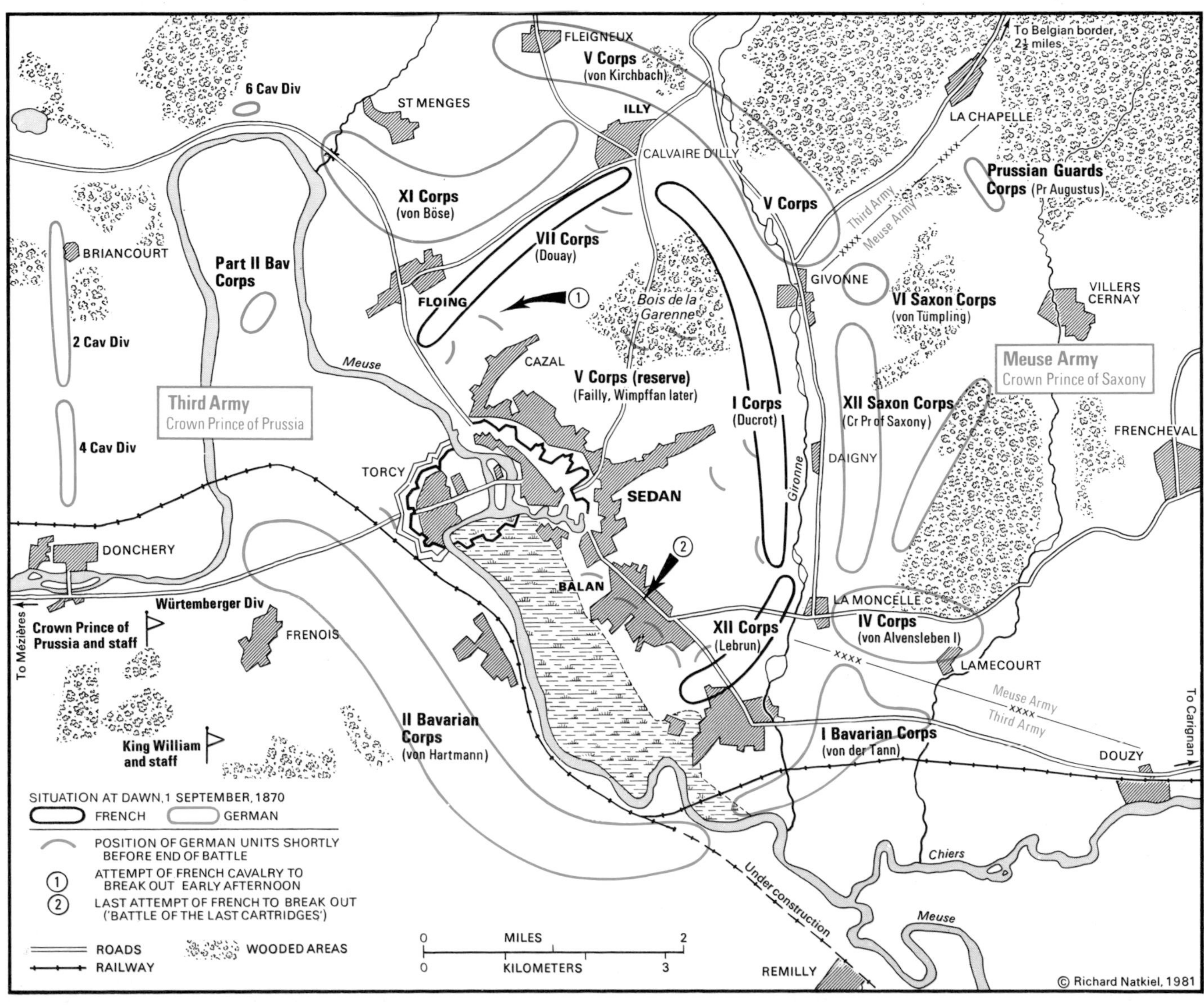

Boer War

The Dutch-speaking republics of the Orange Free State and the Transvaal were thorns in the side of the British, who aspired to rule more than the whole of South Africa. They dreamed of dominating the entire continent on a Cape-to-Cairo axis. President Paul Kruger of the Transvaal stood in their way. In their attempt to move from their positions in the Cape Colony and Natal northward, the British believed that, as the greatest power in the world, they would need but a short time to reduce the Afrikaners. In fact the fight took three years, 1899–1902. Outnumbered and outgunned at all times, the Afrikaners used guerrilla tactics to harass fixed British positions. The British, openly embarrassed internationally, were obliged to call on massive reinforcements brought in from China, India and the British Isles. In the end they won a Pyrrhic victory. Within nine years South Africa became a self-governing Dominion, led by many of the former Boer leaders. The Boer War was a landmark in the history of the British Empire. It marked the beginning of the end of British dominance of the world in the 20th century.

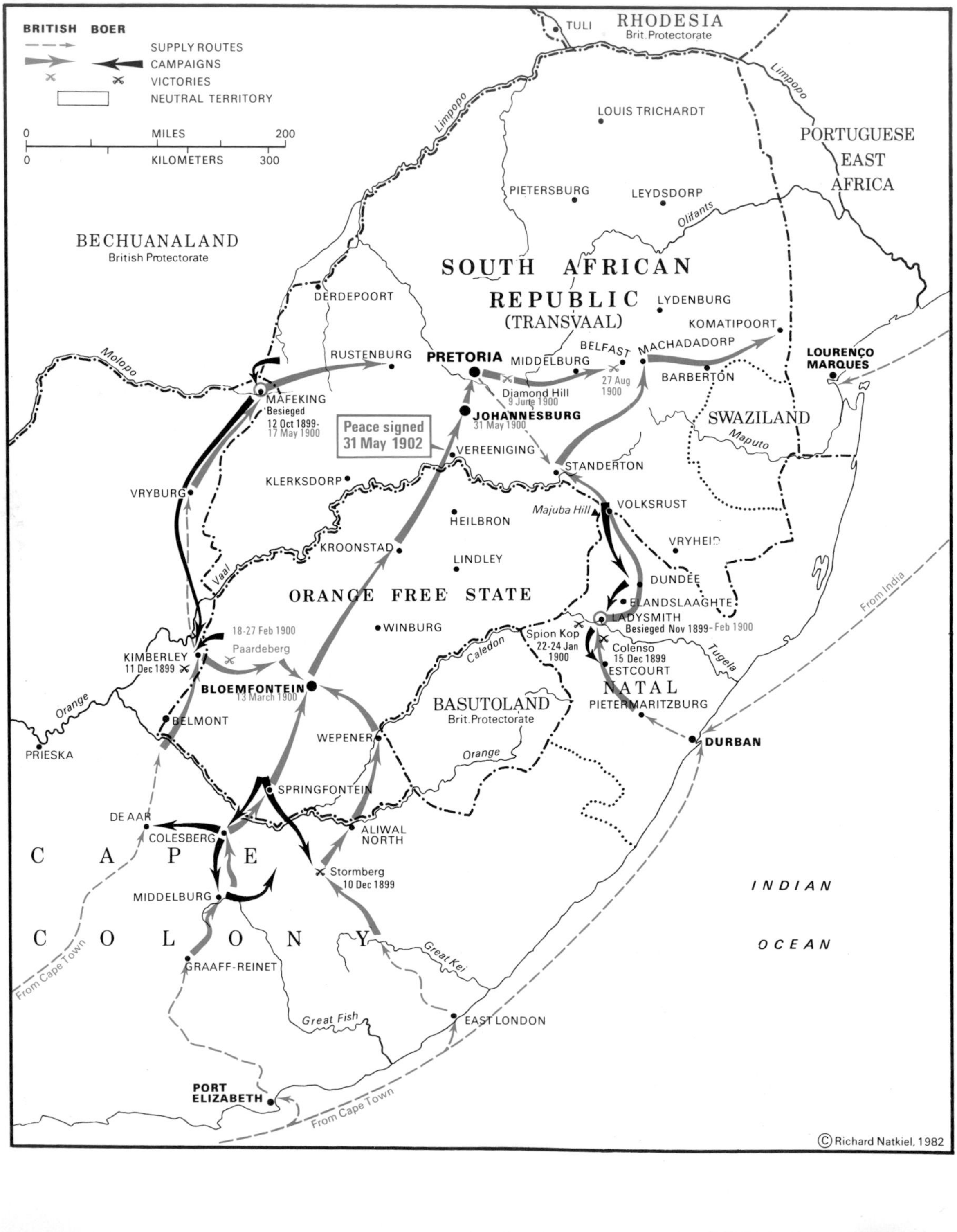

BRITISH BOER
SUPPLY ROUTES
CAMPAIGNS
VICTORIES
NEUTRAL TERRITORY
0 MILES 200
0 KILOMETERS 300
RHODESIA Brit.Protectorate
TULI
Limpopo
LOUIS TRICHARDT
PORTUGUESE EAST AFRICA
PIETERSBURG
LEYDSDORP
Olifants
BECHUANALAND British Protectorate
SOUTH AFRICAN REPUBLIC (TRANSVAAL)
LYDENBURG
DERDEPOORT
KOMATIPOORT
Molopo
RUSTENBURG
PRETORIA
MIDDELBURG
BELFAST
MACHADADORP
LOURENÇO MARQUES
BARBERTON
27 Aug 1900
Diamond Hill 9 June 1900
MAFEKING Besieged 12 Oct 1899-17 May 1900
JOHANNESBURG 31 May 1900
Peace signed 31 May 1902
SWAZILAND
Maputo
VEREENIGING
STANDERTON
KLERKSDORP
VRYBURG
VOLKSRUST
Majuba Hill
HEILBRON
VRYHEID
KROONSTAD
LINDLEY
Vaal
DUNDEE
ORANGE FREE STATE
ELANDSLAAGHTE
LADYSMITH Besieged Nov 1899-Feb 1900
WINBURG
18-27 Feb 1900
Paardeberg
Spion Kop 22-24 Jan 1900
Colenso 15 Dec 1899
Caledon
From India
KIMBERLEY 11 Dec 1899
ESTCOURT
Tugela
BLOEMFONTEIN 13 March 1900
NATAL
Orange
BASUTOLAND Brit.Protectorate
PIETERMARITZBURG
BELMONT
PRIESKA
WEPENER
DURBAN
Orange
SPRINGFONTEIN
DE AAR
COLESBERG
ALIWAL NORTH
CAPE COLONY
Stormberg 10 Dec 1899
MIDDELBURG
INDIAN OCEAN
Great Kei
From Cape Town
GRAAFF-REINET
Great Fish
EAST LONDON
PORT ELIZABETH
From Cape Town
© Richard Natkiel, 1982

Left: The battles of the Boer War gave an important demonstration of the firepower of the most modern firearms.

The Russo-Japanese War

At the turn of the 20th century Russia was one of the world's great powers. Japan had recently emerged from seclusion. Despite Japan's relatively easy victory over China in 1894–95, the world at large discounted growing Japanese naval power, abetted by the British, who had formed an alliance with Japan in 1902. Conversely, most Europeans overestimated the power of Imperial Russia, which was torn by inner dissension, a corrupt and antiquated absolute monarchy, and a backward economic machine, held together by string and Anglo-French capital. The Russo-Japanese War was to be a turning point in the history both of East Asia and the Romanov Dynasty.

Right: The land campaign of the Russo-Japanese War.
Below right: General map of the disputed areas.
Below: Russian artillery horses are unloaded from their rail cars for shipping across Lake Baikal. This gap in the Trans-Siberian railroad slowed the Russian buildup in the east.

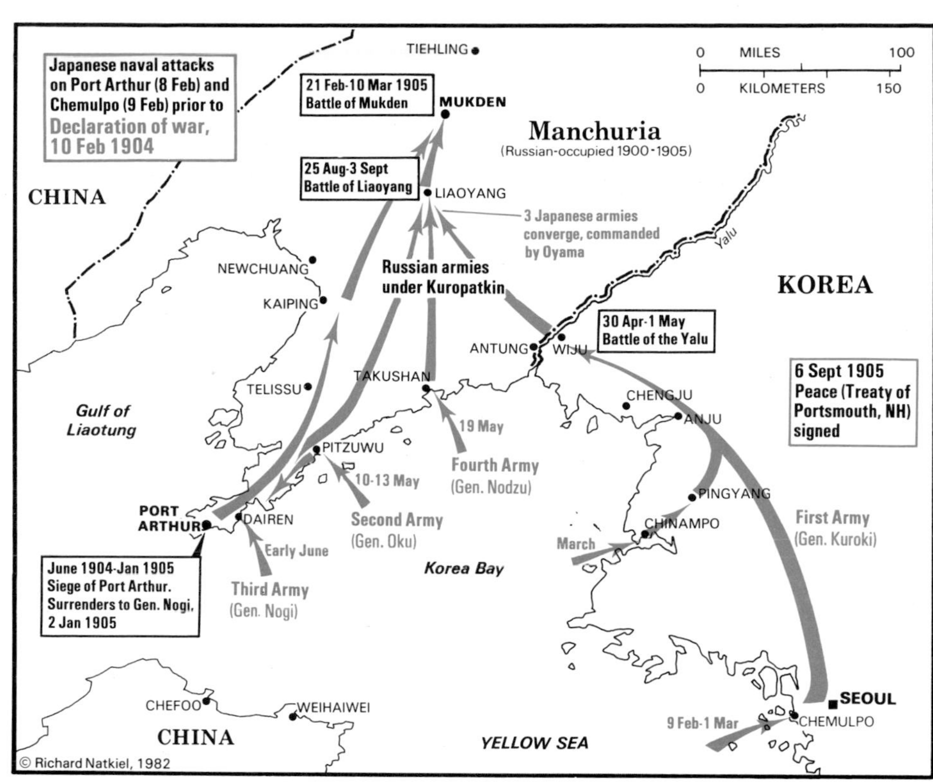

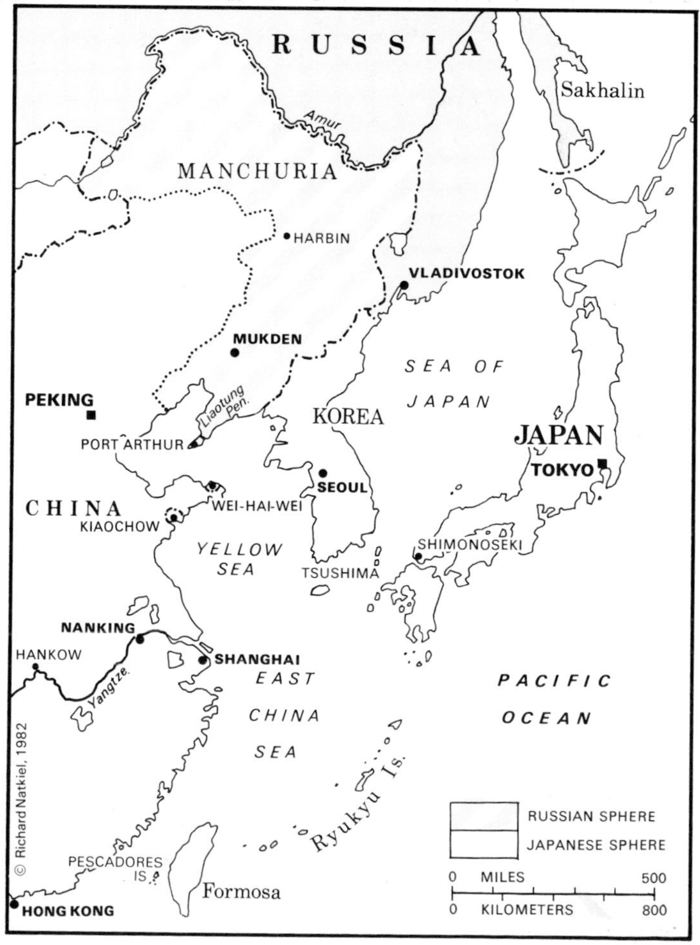

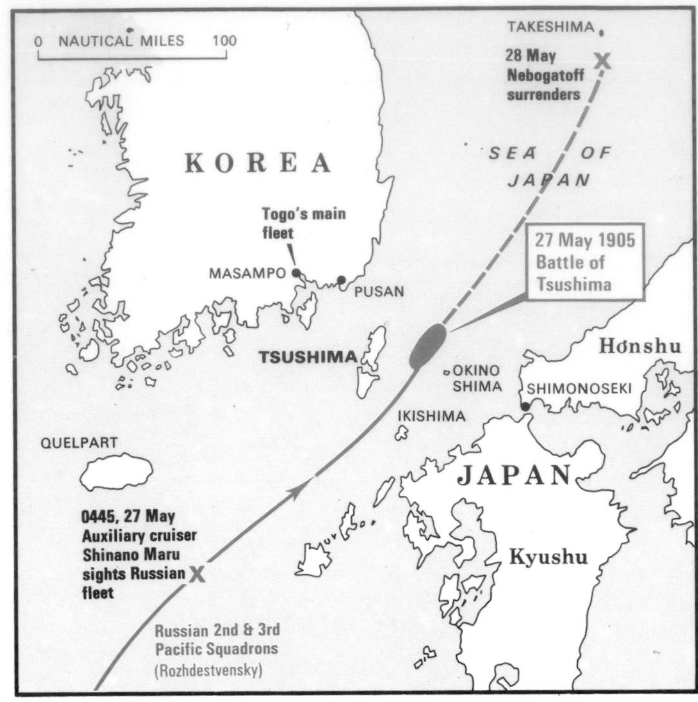

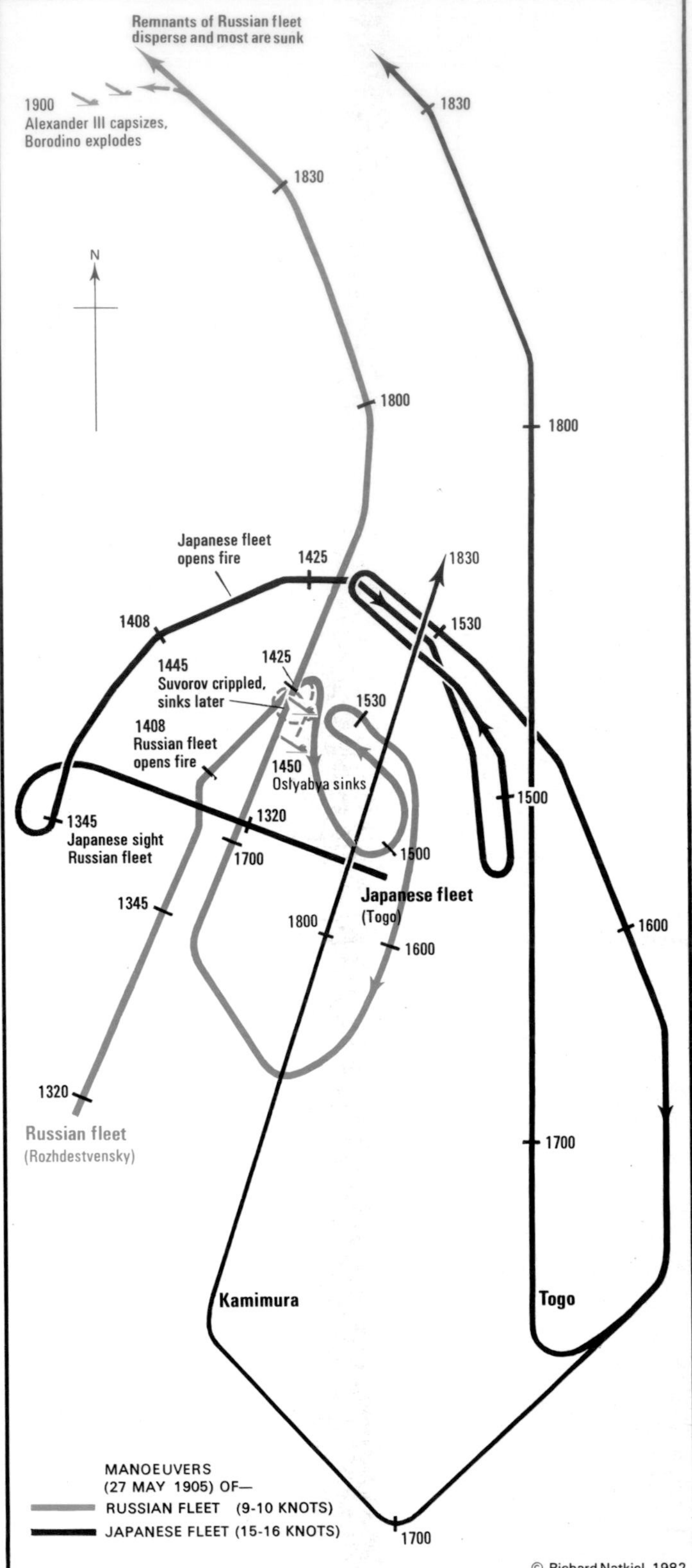

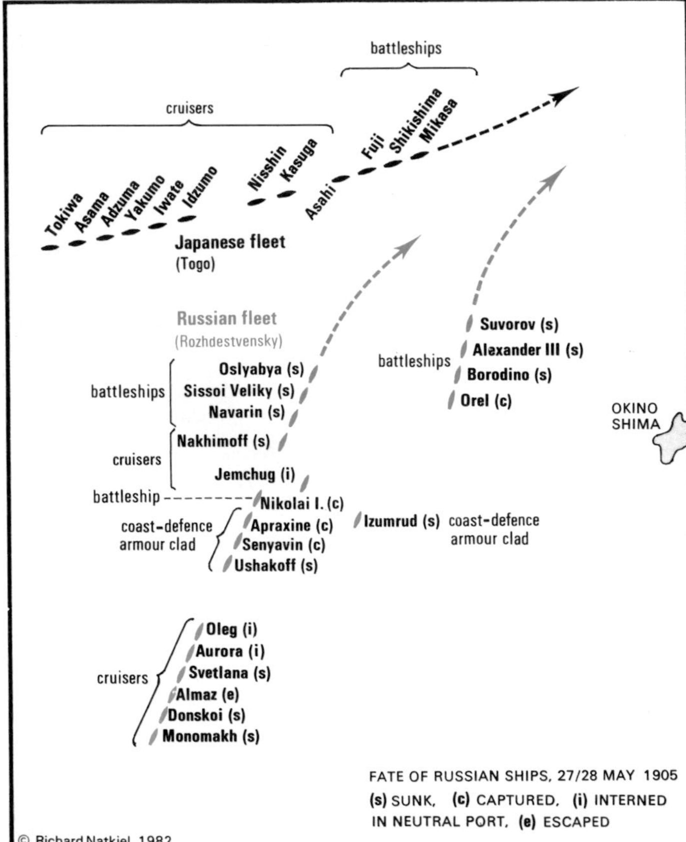

The central point of conflict was Korea and Manchuria, which Japan, quite naturally, saw as part of her sphere of influence. Japan had fought the Chinese to gain hegemony in Korea, only to find herself opposed by the Russians, who were supported by other European powers. Japan first attempted to negotiate with the Russians over Korea and the increasing Russian hold over northern Manchuria through control of the railroads, which passed between Irkutsk on the Trans-Siberian and the Russian port of Vladivostok on the Pacific – the railhead for the longest rail line in the world, recently completed after over a decade of construction. Russia did not take these talks seriously, as she did not believe the Japanese would ever dare to attack a great European power. By 1904 the Japanese fleet was ready. Much of it was new, having been constructed in Britain. The oldest battleships had been launched in 1896. Other ships were still newer. The Russian Fleet, on the other hand, was divided into three parts: Baltic, Black Sea and Pacific Fleets. The Pacific Fleet contained seven battleships, six cruisers and several dozen destroyers and

Left: The maneuvers leading up to the Battle of Tsushima and the events of the battle itself. Togo's success in this full-scale fleet engagement influenced the strategy and tactics of the Japanese Navy until the end of World War II.

torpedo boats. A naval program, abetted by the French, had begun in Russia to modernize the fleet, making her the third largest naval power in the world by 1904, after Britain and France, although Germany and the United States were catching up. Japan learned that six more battleships would be ready for shipment to the Far East in 1904. Therefore, if Japan failed to act soon it might be too late for her ever to challenge Russia in Pacific waters.

The Japanese plan called for an invasion of Korea and then a push into Manchuria. To do this, Russian sea power had to be neutralized. In a surprise attack on 8 February, Admiral Togo bombarded Port Arthur, the Russian naval base on Chinese territory, the nearby Russian commercial port of Dairen (Dalny) and Inchon (Chemulpo), the port of Seoul in Korea. Although 2500 Japanese troops landed at Inchon, only a cruiser and a small gunboat were destroyed there, and there were no naval vessels at Dairen. However, at Port Arthur two Russian battleships and a cruiser were damaged. Although this attack did not rob Russia of its naval supremacy in the Pacific, it did place her on the defensive for the balance of the war. Three Russian cruisers that ventured out from Port Arthur thereafter were destroyed, so the balance of the Russian Fleet was bottled up in the port, well protected by heavy coastal defenses. Apart from the loss of the Russian flagship, the *Petropavlovsk*, to mines, and a similar loss of two Japanese battleships, the Russians showed no inclination to leave their safe harbor. The Japanese were therefore free to exercise their authority on land.

One Japanese army pushed across the Liaotung Peninsula and laid siege to Port Arthur. Two other armies swept through Korea into Manchuria across the Yalu River, and forced the Russian armed forces back to the key rail link of Mukden. From this point the Russians could be supplied by land via the Trans-Siberian Railway. However, the rail line had only one track for most of its length, and bottlenecks built up with wounded returning home, going westward, and fresh troops and supplies coming eastward. The Russians had failed to build sidings along the route. In the ensuing chaos Czar Nicholas II decided to send a new Russian Pacific Fleet to the Far East to relieve Port Arthur and allow reinforcements to reach Manchuria. Leading this new fleet was Admiral Sinovie Rozhdestvensky, whose modest naval skills were matched by a lack of imagination. His Second Pacific Squadron comprised five new battleships, two older ones, one old heavy cruiser, unsuitable for combat, eight cruisers as well as some light cruisers and destroyers. The heart of the squadron's strength lay in its battleships, but these had a slower rate of fire than the Japanese, and slower speeds.

Leaving its Baltic port of Libau on 15 October 1904, Rozhdestvensky ran into trouble from the outset. The crews were untrained, and the newer ships had not yet undergone sea trials and were prone to engine trouble. Three were actually sent back as unfit after the long journey around the world had begun. Furthermore, along the 18,000-mile route there was not one Russian base or coaling station. In addition, as the fleet passed through the English Channel in a fog, there were rumors of Japanese torpedo boats near the English coast. As ridiculous as this may seem, the Russians fired upon unknown ships, some of which turned out to be their own, the others being trawlers of the Hull fishing fleet. The episode, known as the Dogger Bank Incident, made the Russians a laughing-stock, except in Britain, as one trawler had been sunk. The Russians could not expect the British to help them along the route.

At Tangier the fleet split in half, some of it going through the Suez Canal and the rest around the tip of Africa. Morale flagged as it became apparent that neither officers nor men knew what they were doing. By the time they reconverged off Madagascar, news reached them of the shelling and sinking of the Port Arthur fleet by Japanese land guns. The fleet which was being reinforced no longer existed. Later it was learned that Port Arthur itself had fallen to the Japanese after a five-month siege. The journey seemed irrelevant before the Russians were refused permission to land at Singapore and were forced to refuel at the French Indo-Chinese port of Cam Ranh Bay, a trip of 4500 miles from Madagascar – the longest non-stop sea voyage by coal-fired ships to date. A further fleet of ships was sent out from Russia to join Rozhdestvensky, some of them being the very ones rejected for the initial voyage by the Admiral because of their age.

Seeing no point in trying to avoid the Japanese by attempting to sail to Vladivostok, Rozhdestvensky chose to go through the Korean Straits, between Korea and Japan. Admiral Togo was ready and waiting for the Russians, and on 27 May 1905 the fleets engaged at the Battle of Tsushima, named after an island in the straits. Togo's tactics were good, but they were improved upon by the ineptitude of the Russians. Russia lost 34 of the 37 ships of her fleet, and her Admiral was captured by Togo, while he was still unconscious. Those ships attempting to escape were also sunk. After Tsushima the Russo-Japanese War was all but over, as land forces were still engaged in the field in Manchuria. However, the battle forced Russia to the conference table as no land battle could or would have done. By this time the Russian Revolution of 1905 had broken out and there was plenty to occupy the Czar's mind in St Petersburg.

Immediately after the battle the Japanese Government called upon President Theodore Roosevelt of the United States to use his good offices as mediator. Count Witte and Prince Ito came to Washington, which was too hot in the summer of 1905, as it is every summer, so the negotiators repaired to a naval base at Portsmouth, New Hampshire, for talks. The Treaty of Portsmouth was signed on 5 September 1905, ending the war. Japan received Russian railway rights in southern Manchuria as well as the Russian bases of Port Arthur and Dairen. Russia recognized Japan's 'free hand' in Korea. Russia was also obliged to cede southern Sakhalin to Japan. What this meant was that Japan took over the Russian role in East Asia. Within five years Korea became a Japanese colony, and south Manchuria a Japanese preserve. The balance of power had shifted in East Asia. The new American colony, the Philippines, was now at Japan's mercy, and Japan had become the dominant force in the northern Pacific. Furthermore, the myth of white superiority in technical, military and naval matters was broken. Peoples throughout East Asia realized that if one great European power could be crushed by the Asians, the others were vulnerable. The victory of Japan over Russia was the first step in the decolonization of Asia and Africa even during the heyday of Western imperialism.

Thanks to her defeat by Japan, Russia was so weakened internally by international humiliation and national revolution that it was to take but one more push for the Romanovs' 300-year dynasty to crumble. The world balance of power had shifted. The Russo-Japanese War created a new world power, just as the Franco-Prussian War had done. Russia was to look to Europe for imperial expansion, which was one of the causes of World War I. Japan's power in East Asia, however, was to go unchallenged until the outbreak of World War II.

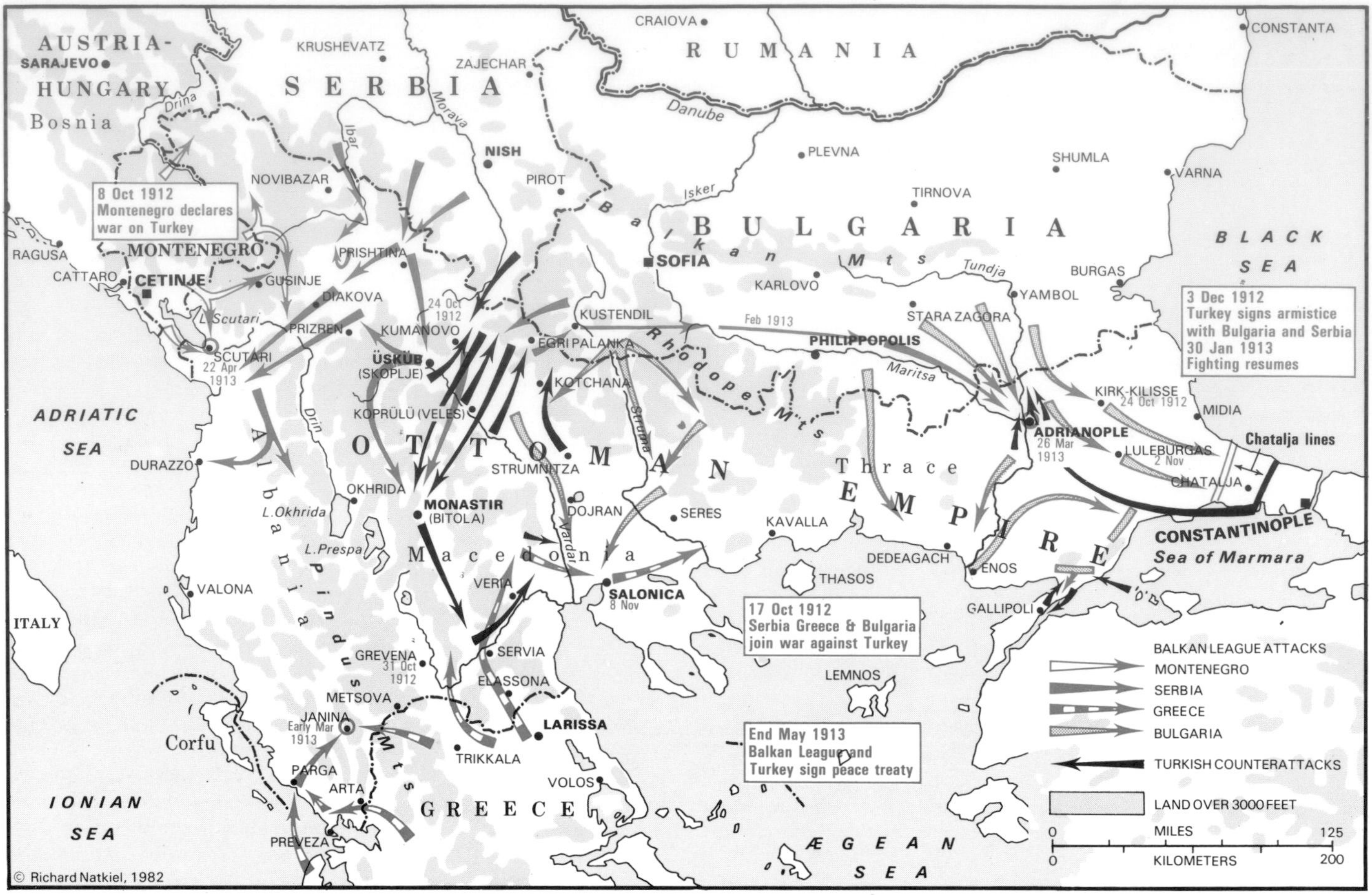

AUSTRIA-HUNGARY
SARAJEVO
Bosnia
KRUSHEVATZ
SERBIA
ZAJECHAR
CRAIOVA
RUMANIA
CONSTANTA
Drina
Ibar
Morava
Danube
NISH
PIROT
NOVIBAZAR
PLEVNA
SHUMLA
VARNA
TIRNOVA
Isker
Balkan Mts
BULGARIA
BLACK SEA

8 Oct 1912
Montenegro declares war on Turkey

RAGUSA
MONTENEGRO
CATTARO
CETINJE
GUSINJE
PRISHTINA
DIAKOVA
SOFIA
KARLOVO
Tundja
BURGAS
YAMBOL
L. Scutari
PRIZREN
KUMANOVO
24 Oct 1912
KUSTENDIL
Feb 1913
STARA ZAGORA
PHILIPPOPOLIS
Maritsa
SCUTARI
22 Apr 1913
ÜSKÜB (SKOPLJE)
EGRI PALANKA
KOTCHANA
Rhodope Mts

3 Dec 1912
Turkey signs armistice with Bulgaria and Serbia
30 Jan 1913
Fighting resumes

KIRK-KILISSE
24 Oct 1912
MIDIA
ADRIATIC SEA
Drin
KOPRÜLÜ (VELES)
Struma
ADRIANOPLE
26 Mar 1913
LULEBURGAS
2 Nov
Chatalja lines
DURAZZO
OTTOMAN EMPIRE
STRUMNITZA
Thrace
CHATALJA
L. Okhrida
OKHRIDA
MONASTIR (BITOLA)
DOJRAN
SERES
KAVALLA
CONSTANTINOPLE
Sea of Marmara
Albania
L. Prespa
Macedonia
Vardar
DEDEAGACH
ENOS
THASOS
VALONA
VERIA
SALONICA
8 Nov
GALLIPOLI
ITALY
Pindus Mts

17 Oct 1912
Serbia Greece & Bulgaria join war against Turkey

GREVENA
31 Oct 1912
SERVIA
ELASSONA
LEMNOS
METSOVA
JANINA
Early Mar 1913
LARISSA
Corfu
PARGA
TRIKKALA
ARTA

End May 1913
Balkan League and Turkey sign peace treaty

IONIAN SEA
VOLOS
GREECE
PREVEZA
ÆGEAN SEA

BALKAN LEAGUE ATTACKS
MONTENEGRO
SERBIA
GREECE
BULGARIA
TURKISH COUNTERATTACKS
LAND OVER 3000 FEET
0 MILES 125
0 KILOMETERS 200

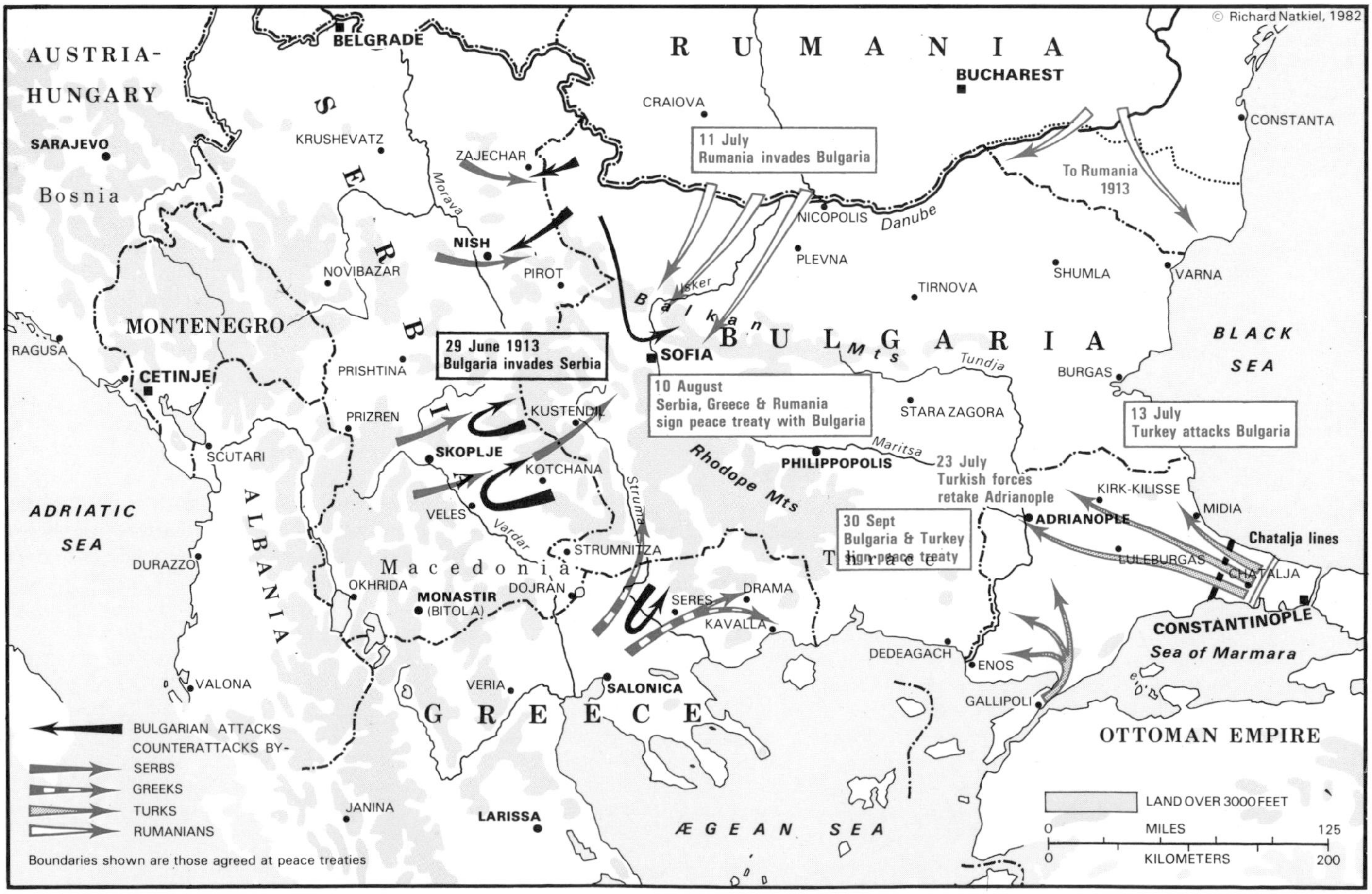

AUSTRIA-HUNGARY
BELGRADE
RUMANIA
BUCHAREST
CRAIOVA
SARAJEVO
KRUSHEVATZ
CONSTANTA
Bosnia
SERBIA

11 July
Rumania invades Bulgaria

ZAJECHAR
Morava
To Rumania 1913
NICOPOLIS
Danube
NISH
PLEVNA
NOVIBAZAR
PIROT
SHUMLA
VARNA
TIRNOVA
Isker
Balkan Mts
MONTENEGRO
BULGARIA
BLACK SEA
RAGUSA
CETINJE

29 June 1913
Bulgaria invades Serbia

PRISHTINA
SOFIA
Tundja
BURGAS

10 August
Serbia, Greece & Rumania sign peace treaty with Bulgaria

STARA ZAGORA
PRIZREN
KUSTENDIL
Maritsa

13 July
Turkey attacks Bulgaria

SKOPLJE
Rhodope Mts
PHILIPPOPOLIS

23 July
Turkish forces retake Adrianople

SCUTARI
KOTCHANA
KIRK-KILISSE
MIDIA
ALBANIA
Struma
ADRIATIC SEA
VELES
Vardar

30 Sept
Bulgaria & Turkey sign peace treaty

ADRIANOPLE
Chatalja lines
STRUMNITZA
Thrace
LULEBURGAS
DURAZZO
Macedonia
CHATALJA
OKHRIDA
MONASTIR (BITOLA)
DOJRAN
SERES
DRAMA
KAVALLA
CONSTANTINOPLE
Sea of Marmara
DEDEAGACH
ENOS
VALONA
VERIA
SALONICA
GALLIPOLI
GREECE
OTTOMAN EMPIRE

BULGARIAN ATTACKS
COUNTERATTACKS BY-
SERBS
GREEKS
TURKS
RUMANIANS

JANINA
LARISSA
ÆGEAN SEA
LAND OVER 3000 FEET
0 MILES 125
0 KILOMETERS 200

Boundaries shown are those agreed at peace treaties

The Balkan Wars

The Ottoman Empire was called 'the sick man of Europe' throughout the 19th century. Occupying a key position at the Dardanelles and much of the Middle East, it was inconvenient for the European powers to fight over its territory. Instead, it was nibbled away. The Turks, who had reached the gates of Vienna over 200 years before, had seen part of their European dominions fall to the Hapsburgs and Romanovs. Serbia, Montenegro and Bulgaria were declared independent in 1878, but were viewed as client states of Russia. To balance the situation in the Balkans, Austria-Hungary occupied Bosnia and Herzegovina at the same time. For thirty years the position remained essentially unchanged until Austria annexed the territory outright in 1908. After Italy seized Libya and the Dodecanese Islands in her war with Turkey in 1911–12, it was feared that the Ottoman Empire might be near collapse. It was this fear that triggered the two Balkan Wars.

In October 1912, encouraged by the Russians, Serbia, Montenegro, Bulgaria and Greece declared war against Turkey – a mad scramble among hated rivals for the remainder of the European portion of the once-proud Ottoman Empire. The war had to be short, as no participant could sustain a long one. Bulgaria reached the gates of Constantinople. Greece reached out and seized Salonica. Albania declared its independence, much to the consternation of Montenegro and Serbia, but all the adversaries of Turkey expanded their territories. However, the Balkan allies distrusted one another, and when Bulgaria realized that Greece and Serbia were conspiring against her to divide Macedonia between them, the Bulgarians became angry, as they had suffered more losses of personnel than any combatant. Before a peace settlement could be reached, a second Balkan War broke out, with the Bulgarians attacking Greece and Serbia. Turkey, seeing her opportunity to recoup losses, also declared war against Bulgaria. Then Rumania, always interested in recapturing the southern Dobrudja from Bulgaria, an area constantly disputed between the two, declared war against Bulgaria as well in 1913. Surrounded by enemies, Bulgaria was thoroughly defeated in a war which lasted only a few weeks.

The Treaty of Bucharest ended the war, which largely maintained the status quo after the First Balkan War, but with some notable exceptions. Albania retained its independence, but most of Macedonia was given to Greece. The balance went to Serbia, both states coming out as the principal victors in the two wars. Rumania gained most of the southern Dobrudja. Turkey actually gained a bit, having pushed her buffer zone around Constantinople out to Adrianople, which she had previously lost. The Ottoman Empire, of course, lost the most – almost all its European possessions – but independence was maintained, as were the strategic Dardanelles.

The importance of the Balkan Wars was obvious. There were no new territories to conquer without involving two or more of the great powers. Austria-Hungary realized that it could expand its influence no further without engaging the Russians directly. The Russians, having been frustrated in the Far East by Japan, could not expand their influence in Europe without taking on Austria-Hungary and her German ally. The stage was set for World War I, which broke out only a few months after the Second Balkan War ended. The incident which began it was in Sarajevo, the capital of Bosnia. The victims were an Austrian Archduke, Franz Ferdinand, and his wife, who died at the hands of a Serbian patriot. Many historians have stated that these two Balkan wars brought about a third Balkan War, which is better known as World War I.

Left: In the Italo-Turkish War of 1911 Italy succeeded in gaining an African Empire against negligible Turkish opposition, which encouraged Turkey's enemies to attack in the Balkans.
Top, far left: The battles of the First Balkan War reduced Turkish territory in Europe to the tiny enclaves in the Gallipoli and Chataljia peninsulas.
Bottom, far left: The campaigns of the Second Balkan War.

The Schlieffen Plan and its Consequences

In 1905 the Chief of the German General Staff, Count Alfred von Schlieffen, proposed a plan that was designed to deal with the threat to Germany of a war on two fronts. Military planners had been concerned for several decades about the combined strength of France and Russia, which would be overwhelming in the event of a war. Schlieffen's plan called for a concentration of German forces against France for a quick victory, followed by rapid rail transportation of German troops to the Eastern Front. Russia's sparse railway system would prevent her from completing mobilization before the German forces could arrive.

In France, seven German armies would converge on the French heartland: two from

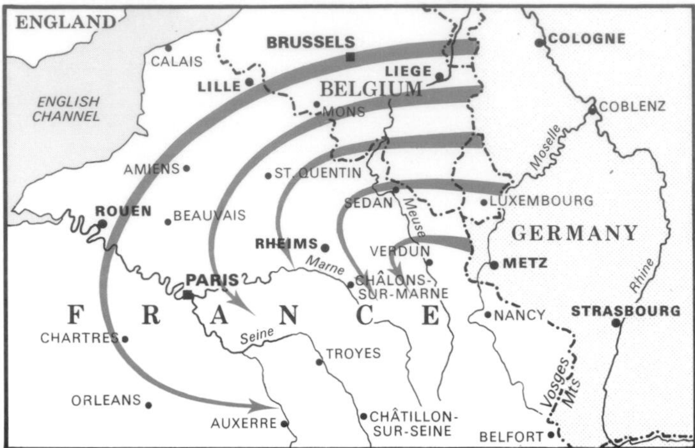

Right: British troops move through a Belgian village in 1914.
Left: The original concept of the Schlieffen Plan.
Below left: How it was modified in action with the German right wing no longer moving to the west of Paris.

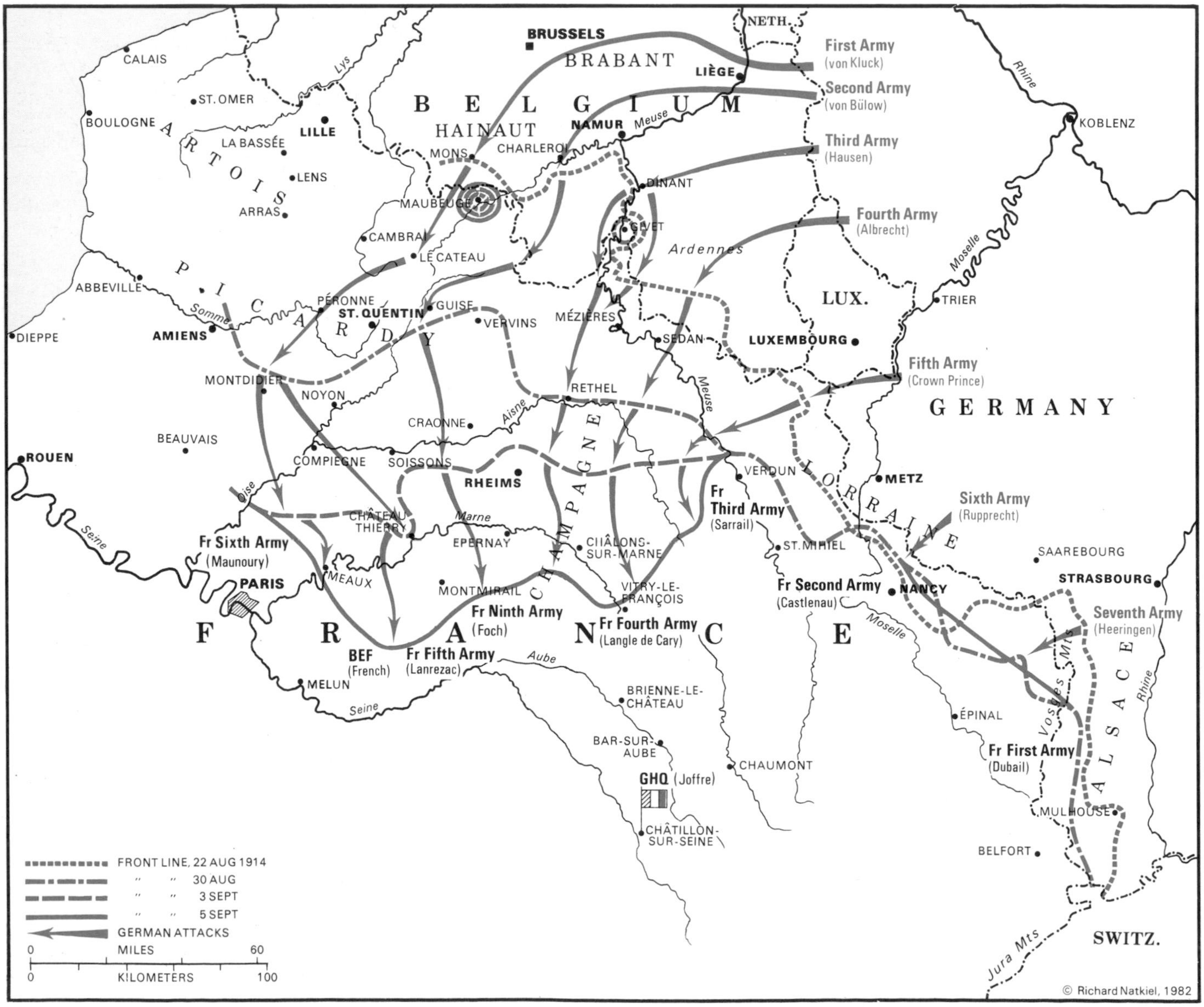

FRONT LINE, 22 AUG 1914
" " 30 AUG
" " 3 SEPT
" " 5 SEPT
GERMAN ATTACKS
0 MILES 60
0 KILOMETERS 100

south of Metz to attack the bulk of the French Army and immobilize it or draw it eastward, five from north of Metz to cross Belgium and turn southwest to encircle Paris. There the rear of the main French forces could be overwhelmed. So said Schlieffen's plan, which allayed long-standing German military anxieties.

The plan was modified by the younger von Moltke, Schlieffen's successor as Chief of Staff, and correspondingly vitiated the force for the Belgian invasion. At the same time, French aid began to effect an astonishing improvement in the Russian railway network. By 1914 the Russians could anticipate mobilizing two-thirds of their huge army in 18 days' time – just three days longer than the Germans would need to mobilize their forces. These changes meant that the Schlieffen Plan was virtually unworkable by the outbreak of the Great War. At the same time, it exerted an inexorable influence on the inception and course of the conflict. The urgency of the mobilization plan contributed to an early decision to go to war, and Germany's determination to help Austria against Russia made it imperative to attack France. The violation of Belgian neutrality inherent in the plan played a large part in Britain's decision to fight Germany. And the European alliance system of 1914 guaranteed that the quarrel originating in a small Balkan State would escalate rapidly into the world war that set the tone for the twentieth century.

The Schlieffen Plan, as modified by the younger von Moltke, went into effect on 3 August 1914, when German cavalry spearheaded the invasion of neutral Belgium by the First, Second and Third German Armies. The fortified Belgian city of Liège was not subdued until 16 August. A week before (8 August) the French Commander-in-Chief, Marshal Joseph J C Joffre, had ordered his First and Second Armies into Lorraine. As planned, the German Sixth Army, commanded by Prince Rupprecht of Bavaria, withdrew under this attack. It was mid-August before Joffre realized that the main German forces were to the north, in Belgium.

Then Rupprecht compromised the German plan by an ambitious decision to take the offensive against the advancing French First and Second Armies in Lorraine. In so doing, he not only pushed the French back out of the trap prepared for them, but suffered heavy losses to his own Sixth Army and the Seventh, which came to his support. The Schlieffen Plan suffered another setback in Belgium, where the German First, Second and Third Armies had to detach part of their forces against Antwerp and Namur. Kluck's First Army was ordered to turn southwestward rather than continue west, as planned, with the result that the British Expeditionary Force (BEF) was able to make a fighting withdrawal from Mons.

But Joffre was unable to capitalize on the weaknesses in the German plan. Seeking to cut off the three northern German armies from their bases, he sent his Third and Fourth Armies into the mountainous, heavily forested Ardennes in what proved an abortive advance. This failure also left the BEF and the French Fifth Army alone to face the German forces wheeling southwestward from Belgium. On 22 August the Fifth Army was overwhelmed by the German Second and Third Armies at Charleroi, and Paris became the fall-back position for the retreating French left wing.

The Battle of the Marne

The French created their Sixth Army to deal with the German threat to their capital when the German right wing turned toward Paris. From German headquarters Moltke was calling for a rapid advance to take advantage of French disarray. He ordered Kluck's First Army to advance west of the Oise and proceed to the west of Paris. The Second Army, under Bülow, was to go directly toward the French capital, while the Third and Fourth Armies were to march on Château-Thierry and Epernay respectively. In the east, the Sixth and Seventh Armies were to block French access to Lorraine and Alsace. The Fifth Army was to besiege Verdun, a vital French fortress blocking the Valley of the Meuse.

Moltke's commanders in the field, Kluck and Bülow, modified this plan with his approval: Kluck's army would move to the east to provide better support to Bülow. Apparently, neither commander paid attention to reports that the French were transporting troops by rail to such locations as Amiens and Montdidier. On 1 September Joffre ordered General Michel-Joseph Maunoury's newly created Sixth Army to retire toward Paris, with the implication that it might be used in an offensive role in conjunction with the capital's garrison. At this point the German forces under Kluck and Bülow were moving ever-farther east of their planned line of advance. The German First Army was crossing the Marne, little hindered by skirmishes on its right flank from Maunoury's patrols. Meanwhile, Joffre formed the Ninth Army under Marshal Ferdinand Foch to fill the gap between his Fourth and Fifth Armies. Then he began to plan a French counteroffensive that would become known as the Battle of the Marne.

The Marne battlefront extended all the way from the environs of Paris to the frontier commanded by Verdun. On 5 September Kluck was heavily engaged by the French Sixth Army near the River Ourcq. His right flank was threatened, and he transferred two corps from the left, with the result that the gap between his army and Bülow's Second grew wider. French General Joseph Galliéni, the Military Governor of Paris,

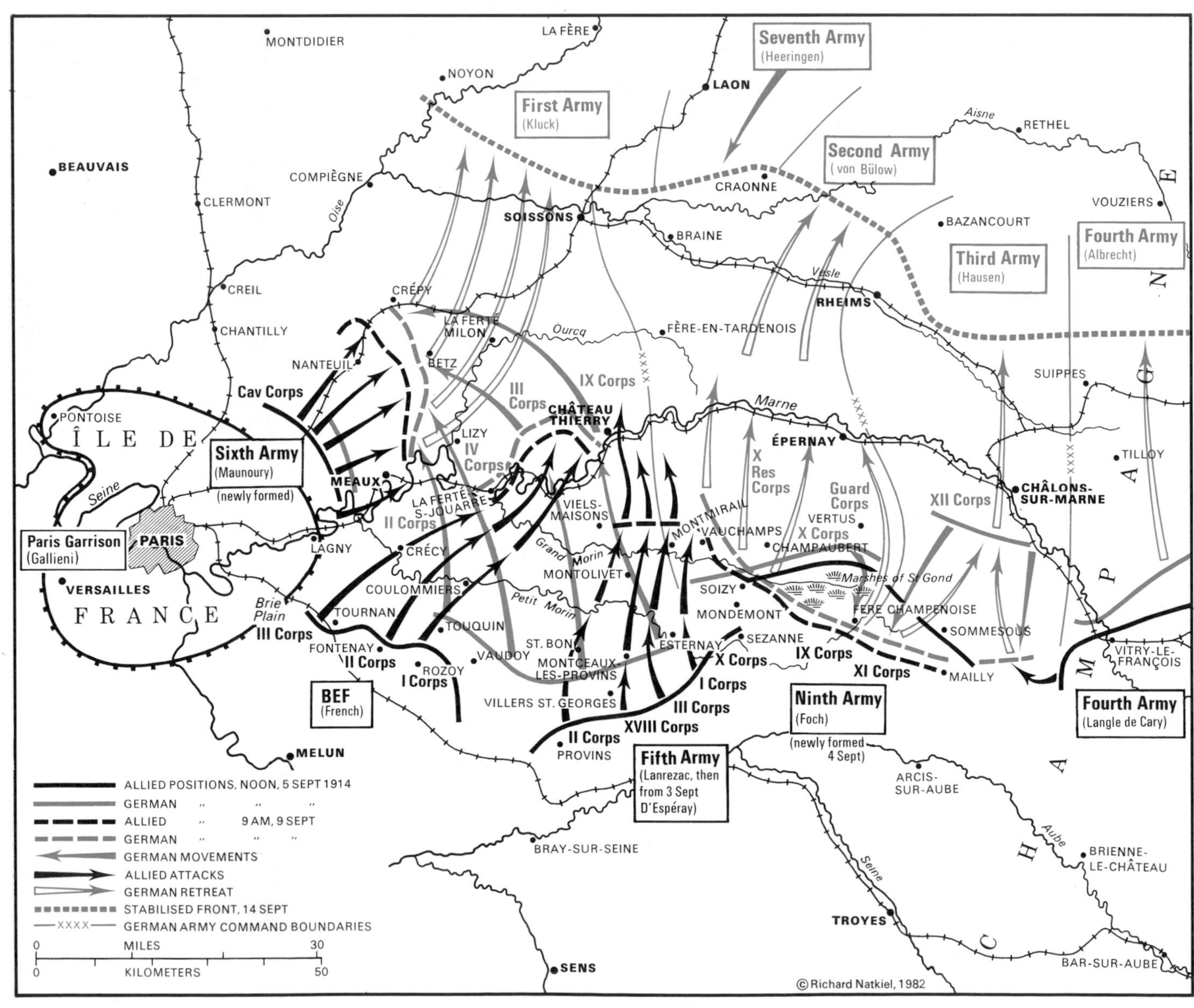

Above: French cavalry escort German prisoners taken during the Battle of the Marne.
Left: The Battle of the Marne, showing the role played by the Paris forces and the BEF and French Fifth Army.

commandeered 1200 taxicabs to deliver reinforcements to Maunoury, but it was the French Fifth Army that delivered the Sixth from the German threat with an attack on Kluck's left wing. (The Germans had believed that the Fifth was in retreat.)

The French counteroffensive was in full cry: by 7 September it had threatened the flank of Bülow's Second Army and forced it to withdraw across the River Petit Morin. Soon after, Bülow had to retire another six or seven miles east, widening the dangerous gap between his forces and Kluck's First Army. Foch's Ninth Army was able to prevent a German Third Army attempt to alleviate the situation.

Joffre appealed to the British commander, Sir John French, to provide BEF support for the French counteroffensive. French complied, leading his small force into the gap between the German First and Second Armies. Their progress was slow, but they met little resistance: within three days the situation had changed dramatically. Joffre ordered his Fifth Army to support the British right flank, and the German officer staff sent by Moltke thought that the situation was so bad that he ordered a withdrawal. The Germans pulled back to the Aisne and dug themselves in. The seven-day Battle of the Marne had been the death knell of the Schlieffen Plan. The swift and victorious strike against France projected by German leaders had failed to materialize. Henceforth, trench warfare would prevail on the Western Front.

The Battle of Tannenberg

The Russians confounded German expectations by mobilizing much faster than anticipated and by sending two armies into East Prussia in August 1914. The First Army, under Pavel Rennenkampf, headed west out of Lithuania and the Second, under Alexander Samsonov, came north from Poland. They were dispatched in haste under pressure of French appeals to the Franco-Russian Treaty of 1892, amended by a secret protocol that provided for mutual support by the fifteenth day of mobilization. The Germans knew nothing about this provision, and the Russian offensive was a complete surprise to them.

The appearance of Rennenkampf's hard-riding Cossack cavalry in East Prussia – the Junker heartland – struck terror into the populace and sent a stream of prominent nobles into Berlin to beg the Kaiser for deliverance. Commander-in-Chief Moltke, already unnerved by the reverses in France, was besieged by petitions to transfer troops from the Western to the Eastern Front. The only German force in place was the Eighth Army, under the less-than-inspired leadership of General Max von Prittwitz. His attempted stand against the Russian First Army at the town of Gumbinnen failed on 21 August, and the German army withdrew to the Masurian Lakes, where it was in danger of being caught between the two Russian armies when Samsonov's force arrived. Moltke summoned 67-year-old General Paul von Hindenburg from retirement and ordered the able Major General Erich Ludendorff, then in Belgium, to serve as his Chief of Staff. Ludendorff made up in brains what he lacked in nobility, and could be counted on to steer Hindenburg in the right direction.

In the interim, the Eighth Army's director of operations, Colonel Max Hoffmann, had conceived a shrewd plan for holding Rennenkampf with a single cavalry division while sending the main German force against Samsonov. He counted on Rennenkampf's native caution, and on the known enmity between the two Russian commanders, who had come to public blows during the Russo-Japanese War. An expert in Russian military matters, Hoffman correctly anticipated that Samsonov and Rennenkampf were not the men to carry off an operation that required the closest cooperation.

Ill-will was not the only factor that handicapped Russian forces in the hasty incursion into East Prussia. Samsonov's route lay through forests, marshes and lakes that were relatively easy to defend. The summer of 1914 had been extremely dry, and the

Below left: The general situation during the East Prussian campaign showing how the position of the Masurian Lakes made communication between the Russian armies difficult.
Below: The decisive Battle of Tannenberg.

Second Army was struggling through ashy sand in which their guns kept bogging down. Food and forage were in short supply, and it was impossible to live off the land. The local population had taken everything movable in its flight from the dreaded Russians – including telegraph poles and much-needed rolling stock. On Rennenkampf's front, too, the men were going hungry. Worse still, they had used up their entire allocation of artillery shells in the battle for Gumbinnen and had not been resupplied.

Rennenkampf was lying low when the German Eighth Army set out to intercept Samsonov. His encoded radio messages (an expedient necessitated by lack of telegraph facilities) were ludicrously easy to decipher. Hindenburg and Ludendorff, who had just arrived to take command of the Eighth Army, knew the First had no intention of moving. The Russians had not even scouted to find out where the Germans were headed. Ludendorff elected to strike at both flanks of Samsonov's army at once and expedited the pace of the Eighth Army's removal south toward the oncoming Russian force. When Samsonov reported increasing opposition to his efforts to link up with Rennenkampf, his command accused him of cowardice and urged him to hasten to the relief of the First Army. The Russian staff believed that German forces were retreating before the First Army: no evidence of a purposeful German movement to the south by every possible means of transport could convince them to the contrary. Samsonov was goaded into pushing his troops still harder in the drive north.

When Rennenkampf finally made a move, it was in the wrong direction – north toward Königsberg, where he believed the Germans had gone. Samsonov's right was stretched ever thinner in its quest for the elusive First Army. His communications were, if possible, worse than Rennenkampf's – a welter of codes, to many of which First Army headquarters lacked keys. He was finally forced to send radio messages *en clair*, which was of material help to German planners. Taking full advantage of rail transport and their own improvements to local roads, three German corps moved rapidly to encircle Samsonov's forces. The German policy of *Auftragstaktik*, which gave commanders in the field latitude to make on-the-spot decisions independently of headquarters, lent flexibility to the German operation. Where circumstances dictated, they set aside directives from on high. For the battle forming near Tannenberg, General Hermann von François was under orders to attack the Russian left wing at Usdau. Instead he only feinted in that direction before falling on the Russian flank at Soldau. The excuse that his artillery had not arrived in time to make the frontal assault was well received at headquarters, since his I Corps' attack was instrumental in the Russian defeat. By now Samsonov's forces were surrounded, and the battle near Tannenberg had lasted two days. On 27 August the Second Army's fate was sealed by the arrival of the I Corps' artillery, emplaced at Usdau for a full-scale assault. The weary and underfed Russian troops began to fall back. Their brief repulse of the German XX Corps only led them deeper into the trap. There was no choice but to recross the frontier – an order that came from Russia too late to save Samsonov's army. Those who could not escape back into Russia gave themselves up by the thousands. Samsonov went into the forest alone and shot himself. It was one of the worst defeats in military history: 310,000 Russian casualties and 90,000 prisoners. Six hundred and fifty guns were lost. Confusion, poor planning and inadequate supply lines had destroyed the Russian offensive.

Rennenkampf's forces had advanced toward the Masurian Lakes and their border, but they came under heavy German attack once the Second Army had been dispatched. Most managed to cross the frontier only because German forces were tiring. Rennenkampf was severely (and unjustly) criticized at home for his failure to stand and fight, despite the fact that his army had suffered 20 percent casualties in the early stage of the incursion. In November 1914 the Czar confirmed his dismissal as commander.

Opposite: Russian officers parade to receive decorations. Behind the ceremonial facade the Russian army was shockingly ill-prepared for war. Not until 1916 was it able to provide rifles for all its men or a reasonable supply of shells for the artillery.

Race to the Sea and the Ypres Salient

After the Battle of the Marne, both sides were slow to realize that the Germans – now on the defensive – had the advantage under the changed rules of modern warfare. Once dug in, they could hold their positions indefinitely with machine guns, barbed wire and other instruments of the new war technology. The Allied offensive was slower than the German advance had been, and hopes for ending the war in a matter of weeks began to seem ephemeral. Before this realization sank in, each side sought to gain positions from which to outflank the other. The battlelines ended north of the Aisne in mid-September 1914; the two months that followed saw the 'race to the sea,' whose dual purpose was to outflank the enemy and command the Channel ports that served as a conduit for British troops and supplies.

General Erich von Falkenhayn, the German Commander-in-Chief who replaced Moltke after the Marne debacle, lacked sufficient forces to win the race. Many of his troops were tied up in Belgium, which had offered unexpectedly stiff resistance to the German incursion. French Commander-in-Chief Joffre clung to his strategy of frontal assault too long to seize the initiative. It remained to the British to carry the war into Belgium, where they sought to outflank the Germans near the Flemish town of Ypres. The BEF had come north by train from the Aisne as the Germans converged from the other direction. The British force was smaller, but represented the elite of the nation's professional army, well trained in rapid rifle fire and fresher than the German troops. They dug in around Ypres.

On 20 October the Germans launched a spirited mass-formation attack that was soon repelled by British rifle fire. The single breach in the British lines was filled by reinforcements, but both sides took heavy casualties. A second German attack on 31 October failed to displace the British. The final battle took place at Nun's Wood, just outside Ypres, on 11 November, when the Prussian Guard was committed to the fight. The concentration of troops in the small salient guaranteed high casualties – the Germans suffered some 135,000, with very little movement to show for it. BEF losses were smaller because their force was less numerous, but they were bad enough to cripple the best fighting force that Britain had to show.

The race to the sea finally ended at Nieuport on the North Sea, which extended the Western Front some hundreds of miles – all the way to the Swiss frontier. Most of Belgium was now occupied by the Germans, but the Belgian Army did not stop fighting.

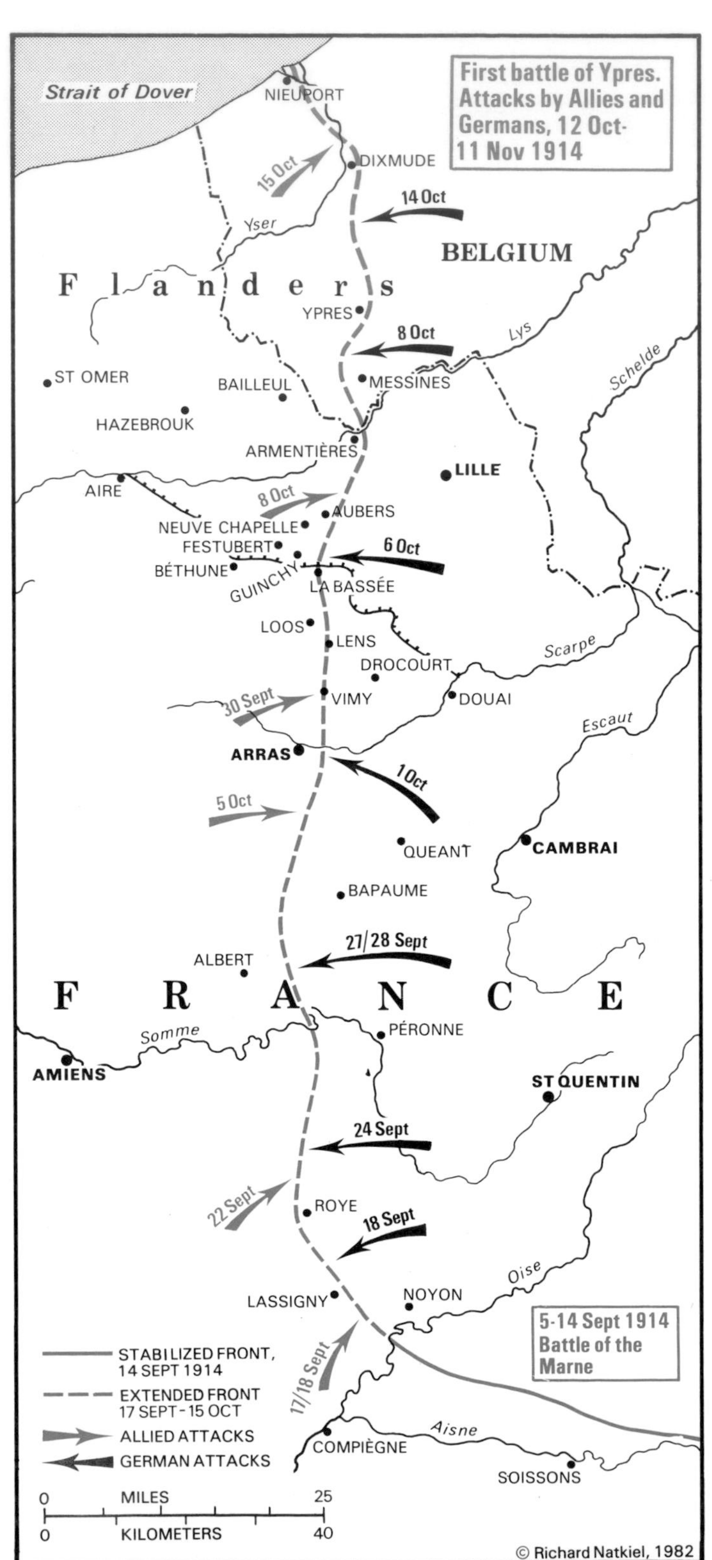

The French war effort was hampered by German occupation of much of northwestern France, where the nation's heavy industry was centered. But the Channel ports essential to British troop and supply movements seemed secure for the time.

Above: Men of the British 19th Brigade come under German artillery fire in September 1914. The well-trained British forces played a part in the early battles of the war out of proportion to their small numbers.
Left: The Race to the Sea. The positions rapidly taken up in this series of outflanking moves, dictated often more by chance than deliberate policy, were to become the battleground for the next three years of war.
Right: The First Battle of Ypres was the final attempt in 1914 to break the stalemate.

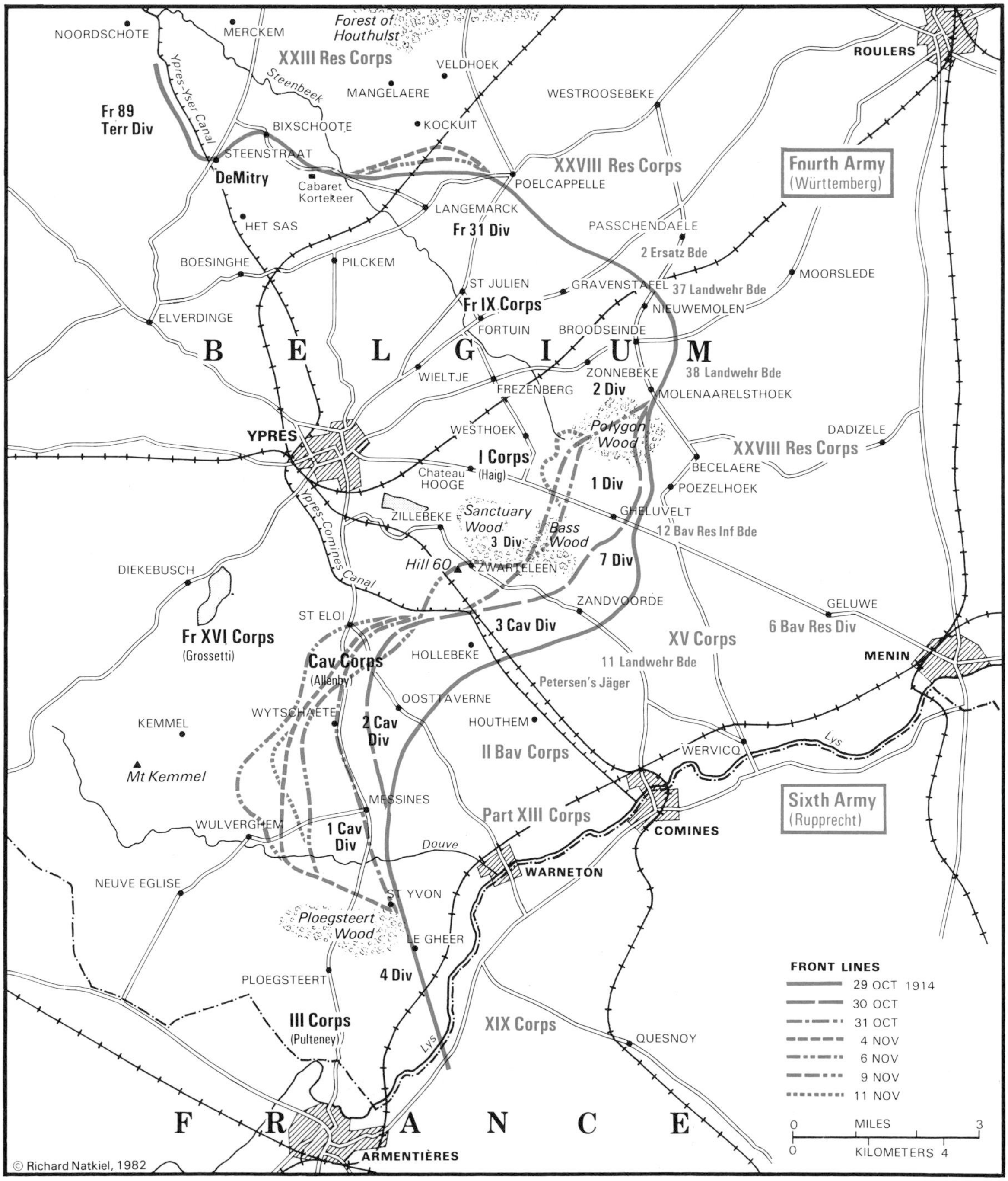

NOORDSCHOTE
MERCKEM
Forest of Houthulst
XXIII Res Corps
VELDHOEK
ROULERS
Ypres-Yser Canal
Steenbeek
MANGELAERE
WESTROOSEBEKE
Fr 89 Terr Div
BIXSCHOOTE
KOCKUIT
STEENSTRAAT
XXVIII Res Corps
Fourth Army (Württemberg)
DeMitry
Cabaret Kortekeer
POELCAPPELLE
LANGEMARCK
HET SAS
Fr 31 Div
PASSCHENDAELE
2 Ersatz Bde
BOESINGHE
PILCKEM
ST JULIEN
GRAVENSTAFEL
37 Landwehr Bde
MOORSLEDE
Fr IX Corps
NIEUWEMOLEN
ELVERDINGE
FORTUIN
BROODSEINDE
B E L G I U M
WIELTJE
ZONNEBEKE
38 Landwehr Bde
FREZENBERG
2 Div
MOLENAARELSTHOEK
YPRES
WESTHOEK
Polygon Wood
DADIZELE
XXVIII Res Corps
I Corps (Haig)
Chateau HOOGE
BECELAERE
1 Div
POEZELHOEK
Ypres-Comines Canal
ZILLEBEKE
Sanctuary Wood
GHELUVELT
12 Bav Res Inf Bde
3 Div
Bass Wood
Hill 60
ZWARTELEEN
7 Div
DIEKEBUSCH
ZANDVOORDE
GELUWE
ST ELOI
3 Cav Div
Fr XVI Corps (Grossetti)
XV Corps
6 Bav Res Div
Cav Corps (Allenby)
HOLLEBEKE
MENIN
11 Landwehr Bde
Petersen's Jäger
OOSTTAVERNE
WYTSCHAETE
2 Cav Div
HOUTHEM
KEMMEL
II Bav Corps
Lys
WERVICQ
Mt Kemmel
MESSINES
Sixth Army (Rupprecht)
Part XIII Corps
WULVERGHEM
1 Cav Div
COMINES
Douve
WARNETON
NEUVE EGLISE
ST YVON
Ploegsteert Wood
LE GHEER
FRONT LINES
29 OCT 1914
30 OCT
31 OCT
4 NOV
6 NOV
9 NOV
11 NOV
PLOEGSTEERT
4 Div
III Corps (Pulteney)
XIX Corps
QUESNOY
Lys
MILES 0 3
KILOMETERS 0 4
F R A N C E
ARMENTIÈRES

Coronel and the Falklands

In the fall of 1914 two of the most important naval battles of the Great War were taking shape in the Pacific. A key factor underlying the global conflict was German colonial and naval expansion, which the British had viewed with alarm for several decades. Germany's determination to find 'a place in the sun' had been implemented as far afield as Tsingtao, China, which served as a base for the German Far Eastern naval squadron. The British saw a threat to their Empire in every German advance and welcomed Japan as an ally in the Far Eastern Theater. Japan's entry into the war forced the Germans to abandon their base at Tsingtao, but Admiral Graf von Spee took his entire force across the Pacific to harass British shipping.

The far-flung intelligence network of the British Admiralty soon located the Germans off the coast of Chile, and Admiral Christopher Cradock, the British commander of the South American squadron, was ordered out with four vessels to attack them. Cradock boasted two armored cruisers, *Monmouth* and *Good Hope*, plus a lighter cruiser and an armed merchantman. The Germans had two armored cruisers of their own – *Gneisenau* and *Scharnhorst* – that were faster and more heavily gunned and armored than the British. In fact, they were among the most powerful ships at sea. Three lighter cruisers accompanied them.

Cradock sighted the larger German force on 1 November 1914 off Coronel, the principal coaling station on the South American coast. As ordered by his Admiralty, he attacked immediately. The Germans' superiority in strength and numbers was enhanced by wind and evening-sun directions that worked against the British. The conclusion was foregone: both the *Good Hope* and the *Monmouth* were sunk with all hands, and the two smaller vessels, *Otranto* and *Glasgow*, fled under cover of darkness two hours after battle was joined. The German ships left the scene unharmed to resume their commerce raiding in the area.

At the British Admiralty the finger of blame was pointed variously at Cradock and at Winston Churchill, First Lord of the Admiralty, whose competence was thrown into question. The British were not accustomed to losing at sea, and Churchill moved quickly to retrieve the situation and his own reputation. Two battlecruisers, *Inflexible* and *Invincible*, were dispatched to the Falkland Islands in the South Pacific, where the British had a colony and naval base. So rapid was their progress that their tripod masts were looming over the Falklands before the Germans knew they had left England.

The battlecruisers' presence was an unpleasant shock to Spee and his squadron when they arrived on 8 December to raid the colony. The Germans withdrew as soon as they saw the big ships preparing to go out of harbor, but British Admiral Frederick Sturdee gave chase and drew within range after an all-day pursuit. His speed was

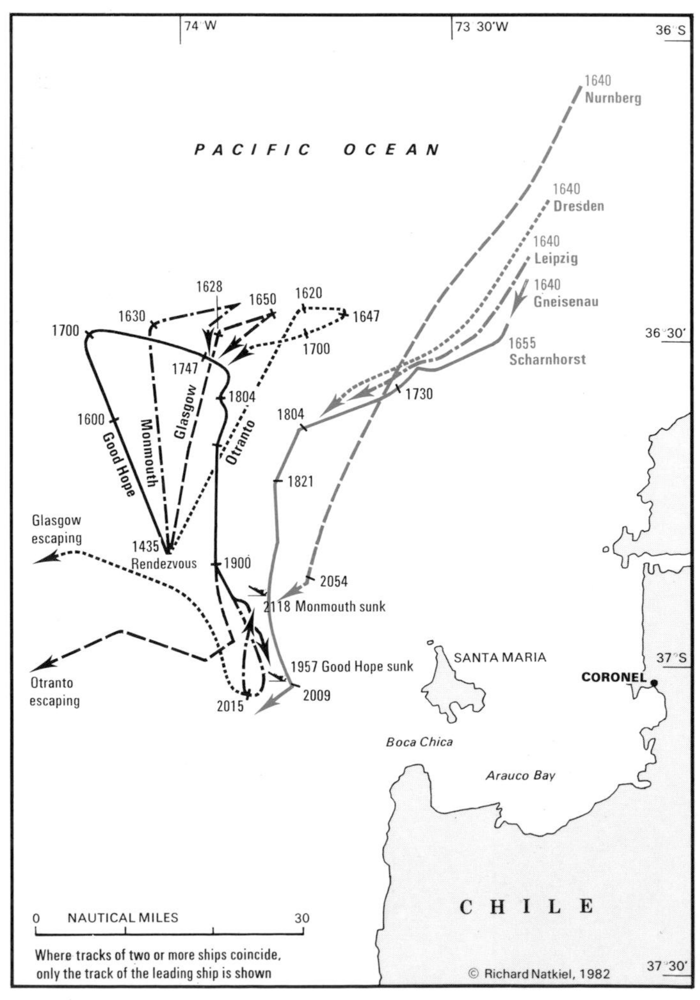

Where tracks of two or more ships coincide, only the track of the leading ship is shown

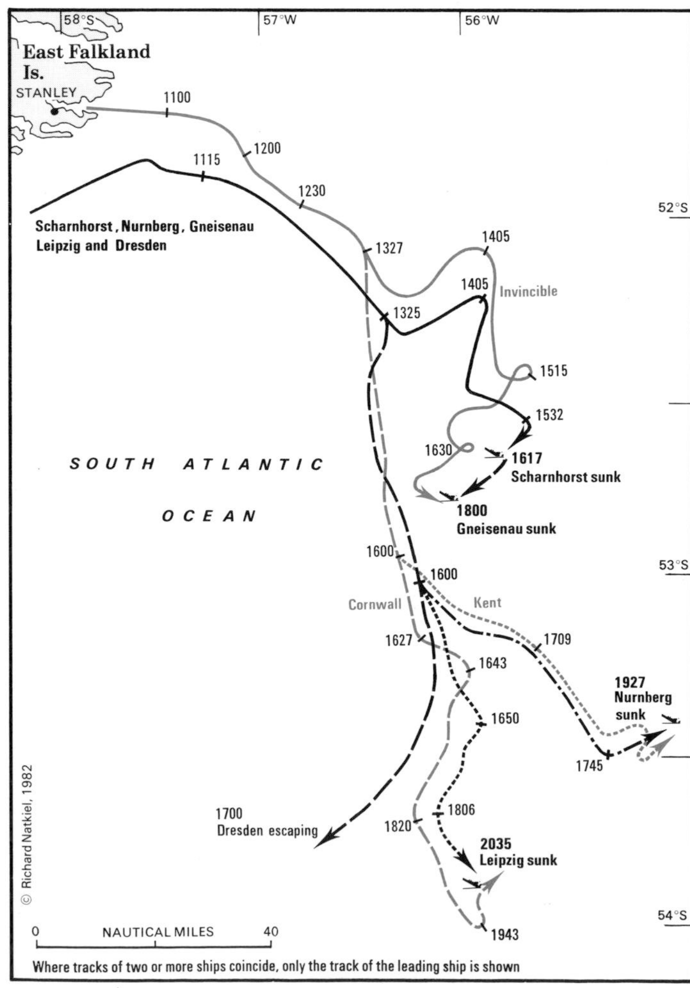

Where tracks of two or more ships coincide, only the track of the leading ship is shown

Below left: Maps of the Battles of Coronel (left) and the Falklands.
Right: Admiral Graf von Spee (left), commander of the German forces at Coronel and the Falklands.
Bottom: The last moments of the *Scharnhorst* (foreground) and the *Gneisenau*.

superior to that of the *Gneisenau* and *Scharnhorst*, and he took advantage of it to stay beyond reach of the German guns as he directed a punishing bombardment against their ships. Both German armored cruisers went to the bottom.

The three lighter cruisers that made up Sturdee's squadron overwhelmed two other German vessels, the cruisers *Leipzig* and *Nurnberg*. Only the *Dresden* escaped, and a few months later it too was hunted down.

Sturdee was made a baronet as a result of this battle, and Winston Churchill's prestige was restored with that of the British Admiralty. It would soon be jeopardized again by the abortive Gallipoli adventure against Turkey, which had entered the war on the German side in October 1914.

Gallipoli

Turkey's entrance into the war on behalf of Germany created serious supply problems for Russia, one of whose sea routes to her Allies was cut off by the closing of the Dardanelles Strait. British leaders, seeking a way to expedite the war that had bogged down on the Western Front, saw a campaign against Turkey as offering several advantages. A successful attack on the Gallipoli Peninsula would secure the fall of Constantinople, knock Turkey out of the war and open a supply route to the numerous but poorly equipped Russian Army. Both Lord Kitchener, the British War Minister, and Winston Churchill of the Admiralty favored the plan.

Churchill proposed at first that ships alone could do the job; only when ministerial opinion was engaged on behalf of the project did he amend this view to include troop involvement. Once a concerted sea/land action was agreed upon, the island of Mudros was selected as the base of operations. There fleet and land forces from Alexandria were concentrated under Sir Ian Hamilton. Participating military forces included the British 29th Division, the Royal Navy, Australians and New Zealanders (Anzacs) and a French Expeditionary Force.

In January 1915 French and British ships under Admiral Carden gathered at Lemnos Island, 60 miles from the entrance to the Dardanelles, which were thickly mined and guarded by Turkish forts on both sides. The first attack was launched on 19 February against the forts at the entrance, the second on 26 February. When the guns of the forts were silenced, landing parties demolished them, except at Kum Kale on the Asiatic coast where they were driven back. On 4 March the fleet passed up the Strait, which was partially swept of mines, to Fort Dardanus opposite Kilia Bahr. But Allied bombardments had alerted the Turks to an impending attack: they had strengthened shore defenses and improved their mining techniques.

The initial naval attack on Fort Dardanus was unsuccessful, as the Turks were able to shell the ships from concealed positions along both shores. Admiral Carden resigned, and was replaced by Rear Admiral Sir John de Robeck. On 18 March three Allied ships – *Irresistible*, *Ocean* and *Bouvet* – were destroyed by mines, and *Inflexible* and *Gaulois* were put out of action. Commanding admirals were dissuaded from additional close bombardments. Clearly, it was time to implement the land side of the operation.

The southern end of the peninsula was chosen as the point of attack. Some 75,000 troops took part in the initial landings of 25 April 1915, including 30,000 from Australia and New Zealand and 17,000 from France. The shoreline was rent by ravines and gullies, presenting only a few small strips of beach backed by cliffs. Five landing points, designated east to west 'S,' 'V,' 'W,' 'X' and 'Y' Beaches, were selected from which to attack the heights in the peninsula's center. But these commanding positions were heavily entrenched by the Turks, and the difficult terrain, unmapped and unknown to the Allies, concealed nests of gunners and snipers. The landings themselves were largely well planned and carried out, but once ashore the troops were beset by confusion and irresolute leadership.

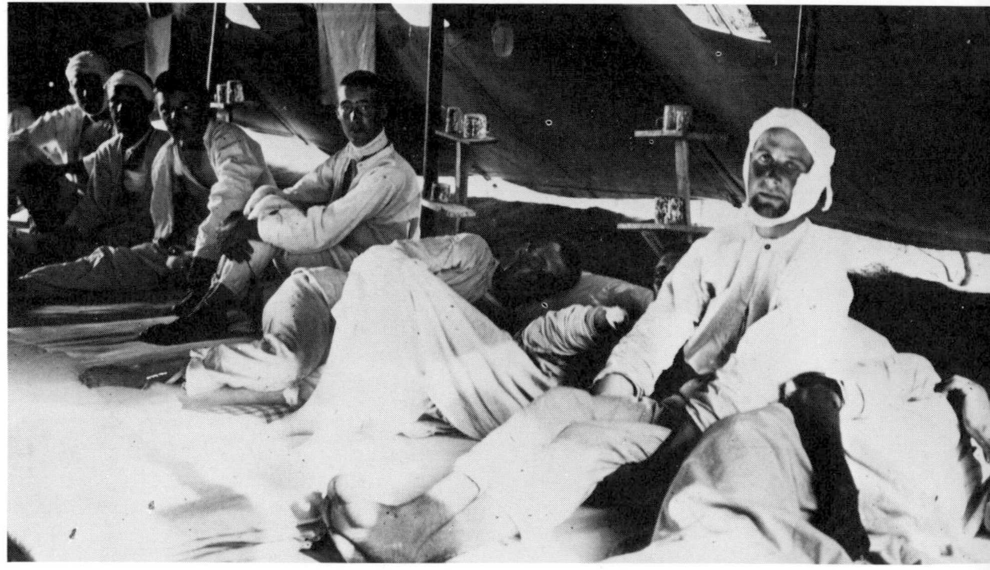

The Anzacs made a separate landing north of the promontory of Gaba Tepe (later called Anzac Cove). They gained only a little ground, which was taken and held for the next three months at terrific cost. British howitzers – even naval guns – had little effect against the Turkish positions on the heights, manned by 80,000 men under German General Liman von Sanders. Allied

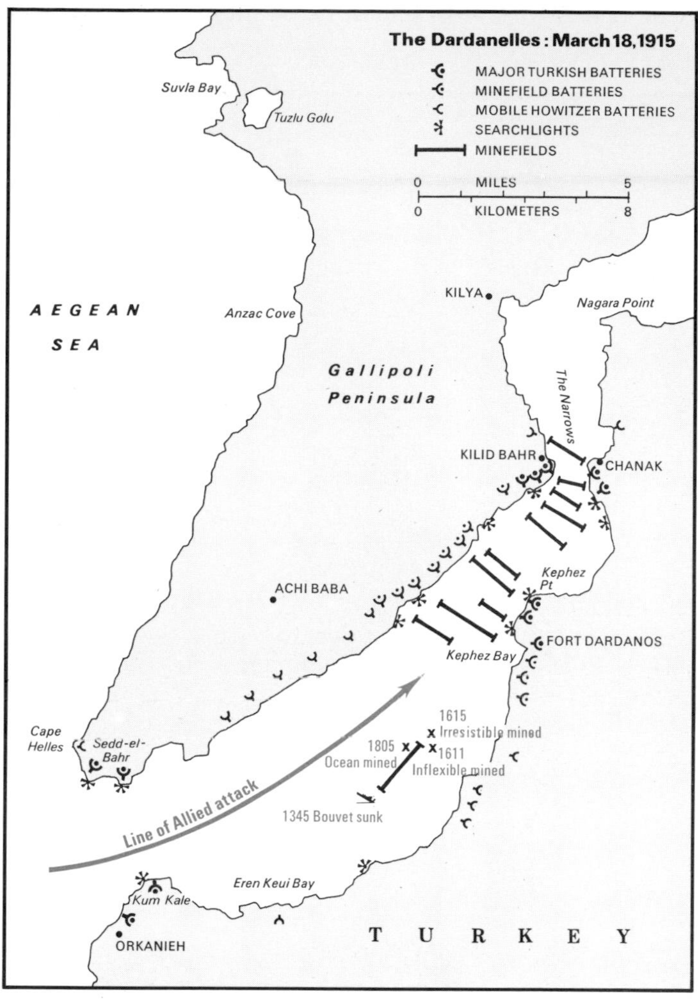

troops dug in near the coast to face months of inconclusive but costly engagements. Reinforcements were sent to both sides, and the sweltering summer brought high Allied casualties – the price of hesitation after the initial thrust.

In London, Kitchener, Churchill and the British Cabinet clung tenaciously to the hope of a strategic victory in the east through the first great amphibious operation of modern times. Increasing numbers of troops were sent in, and some gains were made on the southern peninsula during June. On August 6–10 a heroic effort was made to carry the heights of Sari Bahr, without which the precarious holdings along the peninsula were useless. Fresh troops were landed at Suvla Bay, north of Anzac Cove, with orders to advance inland against the high ground, but poor leadership resulted in yet another failure. While Allied officers and men milled around near the landing point to consolidate, the Turks had time to prepare for the coming attack, which they repulsed easily. By September it was clear that the Gallipoli campaign was a disaster, but it was not until year's end that British authorities could accept the fact and order a withdrawal.

Sir Ian Hamilton was replaced by General Monro, who planned a successful evacuation, completed without loss of life by 9 January 1916. It had been an expensive year for the Allied cause. The way to Constantinople was still blocked – and would be throughout the war. The door to Russia remained shut. Instead of a morale-building victory, the French and British had found in the Gallipoli campaign a synonym for failure.

Top: Maps of the naval attack on the Dardanelles (left) and the subsequent Gallipoli landings.
Above: A British trench taken by the Turks after a typically fierce struggle.
Opposite, top: A Turkish shell bursts on 'V' Beach at Gallipoli.
Opposite, lower: British POWs in a Turkish hospital.

Second and Third Battles of Ypres

The stasis on the Western Front in early 1915 led commanders on both sides to cast about for sites where even a minor victory might be achieved. Little came of any of the efforts that ensued, though all cost heavily in lives. In Champagne the French launched a February offensive that gained almost no ground with an expenditure of 50,000 troops. A month later the British attacked at Neuve Chapelle with little more success.

The Germans chose to stay on the defensive until 22 April, when they launched an attack against British and French entrenchments at Ypres. For the first time on the Western Front, poison gas was used as a weapon (the Germans had previously tested it against the Russians). Allied forces, overcome by astonishment and fear, left a wide gap in their lines as they fled the choking gas overspreading their trenches. The Germans moved in with very few losses, but the shock value of the poison-gas attack was dissipated by their lack of sufficient troops to follow it up decisively.

The historic Flemish town of Ypres had been entirely destroyed in the first conflict on these grounds the year before, but the strategic salient was destined to serve as a battleground throughout the war. In 1917 the region was racked again by the Third Battle of Ypres (or Passchendaele), precipitated in part by the Allied need to distract the Germans from deteriorating morale in the French Army. By spring of that year, French forces had suffered horrendous casualties; with no end in sight, many units began to mutiny. Over 54 divisions were involved before General Henri-Philippe Pétain took over from General Robert Nivelle, who had succeeded Joffre as commander-in-chief. Pétain's efforts to restore morale began to have their effect, but it was doubtful that the French could withstand a serious German assault.

British Field Marshal Sir Douglas Haig already decided on a third attack in the ravaged Ypres salient. The Allies were desperate to end the stalemate on the Western Front, and Royal Navy support

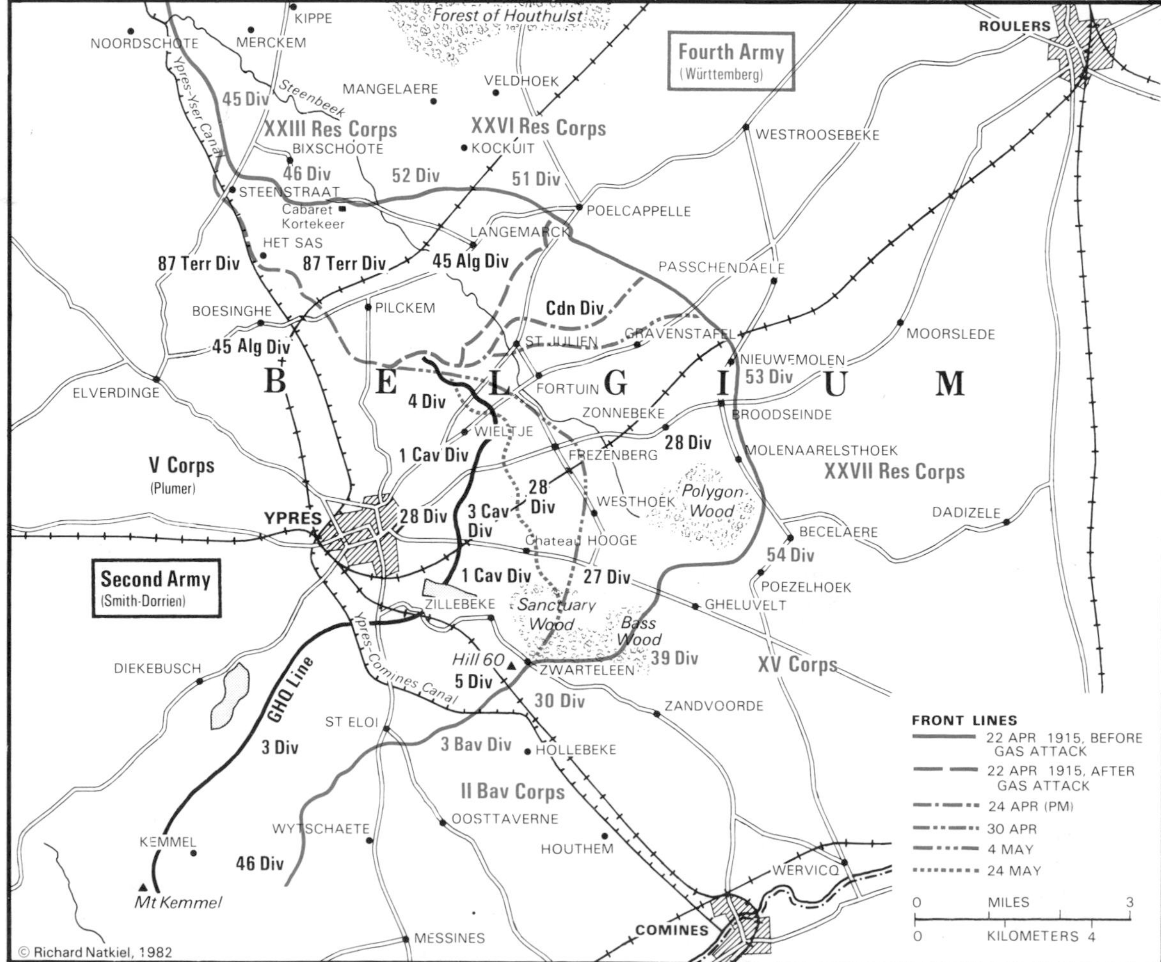

Above: Men of the British 51st Division cross a communication trench as they move up to the front. Left: The Second Battle of Ypres.

Below right: The Third Battle of Ypres. Note the gradual extension of the front allocated to the methodical General Plumer's Second Army. Below left: A British tank tows a captured German gun. Ground conditions in the Ypres Salient were usually too poor to allow tanks to operate effectively.

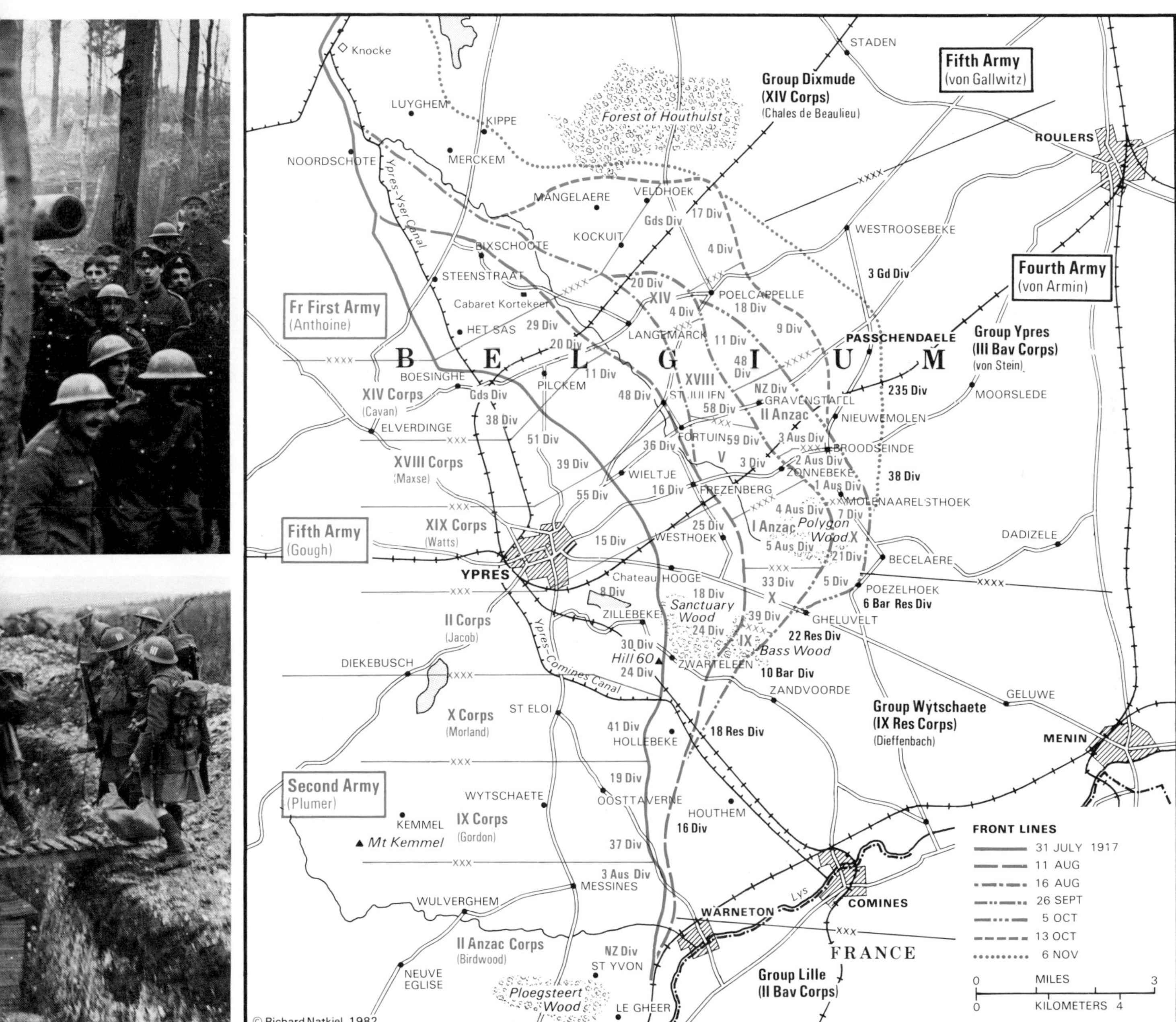

was enlisted in the interest of destroying submarine bases in Belgium. The French mutinies only confirmed this course, as the offensive would prevent the Germans from exploiting the problem.

Haig's objective was to widen his narrow salient at Ypres and use it as a jumping-off place to Ostend (a German submarine base) and other North Sea ports. Months before the attack, British sappers began tunneling under the German-held Messines Ridge, which commanded the area, to plant explosives. In early June they were detonated, and a short attack on the ridge secured it to the British.

The main battle began on 31 July after a week of preliminary bombardment. In the next four days the British advanced two miles at a cost of 32,000 casualties. The pattern set in earlier struggles for this ground was repeating itself: heavy losses for miniscule gains. Constant rain hampered the combatants' every move. On 6 August the British won a little ground near Langemarck, but the Germans were unperturbed.

In late September the weather broke for a few days, enabling Plumer's Second British Army to progress into the Menin Road and Polygon Wood sectors. It was a brief reprieve: both rain and mud returned, accompanied by the chill of October. Within a few weeks the mud was waist-high in many areas.

The three Allied commanders involved were ready to relinquish the fight, but Haig insisted on a final drive toward the village of Passchendaele. The last attack mired down in mud and blood on 10 November, with an appalling quarter of a million casualties on each side for the entire offensive.

Verdun

By 1916 it was clear to both sides that a war of attrition was in progress in which victory might be achieved by exhausting the enemy's manpower reserves. German commander Falkenhayn chose Verdun as the likeliest target on which to test German artillery against French infantry in great numbers. The strong French frontier fortress on the River Meuse had seen little fighting, and it was possible that defenses were not rigorous. Germany had numerous railways leading into the area – far more than the French. It would be a test case in body counts, rather than a true strategic assault on the ancient guardian of the Meuse with its circle of outlying forts.

The opening German bombardment of 21 February was the heaviest of the war to date, concentrated on several French divisions holding an eight-mile front on the riverbank. Next day, the French began to withdraw from this first line of defense, and reinforcements were ordered into Verdun. The second French line was breached on 24 February, and the Germans advanced to the third. Here a line of trenches joined two strong forts – Douaumont and Vaux – four miles from Verdun. Douaumont's garrison was insufficient to withstand the German attack: the fort fell to the enemy.

Pétain, who had been appointed commander of the French defense, called for more artillery and widened the highway leading to Verdun. It became the vital artery called the *Voie Sacrée*, which brought in essential supplies and reinforcements and gave passage out for the wounded. Early in March, a determined German assault on both sides of the river gained new ground with heavy losses to both sides. Not until 6 June, after a grueling three-month siege, did the fort at Vaux fall to the Germans.

The struggle for Verdun ebbed and flowed for the rest of the year, but the German effort faltered in the wake of Allied offensives on other fronts that drew off troops from the frontier. Not until December did the assault trail off in futility. Verdun itself was never captured, but the French Army suffered some 360,000 casualties in defending it. German losses, too, were far heavier than Falkenhayn had envisioned when he mapped out his sitting-duck strategy. In the event, Verdun became a microcosm of World War I itself.

Above right: No Man's Land at Verdun.
Right: Casualties of the bitter fighting in one of the tunnels at Fort Vaux.
Opposite, top: The Verdun battle.
Opposite, bottom: French reinforcements arrive along the *Voie Sacrée* to help the defenders of Verdun.

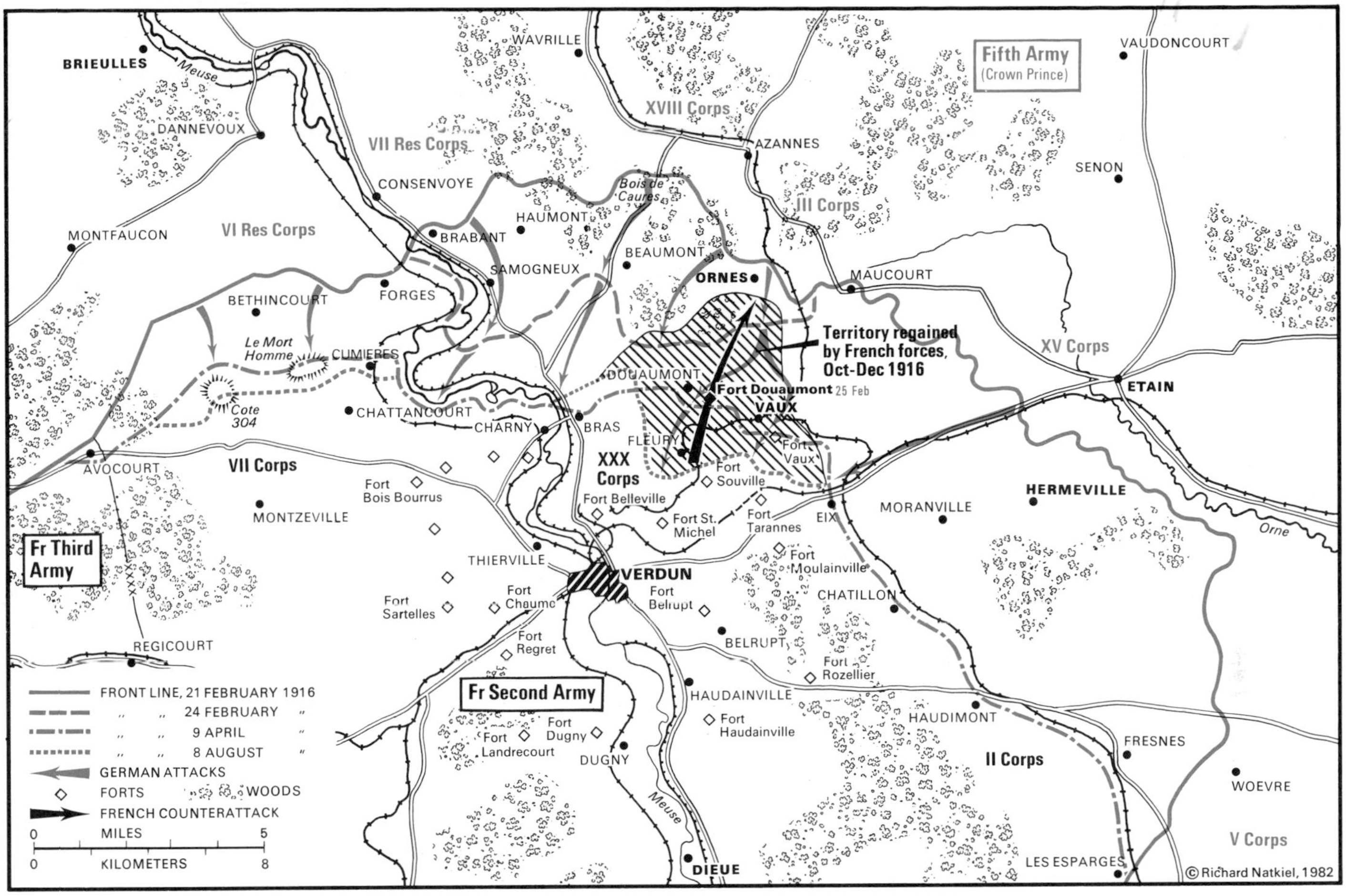

Fifth Army
(Crown Prince)
XVIII Corps
VII Res Corps
VI Res Corps
III Corps
XV Corps
VII Corps
XXX
Corps
Fr Third
Army
Fr Second Army
II Corps
V Corps
Territory regained
by French forces,
Oct-Dec 1916
Fort Douaumont 25 Feb
BRIEULLES
DANNEVOUX
WAVRILLE
AZANNES
VAUDONCOURT
SENON
CONSENVOYE
HAUMONT
Bois de
Caures
BRABANT
MONTFAUCON
SAMOGNEUX
BEAUMONT
ORNES
MAUCOURT
FORGES
BETHINCOURT
Le Mort
Homme
CUMIERES
Cote
304
CHATTANCOURT
DOUAUMONT
VAUX
ETAIN
CHARNY
BRAS
FLEURY
Fort
Vaux
Fort
Souville
AVOCOURT
Fort
Bois Bourrus
Fort Belleville
HERMEVILLE
MONTZEVILLE
Fort St.
Michel
Fort
Tarannes
EIX
MORANVILLE
Orne
THIERVILLE
VERDUN
Fort
Moulainville
Fort
Sartelles
Fort
Chaume
Fort
Belrupt
CHATILLON
REGICOURT
Fort
Regret
BELRUPT
Fort
Rozellier
HAUDAINVILLE
HAUDIMONT
Fort
Landrecourt
Fort
Dugny
Fort
Haudainville
FRESNES
DUGNY
Meuse
WOEVRE
DIEUE
LES ESPARGES
FRONT LINE, 21 FEBRUARY 1916
" " 24 FEBRUARY "
" " 9 APRIL "
" " 8 AUGUST "
GERMAN ATTACKS
FORTS
WOODS
FRENCH COUNTERATTACK
0 MILES 5
0 KILOMETERS 8
©Richard Natkiel, 1982

The Battle of the Somme

In the summer of 1916 the British share of the Western Front had stretched south to the River Somme: here the Anglo-French command planned a major offensive involving eight French and 14 British divisions along a 26-mile front. Another eight divisions would be held in reserve.

In the preliminary artillery barrage, which lasted almost a week, over a million shells were dispatched against the German trenches. On 1 July the bombardment ended, and German troops swarmed from their deep dugouts to take up machine-gun positions in the ruined trenches and the shell-pitted ground around them. The British assembled rapidly before their own trenches and moved off in dense lines across the No Man's Land created by the heavy shelling – terrain that grew ever more difficult as they approached the German positions. The French remained at their posts to follow within a few hours.

Anglo-French forces had expected little resistance after the devastating six-day bombardment, but the Germans were ready for them by the time they traversed the quarter-mile belt of No Man's Land. Machine-gun and rifle fire mowed down the first British line and then the second. German artillery opened up against the British side of the sector, but the troops there kept on coming. The sacrifice of men that day recalled Japanese assaults against Russia 15 years before: 20,000 British soldiers lost their lives; 40,000 were wounded.

Casualties were totally disproportionate to the small gains made. Part of the German first line was taken, and the French were successful against the second line with a night attack. But when three reserve cavalry divisions tried to exploit the gap, they were decimated by machine-gun fire. The Allied command resigned itself to another battle of attrition that lasted until November. In September there was a notable offensive – the Battle of Flers Courcelette – which saw the first use of tanks in the war, but they were too few and too slow to exploit their initial deep penetration.

The last major engagement was to take place on the Ancre in November, but it bogged down in mud and came to nothing. All told, the Battle of the Somme accounted for over half a million Allied casualties, with a comparable cost to Germany. British generals were much criticized for their inept handling of the offensive, but German observers reported that their army was wrecked on the Somme by the loss of countless NCOs and junior-grade officers.

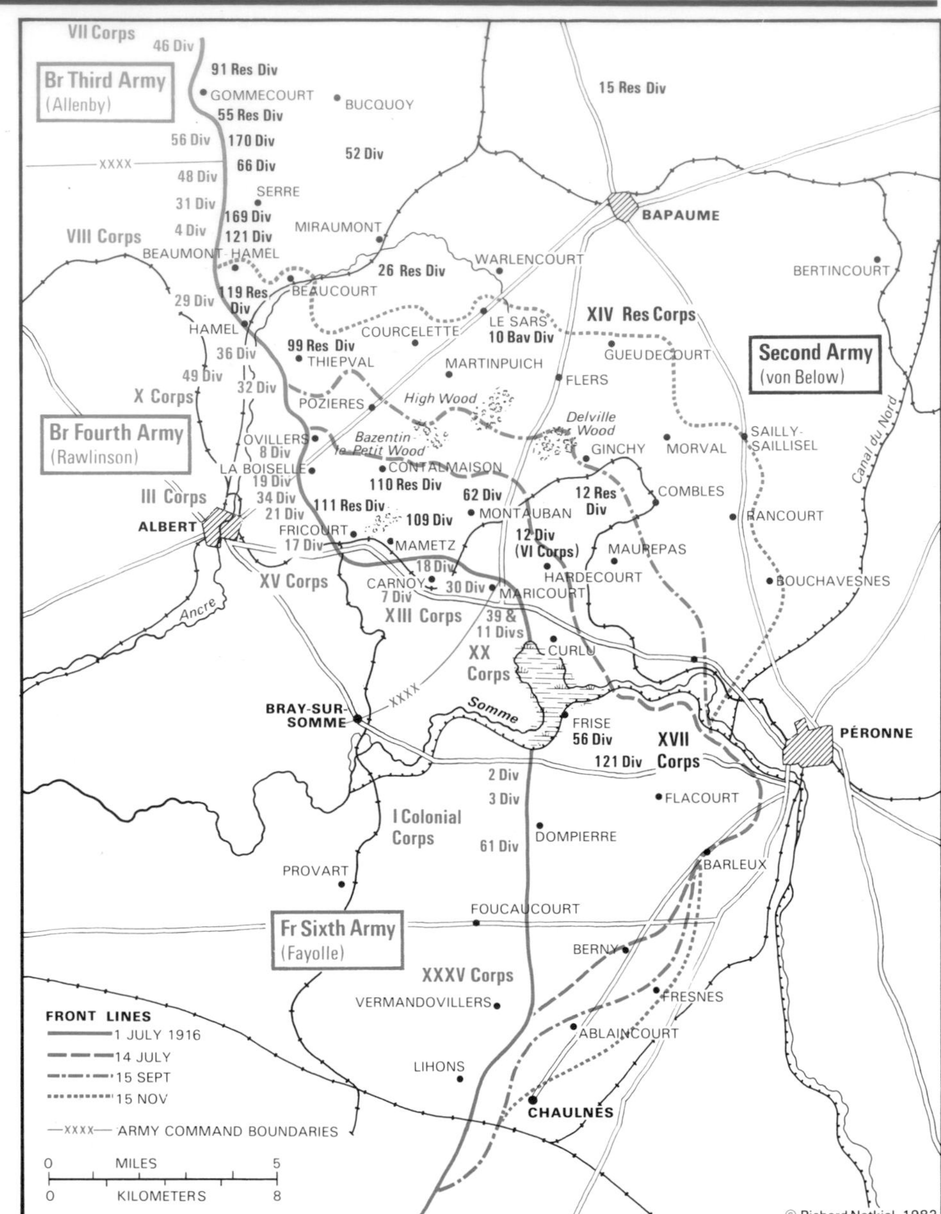

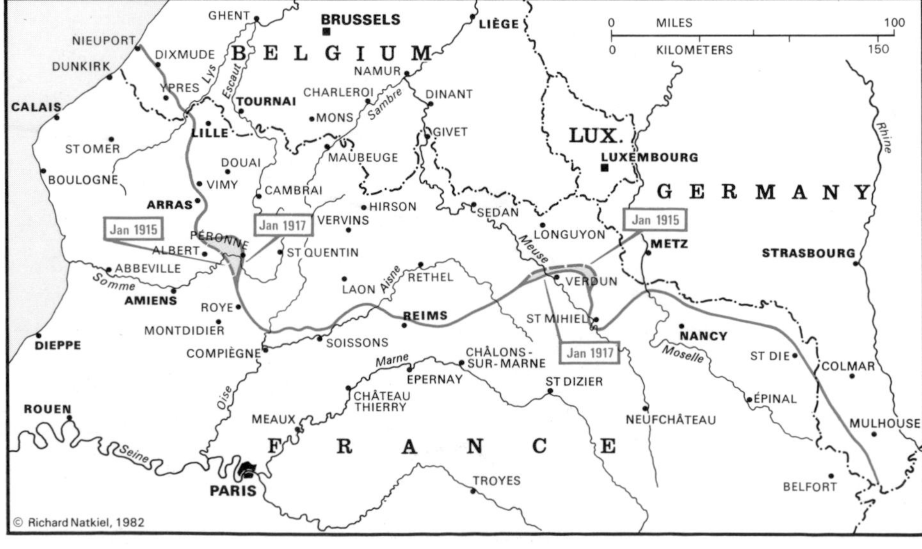

Left: The Battle of the Somme.
Bottom left: The Western Front showing the scant changes brought about by the German and Allied attacks of 1916.
Below: Heavily laden British troops move up to the front.

Bottom: Men of the Lafayette Escadrille, a unit composed of American volunteers serving with the French air force which served in the Somme sector during the battle.

The Battle of Jutland

Prior to mid-1916 the German High Seas Fleet had avoided a full-scale battle against the larger British Grand Fleet in the hope of pitting its whole strength against only part of the British force at some future date. On 30 May 1916 Admiral John Jellicoe, commander-in-chief of the Grand Fleet, learned via intercepted radio signals that the German fleet was on its way out of harbor at Wilhelmshaven.

The Grand Fleet left Scapa Flow on an intercepting course, with Admiral Beatty's battlecruiser squadrons supported by four fast new battleships as scouts. Cruisers from Beatty's squadron made contact off Jutland with German cruisers, and the British battlecruisers soon sighted their German counterparts, which were screening the advance of the German battleships. The two scouting groups joined battle that afternoon.

German guns and armor proved superior to British in this preliminary engagement: two of Beatty's battlecruisers were blown up. Beatty had sighted the German battleships approaching from the south, but he failed to keep Jellicoe informed of the

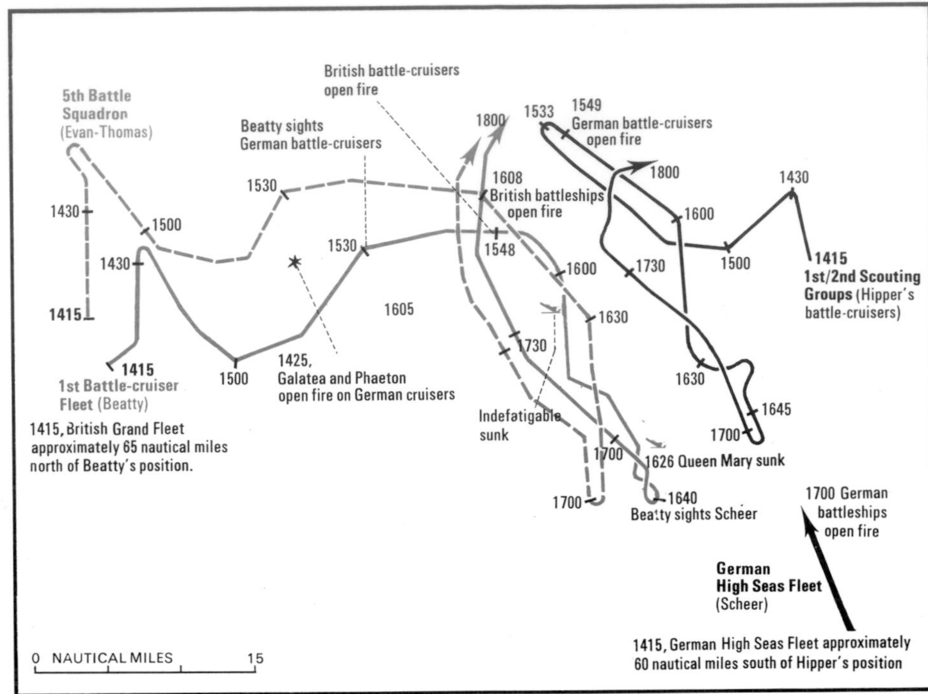

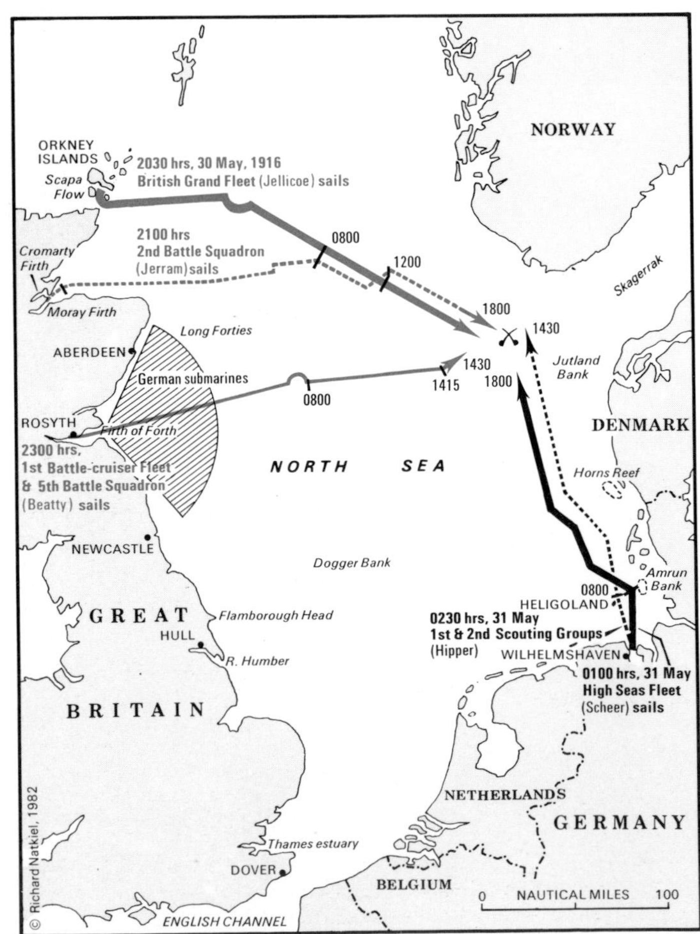

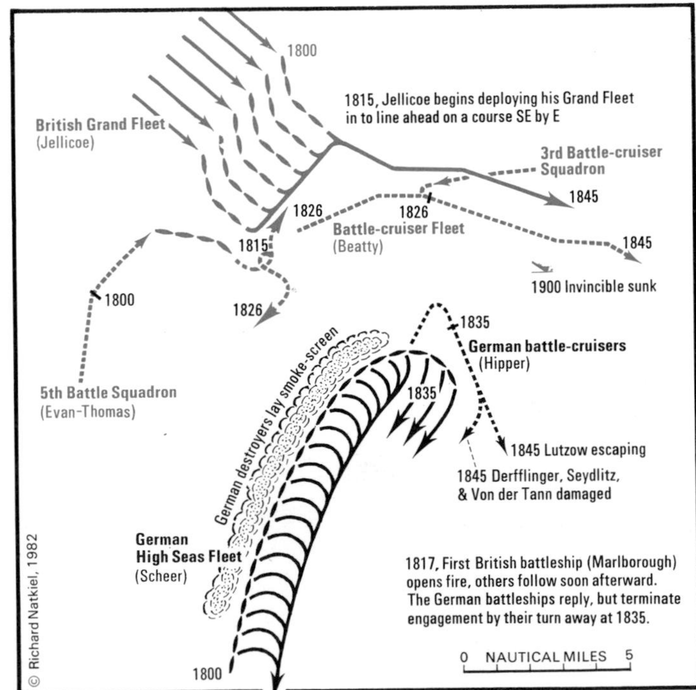

Maps of the two fleets' courses in the advance to battle (left), the engagement of the battlecruiser vanguards (top) and the deployment of the British main body ahead of the Germans. Top right: The British light cruiser *Southampton*. Right: The battlecruiser *Indefatigable* sinks.

enemy's position and course. Jellicoe was awaiting the moment when he could deploy his battlefleet of 24 Dreadnoughts, which were cruising in six parallel lines in search of the enemy. Jellicoe would have to deploy into line-ahead formation if all his ships were to use their guns: timing was of the essence, as he could not do this until he had the enemy's position and bearing.

At 1815 the German battlecruisers encountered those that had remained to screen Jellicoe, and another British battlecruiser was destroyed before the British commander realized the likely location of the main German force. Jellicoe began his deployment into line ahead and 20 minutes later encountered German Admiral Reinhard Scheer, with his battleships in line ahead. Jellicoe passed ahead of the German fleet at right angles and concentrated his fire on Scheer's leading ships.

Scheer ordered an 'all-together' reversal of course – an extremely difficult maneuver – only to find himself in the same peril half an hour later. The Germans withdrew with the help of a smokescreen; then German destroyers attacked with torpedoes. Jellicoe turned away, losing contact with the enemy, and was roundly criticized later. Churchill came to his defense on the ground that Jellicoe had carried a massive responsibility.

During the night Jellicoe sought to interpose his ships between the fleeing Germans and their bases. This attempt was foiled by an Admiralty failure to transmit vital German radio messages and by British commanders' negligence in reporting engagements during the night. The loss of three battlecruisers and three armored cruisers seemed a sorry end to the long-awaited confrontation with the German fleet. The only consolation was that the Germans were the ones who had fled the scene.

Below: The German fleet's second and nearly disastrous move toward the British and the subsequent retreat.
Bottom left: The German flight back to base.
Bottom right: Admiral Scheer (center), commander of the High Seas Fleet.

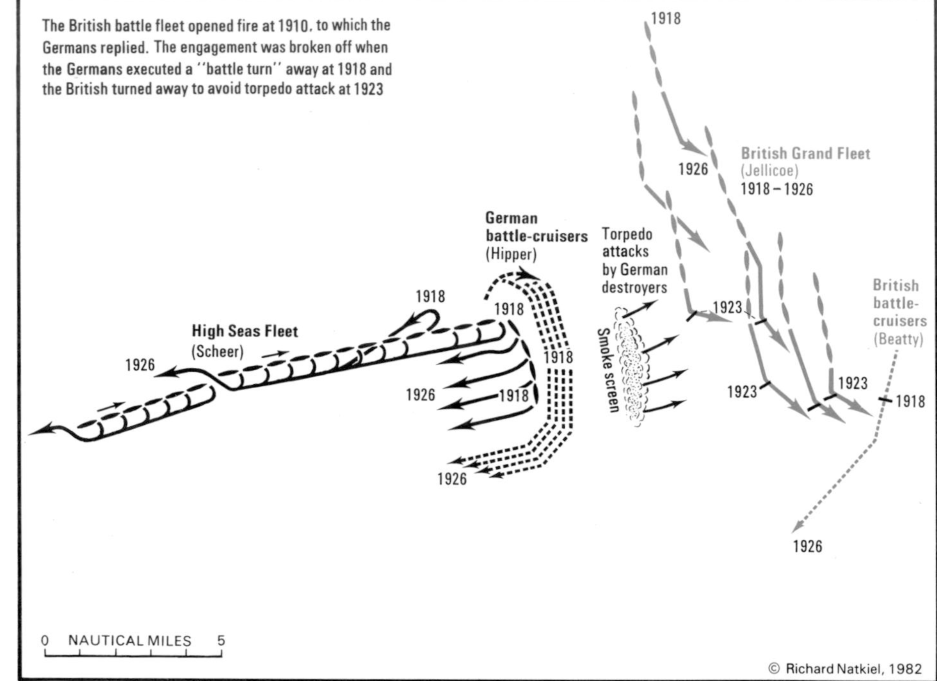

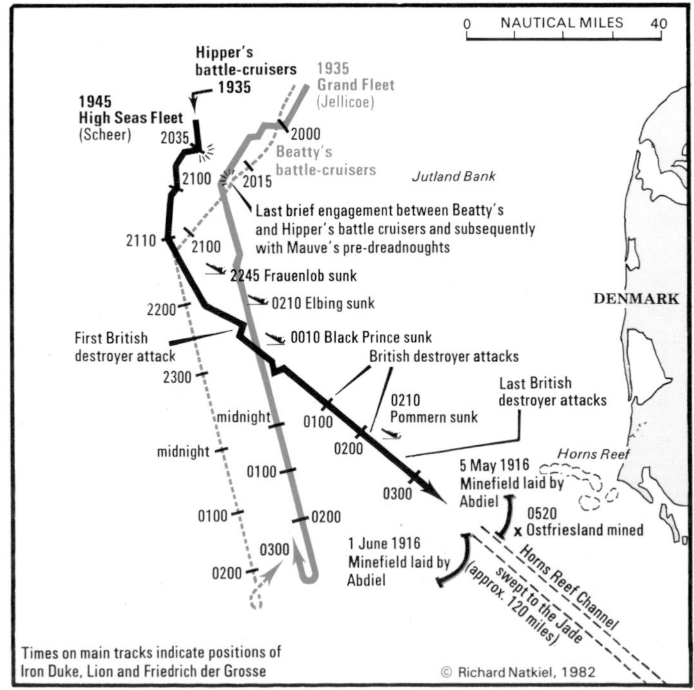

The Brusilov Offensive

During 1915 the Russian Army had been retreating on the Eastern Front. By 1916 many of its equipment shortages had been overcome, and the Russians were contemplating a real offensive. While this was still in the planning stage, an urgent appeal for help came from the Italians, whose army had been heavily attacked by the Austrians in the Trentino district. As a result, General Alexei Brusilov, the new commander of the Southern Front defending the Ukraine, had unusual freedom of action to attack the Austrians at short notice.

Brusilov was well prepared for such an eventuality. He had already ordered his commanders to dig their trenches closer to the Austrian lines (No Man's Land on the Eastern Front could be up to several miles wide – too far, in Brusilov's opinion, to launch an attack). He had also abandoned the practice of massing reserves in advance of a battle, believing that this only alerted the enemy to his intentions and enabled them to bring up three times as many men via their superior railroad facilities.

The attack that would be called the Brusilov Offensive began on 4 June 1916. The Russians faced the Austrian Fourth and Seventh Armies on the flanks, the Second and Southern Armies in the center. The Southern Army alone included German divisions. A strong artillery bombardment demoralized the Austrians before the assault, and they were in headlong retreat soon after the Russians struck. The breakthrough was accomplished with bewildering speed and seemed at first the most successful Russian operation of the war to date. But the failure to mass reserves led to a faltering of Brusilov's offensive. The Germans collected forces around Kovel and threatened the Russians from the north. When they attacked, Brusilov had to retreat: in the process his force suffered some one million casualties.

The offensive had heartened the Allies, perhaps weakened the German assault on Verdun and destroyed the morale of the ill-assorted Austrian Army entirely. But the disproportionate casualties in this and subsequent Russian operations paved the way for the revolution of the following year.

Above: General Brusilov.
Below: The substantial territorial gains made by Brusilov's offensive.
Below left: A Russian heavy gun in a prepared position.

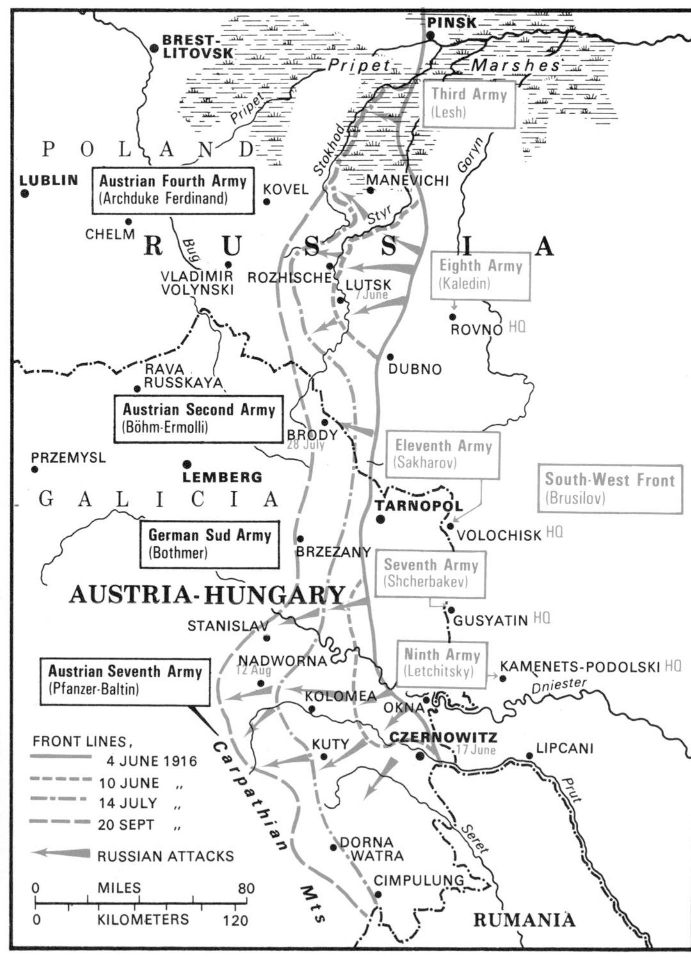

German Offensives, Spring 1918

Early in 1918 the Germans were able to transfer 70 divisions from the Eastern to the Western Front as a result of the Russian Revolution. General Ludendorff and his colleagues believed this would enable them to overwhelm exhausted Allied forces before significant numbers of American troops were ready for battle. The plan was to attack the British Fifth and Third Armies, breaking through north and south of Peronne, then driving a wedge between French and British forces. The Germans regarded the British forces as the strongest on the Allied side and believed that the war would be won if they could be defeated.

The attack was to involve specially trained storm troops and new tactics. Artillery would bombard the rear areas primarily with gas shells (to disrupt communications) rather than with conventional ordnance for destroying defenses. The storm troops were to infiltrate through the front line without attacking its strongpoints. This *Kaiserschlacht* (Kaiser's Battle) began on 21 March.

The initial gas-shell bombardment was highly effective, and fog provided cover for early infantry attacks. Within three days the Germans had penetrated the British line on a wide front to advance 14 miles – a huge gain by Western-Front standards. Allied generals disagreed on strategy: Pétain favored a retreat toward Paris, while Haig saw hope for a counteroffensive if the French were less reluctant to send in their reserves. Marshal Foch had to assume the role of overall co-ordinator to resolve Allied differences.

By 5 April the Germans had lost their initial momentum, but retained possession of a wide salient that stretched to nine miles east of Amiens. To retain this advantage, they attacked the British First Army for the remainder of April and were finally stopped again only by a desperate defense. German generals turned their attention to the French hoping to draw off Allied reserves before making a final decisive attack on the more-formidable British forces.

In fact the attack on the French was far more successful in its early stages than the Germans had expected.

On 27 May the Chemins des Dames Ridge fell to a German assault that reached Château-Thierry a week later. Then this drive too began to die out. The last two German offensives were made with very low reserves and high casualties among the best units. German morale was in decline even as Allied forces were heartened by the presence of fresh American units in ever-growing numbers. On 18 July Foch was ready to begin his counteroffensive east from Villers Cotterêts. Inexorably, he pushed the Germans back until early August: then a massive Anglo-French attack took the Great War into its final phase.

Below: The actual development of the battle, showing how the Germans reinforced their success on the left, failing to maintain their move on the communications center at Amiens.

Right: The German plan for the *Kaiserslacht*.
Far right: General map of the whole series of German offensives of 1918.
Below right: General Ludendorff, planner of the offensives.
Bottom right: Storm troops push past rudimentary defenses in the early stages of the March fighting.

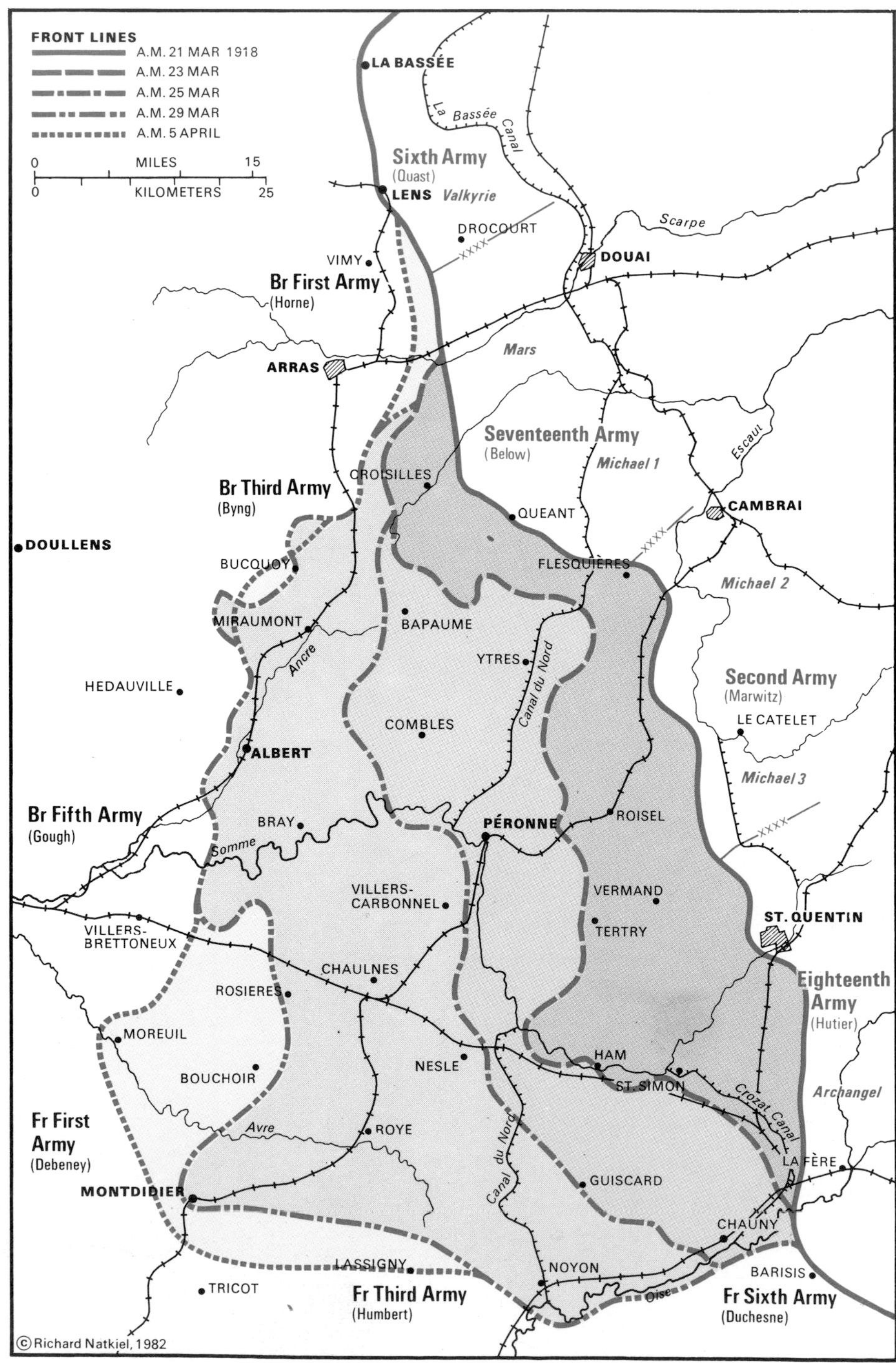

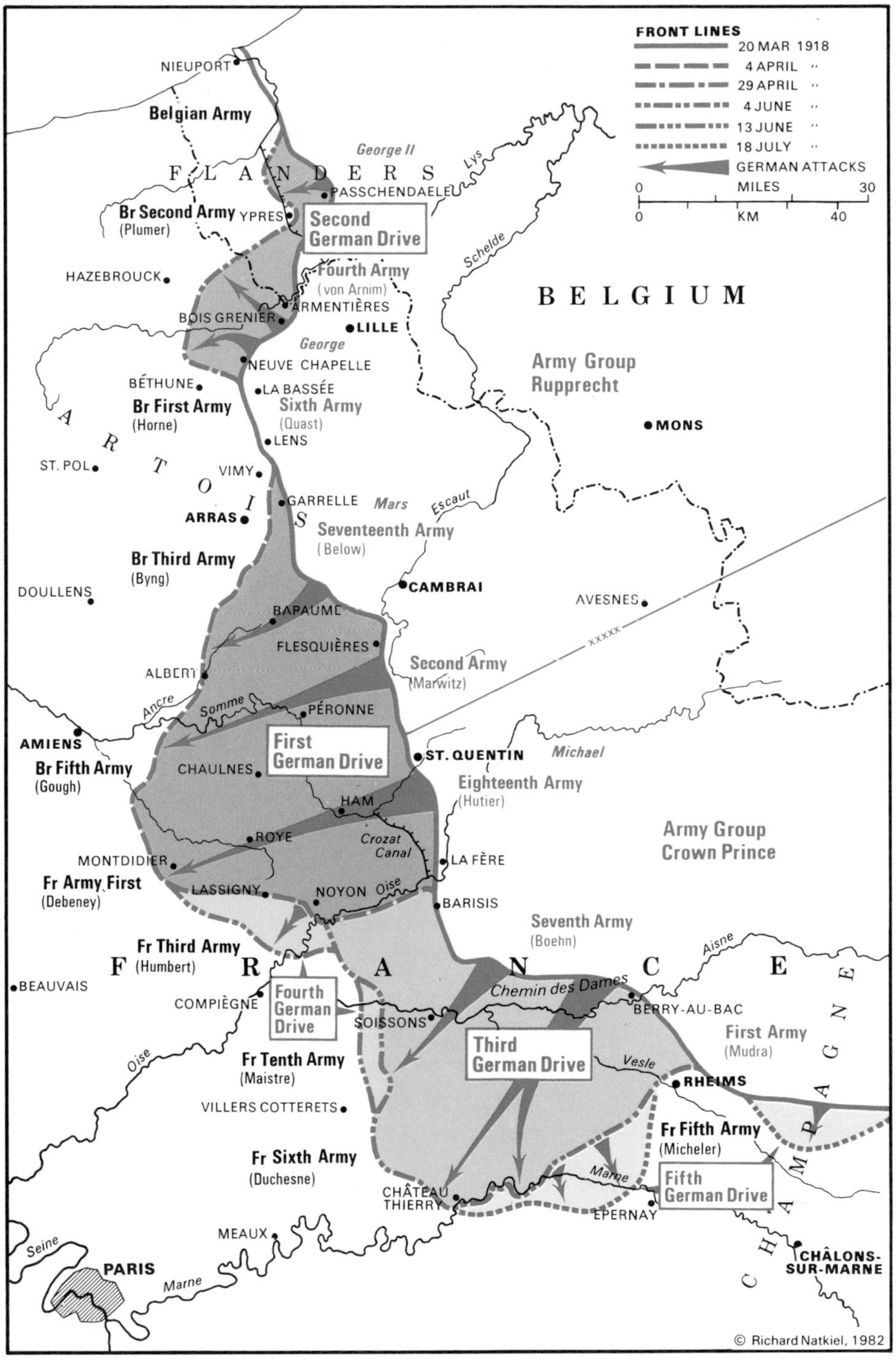

FRONT LINES
20 MAR 1918
4 APRIL "
29 APRIL "
4 JUNE "
13 JUNE "
18 JULY "
GERMAN ATTACKS
MILES
0 30
0 KM 40
NIEUPORT
Belgian Army
George II
FLANDERS
PASSCHENDAELE
Lys
Br Second Army (Plumer)
YPRES
Second German Drive
Fourth Army (von Arnim)
HAZEBROUCK
Schelde
BELGIUM
BOIS GRENIER
ARMENTIÈRES
LILLE
George
NEUVE CHAPELLE
BÉTHUNE
LA BASSÉE
Army Group Rupprecht
Br First Army (Horne)
Sixth Army (Quast)
LENS
MONS
ARTOIS
ST. POL
VIMY
GARRELLE
Mars
Escaut
ARRAS
Seventeenth Army (Below)
Br Third Army (Byng)
DOULLENS
CAMBRAI
AVESNES
BAPAUME
FLESQUIÈRES
ALBERT
Second Army (Marwitz)
Ancre
Somme
PÉRONNE
AMIENS
First German Drive
ST. QUENTIN
Michael
Br Fifth Army (Gough)
CHAULNES
Eighteenth Army (Hutier)
HAM
Army Group Crown Prince
ROYE
Crozat Canal
MONTDIDIER
LA FÈRE
Fr Army First (Debeney)
LASSIGNY
NOYON
Oise
BARISIS
Seventh Army (Boehn)
Fr Third Army (Humbert)
FRANCE
Aisne
BEAUVAIS
COMPIÈGNE
Fourth German Drive
Chemin des Dames
SOISSONS
BERRY-AU-BAC
First Army (Mudra)
Third German Drive
Oise
Fr Tenth Army (Maistre)
Vesle
RHEIMS
VILLERS COTTERETS
CHAMPAGNE
Fr Fifth Army (Micheler)
Fr Sixth Army (Duchesne)
Marne
CHÂTEAU THIERRY
Fifth German Drive
EPERNAY
MEAUX
Seine
PARIS
Marne
CHÂLONS-SUR-MARNE
© Richard Natkiel, 1982

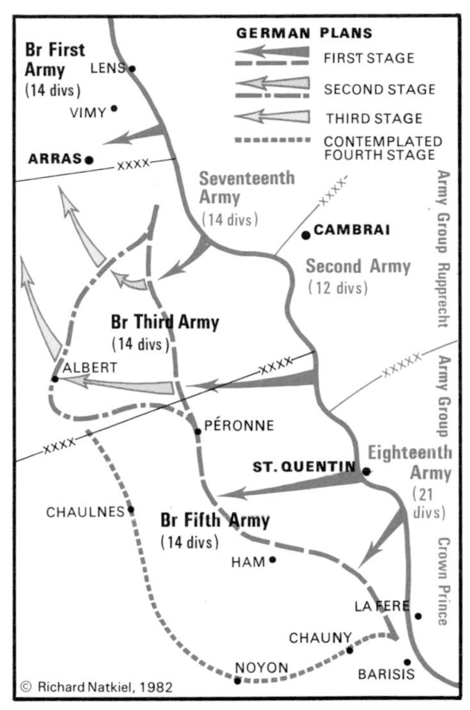
GERMAN PLANS
FIRST STAGE
SECOND STAGE
THIRD STAGE
CONTEMPLATED FOURTH STAGE
Br First Army (14 divs)
LENS
VIMY
ARRAS
Seventeenth Army (14 divs)
CAMBRAI
Second Army (12 divs)
Army Group Rupprecht
Br Third Army (14 divs)
ALBERT
PÉRONNE
ST. QUENTIN
Eighteenth Army (21 divs)
Army Group Crown Prince
CHAULNES
Br Fifth Army (14 divs)
HAM
LA FÈRE
CHAUNY
NOYON
BARISIS
© Richard Natkiel, 1982

The Battle of Belleau Wood

The speed and smoothness of American mobilization threw the Germans out of reckoning in the last year of the war. They had counted on defeating the Allies before American troops were ready to fight in France in sufficient numbers to make a difference. By 3 June 1918 German spring offensives had rolled all the way to Château-Thierry – which was practically undefended. The French mustered what reserves they could, augmented by the US 2nd and 3rd Divisions, infantry and marines.

Near Belleau Wood 85,000 American troops counterattacked the Germans in a six-day battle that began in surrounding wheatfields and ended at the German trenches. US riflemen were equal to the battle (known also as the Battle of Château-Thierry) and prevented the Germans from gaining a foothold on the south bank of the River Marne. Both their presence and their competence were a shock to the German High Command, one that would soon intensify.

Once America had entered the war, however reluctantly, all her considerable resources were brought to bear on assembling and transporting troops, keeping them supplied and completing their training on arrival in France. In an astonishingly short time the American Expeditionary Force had its own supply dumps, warehouses, railroads and recreation camps and was ready to take up a long sector on either side of Verdun.

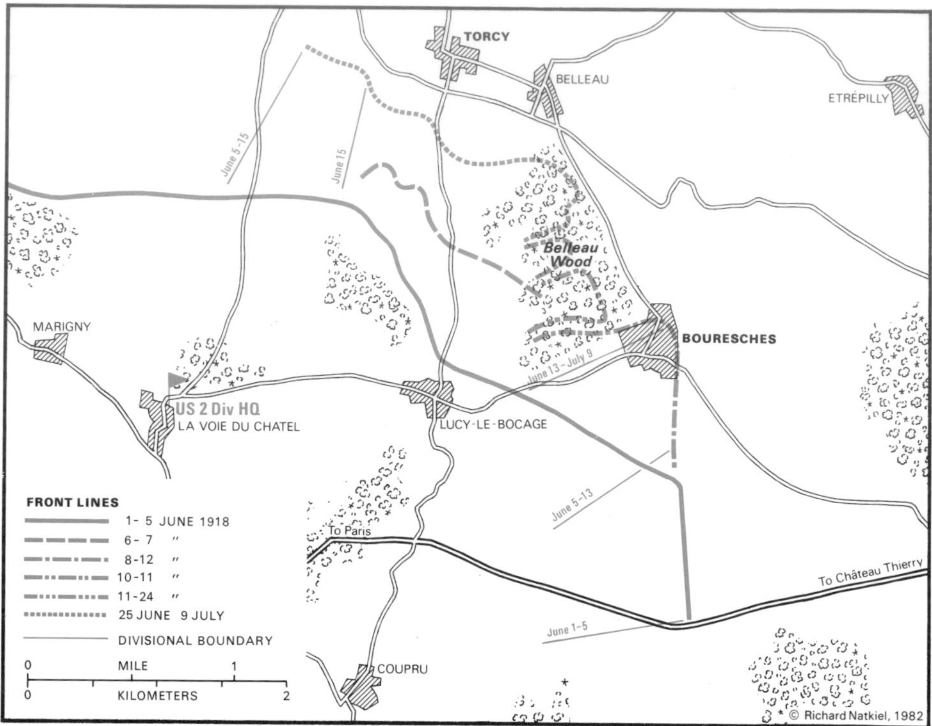

Above: Despite the comparatively limited gains made, the American offensive at Belleau Wood was an important boost to Allied morale.
Below: American machine gunners engage a German aircraft near Villiers-Tournelle, 20 May 1918. Their weapon is a French-made Hotchkiss, a token of American unpreparedness for the war.

Right: US infantry advance through the shattered remains of the town of Varennes in the Argonne region, 26 September 1918, as the final Allied offensives of the war gathered momentum.
Below: Location of Belleau Wood on the Western Front.

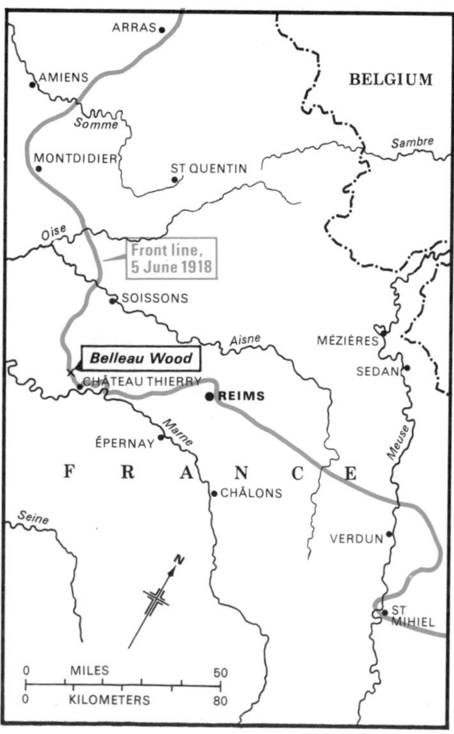

'The Black Day of the German Army'

The Allies were ready to launch their final offensives by 8 August 1918; the first objective was to clear the Germans from the Paris-Amiens railroad. They proposed to do this with the help of tanks, which had proved themselves at the Battle of Cambrai the previous year.

The British had 554 tanks, 14 infantry divisions, cavalry and over 2000 guns to throw into the battle, which they launched under cover of fog after a secret all-night assembly near Amiens. The fact that the tanks were undergunned and easily knocked out by artillery made no difference to their devastating effect on German morale – already at its lowest ebb of the war. The threat of innumerable tanks bearing down on them through the fog plus vigorous artillery/infantry attacks was enough to make thousands of German soldiers throw down their arms and either flee or surrender. Allied forces, which included many Australian and Canadian troops, were fresh and determined; German soldiers were worn down by their frustrating spring offensives and prey to anxiety about their families at home, whom they knew to be starving. Before the day was out, six German divisions were in ruins, and the Allies had advanced seven miles on a wide front.

The battle was known to the British as that of Amiens, to the French as that of Montdidier: to the Germans, it would remain, in Ludendorff's words, 'the Black Day of the German Army.'

Allied progress slowed down the following day with the destruction or disablement of most of the British tanks. German reinforcements began to arrive, and the French on the right wing were making little headway. On 10 August the French Third Army joined the fray, and a day later the Australians and Canadians were ordered to the Somme between Peronne and Ham. The French First Army, which had its own tanks, had recaptured Montdidier and was now to occupy Ham. But stiffening resistance and dwindling armaments led the commander of the British Fourth Army to postpone a fresh offensive.

A few days later the entire Allied line north of the Marne was advancing. The British gained ground along the Somme, and the French made progress south of the Oise. On 12 September the US First Army, under General John J Pershing, attacked the St Mihiel salient as the Germans were evacuating it; the result was a victory that involved few casualties and encouraged the previously untried troops. The Germans retreated to their last defense – the Hindenburg Line.

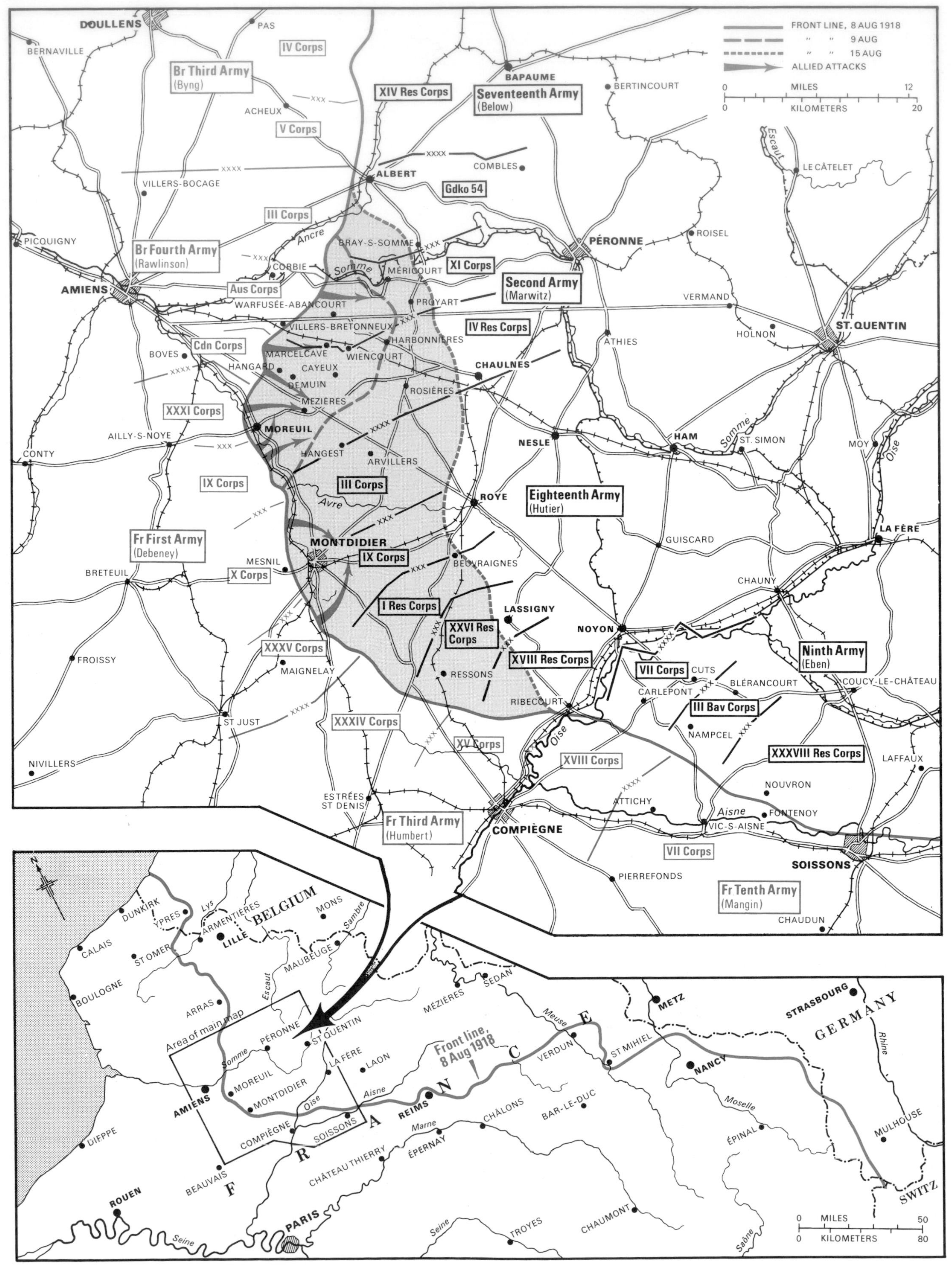
FRONT LINE, 8 AUG 1918
" " 9 AUG
" " 15 AUG
ALLIED ATTACKS
0 MILES 12
0 KILOMETERS 20
DOULLENS
PAS
BERNAVILLE
IV Corps
Br Third Army
(Byng)
ACHEUX
V Corps
XIV Res Corps
BAPAUME
Seventeenth Army
(Below)
BERTINCOURT
Escaut
LE CÂTELET
COMBLES
ALBERT
Gdko 54
VILLERS-BOCAGE
III Corps
PICQUIGNY
Br Fourth Army
(Rawlinson)
Ancre
BRAY-S-SOMME
PÉRONNE
ROISEL
CORBIE
Somme
MÉRICOURT
XI Corps
AMIENS
Aus Corps
Second Army
(Marwitz)
PROYART
VERMAND
WARFUSÉE-ABANCOURT
VILLERS-BRETONNEUX
IV Res Corps
HOLNON
ST. QUENTIN
BOVES
Cdn Corps
MARCELCAVE
HARBONNIÈRES
ATHIES
HANGARD
CAYEUX
WIENCOURT
CHAULNES
DEMUIN
MEZIÈRES
ROSIÈRES
XXXI Corps
MOREUIL
AILLY-S-NOYE
NESLE
HAM
ST. SIMON
MOY
Oise
CONTY
HANGEST
ARVILLERS
IX Corps
III Corps
Avre
ROYE
Eighteenth Army
(Hutier)
LA FÈRE
Fr First Army
(Debeney)
MONTDIDIER
IX Corps
GUISCARD
MESNIL
BEUVRAIGNES
BRETEUIL
X Corps
CHAUNY
I Res Corps
LASSIGNY
XXVI Res Corps
NOYON
Ninth Army
(Eben)
FROISSY
XXXV Corps
XVIII Res Corps
VII Corps
CUTS
MAIGNELAY
RESSONS
BLÉRANCOURT
COUCY-LE-CHÂTEAU
CARLEPONT
RIBECOURT
III Bav Corps
ST JUST
XXXIV Corps
NAMPCEL
XV Corps
XXXVIII Res Corps
LAFFAUX
NIVILLERS
XVIII Corps
NOUVRON
ESTRÉES
ST DENIS
ATTICHY
Aisne
FONTENOY
Fr Third Army
(Humbert)
COMPIÈGNE
VIC-S-AISNE
VII Corps
SOISSONS
PIERREFONDS
Fr Tenth Army
(Mangin)
CHAUDUN
DUNKIRK
YPRES
Lys
ARMENTIÈRES
LILLE
BELGIUM
MONS
Sambre
CALAIS
ST OMER
MAUBEUGE
BOULOGNE
SEDAN
ARRAS
Escaut
MÉZIÈRES
METZ
STRASBOURG
GERMANY
Area of main map
PÉRONNE
ST QUENTIN
Meuse
E
Front line, 8 Aug 1918
VERDUN
ST MIHIEL
Rhine
Somme
LA FÈRE
LAON
C
NANCY
MOREUIL
AMIENS
MONTDIDIER
Aisne
N
REIMS
CHÂLONS
BAR-LE-DUC
Moselle
Oise
A
COMPIÈGNE
SOISSONS
Marne
ÉPINAL
MULHOUSE
DIEPPE
R
ÉPERNAY
CHÂTEAU THIERRY
BEAUVAIS
F
ROUEN
SWITZ
PARIS
Seine
TROYES
CHAUMONT
Seine
Saône
0 MILES 50
0 KILOMETERS 80

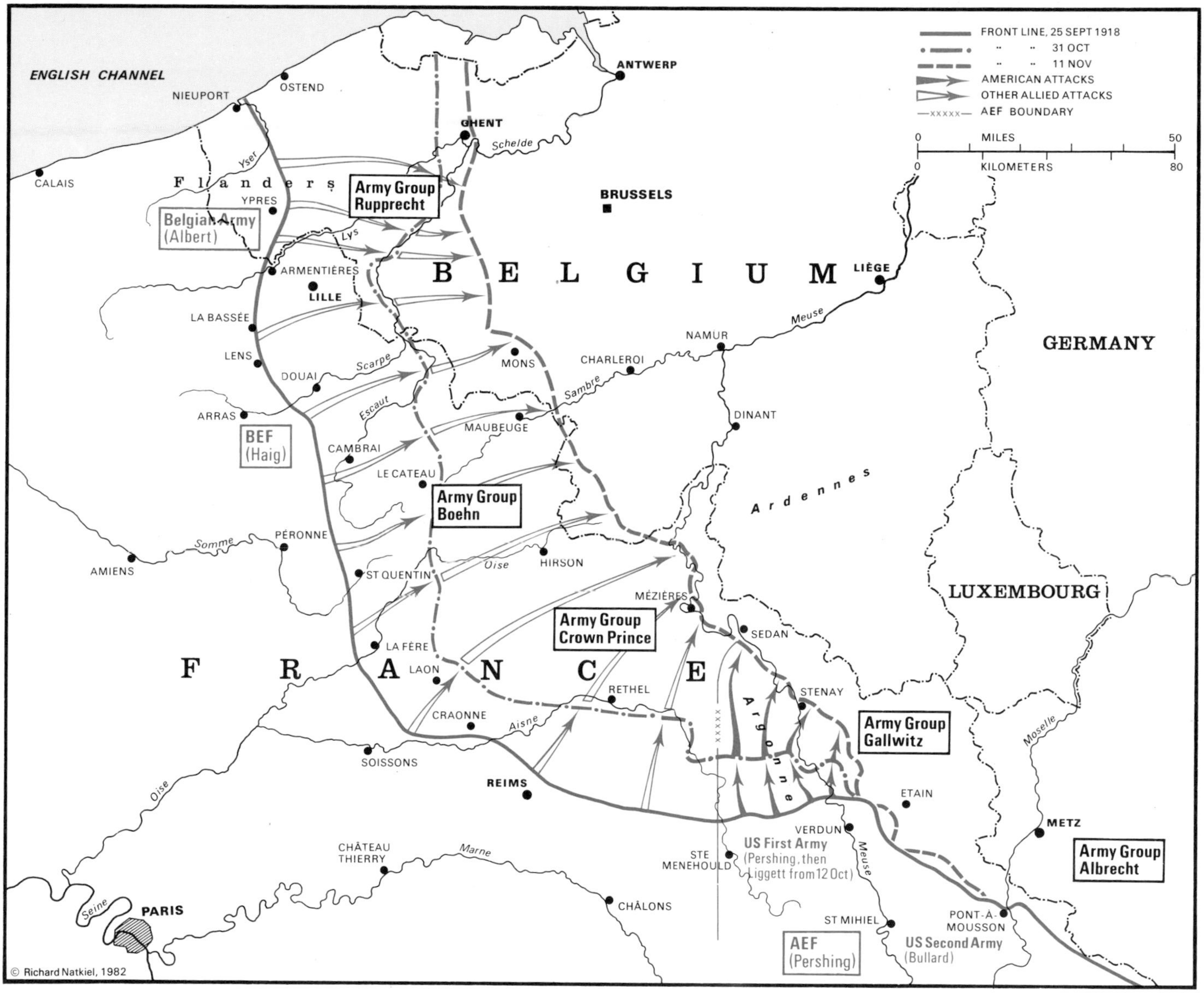

FRONT LINE, 25 SEPT 1918
" " 31 OCT
" " 11 NOV
AMERICAN ATTACKS
OTHER ALLIED ATTACKS
AEF BOUNDARY
0 MILES 50
0 KILOMETERS 80

ENGLISH CHANNEL
NIEUPORT
OSTEND
ANTWERP
GHENT
Schelde
CALAIS
Yser
Flanders
YPRES
Army Group Rupprecht
BRUSSELS
Belgian Army (Albert)
Lys
ARMENTIÈRES
LILLE
BELGIUM
LIÈGE
LA BASSÉE
Meuse
NAMUR
GERMANY
LENS
CHARLEROI
DOUAI
Scarpe
MONS
Sambre
ARRAS
Escaut
MAUBEUGE
DINANT
BEF (Haig)
CAMBRAI
LE CATEAU
Ardennes
Army Group Boehn
PÉRONNE
Somme
AMIENS
HIRSON
ST QUENTIN
Oise
LUXEMBOURG
MÉZIÈRES
Army Group Crown Prince
SEDAN
LA FÈRE
FRANCE
LAON
RETHEL
STENAY
Argonne
CRAONNE
Aisne
Army Group Gallwitz
Moselle
SOISSONS
REIMS
ETAIN
Oise
VERDUN
METZ
CHÂTEAU THIERRY
Marne
STE MENEHOULD
US First Army (Pershing, then Liggett from 12 Oct)
Meuse
Army Group Albrecht
CHÂLONS
Seine
PARIS
ST MIHIEL
PONT-À-MOUSSON
AEF (Pershing)
US Second Army (Bullard)

Opposite: 'The Black Day of the German Army'.
Above: The series of Allied offensives that defeated the German Army and won the war.
Left: American tanks on the advance.

The big Allied breakthrough came on 26 September, when the French Fourth Army and the US First Army attacked between Reims and the River Meuse. Two more British armies converged near Lens; the French and surviving Belgian units made an offensive around Armentières; the French First and the British Fourth Armies attacked near Epehy. The latter assault, made with British tanks, was decisive: the Hindenburg Line was broken.

Ludendorff advised the Kaiser to seek an armistice, and the German Army was in retreat throughout the last weeks of the war. The German commander-in-chief resigned before the Armistice was signed, in protest against its terms, and emerged from the war with his reputation intact. He had simultaneously avoided total defeat and implied that he would have preferred to finish the fight.

Vittorio Veneto and the Palestine Campaign

After their retreat from Caporetto the Italians had made a stand on the Piave, bolstered by 11 British and French Divisions transferred from the Western Front. Austrian and German forces overextended their supply lines in their subsequent advance and abandoned their efforts to break through late in 1917. Under General Diaz Italian troops spent the next six months regrouping as both the Germans and the Allies withdrew most of their units.

Under German pressure the Austrians renewed their attacks from 15–24 June 1918, but the offensive was ill-conceived and General Boroević's group, attacking over the Piave, was soon repulsed. In the Monte Grappa sector, the Austrians under Conrad were thrown back by Anglo-French forces that had remained on the Italian front. Four months later the Italians were ready to advance.

The Fourth Army made diversionary attacks around Monte Grappa and crossings of the Piave were successfully accomplished to the east. British and French troops made

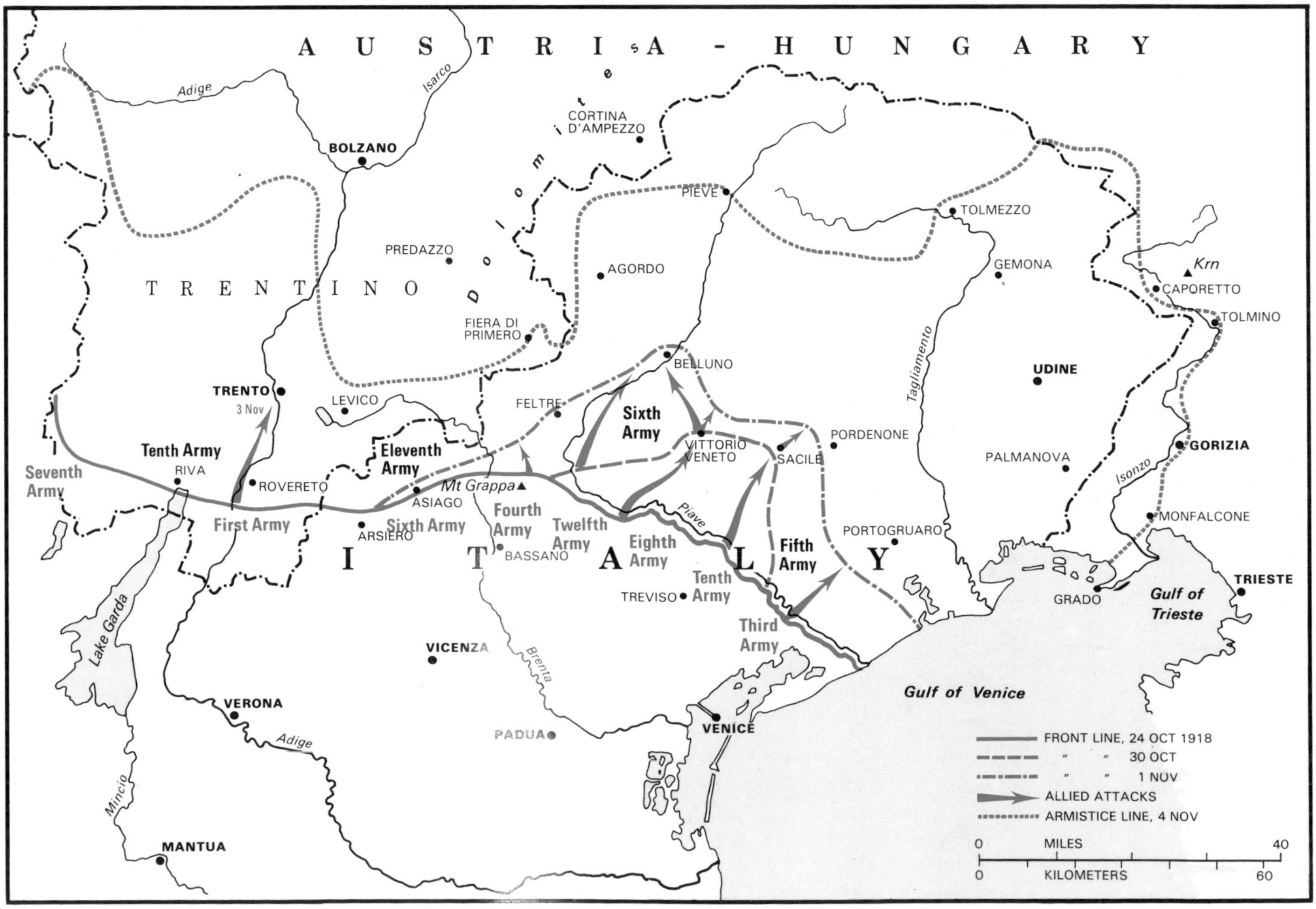

AUSTRIA-HUNGARY
TRENTINO
ITALY
Dolomites
Adige
Isarco
BOLZANO
CORTINA D'AMPEZZO
PIEVE
TOLMEZZO
PREDAZZO
AGORDO
GEMONA
Krn
CAPORETTO
TOLMINO
FIERA DI PRIMERO
BELLUNO
UDINE
Tagliamento
TRENTO
3 Nov
LEVICO
FELTRE
Sixth Army
PORDENONE
VITTORIO VENETO
SACILE
PALMANOVA
GORIZIA
Isonzo
Tenth Army
Seventh Army
RIVA
ROVERETO
Eleventh Army
Mt Grappa
ASIAGO
First Army
ARSIERO
Sixth Army
Fourth Army
Twelfth Army
BASSANO
Eighth Army
Piave
Fifth Army
PORTOGRUARO
MONFALCONE
TRIESTE
GRADO
Gulf of Trieste
TREVISO
Tenth Army
Third Army
Lake Garda
VICENZA
Brenta
Gulf of Venice
VERONA
PADUA
VENICE
Adige
Mincio
MANTUA
FRONT LINE, 24 OCT 1918
" " 30 OCT
" " 1 NOV
ALLIED ATTACKS
ARMISTICE LINE, 4 NOV
0 MILES 40
0 KILOMETERS 60

the most important initial gains; by 30 October the Austrians were in retreat, pursued by Italian cavalry. This Battle of Vittorio Veneto was officially over with the armistice of 3 November.

In Palestine, British General Edmund Allenby had taken command after the British defeat in the Second Battle of Gaza. His mandate was to capture Jerusalem 'in time for Christmas.' Well supplied with cavalry, Allenby sent them inland from the coastal plain to outflank the enemy while his artillery and infantry took the northern road. German commander Falkenhayn (transferred to the Middle East after his failure to win dramatic victories on the Western Front) was unable to muster sufficient Turkish forces to hold Allenby's thrice-larger force. In early November the British took Gaza, then Beersheba, then Jaffa. Turkish defenders in Jerusalem were deprived of their supply line by the capture of a critical railroad junction: they surrendered on 9 December 1917.

Allenby's campaign was much strengthened by Arab irregular and guerrilla forces. A 1916 revolt in the Hejaz had resulted in their becoming a powerful force under the inspired leadership of British officer T E Lawrence (Lawrence of Arabia), who was sent to the Hejaz in December 1916.

By September of 1918 Allenby felt strong enough to launch an offensive that would ultimately force Turkey out of the war. His infantry first drove the Turks back to the key railroad junction of Tulkarm, while his cavalry rode swiftly through the night to Beth Shean and Nazareth, where they cut off the Turkish retreat. Two enemy armies were destroyed, and a third fled across the Jordan and fragmented.

Damascus fell on 1 October, and French units captured Beirut on the 7th. Turkey reeled back in Mesopotamia and surrendered her entire army on the Tigris. Aleppo was taken on 25 October, and Turkey was forced to sign an armistice five days later. It was one more inducement to the German High Command to call for an end to the war.

Above left: Medical personnel evacuate wounded from the front, Palestine 1918.
Left: The Battle of Vittorio Veneto. In a little over a week from the start of the battle to the armistice the Italian and Allied forces took some 300,000 prisoners.
Right: The British campaign in Palestine led by General Allenby was one of the most imaginatively directed of World War I.

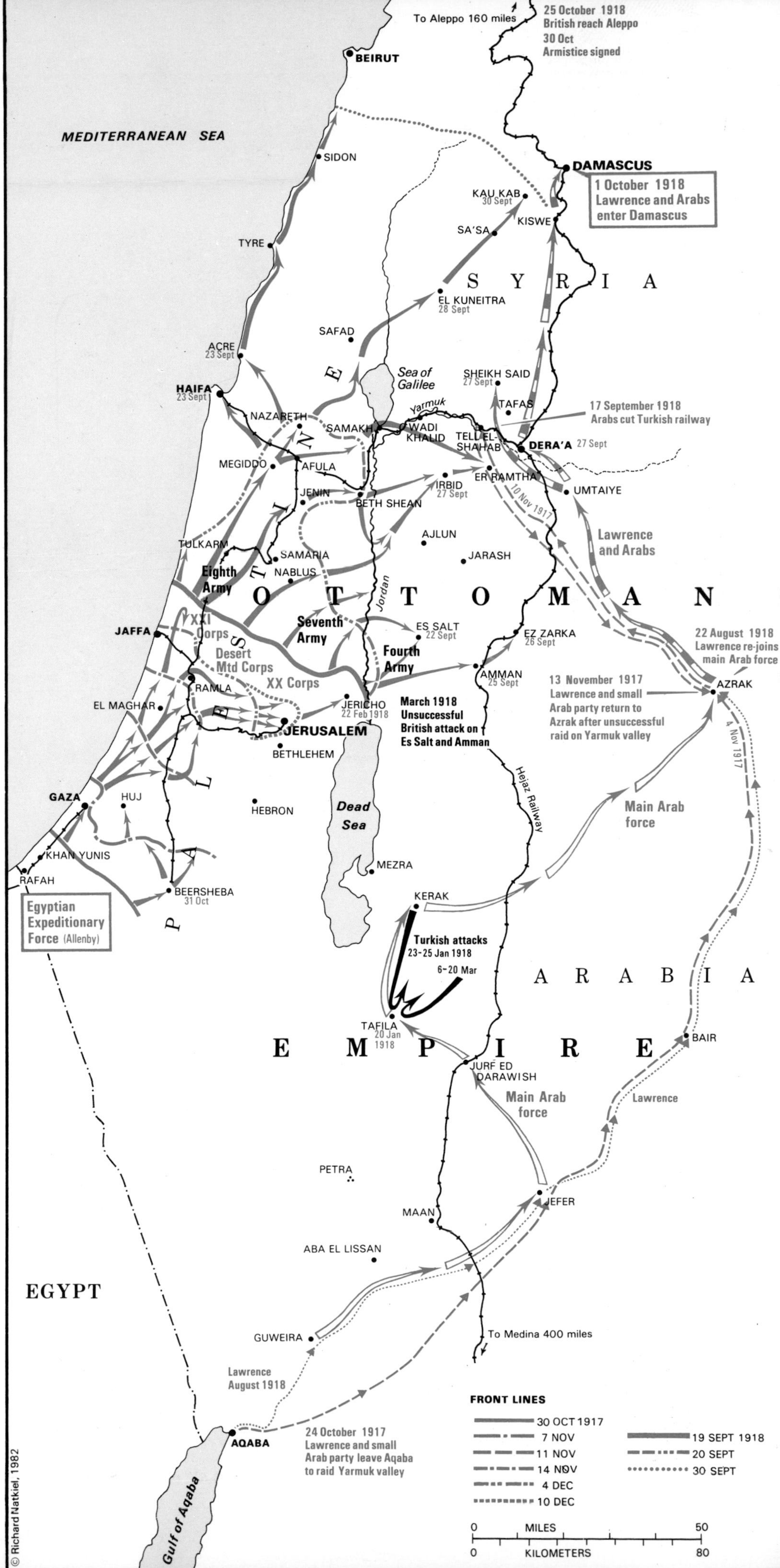

The Russian Revolution

In the spring of 1918 the Treaty of Brest-Litovsk took Russia out of World War I as a result of the Bolshevik takeover of Petrograd (renamed Leningrad). Russia's former allies, anti-Bolshevik in principle, were outraged at this abandonment, and German domination of Eastern Europe was guaranteed. The Germans set up states amenable to their interests in Poland and the Ukraine, but when the German Government was overthrown by the armistice of November 1918, a power vacuum opened in and around the new Soviet Union. The Bolsheviks controlled little more than a corridor between Leningrad and Moscow, for all practical purposes. Finland and the Baltic States were created from the western Russian provinces, and an enlarged Rumania hastened to claim Bessarabia. The newly formed state of Poland looked toward eastward expansion at Russia's expense.

The Allies, for their part, were hoping that the civil war between Czarist adherents and the Bolsheviks would lead to Lenin's collapse. To that end, they sent invasion forces to the northern ports of Murmansk and Archangel, as well as the Black Sea ports, to support the White Army cause. Leon Trotsky's newly formed Red Army struck back promptly: it was at the gates of Warsaw before the French, led by General Maxime Weygand and Captain Charles de Gaulle, intervened. With this support, the Polish Army was able to capture large sections of White Russia. But the Ukrainians were less fortunate in their Allied support. By the spring of 1920 their combined forces had been thrown back and dispersed. The Allies were more than ready to recall their troops, and the cohesiveness and strength of the Red Army made it a force to be reckoned with: in the end, it swept the field.

Far left, below: Lenin pictured in 1917.
Below: Soldiers and sailors on the streets of Petrograd in the early days of the revolution.

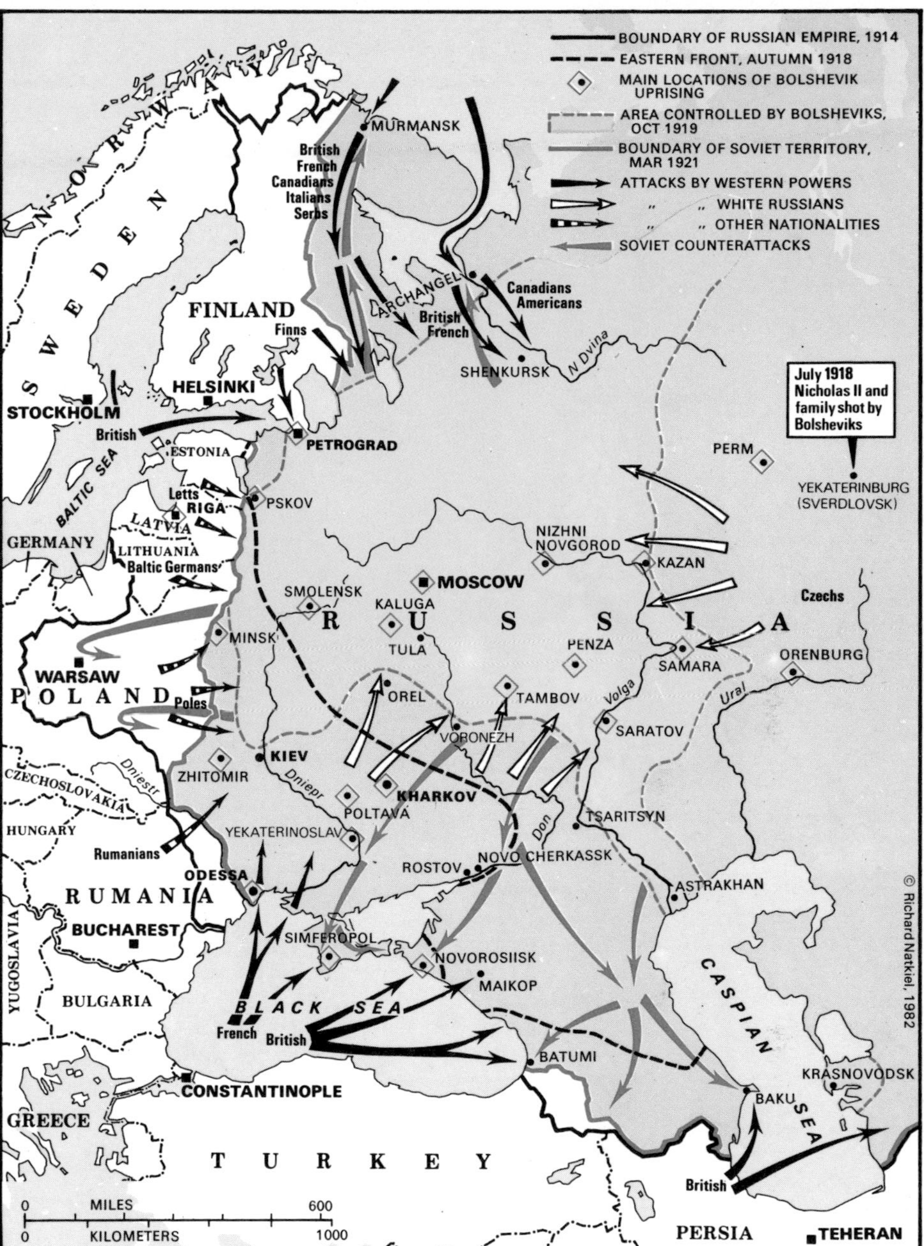

Left: Czar Nicholas, Czarina Alexandra, and Prince Alexei.
Second left: German and Russian soldiers fraternising immediately after the beginning of the revolution.

Above: The Russian Civil War. The vigorous leadership of Trotsky gave the Red Army vital advantages over its disunited enemies.
Below: Popular demonstration in June 1917.

The Long March of the Chinese Communists: 1934–35

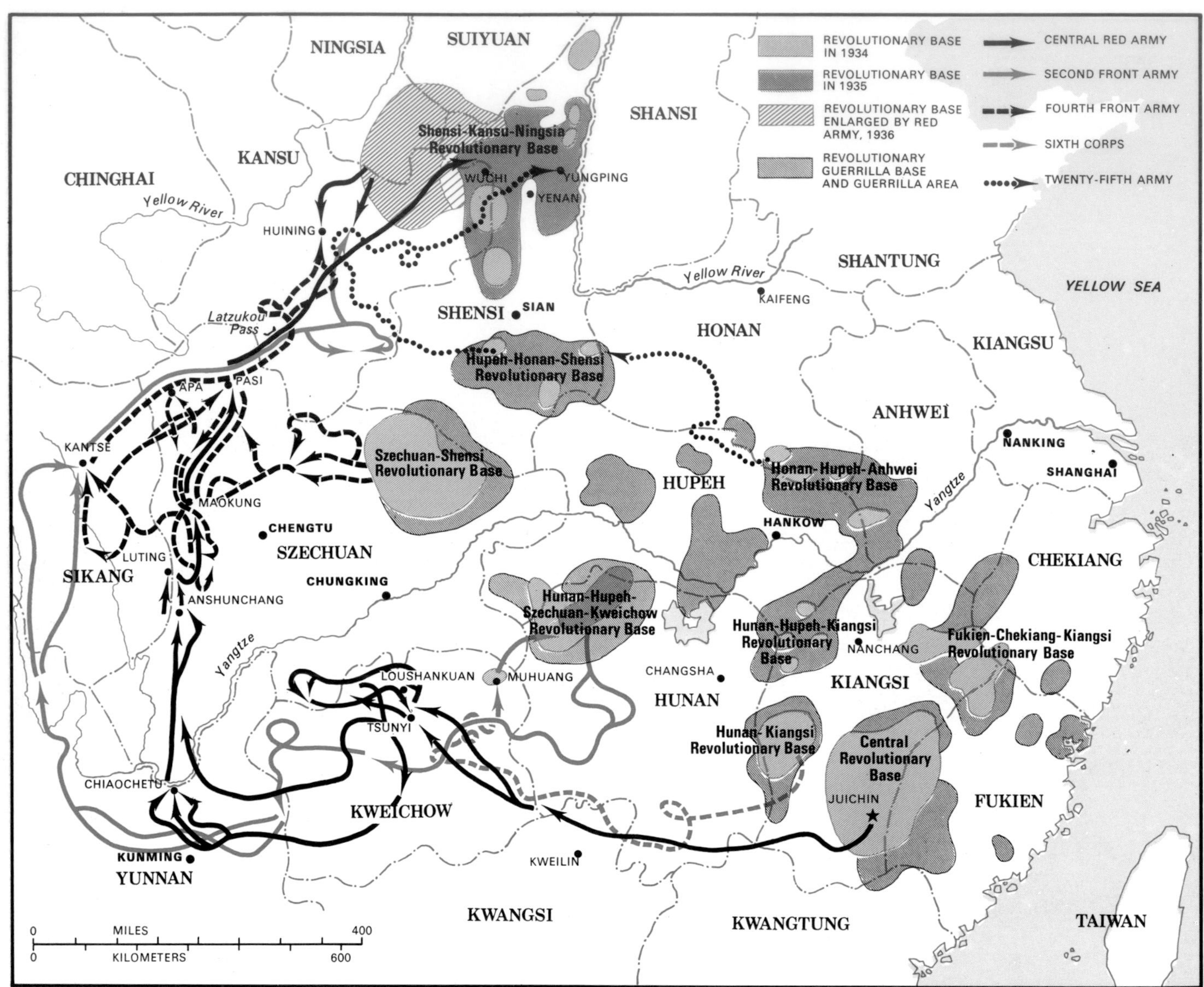

The power vacuum created in China by the fall of the Manchu Dynasty (1911) was filled largely by local warlords competing with the Nationalist Party – the Kuomintang – and later with the Chinese Communist Party. Founded in 1921, the Communist Party maintained fairly stable relationships with Chiang Kai-Shek's Kuomintang until 1927, when the nationalist group moved strongly against it.

Subsequent attempts to establish Communist enclaves in the cities proved unsuccessful, and the Communists began to concentrate on winning over the rural peasantry. This change of focus was spearheaded by their leader Mao Tse-tung, who proclaimed the establishment of a Chinese Soviet Republic from his main stronghold in Kiangsi Province in 1931. The nationalists believed that this threat exceeded that of the Japanese (who had taken over Manchuria in October 1931), and Chiang Kai-shek launched a series of Bandit Suppression Campaigns against Communist revolutionary bases.

In 1934 the Communists found it necessary to move their entire operation to a less vulnerable area: that October they broke out of Kiangsi and began what is known as the Long March. It lasted until November 1935, with some units covering 6000 miles in their journey to the chosen location of Yenan. There Mao established a moderate socialist regime with relatively little opposition from the inhabitants. Many Chinese Communists became casualties on the grueling March, but they were still a strong force when they reached their goal in Shensi Province. In the process, they had gained support throughout China by their commitment to fighting the Japanese invaders; many Chinese were dissatisfied with Chiang's concern about fighting Communism first. When some of Chiang's forces mutinied in Sian late in 1936, he himself fell into Communist hands for some time and had to give assurances of greater activity against the Japanese. These promises had to be made good in 1937, when Japan attacked in force.

Below left: The Long March. Although the Communist forces suffered heavily during the march, they also gained new recruits, and left activists at work in the areas they passed through.

Below: Chinese soldiers attack during a battle with the Japanese.
Bottom: A student protest during the 1930s. Students, particularly in Peking, were an important influence in arguing that Chiang Kai-shek should do more to fight the Japanese.

The Italian Invasion of Ethiopia

Ethiopia (Abyssinia) was an East African Christian kingdom that had maintained its independence for centuries despite covetous incursions by its neighbors. In 1896 it had repelled an Italian invading army at Adowa, and the Italians were still smarting from that defeat. By 1930 Mussolini was well entrenched and looking for foreign conquests, and Haile Selassie had become Emperor of Ethiopia; he introduced modernizing reforms, but invited no Italian experts into the country to give technical assistance.

The early 1930s saw a series of border incidents involving Ethiopia's frontiers with the neighboring Italian colonies of Eritrea and Somaliland. One such confrontation, at the Oasis of Walwal in December 1934, was submitted to the League of Nations for arbitration, but Mussolini continued to reinforce his East African colonies. By the time arbitrators handed down their opinion that neither side had been to blame, Mussolini was preparing to invade Ethiopia as soon as the rainy season ended. France gave tacit acquiescence.

On 3 October 1935 Italian troops invaded from Eritrea and captured Adowa; forces from Somaliland were slower in their progress. The League of Nations invoked economic sanctions against Italy, but key states, including Switzerland and Austria, failed to comply with them so they were unavailing. Poor roads made for a slow Italian advance, but superior weaponry, including aircraft and poison gas, guaranteed the eventual defeat of the Ethiopians. On 5 May 1936 the capital, Addis Ababa, fell, and Haile Selassie fled the country, to return only in 1941 when the British drove out the Italians.

Below center: Nationalist troops in Toledo shortly after its capture on 28 September 1936. Cadets at the military academy in Toledo had been important early supporters of the Nationalist cause.

Below: The conquest of Ethiopia. The ineffectiveness of League of Nations sanctions only encouraged Hitler and Mussolini in their plans.

The Spanish Civil War

Civil unrest in Spain in 1931 saw the overthrow of the Spanish monarchy in favor of a republic, whose left-wing government hastened to introduce such unpopular measures as separation of Church and State, state education and break-up of the large estates. Right-wing parties were returned in a 1933 election, but their efforts to undo the work of the new regime were interrupted by the victory of a 'popular front' from the left in 1936.

The previous reforms were extended despite violent resistance from Spanish fascists, who were known as the Falangists. Political assassinations were followed by a revolt originating among army officers in Spanish Morocco. In October 1936 the insurgent General Francisco Franco was declared 'Chief of the Spanish State.' Cadiz, Seville, Zaragoza and Burgos declared themselves for Franco, who made his headquarters in the latter city. Soon Fascist Italy and Nazi Germany were sending troops to support the insurgent Nationalist regime in Spain, while Russia funneled men and supplies to the embattled Republican Government. An International Brigade of volunteers from various countries also rallied to the Republican cause, in the belief that it

Above: General Franco leads a triumphal parade through the streets of Zaragoza.
Below: The campaigns of the Spanish Civil War.

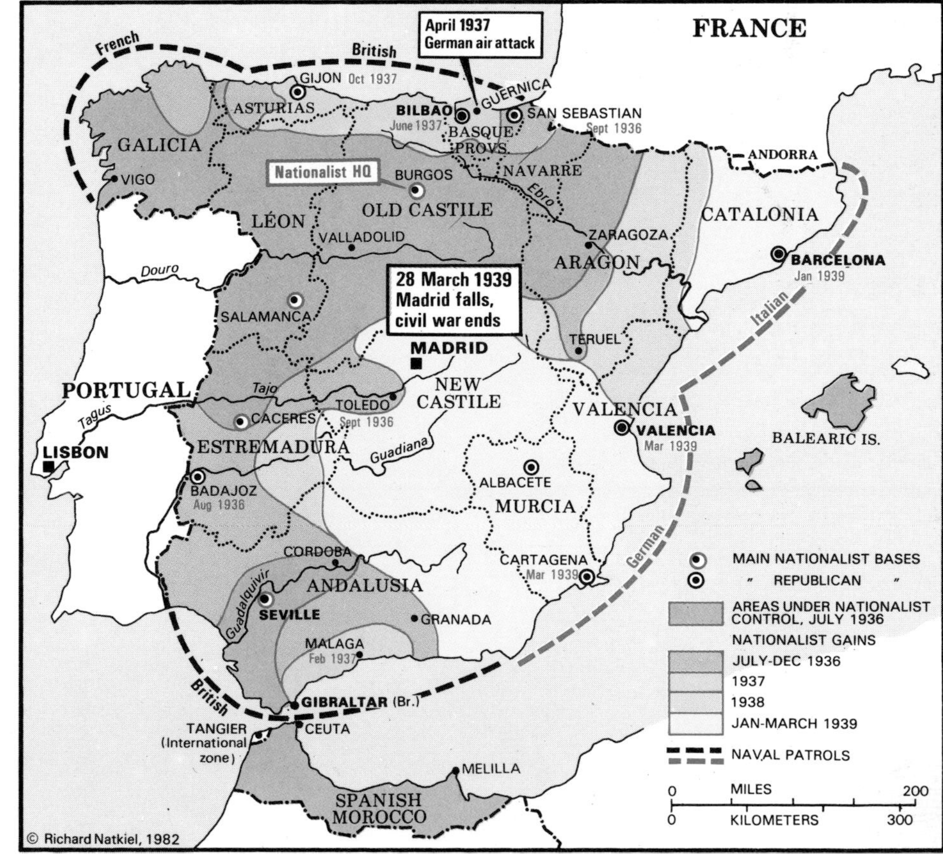

Below: Republican troops man the barricades during fighting in a Catalonian town.

was the first great conflict with European Fascism.

By the end of 1936 Franco's Nationalists held about half of Spain, with the help of their superior military force and supply routes through Portugal. Within two years, increased German and Italian help (ineffectually obstructed by the French and British) extended these gains. Meanwhile, Soviet intrigues vitiated the Republican effort on various fronts and ended in the cutting off of all aid from Moscow. Madrid was besieged and Catalonia invaded by the Nationalists. Early in 1939, with the loss of Barcelona, Valencia, and Madrid, the government's resistance ended after three-quarters of a million had died, many by execution.

The Spanish Civil War had far-reaching implications for international relations: it helped strengthen the relationship between Germany and Italy – and weaken the possibility of anti-German agreements between France and the USSR, because of the French refusal to help the Republicans. Both Britain and France appeared weak and vacillating in supporting their interests. And Hitler and Mussolini received an object lesson in the effectiveness of swift and ruthless military action. German and Italian forces gained valuable fighting experience, and the German Luftwaffe gave an intimidating display of power that contributed to the Anglo-French appeasement policy that would prevail until Nazi Germany unleashed its 'Lightning War' in 1939.

The German Invasion of Poland

Hitler's aggressions against Czechoslovakia and Lithuania in March 1939 made it clear that Poland would be his next objective. Britain and France clung to their policy of appeasement; they tried to persuade the Poles to make concessions like those of Munich in the hope that Hitler would curb his bellicosity. The fact that Germany revoked both its 1934 non-aggression pact with Poland and its 1935 naval agreement with England did nothing to foster this hope.

In the summer of 1939 Soviet Russia was being courted by all concerned as a potential ally. French and British overtures were mismanaged, leading only to the conviction that Josef Stalin would demand a free hand in Eastern Europe as the price of his aid. German diplomacy was more

Left: German troops destroy a Polish frontier post on the first day of the attack.
Below: Ribbentrop (left), a German official, Stalin and Molotov at the conclusion of the Soviet-German Non-Aggression Pact.

Left: Hitler and his generals look on as German forces close in on Warsaw.
Below: German troops make their formal entry into the Polish capital, Warsaw. The city was subjected to heavy bombing before the surrender was agreed.

successful: Foreign Minister Joachim von Ribbentrop returned to Berlin with both an economic agreement and a Non-Aggression Pact with the USSR.

Hitler felt confident – with good reason – when he launched his 1 September attack against Poland with an astonishing 53 divisions. These included panzer corps formed from tank and motorized units. The German Army Commander-in-Chief, Field Marshal Walther von Brauchitsch, was given a free hand in the Polish campaign. Traditional artillery and infantry *en masse* were augmented by the armored units and an overwhelming superiority in the air: the German Luftwaffe had some 1600 modern planes as against the Poles' 500 outdated aircraft.

The rationale for the blitzkrieg that began on 1 September was an alleged Polish attack on a German radio station near the border at Gliewitz. In fact, the photos exhibited to foreign journalists had only one valid component – the bodies in Polish uniform scattered on the ground. They were later found to be those of concentration camp inmates.

Britain and France responded to the German invasion with an unheeded ultimatum, followed on 3 September by declarations of war. Australia,Canada and New Zealand followed joined on 6 September by South Africa. World War II was already gathering its juggernaut momentum.

The Poles were late in mobilizing, having fielded only 23 infantry divisions when the German war machine fell upon them. Artillery was in short supply, there was a single weak armored division and Polish cavalry committed mass suicide in courageous attacks on German tanks. The sparse Polish forces were unwisely deployed along the frontier: the outcome was apparent within a few days. The lone counterattack against the Germans – along the Bzura River from 9–15 September – was bravely fought but unavailing. The last real resistance collapsed with the city of Warsaw in late September.

The Soviets had already moved in to claim their share of the Polish partition secretly agreed to the previous August. The German-Soviet Treaty of Friendship proclaimed on 19 September was anticlimactic – and short-lived.

Opposite, top right: The agreed partition of Poland between Germany and the USSR.
Above left: The deployments and the early battles. The Polish forces formed up too near the borders, a further complication for their inferior mobilization system.
Left: The concluding moves of the campaign.

The Russo-Finnish War

The Winter War of 1939–40 between Russia and Finland is best remembered for the fierce resistance of outnumbered Finnish forces to the might of the Red Army. The Finns never had more than 200,000 troops, but they inflicted over 200,000 casualties on Soviet forces that ultimately included 1,200,000 men.

The opening gun was a Soviet demand for territorial concessions similar to those that were finally granted. These demands originated in Soviet concerns about Baltic security, which affected the entire area contiguous with northwestern Russia at this time. The Finns were wary of the Soviet offer to negotiate the matter, correctly assuming that other demands would follow; they hoped that Soviet willingness to begin talks indicated a lack of determination. Negotiations that began in early October 1939 broke down in a matter of weeks, and the Soviet attack was launched on 30 November.

Twenty-six Red Army divisions and massive numbers of tanks and artillery rolled across the Finnish frontier to face nine defending divisions with few guns, little ammunition and almost no armor. What the Finns did have was determination, good training and high mobility under winter conditions. Throughout December they beat off every Soviet attack – largely by isolating unwieldy columns and defeating them in detail.

Marshal S K Timoshenko was appointed commander of Soviet forces early in January 1940; he focused on more effective use of firepower, and the Soviets began to gain the advantage they should have had through sheer force of numbers. Pressure on the Finns mounted throughout February: by early March they had lost a series of all-out battles and had to agree to an armistice.

Like the Spanish Civil War, the Russo-Finnish conflict had repercussions far beyond the narrow borders of the embattled country. The League of Nations was entirely discredited when the Soviet Union ignored its attempts to mediate and showed no concern about its own subsequent expulsion. Britain and France made a poor showing with their indecisiveness about helping Finland: as a result, French Premier Daladier's government fell to the more vigorous Paul Reynaud. Perhaps most importantly, the war created a false impression of Red Army incompetence that may have been instrumental in leading Hitler to turn on his Soviet ally. By the time he did so, much-needed reforms had strengthened the Russian Army much beyond its unimpressive performance in the Winter War.

Above: Soviet annexations in Eastern Europe 1939–40, Stalin's effort to create a buffer between the USSR and Germany while Hitler was still occupied by the war with Britain and France.

Left: A Russian column passes antitank obstacles on the way to the front on the Karelian Isthmus in December 1939.

Above right: The Russo-Finnish War, showing the comparatively limited concessions which the Soviets eventually obtained.

Right: Finnish infantry in a defensive position.

Far right: Soviet Marshal Timoshenko.

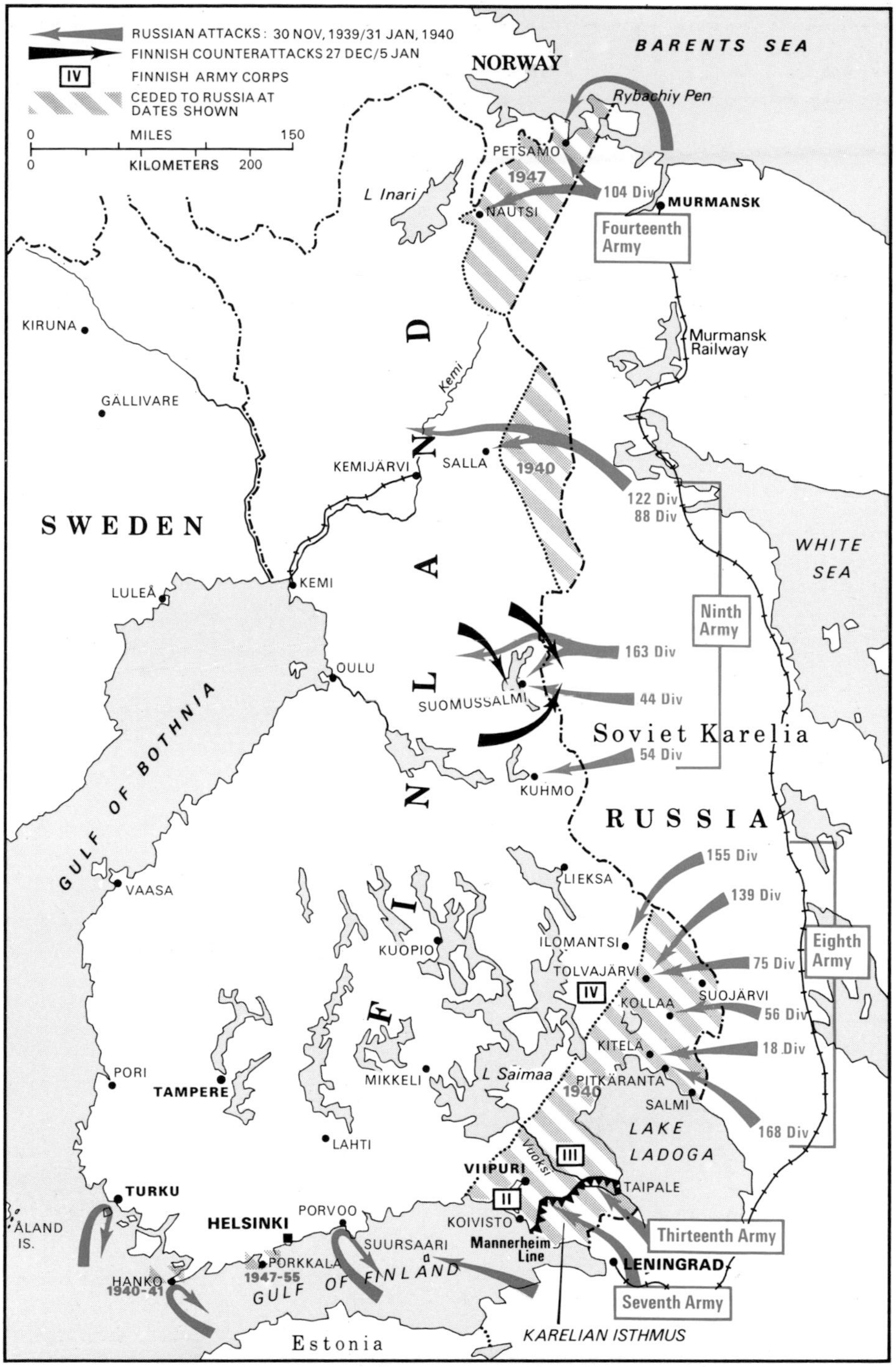

RUSSIAN ATTACKS: 30 NOV, 1939/31 JAN, 1940
FINNISH COUNTERATTACKS 27 DEC/5 JAN
IV FINNISH ARMY CORPS
CEDED TO RUSSIA AT DATES SHOWN
0 MILES 150
0 KILOMETERS 200
BARENTS SEA
NORWAY
Rybachiy Pen
PETSAMO
1947
104 Div
L Inari
NAUTSI
MURMANSK
Fourteenth Army
KIRUNA
Murmansk Railway
GÄLLIVARE
Kemi
KEMIJÄRVI
SALLA
1940
122 Div
88 Div
SWEDEN
WHITE SEA
LULEÅ
KEMI
Ninth Army
163 Div
OULU
44 Div
SUOMUSSALMI
Soviet Karelia
54 Div
GULF OF BOTHNIA
KUHMO
FINLAND
RUSSIA
155 Div
LIEKSA
VAASA
139 Div
ILOMANTSI
KUOPIO
Eighth Army
75 Div
TOLVAJÄRVI
IV
SUOJÄRVI
KOLLAA
56 Div
KITELÄ
18 Div
PORI
TAMPERE
MIKKELI
L Saimaa
PITKÄRANTA
1940
SALMI
LAKE LADOGA
168 Div
LAHTI
Vuoksi
III
VIIPURI
TURKU
II
TAIPALE
ÅLAND IS.
HELSINKI
PORVOO
KOIVISTO
Thirteenth Army
SUURSAARI
Mannerheim Line
HANKO 1940-41
PORKKALA 1947-55
GULF OF FINLAND
LENINGRAD
Seventh Army
Estonia
KARELIAN ISTHMUS

The Conquest of Norway and Denmark

The German invasion of Scandinavia in April 1940 marked the end of the Phony War. Prior to this, British and French strategy had been to avoid costly battles on the Western Front in favor of blockade and encirclement. The bungled plans to assist Finland and the related Allied interest in Norway were based on such tactics, which originated in the dread of another world war as destructive of life as the first.

Germany's objective in Scandinavia was not only to frustrate Allied plans, but to protect iron-ore imports that passed from Sweden to Germany via the Norwegian port of Narvik. Hitler was convinced that the Allies would intervene after the *Altmark* incident of February 1940, in which a German ship carrying British prisoners was boarded in Norwegian waters by the British. The Germans had minor in-country support in the form of the Norwegian Nazi Party, led by Vidkun Quisling.

Rapid plans were made by both sides in the early months of 1940. The Norwegian campaign was to see the first extensive naval engagements of World War II. The Germans moved first by a matter of hours, suffering heavy losses in their naval escort force, but gaining an initiative that they held throughout the campaign. On 9 April 1940 they made simultaneous landings at Oslo, Kristiansand, Stavanger, Bergen, Trondheim and Narvik. Their rapid capture of several strategic airfields enabled them to reinforce their assault units and retain dominance of coastal waters, even when the full strength of the British Royal Navy was deployed.

Norwegian defense forces were sparse and underarmed in the wake of early German attacks on their arms depots. Reserve mobilizations came too late to make much difference. And Allied organization proved woefully inadequate; those troops that did land lacked proper armaments and supplies. German air power closed the books on a free Norway before the summer of 1940.

Both Norway and Denmark would remain under German occupation for the rest of the war, providing valuable Atlantic bases for German strikes against Arctic convoys to the USSR. On the debit side, a disproportionate number of German troops were tied up in Norway (where resistance never really ended), and naval losses there in 1940 helped undo the plan to invade Britain by sea after the fall of France.

Right: Allied warships and transports in a Norwegian port shortly after a German air attack. The narrow fiords gave little room for evasive maneuvers.

Right: The campaign in Norway. The German capture of Fornebu airfield at Oslo and Sola at Stavanger at the very outset gave their forces an advantage they never relinquished.

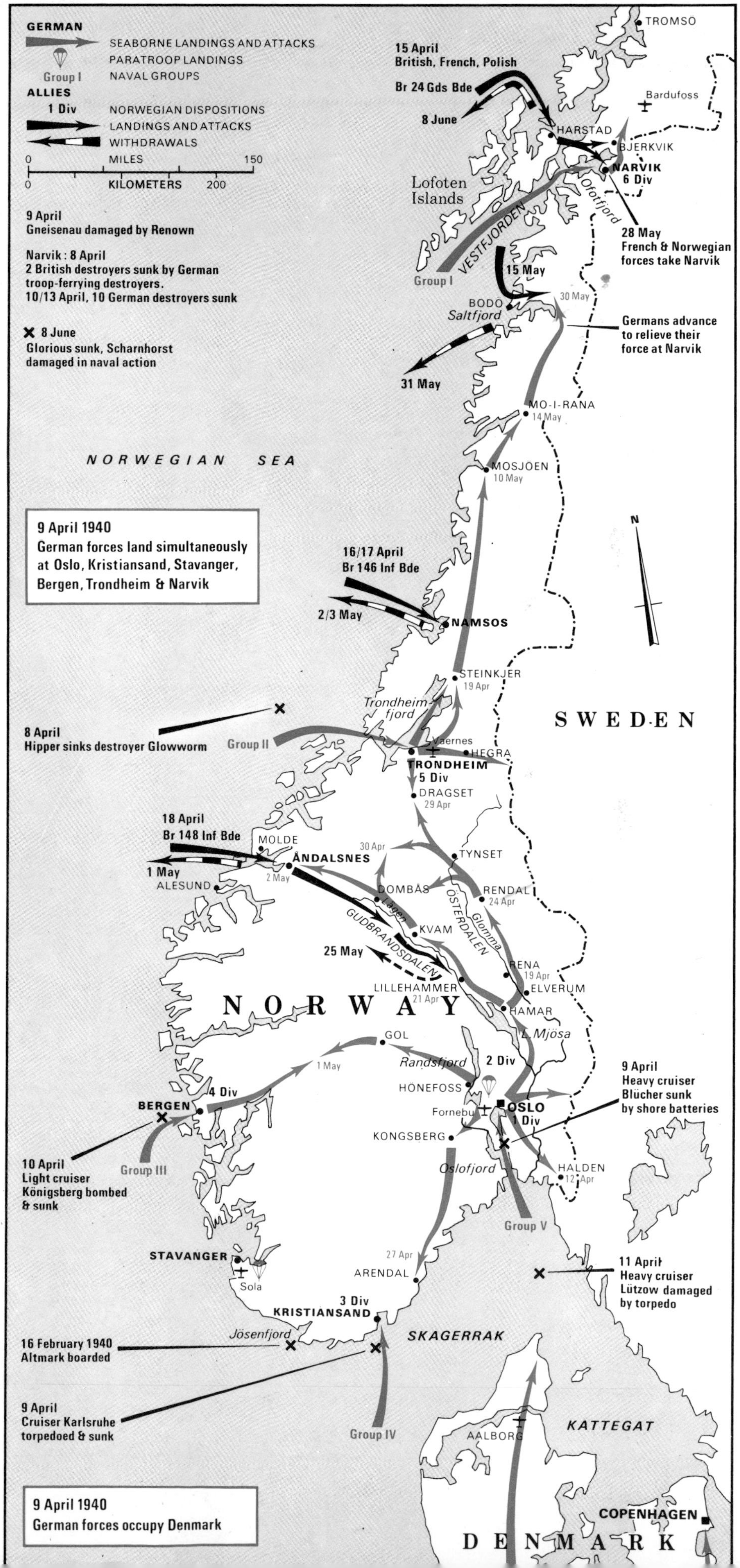

The Battle for France

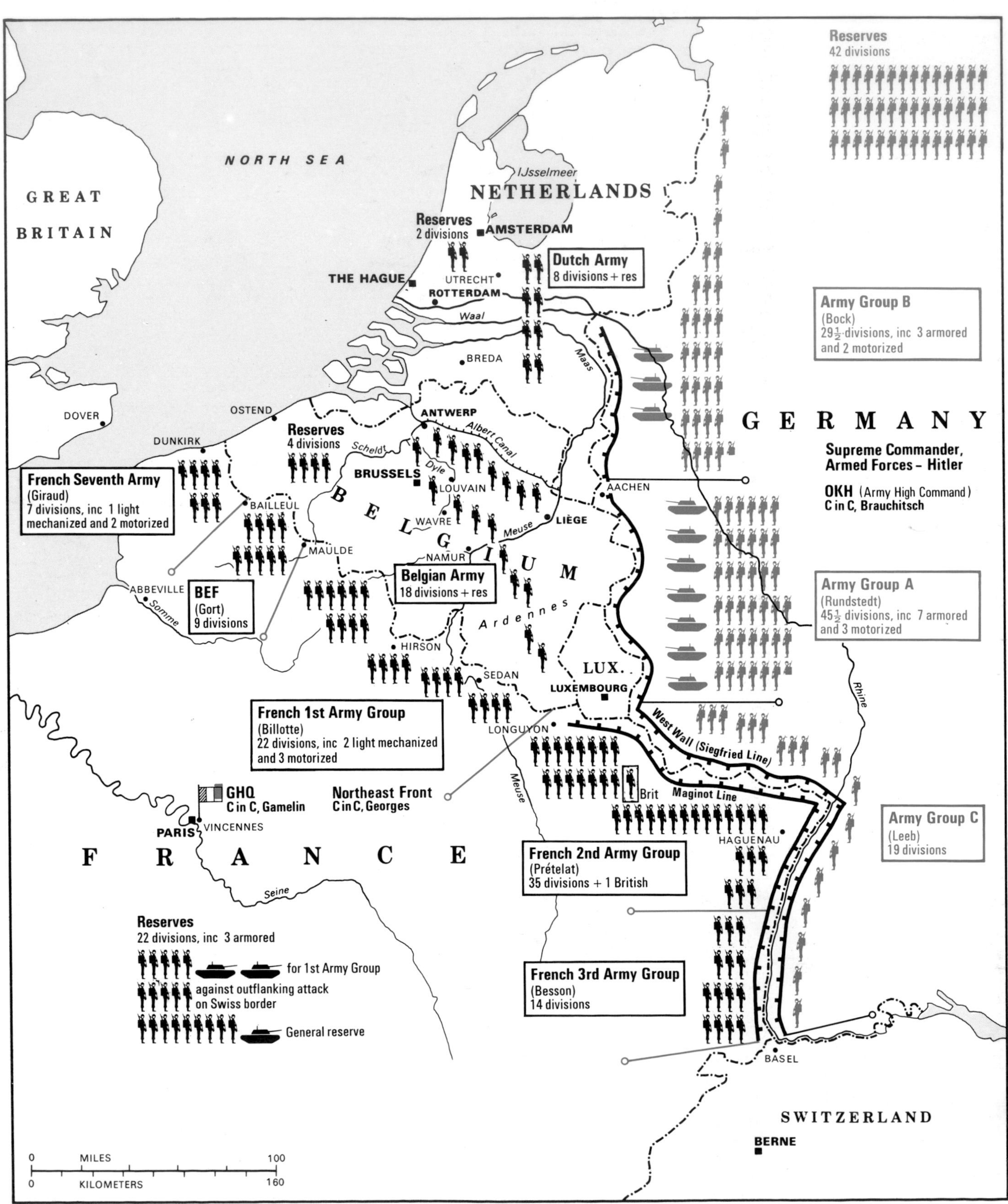

Left: German troops enter The Hague.
Opposite: The evenness of the initial line-up for the Battle of France conceals the German's qualitative superiority in every meaningful category.
Below left: The overrunning of the Low Countries.

Between the fall of Poland and the invasion of Scandinavia, there was little activity along the Western Front. But many preparations were going on during the period that has been called the Phony War. Hitler first wanted to attack France in November 1939, but was persuaded to wait until May of the following year. In the interim, the German High Command explored various ways of defeating France without a frontal assault on the Maginot Line fortifications. Limited advances into Belgium and Holland were considered, as were variations on the 1914 Schlieffen Plan. All seemed too easy to counter.

At last, General Fritz von Manstein was instrumental in coming up with the plan code-named Sickle-stroke. He proposed that attacks into Belgium and Holland should be made by Army Group B to draw Anglo-French forces forward of their prepared positions on the Franco-Belgian border. Simultaneously, Army Group A would make the major German advance, led by powerful tank forces, through Luxembourg and the hilly Ardennes region to the Meuse River. Having crossed the Meuse, the army would make a drive for the Channel, cutting off the Belgians, the Dutch and all Allied forces that had advanced to help them.

The British and French had prepared for no such contingency, largely because they believed the Ardennes terrain impassable to a major force, especially one with tanks. Instead, they were expecting some variation on the Schlieffen Plan. The Maginot Line was garrisoned and the remaining forces deployed along the Franco-Belgian border should the Belgians ask for help. Belgian and Dutch co-operation were obviously key factors in the success of this plan, but there was no guarantee of it prior to 10 May because the smaller countries feared to compromise their neutrality and invite a German attack.

The defense of France was beset with other problems, including poor communications, bad headquarters siting and uncertain leadership in the person of General Maurice Gamelin, who was 68 years old and in declining health. Relations between the French and the British were far from ideal.

The ground forces involved were fairly equal in numbers: the Allies had 149 divisions against 136 German, with 3000 tanks against 2700. However, German armor, training and leadership were all superior. (The British had not a single tank division in place when the fighting began, and French tanks were not deployed in powerful panzer corps, but wastefully, in support of

Right: Rouen burns in the wake of the German attack.
Bottom: The Germans close in on Dunkirk.
Far right: Final stages of the Battle of France.
Below right: British signallers at work.
Below, far right: The division of France into occupied and unoccupied zones.

small infantry units.) The German Air Force had no peer in the world: over 3000 modern planes with well-trained pilots and crews. Against this, the Allies had an unimpressive assortment of 2000 aircraft, including British-based RAF units. Germany's dive-bombing Stukas were especially effective in an air-support role.

The German attack began on 10 May 1940, when all eyes turned toward the Low Countries. A host of paratroopers descended on important border defenses in both Holland and Belgium, as ground forces launched simultaneous attacks. Air raids on Holland, especially Rotterdam, stymied Dutch defense efforts, and the government fled to England after its surrender of 14 May. In Belgium the Germans made equally swift progress, forcing Anglo-French evacuation of the Dyle Line by 15 May.

The German master stroke was the successful penetration through the Ardennes and subsequent capture of vital bridgeheads over the Meuse. Local French forces failed to counterattack, and German tanks rolled toward the sea almost unchecked. General Maxime Weygand replaced Gamelin as French commander-in-chief and tried unsuccessfully to organize a counterattack. Thereafter, Allied forces were in retreat toward the sea. An inexplicable order from Hitler and Rundstedt almost stopped the German advance from 23–26 May, which gave Allied forces the chance to fall back to the Dunkirk perimeter. There some 338,000 men (including 120,000 French) were evacuated in a nine-day operation that cost heavily in transport ships and covering aircraft.

Meanwhile, Weygand was trying to organize remaining French forces for the defense of the Somme line, which came under heavy attack on 5 June. The line was soon broken, despite courageous resistance by many French units, and the German advance flowed on. Premier Reynaud and his government resigned, and his successor, Marshal Pétain, announced on 17 June that he was seeking an armistice. It was signed five days later in the same railroad carriage as had been used for the armistice negotiations in 1918 at the end of World War I.

France was split into occupied and unoccupied zones, the unoccupied sector being ruled from Vichy by the Pétain government, which was stigmatized by close co-operation with the German victors. A junior general and would-be statesman named Charles de Gaulle escaped to Britain with a small following and proclaimed himself leader of the Free French, declaring that France had lost a battle, but not the war.

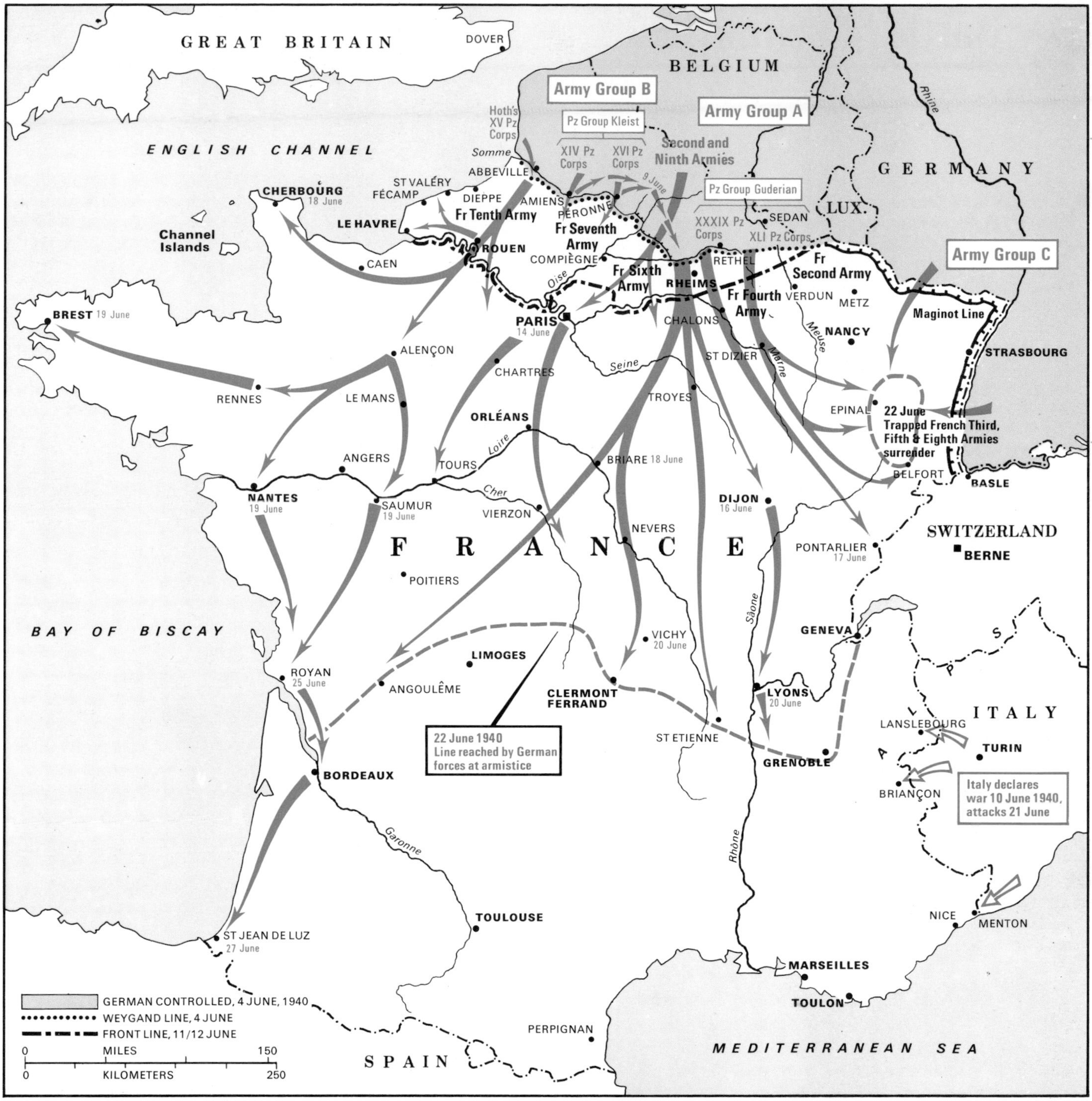
GREAT BRITAIN
DOVER
BELGIUM
Army Group B
Army Group A
Hoth's XV Pz Corps
Pz Group Kleist
XIV Pz Corps
XVI Pz Corps
Second and Ninth Armies
9 June
Pz Group Guderian
XXXIX Pz Corps
XLI Pz Corps
SEDAN
LUX.
GERMANY
Rhine
Army Group C
ENGLISH CHANNEL
Somme
ABBEVILLE
ST VALÉRY
FÉCAMP
DIEPPE
AMIENS
PERONNE
CHERBOURG 18 June
LE HAVRE
Channel Islands
Fr Tenth Army
Fr Seventh Army
ROUEN
CAEN
COMPIÈGNE
Oise
Fr Sixth Army
RHEIMS
RETHEL
Fr Second Army
VERDUN
METZ
Fr Fourth Army
Maginot Line
BREST 19 June
PARIS 14 June
CHALONS
NANCY
STRASBOURG
ALENÇON
CHARTRES
Seine
ST DIZIER
Marne
Meuse
RENNES
LE MANS
TROYES
EPINAL
22 June Trapped French Third, Fifth & Eighth Armies surrender
ORLÉANS
Loire
ANGERS
TOURS
BRIARE 18 June
BELFORT
BASLE
NANTES 19 June
SAUMUR 19 June
Cher
VIERZON
DIJON 16 June
SWITZERLAND
BERNE
NEVERS
PONTARLIER 17 June
FRANCE
POITIERS
Saône
BAY OF BISCAY
GENEVA
VICHY 20 June
LIMOGES
ROYAN 25 June
ANGOULÊME
CLERMONT FERRAND
LYONS 20 June
ALPS
ITALY
LANSLEBOURG
TURIN
22 June 1940 Line reached by German forces at armistice
ST ETIENNE
GRENOBLE
BORDEAUX
BRIANÇON
Italy declares war 10 June 1940, attacks 21 June
Garonne
Rhône
TOULOUSE
NICE
MENTON
ST JEAN DE LUZ 27 June
MARSEILLES
TOULON
GERMAN CONTROLLED, 4 JUNE, 1940
WEYGAND LINE, 4 JUNE
FRONT LINE, 11/12 JUNE
0 MILES 150
0 KILOMETERS 250
PERPIGNAN
SPAIN
MEDITERRANEAN SEA

BRITAIN
BELGIUM
GERMANY
PARIS
FRANCE
(German occupied)
SWITZ
VICHY
(Vichy)
ITALY
BORDEAUX
MARSEILLES
SPAIN

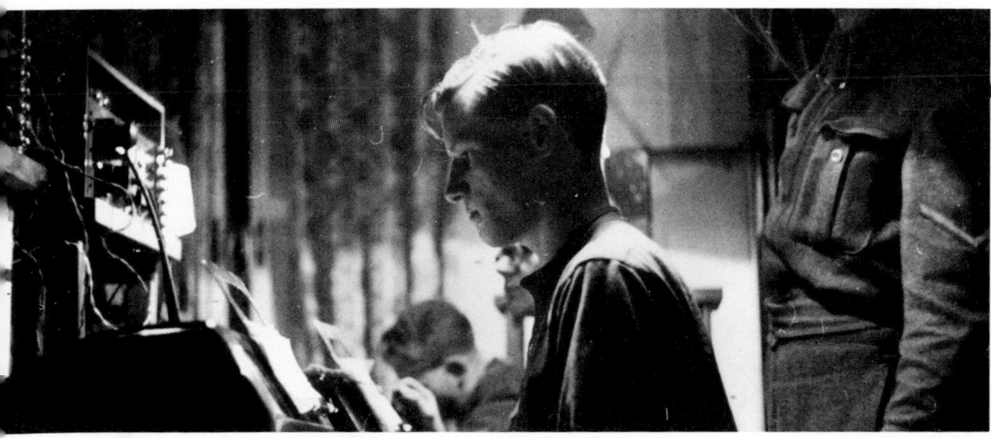

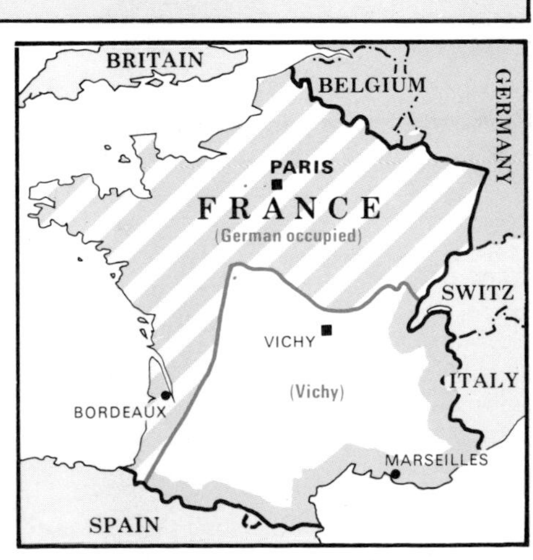

The Battle of Britain

On 16 July 1940 Hitler directed the German armed forces to prepare for an invasion of England across the Channel. The Luftwaffe was to make preliminary strikes aimed at destroying the RAF on the ground so it could not protect the Royal Navy when the crossings began.

Britain's survival of this threat would depend upon keeping the RAF largely intact and gaining time to re-equip after the losses of Dunkirk; if the Germans could be held off through the summer, stormy fall weather might make the invasion impossible.

A major British advantage was the line of radar stations along the coast. Another was good leadership in the person of Air Chief Marshal Hugh Dowding, and a rapid communications system that co-ordinated radar and other information from various RAF sectors for optimum fighter direction.

It was fortunate for Britain that Germany failed to appreciate the role of radar in the British defense network: little was done to destroy the vital stations. While the Germans lacked information they needed on the extent of damage done, RAF planners had access to all the data on enemy planes destroyed, weak links in their own defense lines and other intelligence that helped them husband their resources. The RAF's main shortage was of trained fighter pilots, but operations over their home ground – or waters – enabled them to rescue and return to service those pilots who were shot down unwounded. (Many RAF flyers took to the air again on the same day they had been knocked out of the sky.) The Germans had no such second chance in most cases. An additional drawback was the short range of their principal fighter, the Messerschmitt Bf 109, which could stay over England for a matter of a few minutes only.

German air power and experience would have offset all these negatives if the German High Command had done its job with competence. But Reichsmarshall Hermann Göring made many mistakes in his leadership of the Luftwaffe. Its all-out attacks did not begin until 13 August – more than two months after Dunkirk – and then they were misapplied. Instead of concentrating on British airfields – which would have made the invasion possible by destroying the RAF – the Germans turned their attention to London, Coventry and other cities of limited strategic importance. And the British people, instead of being demoralized by the 'Blitz' that began in early September, were unified in their resolve to repel the German aggressors.

The last major daytime attack on London fell in mid-September (although night raids would continue into 1941). Coventry would be devastated in November and 19 other towns and cities would be bombed in the Battle of Britain, but the German invasion would never be carried out.

Right: The German and RAF deployments during the Battle of Britain.
Below: A burning London building collapses after a German raid. Compared to the raids later mounted by the British and Americans on German cities and industries, the German attacks were rather ineffective.

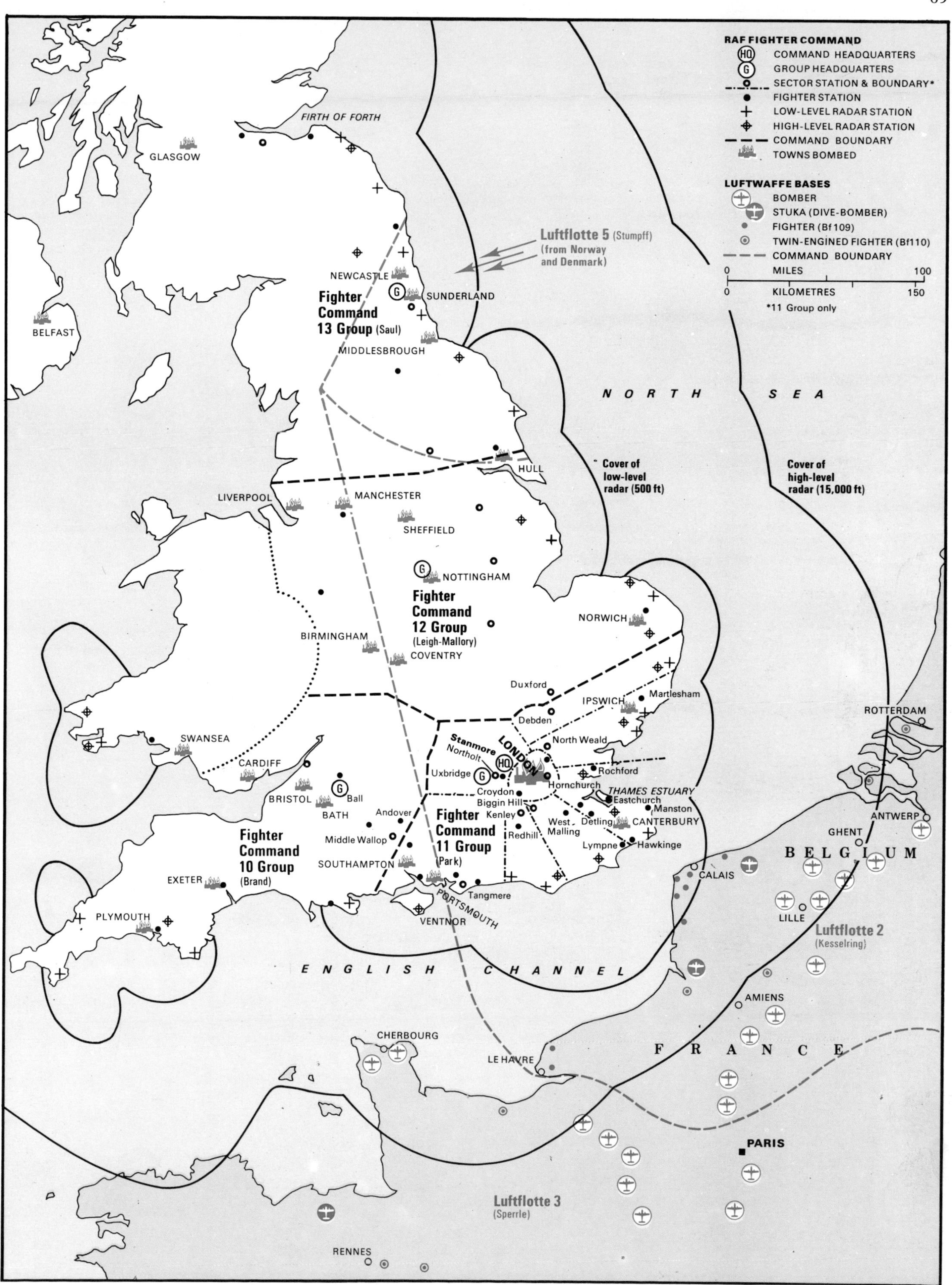
RAF FIGHTER COMMAND
COMMAND HEADQUARTERS
GROUP HEADQUARTERS
SECTOR STATION & BOUNDARY*
FIGHTER STATION
LOW-LEVEL RADAR STATION
HIGH-LEVEL RADAR STATION
COMMAND BOUNDARY
TOWNS BOMBED
LUFTWAFFE BASES
BOMBER
STUKA (DIVE-BOMBER)
FIGHTER (Bf109)
TWIN-ENGINED FIGHTER (Bf110)
COMMAND BOUNDARY
0 MILES 100
0 KILOMETRES 150
*11 Group only
FIRTH OF FORTH
GLASGOW
Luftflotte 5 (Stumpff)
(from Norway and Denmark)
NEWCASTLE
SUNDERLAND
BELFAST
Fighter Command 13 Group (Saul)
MIDDLESBROUGH
NORTH SEA
HULL
Cover of low-level radar (500 ft)
Cover of high-level radar (15,000 ft)
LIVERPOOL
MANCHESTER
SHEFFIELD
NOTTINGHAM
Fighter Command 12 Group (Leigh-Mallory)
NORWICH
BIRMINGHAM
COVENTRY
Duxford
IPSWICH
Martlesham
Debden
ROTTERDAM
North Weald
SWANSEA
Stanmore
Northolt
LONDON
CARDIFF
Uxbridge
Rochford
Hornchurch
Croydon
THAMES ESTUARY
Biggin Hill
Eastchurch
BRISTOL
Ball
Manston
BATH
Andover
Kenley
West Malling
Detling
CANTERBURY
Fighter Command 11 Group (Park)
Redhill
ANTWERP
GHENT
Fighter Command 10 Group (Brand)
Middle Wallop
Lympne
Hawkinge
BELGIUM
SOUTHAMPTON
CALAIS
EXETER
Tangmere
PORTSMOUTH
LILLE
PLYMOUTH
VENTNOR
Luftflotte 2 (Kesselring)
ENGLISH CHANNEL
AMIENS
CHERBOURG
LE HAVRE
FRANCE
PARIS
Luftflotte 3 (Sperrle)
RENNES

SOFIA
Twelfth Army
(List)
YUGOSLAVIA
KYUSTENDIL
XL Pz Corps
KRIVA PALANKA
PLOVDIV
Maritza
Drin
SHKODËR
DELČEVO
BULGARIA
SKOPJE
8 Apr
Vardar
KOČANI
Struma
XVIII Corps
VELES
6 Apr
NEVROKOP
ALBANIA
STRUMICA
Rupel Pass
XXX Corps
TURKEY
DURRËS
TIRANË
PRILEP
Beles Mts
Nestos
EKHINOS
DOJRAN
XANTHI
Thrace
ELBASAN
Shkumbin
L Okhrida
MONASTIR
9 Apr
SERRAI
DRAMA
KOMOTINÍ
Monastir Gap
L Prespa
Axios
KILKIS
Macedonia
KAVALLA
Ital Ninth Army
L Vegorritis
ALEXANDROÚPOLIS
EDHESSA
Gr Second Army
FLORINA
Vermion Mts
THASOS
16 Apr
Ital Eleventh Army
AMINDAION
THESSALONIKI
9 Apr
SAMOTHRACE
19 Apr
VALONA
KORCË
KLISSOURA
VEROIA
PTOLEMAÏS
Aliákmon
Piéria Óri
TEPELENË
Vijosë
KOZÁNI
KATERÍNI
PINDUS MOUNTAINS
23 April
SÉRVIA
16 April
GJIROKASTËR
Venetikos
Mt Olympus
LÍMNOS
SARANDË
Gr First Army
'W' Force
(Wilson)
Mt Ossa
CORFU
IOÁNNINA
20 Apr
TRIKKALA
LÁRISA
19 Apr
Pinios
PLAIN OF THESSALY
VÓLOS
PARAMITHIÁ
Surrenders
23 April
LESBOS
4 May
ÁRTA
GREECE
ÆGEAN
LAMIA
SKÍROS
Thermopylai
MOLOS
LEVKÁS
BRÁLLOS
SEA
20 April
Akhelóos
Evvoia
(Eubœa)
KHÍOS
4 May
KEFALLINÍA
MESOLÓNGION
26 Apr
THEBES
Gulf of Corinth
PÁTRAI
ATHENS
27 Apr
RAFINA
IONIAN
CORINTH
26 Apr
PIRAEUS
PORTO RAFTI
ÁNDROS
ZÁKINTHOS
PÍRGOS
Peloponnesos
TÍNOS
NÁUPLIA
TRÍPOLIS
SEA
KALAMATA
28 Apr
NAXOS
MONEMVASÍA
MÍLOS
C Matapan
KÍTHIRA
British evacuation routes
Suda Bay
CANEA
HERÁKLION
CRETE
STABILI ED FRONT IN ALBANIA, 6 APRIL 1941
METAXAS LINE
ALIAKMON LINE
THE FRONT AT DATES SHOWN
GERMAN AIRBORNE LANDING, 26 APRIL
HEIGHT IN FEET
OVER 6000
3000–6000
1200–3000
UNDER 1200
0
MILES
100
0
KILOMETERS
160

The Conquest of Greece

Hitler's master plan for 1941 called for attacking the USSR and securing dominion over southeastern Europe and its natural resources. Hungary, Rumania and Bulgaria were drawn into the Axis orbit in the winter of 1940–41; Greece and Yugoslavia remained problematic. Italy had occupied Albania in 1939 and started a war against Greece the following October, but Mussolini's ambitions had outrun his troops' abilities; by March 1941 the Italians had suffered many defeats and lost control of most of Albania.

By this time Greece was getting help from Britain, and Hitler was faced with the possible defeat of his Italian ally and British access to the oil fields of Rumania – both unacceptable prospects. The Führer implemented his plan to subdue Greece (in preparation since late 1940). It would be a mountain campaign, employing three full corps, strong armored units and overwhelming air support.

Allied forces in Greece included those already engaged with the Italians, plus seven undermanned Greek divisions, almost two full New Zealand and Australian divisions and a British armored brigade. British leaders hoped to base their defense on the mountainous Aliakmon Line, with sufficient forces to cover the Monastir Gap, but the Greek Commander-in-Chief, General Papagos, rejected this sound advice. He held out for protecting Greek Macedonia, with the result that resources were drained off to the weaker Metaxas Line. The Germans planned to destroy this force in direct attacks, and push other units through the Monastir Gap to outflank the defense lines.

The powerful German attack began on 6 April; within four days the Aliakmon Line was being evacuated. General Archibald Wavell's decision not to bring in reinforcements from Egypt meant the end of the struggle for Greece. German paratroops descended on the island of Crete on 20 May, and the last British bastion was evacuated after 10 days of fierce fighting.

Left: The campaign in Greece. Note the German drive through the Monastir Gap which split the Allied forces and compelled their retreat.
Top right: Greek and German officers begin surrender negotiations. About 50,000 Allied soldiers were evacuated from the Greek mainland before the German victory was complete.
Right: German troops pass through Lamia as the advance to Athens continues.

Operation Barbarossa and the Finnish Front

By early 1941 the USSR had been warned by many sources that Hitler was about to turn against his Soviet ally. Stalin's secret agents made reports to this effect, and a sympathetic German printer showed Soviet diplomats in Berlin copies of a new Russian phrasebook he had been ordered to print in quantity: it contained such phrases as 'Hands up or I'll shoot!' and 'Are you a Communist?' In fact, in December 1940 Hitler had issued a general directive that proposed nothing less than the destruction of the entire Red Army.

German strategy was based on the fact that prevailing Russian military doctrine had placed most of the nation's army near the frontiers in preparation for offensive action. Deep penetrations by German armor would make it possible to cut off the retreat of these Soviet formations. Then German forces would press eastward to establish a line running from Archangel to Astrakhan. Stalin and his advisers made no move to counter the ominous preparations of the Germans, lest they provoke the attack: thus their forces were taken by surprise when Operation Barbarossa was unleashed on 22 June 1941.

Heavy German air attacks, directed mainly at airfields close to the frontier, shattered the Red Air Force on Day One. Army Group Center made a pincer movement from East Prussia and Poland toward Minsk, cutting off parts of two Soviet armies; they surrendered en masse. Meanwhile, Army Group South entered the Ukraine with Rumanian troops and overcame other large Soviet forces. General S M Budenny, a trusted intimate of Stalin since revolutionary days, engaged in catastrophic battles rather than retreat on the Southwest Front.

By mid-November the invaders had captured Rostov and the Perekop Isthmus commanding the Crimea. A large tank battle near Smolensk, and another engagement at Bryansk, enabled the Germans to take Orel, Tula and Vyazma. The Baltic States were occupied, and some formations had penetrated east of Leningrad. The widely hailed 'Stalin Line' had proved ephemeral in the face of the German war machine.

The Finns took part in the German campaign against Russia to recover the territory they had lost the previous year. Their principal role was to provide a front from which Army Group North could launch itself against Leningrad. Finnish manpower and training had both increased after the Winter War, and the Finns made early gains from their initial joint attack of 29 June right through the summer. They advanced successfully north of Lake Ladoga and in the Karelian Isthmus, almost to the walls of Leningrad. There Mannerheim's orders halted them. The fall of 1941 saw additional advances toward Lake Onega and farther north, but by December Finnish efforts had turned toward the defensive.

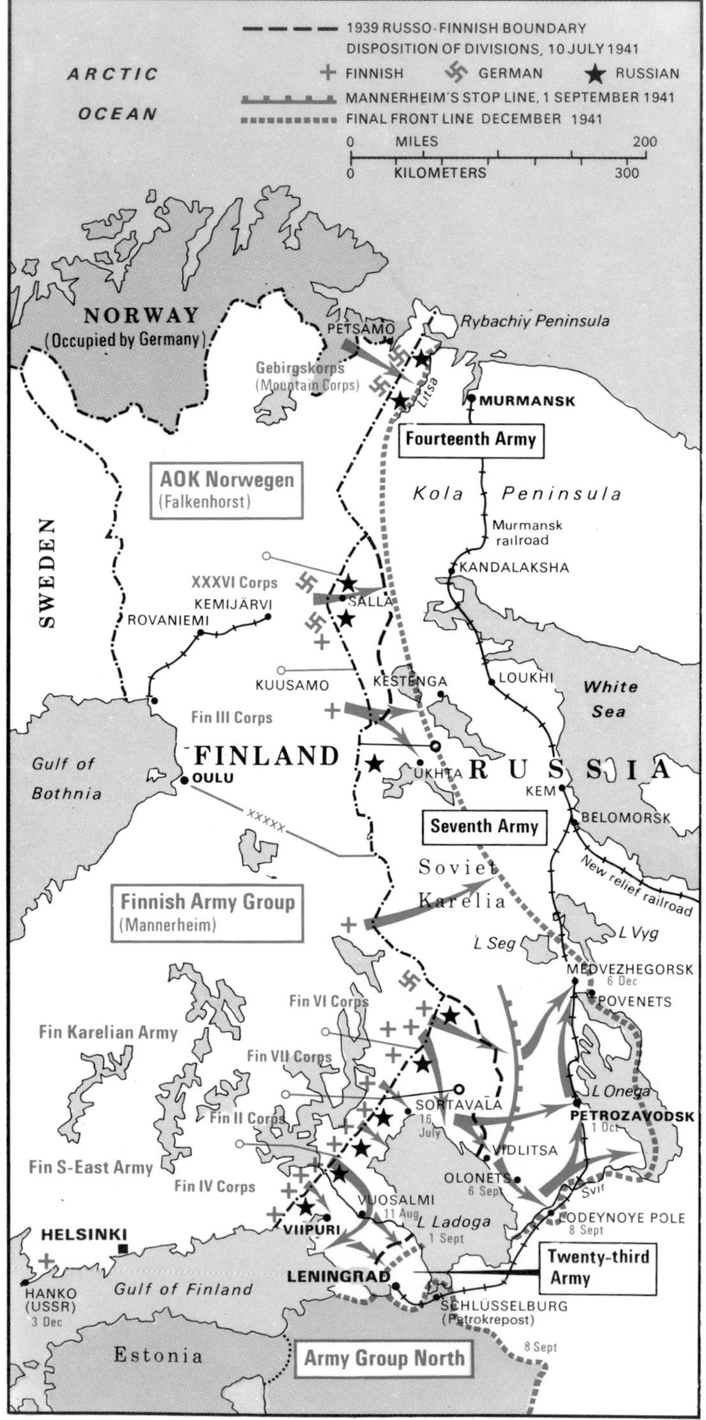

Right: The line-up at the start of the German invasion.
Bottom: A Russian tank commander receives his orders by messenger. In 1941 few Russian tanks had radios.
Below left: Operations on the Finnish front.
Below: A primitive sound-location device forms part of Leningrad's air defenses in 1941.

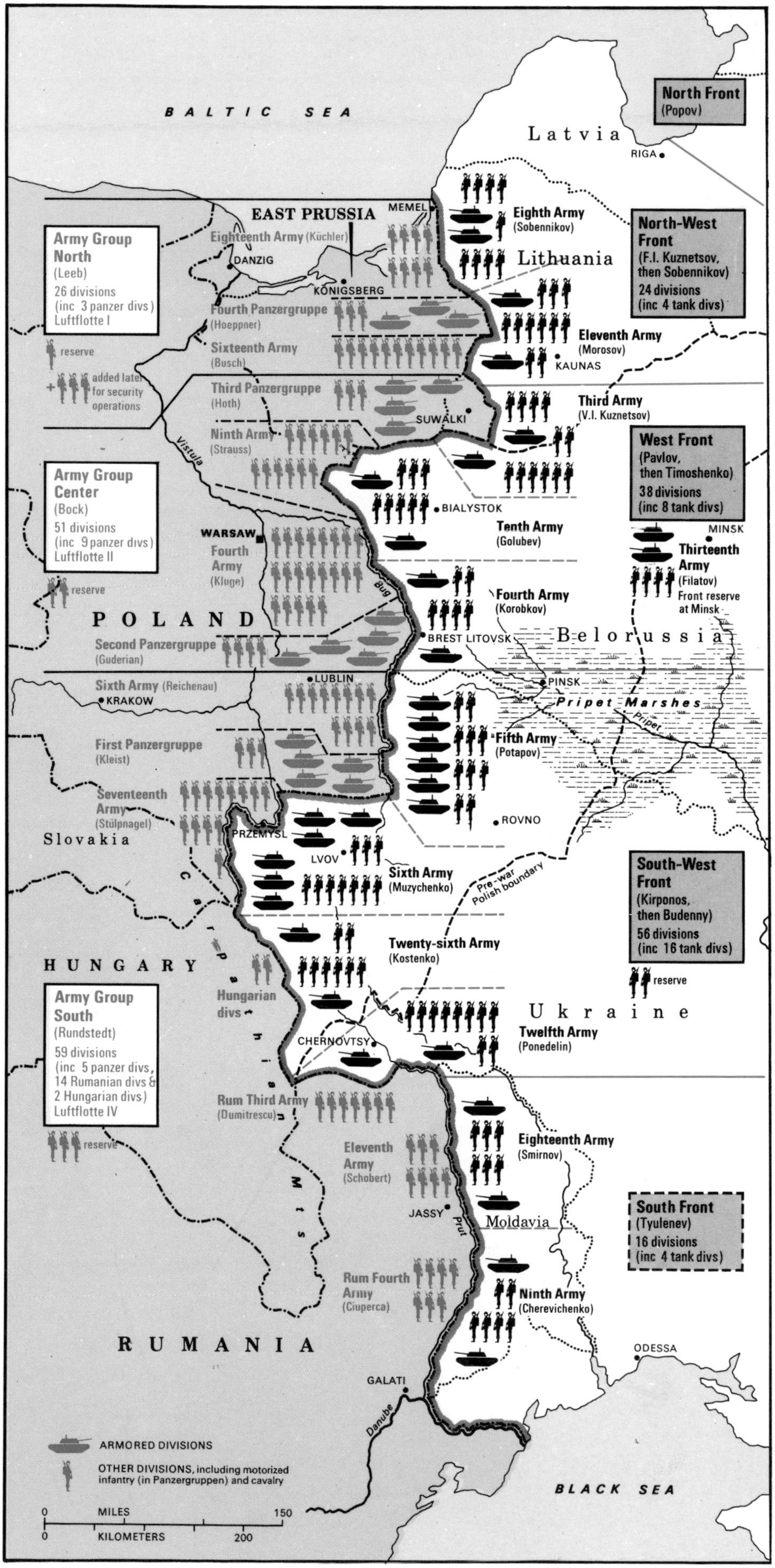

BALTIC SEA

Latvia

RIGA

North Front
(Popov)

EAST PRUSSIA

MEMEL

Army Group North
(Leeb)
26 divisions
(inc 3 panzer divs)
Luftflotte I

Eighteenth Army (Küchler)

DANZIG

KÖNIGSBERG

Fourth Panzergruppe (Hoeppner)

Sixteenth Army (Busch)

reserve

added later for security operations

Eighth Army (Sobennikov)

Lithuania

North-West Front
(F.I. Kuznetsov, then Sobennikov)
24 divisions
(inc 4 tank divs)

Eleventh Army (Morosov)

KAUNAS

Third Panzergruppe (Hoth)

SUWALKI

Third Army (V.I. Kuznetsov)

Ninth Army (Strauss)

Vistula

West Front
(Pavlov, then Timoshenko)
38 divisions
(inc 8 tank divs)

Army Group Center
(Bock)
51 divisions
(inc 9 panzer divs)
Luftflotte II

BIALYSTOK

Tenth Army (Golubev)

MINSK

Thirteenth Army (Filatov)

Front reserve at Minsk

WARSAW

Fourth Army (Kluge)

Bug

reserve

Fourth Army (Korobkov)

POLAND

BREST LITOVSK

Belorussia

Second Panzergruppe (Guderian)

LUBLIN

PINSK

Sixth Army (Reichenau)

KRAKOW

Pripet Marshes

Pripet

First Panzergruppe (Kleist)

Fifth Army (Potapov)

Seventeenth Army (Stülpnagel)

ROVNO

Slovakia

PRZEMYSL

LVOV

Sixth Army (Muzychenko)

Pre-war Polish boundary

South-West Front
(Kirponos, then Budenny)
56 divisions
(inc 16 tank divs)

Twenty-sixth Army (Kostenko)

reserve

HUNGARY

Carpathian Mts

Army Group South
(Rundstedt)
59 divisions
(inc 5 panzer divs, 14 Rumanian divs & 2 Hungarian divs)
Luftflotte IV

Hungarian divs

Ukraine

Twelfth Army (Ponedelin)

CHERNOVTSY

reserve

Rum Third Army (Dumitrescu)

Eighteenth Army (Smirnov)

Eleventh Army (Schobert)

JASSY

Prut

Moldavia

South Front
(Tyulenev)
16 divisions
(inc 4 tank divs)

Rum Fourth Army (Ciuperca)

Ninth Army (Cherevichenko)

RUMANIA

ODESSA

GALATI

Danube

ARMORED DIVISIONS

OTHER DIVISIONS, including motorized infantry (in Panzergruppen) and cavalry

BLACK SEA

0 MILES 150
0 KILOMETERS 200

Moscow: Attack and Counteroffensive

The Russians made a spirited defense at Smolensk that delayed the German advance to Moscow despite its ultimate failure. Thus the Russians were able to evacuate much of their factory equipment and key workers, sending them east before the Germans arrived. Railroads, too, were evacuated, frustrating Hitler's hopes of a transportation breakdown: the Soviets retained the advantage in locomotives and freight cars per mile of track.

On 2 October 1941 the capture of Moscow was ordered; 51 divisions, including 13 armored units, were to encircle the city. The fighting grew fiercer and more desperate as the Germans closed in on the capital. Commanders on both sides knew that the delay at Smolensk had left little time to capture Moscow before winter set in. But German troops did not succeed in surrounding the city; its lines of communication to the east remained open, permitting Russian reinforcement by rail from Siberia.

The whole population of Moscow took part in the effort to repel the German invaders. Workers were sent to the front with a week's training; women dug trenches and handled supplies. The anniversary of the Russian Revolution was celebrated underground in subway stations as intensive bombing raged overhead. German planes, however, failed to play an effective ground-support role, so much of their potential was thrown away.

By the end of November, German units had reached the western suburbs, but two attempts to take the whole city by storm had failed. Encirclement was still incomplete, as an early winter began with temperatures dropping to 40 degrees below zero.

Because the German High Command had expected a quick summer victory, troops were not equipped with winter clothing or maintenance supplies for their vehicles. Motorized divisions were immobilized, as tanks and trucks froze up and cylinders cracked. The men suffered severely in the Arctic cold, and frantic efforts in Berlin to issue appropriate supplies were too little too late.

Meanwhile, Russian reinforcements were arriving from Siberia, and the apparent success of the German invasion was shown to be illusory. Moscow and Leningrad remained unconquered, despite the vast damage inflicted on the Red Army. The Soviet armaments industry was rebuilding itself far from the front. Materiel from the West was coming into the country from points as diverse as Archangel, Murmansk, Vladivostok and Persia. On 8 December Hitler called off the siege of Moscow for the winter.

Napoleon's disaster of 1812 was destined to be played out again with the Germans filling his role. The Russians were preparing a counteroffensive in the form of a massive infiltration that avoided the strongest enemy concentrations. Passing over the fields rather than roads, making good use of Cossacks, ski troops and guerrilla forces, the Soviets threatened the invaders from flank and rear on various fronts. German efforts were hampered by lack of supplies and Luftwaffe support – some aircraft engines could not operate in the freezing temperatures. Sparse German railroad links were plagued by a change of gauge, and the Russian roads were notoriously poor. The armies at center were pushed back the farthest: Soviet recapture of Kalinin and Tula removed the immediate threat to Moscow.

The offensive continued through February, with both sides becoming widely scattered and almost worn out. The

Right: The German advance from the start of the invasion until 30 September, showing the great encirclements made in the battles for Minsk and Kiev and the southward diversion of Guderian's Second Panzergroup to take part in the Kiev fighting – a major cause of delay in the advance to Moscow. Below: Muscovite citizens prepare the capital's defenses.

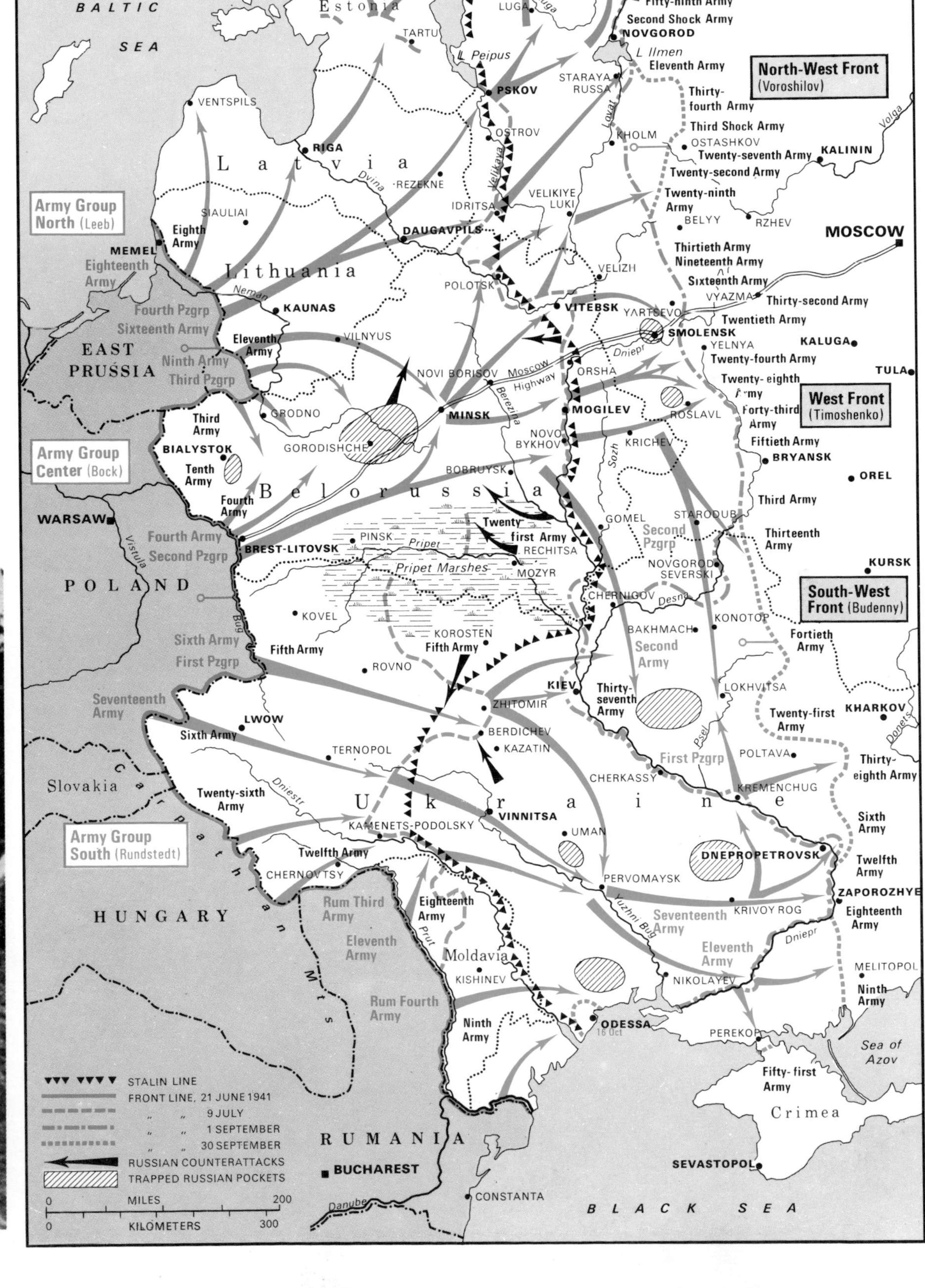

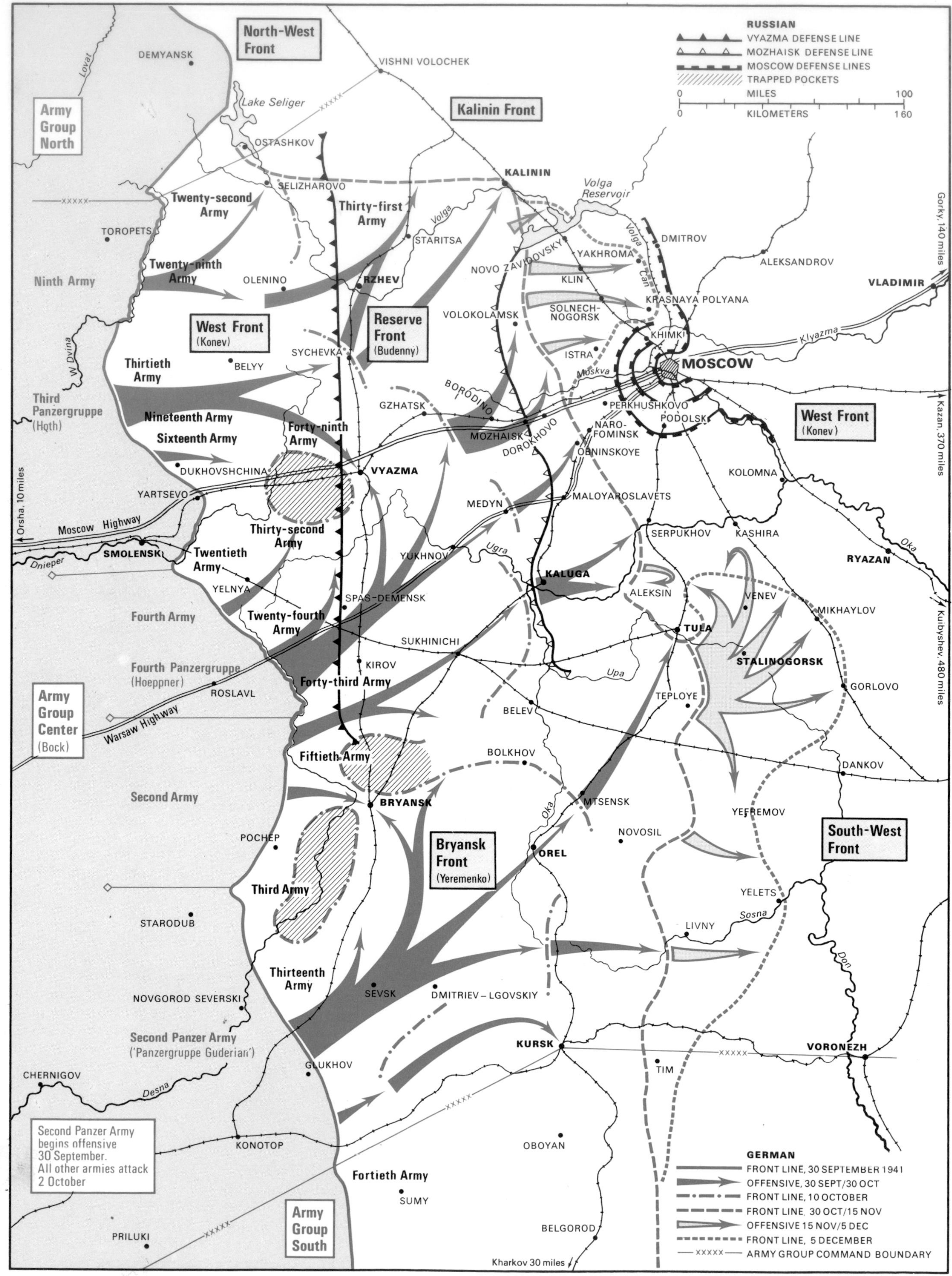
RUSSIAN
VYAZMA DEFENSE LINE
MOZHAISK DEFENSE LINE
MOSCOW DEFENSE LINES
TRAPPED POCKETS
MILES
KILOMETERS
0
100
0
160
North-West Front
Kalinin Front
Army Group North
Ninth Army
Third Panzergruppe (Hoth)
Fourth Army
Fourth Panzergruppe (Hoeppner)
Army Group Center (Bock)
Second Army
Second Panzer Army ('Panzergruppe Guderian')
Army Group South
Twenty-second Army
Twenty-ninth Army
Thirty-first Army
West Front (Konev)
Reserve Front (Budenny)
Thirtieth Army
Nineteenth Army
Sixteenth Army
Forty-ninth Army
Thirty-second Army
Twentieth Army
Twenty-fourth Army
Forty-third Army
Fiftieth Army
Bryansk Front (Yeremenko)
Third Army
Thirteenth Army
Fortieth Army
West Front (Konev)
South-West Front
DEMYANSK
VISHNI VOLOCHEK
Lake Seliger
OSTASHKOV
SELIZHAROVO
KALININ
Volga Reservoir
TOROPETS
STARITSA
Volga
OLENINO
RZHEV
NOVO ZAVIDOVSKY
YAKHROMA
DMITROV
Volga Can.
KLIN
ALEKSANDROV
VLADIMIR
Gorky, 140 miles
KRASNAYA POLYANA
SOLNECH-NOGORSK
VOLOKOLAMSK
KHIMKI
Klyazma
W Dvina
SYCHEVKA
BELYY
ISTRA
MOSCOW
Moskva
BORODINO
GZHATSK
PERKHUSHKOVO
PODOLSK
NARO-FOMINSK
MOZHAISK
DOROKHOVO
OBNINSKOYE
Kazan, 370 miles
DUKHOVSHCHINA
VYAZMA
KOLOMNA
YARTSEVO
MEDYN
MALOYAROSLAVETS
Orsha, 10 miles
Moscow Highway
SMOLENSK
Dnieper
SERPUKHOV
KASHIRA
YUKHNOV
Ugra
RYAZAN
Oka
KALUGA
YELNYA
ALEKSIN
VENEV
SPAS-DEMENSK
MIKHAYLOV
TULA
SUKHINICHI
Kubyshev, 480 miles
STALINOGORSK
KIROV
Upa
ROSLAVL
TEPLOYE
GORLOVO
Warsaw Highway
BELEV
BOLKHOV
DANKOV
BRYANSK
MTSENSK
YEFREMOV
Oka
POCHEP
NOVOSIL
OREL
YELETS
STARODUB
Sosna
LIVNY
Don
SEVSK
DMITRIEV – LGOVSKIY
NOVGOROD SEVERSKI
KURSK
VORONEZH
GLUKHOV
TIM
CHERNIGOV
Desna
KONOTOP
OBOYAN
SUMY
PRILUKI
BELGOROD
Kharkov 30 miles
Second Panzer Army begins offensive 30 September. All other armies attack 2 October
GERMAN
FRONT LINE, 30 SEPTEMBER 1941
OFFENSIVE, 30 SEPT/30 OCT
FRONT LINE, 10 OCTOBER
FRONT LINE, 30 OCT/15 NOV
OFFENSIVE 15 NOV/5 DEC
FRONT LINE, 5 DECEMBER
ARMY GROUP COMMAND BOUNDARY

Left: The Germans close in on Moscow. Below: The Soviet counterattack. German success in supplying surrounded positions by air, notably at Demyansk in the north of the sector, may have inspired Hitler to try to repeat this when his Sixth Army was cut off at Stalingrad a year later.

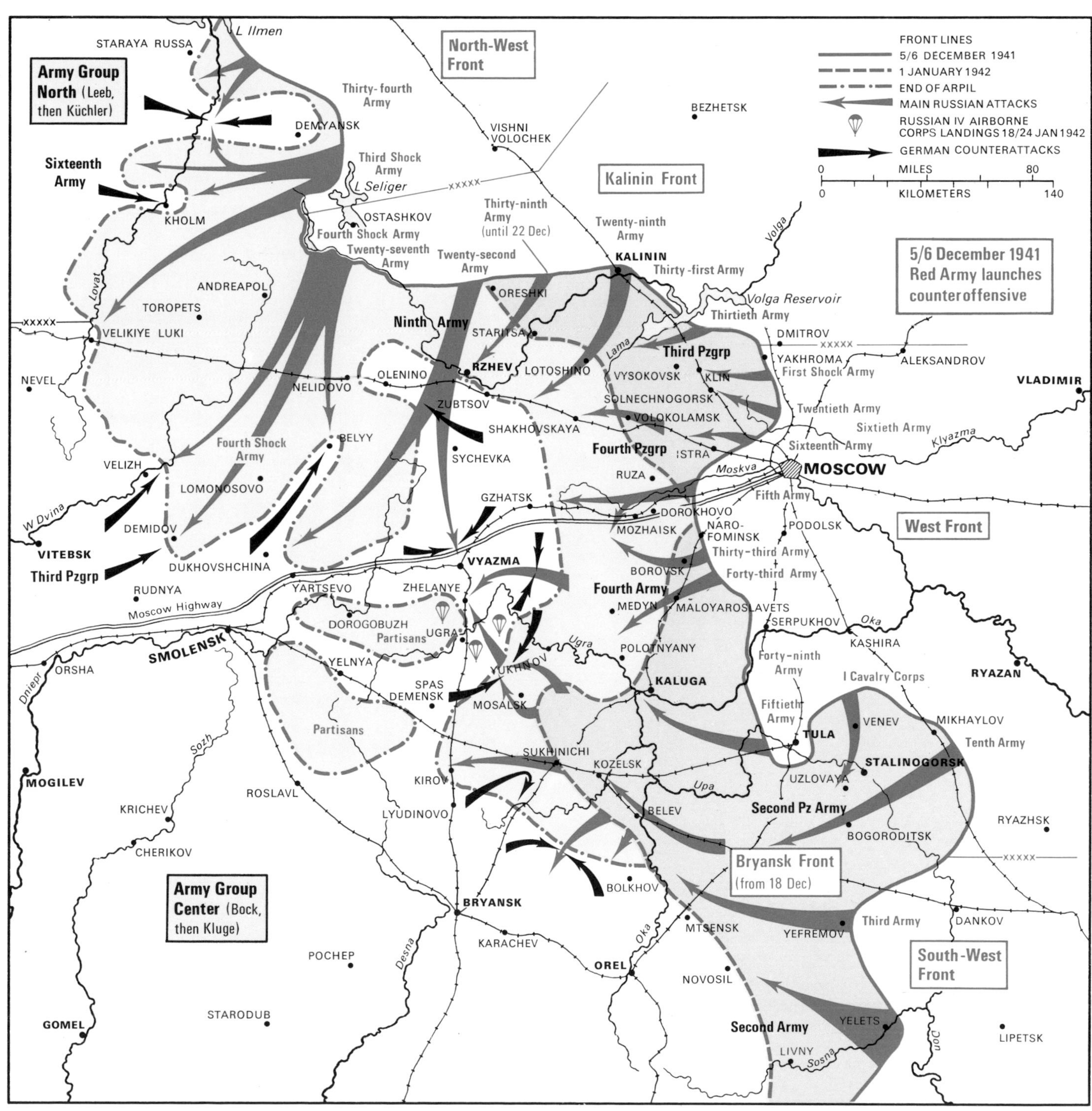

Russians had come back as far as Velikiye Luki and Mozhaisk. In the north, the Germans had fallen back from Tikhvin and Lake Ladoga, over which the Soviets built an ice road to Leningrad. The Kerch Isthmus was retaken in the south, opening the way to reoccupation of the Crimea, where the Soviet Navy – much weakened in the war's early days – played a supporting role.

The Germans took to their strongly fortified defensive positions ('hedgehogs') to await the arrival of fresh troops. Orders from Hitler were not to retreat in the face of the Russian offensive. Many German positions proved defensible with the help of supplies brought in by air, and the no-retreat policy may well have prevented a total disaster (although it was highly unpopular with German generals and their troops). Unfortunately, its comparative success confirmed the Führer's belief in his military genius and made him increasingly oblivious to the advice of his generals in the field.

The Battle of the Atlantic

HALIFAX
GIBRALTAR
SIERRA LEONE
Pan-American Neutrality Zone

BATTLE OF THE ATLANTIC, SEPT. 1939–MAY 1940

- ALLIED AND NEUTRAL MERCHANT SHIPS SUNK
- U-BOATS SUNK
- CONVOY ROUTES, ESCORTED
- " " , UNESCORTED
- GERMANY, 3 SEPT. 1939
- GERMANY AND GERMAN OCCUPIED TERRITORY, 31 MAY 1940

MERCATOR PROJECTION

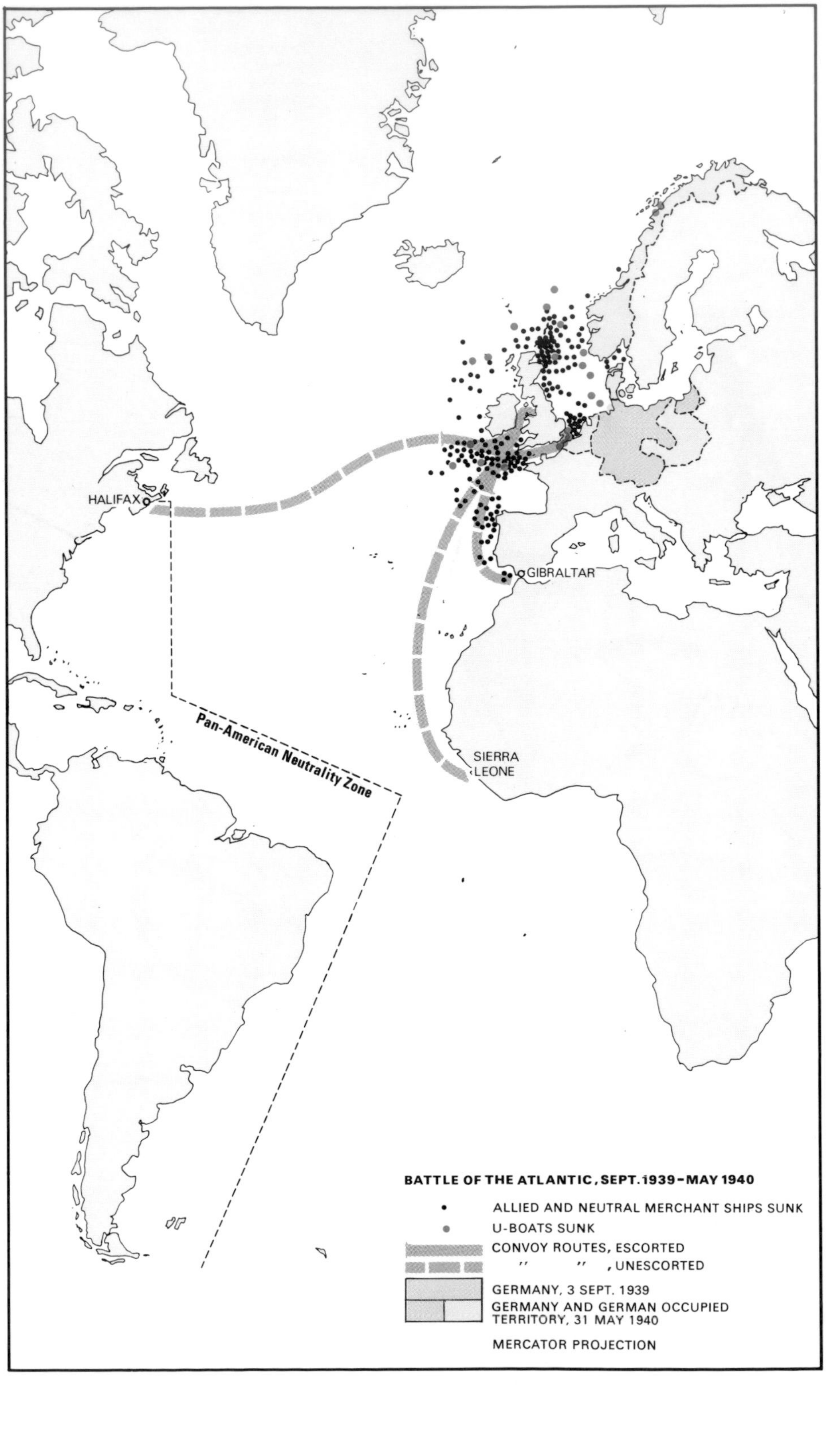

In the early days of World War II, Germany made little use of the U-boats that had been so successful in the previous war. Inter-war submarine construction had not kept pace with that of surface ships, and Hitler was reluctant to deploy the U-boats in force for an unrestricted campaign on account of neutral opinion. The British introduced a convoy system early in the conflict, but they lacked enough escorts to cover all ships, many of which sailed independently. It was among these 'independents' that the U-boats took their greatest toll in the early months of the war.

June 1940 brought a complete change in the war for the sea roads. British naval responsibility increased with the loss of support from the French fleet and Italy's entry into the war. The German position was enhanced by the acquisition of U-boat and air bases in western France and Norway. German U-boats enjoyed a good intelligence network – the B-Dienst signals service – while the British were still struggling to master the secrets of the German Enigma cipher. They did have Asdic equipment for detecting submerged submarines, but radar was far from refined and U-boats on the surface could be detected only

The maps show the gradually increasing range of operations of the U-boats and the British escorts and the transformation in German prospects by the acquisition of bases in western France after June 1940.

visually – a particular problem at night. The British had few patrol aircraft, armed only with ineffective antisubmarine bombs. Thus the Battle of the Atlantic was a war of intelligence, technology, air support and industrial production of merchant ships, escorts and submarines, not one of merchant ship and submarine losses alone.

For the second half of 1940 (known to German submarine crews as 'the happy time') the U-boats were in the ascendant. 'Wolf pack' tactics, whereby groups of U-boats made co-ordinated attacks on convoys under cover of darkness, were highly effective. Still, many German submarines were lost in this period, and rebuilding did not keep pace. By March 1941 U-boat strength had reached an all-time low, and British radar and escort personnel had improved their techniques. That month Churchill formed a high-level Battle of the Atlantic Committee to oversee all aspects of the struggle; it would contribute greatly to future Allied success by ensuring that scientific and intelligence developments were adopted quickly and were fully integrated with operational plans.

During the remainder of 1941, the Germans tripled their U-boat fleet again,

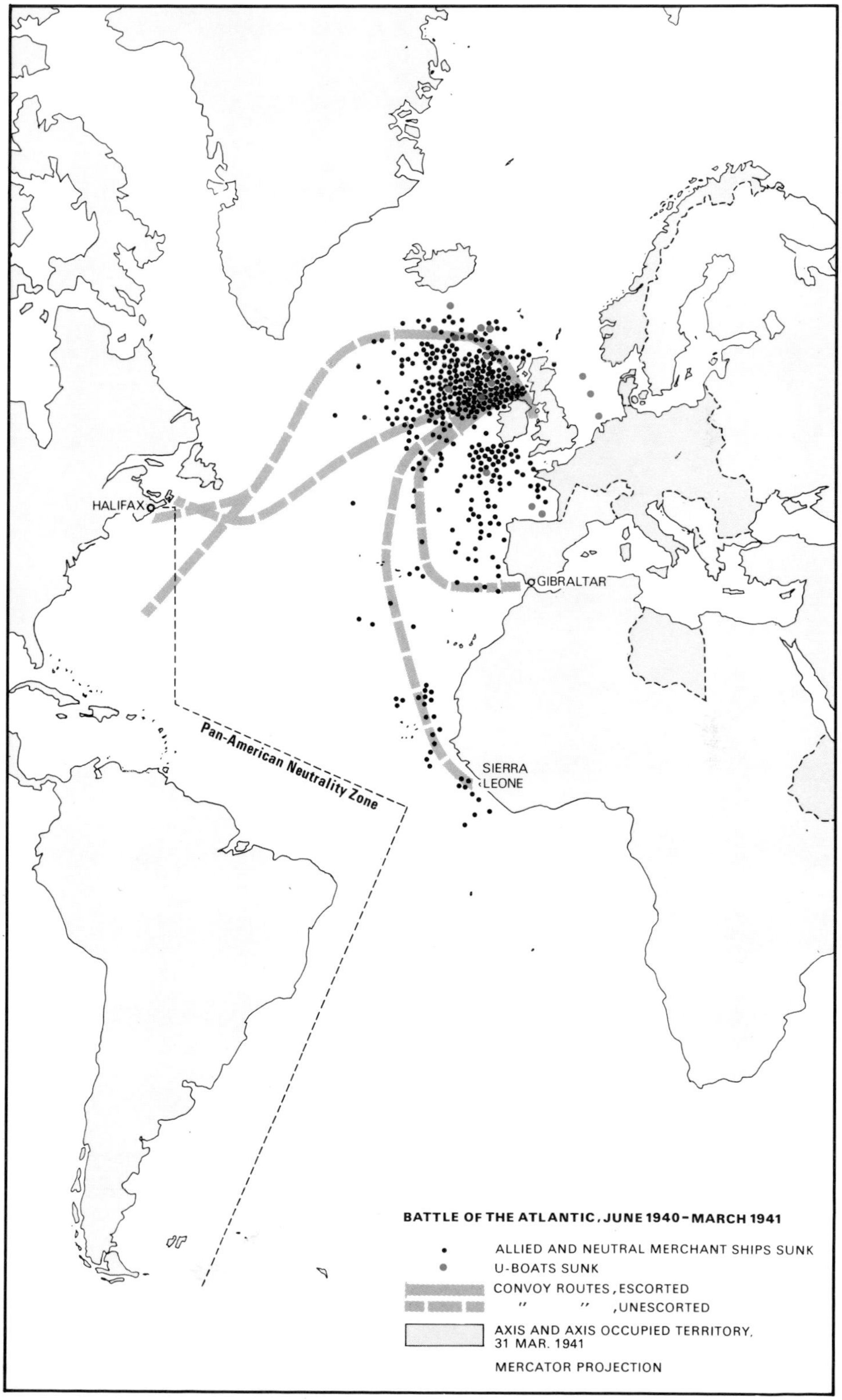

HALIFAX
GIBRALTAR
SIERRA LEONE
Pan-American Neutrality Zone

BATTLE OF THE ATLANTIC, JUNE 1940 – MARCH 1941

ALLIED AND NEUTRAL MERCHANT SHIPS SUNK
U-BOATS SUNK
CONVOY ROUTES, ESCORTED
" " , UNESCORTED
AXIS AND AXIS OCCUPIED TERRITORY, 31 MAR. 1941
MERCATOR PROJECTION

Left : Admiral King, Chief of Staff of the US Navy (left), and Admiral Pound, British First Sea Lord.

BATTLE OF THE ATLANTIC, APRIL 1941–DEC. 1941

- ALLIED AND NEUTRAL MERCHANT SHIPS SUNK
- U-BOATS SUNK
- U BOAT SUPPLY SHIPS SUNK
- CONVOY ROUTES
- ALLIED AIR COVER ZONES
- AXIS AND AXIS OCCUPIED TERRITORY, 31 DEC. 1941

MERCATOR PROJECTION

American Western Hemisphere Defence Zone 18 April 1941
Pan-American Neutrality Zone
MURMANSK
REYKJAVIK
ST. JOHNS
HALIFAX
GIBRALTAR
SIERRA LEONE

but better Allied performance achieved a balance. Far fewer shipping losses could be credited to the submarines. The US was providing increasing help in the form of both war matériel and actual escort service in some areas, and a British intelligence breakthrough in May enabled diversion of threatened convoys and U-boat interception. This second phase of the Battle of the Atlantic lasted until the US entered the war.

At this point U-boats were deployed off the US East Coast, where they found easy

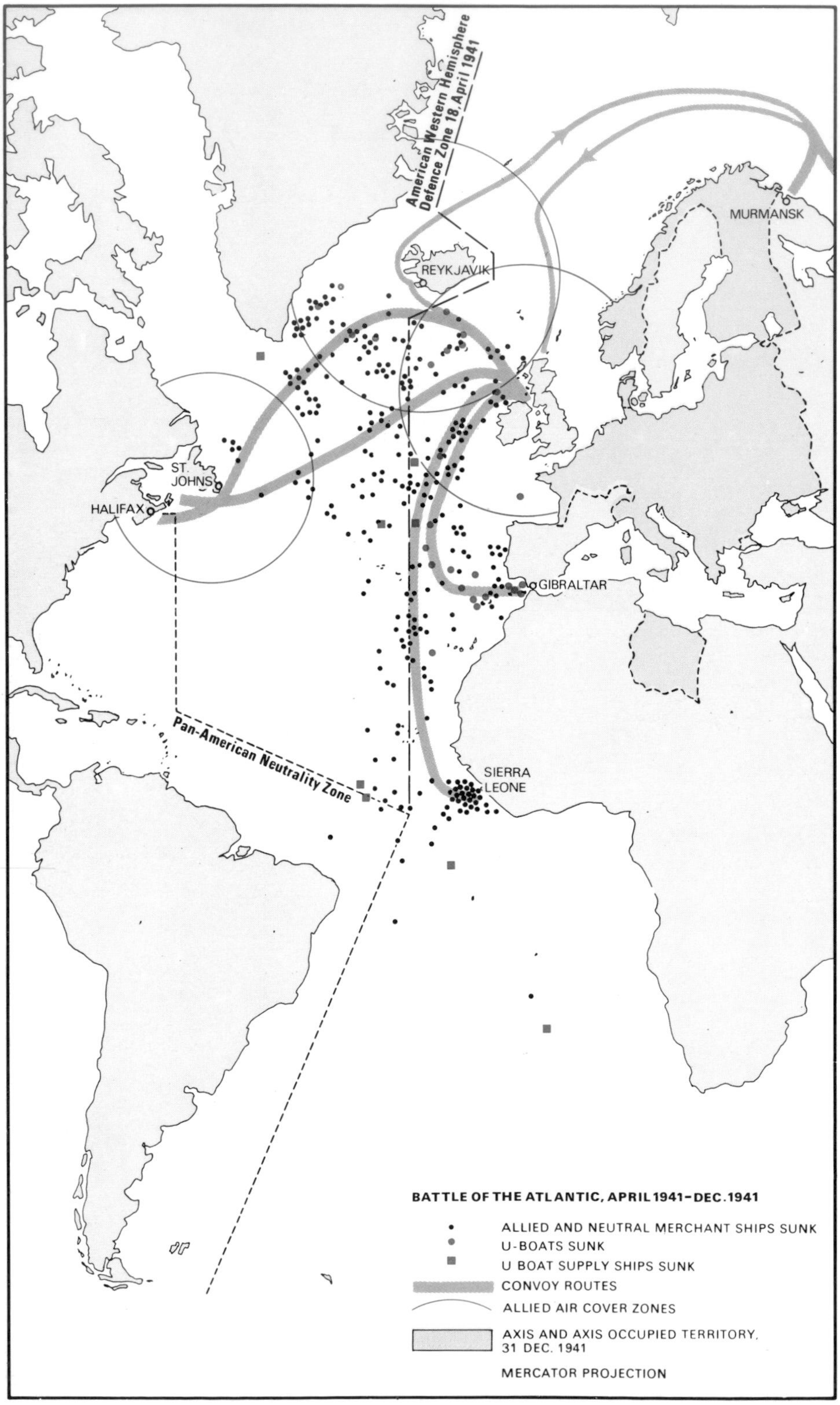

Right: The German heavy cruiser *Prinz Eugen* enters Brest in June 1941 after parting company from the battleship *Bismarck* before she was caught and sunk by the British.

targets. Ships sailed without escorts, showed lights at night, even sent uncoded radio signals. Insufficient US Navy patrols were easily evaded by experienced German commanders. But American strategists soon realized the need for effective convoys; by July 1942 the East Coast was protected as far south as the Caribbean. The U-boats returned their attention in part to the struggle for the main North Atlantic routes while others operated off Trinidad and, with increasing difficulty, in the Mediterranean.

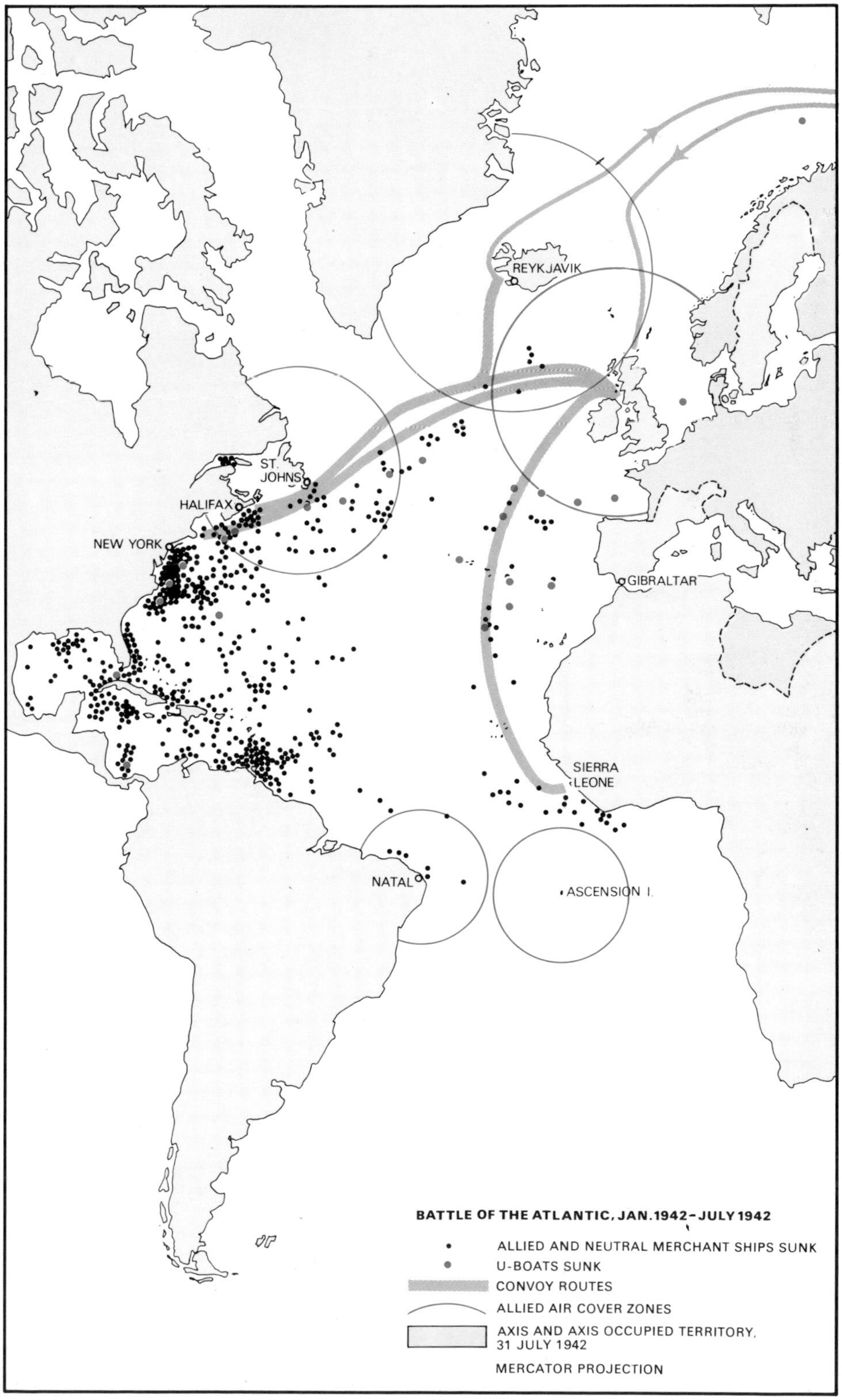

REYKJAVIK
ST. JOHNS
HALIFAX
NEW YORK
GIBRALTAR
SIERRA LEONE
NATAL
ASCENSION I.

BATTLE OF THE ATLANTIC, JAN.1942–JULY 1942

- ALLIED AND NEUTRAL MERCHANT SHIPS SUNK
- U-BOATS SUNK
- CONVOY ROUTES
- ALLIED AIR COVER ZONES
- AXIS AND AXIS OCCUPIED TERRITORY, 31 JULY 1942

MERCATOR PROJECTION

Above left: *U.203* sets out on patrol from Brest in April 1943, at the turning point of the battle of the Atlantic.

Pearl Harbor

The Imperial Japanese Navy attack on Pearl Harbor, Hawaii, was led by Admiral Chuichi Nagumo and achieved complete surprise. Warplanes from his six carriers struck the US Pacific Fleet base at 7:55 AM on 7 December 1941, destroying 188 planes (most of them on the ground) and five of the eight battleships in harbor. Japanese pilots were well trained and well equipped – their Zero fighters would be formidable adversaries in the months to come.

Two factors marred the Japanese achieve-

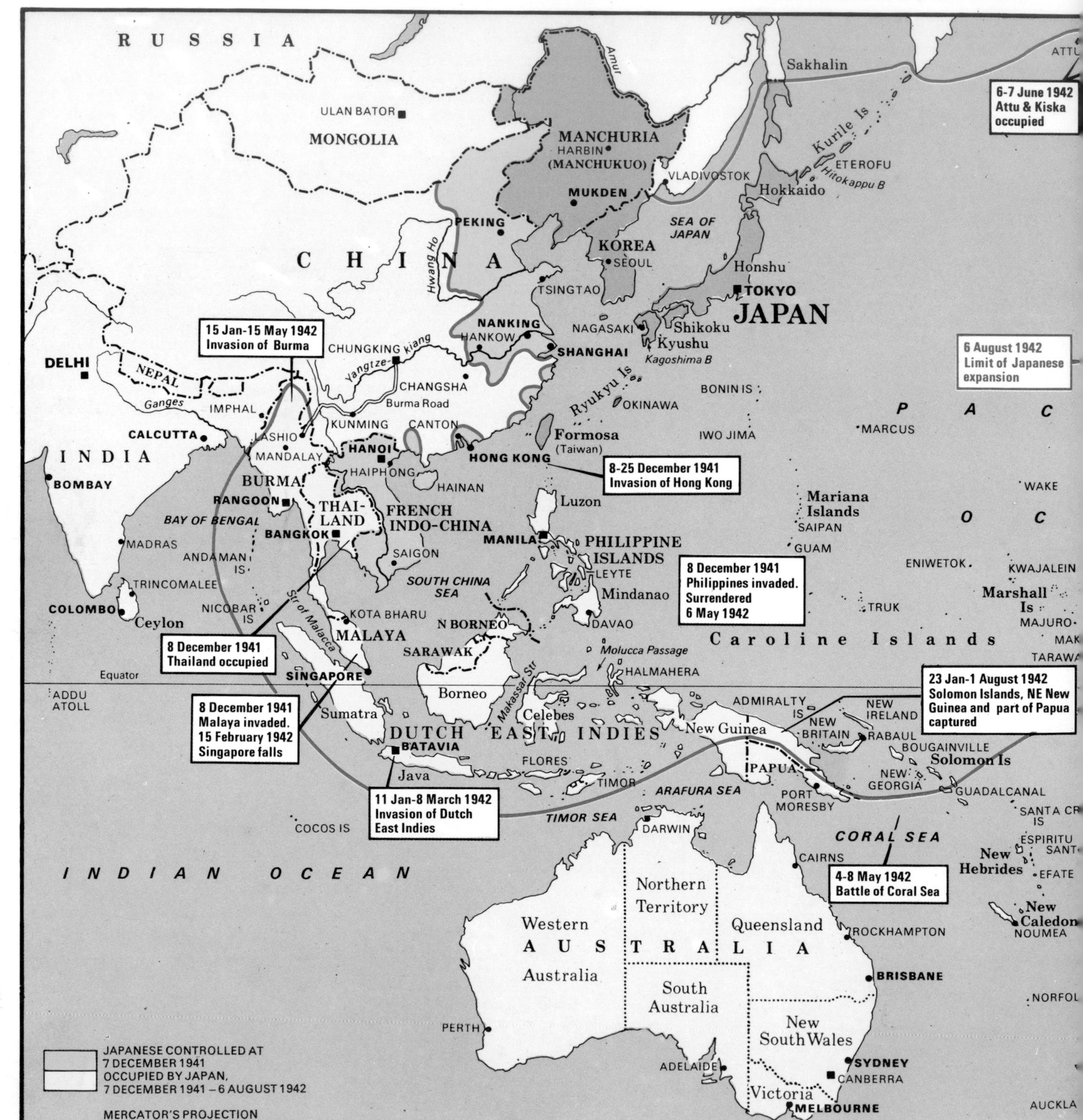

Below: Japanese Admiral Yamamoto was almost uncannily accurate in his prediction that his country would achieve success after success for six months following the outbreak of war. Japanese expansion went almost unchecked until the US victory at Midway.
Below right: Zero fighters ready for takeoff at the start of the Pearl Harbor attack.
Bottom right: The burning battleship *Nevada*

ment: the absence of all the Pacific Fleet carriers (which would become crucial to the Pacific War) and the failure to strike the base's massive oil-storage facilities. These omissions would combine to form a solid foundation on which US industrial power could build a comeback from the devastating surprise attack. The Japanese themselves were aware that they must win the war in the Pacific quickly or not at all, in the absence of a comparable industrial and natural-resource power base. Admiral Yamamoto had already foreseen this problem and given warning to his associates.

Nevertheless, US authorities had little ground for complacency in the aftermath of Pearl Harbor. A top-level cipher to the Japanese ambassador in Washington had been intercepted and passed so ineptly that the resultant warning did not reach Pearl Harbor until midday – hours after the attack. A peacetime mentality had rendered the base highly vulnerable: planes on Oahu airfields were crowded together; ammunition boxes were locked; a submarine report from a patrol ship and a radar warning were both disregarded.

The US declaration of war was now inevitable, and what President Roosevelt described as 'a day of infamy' became the rallying cry for American military and civilian efforts throughout the war.

ATKA
Aleutian Islands
3-6 June 1942
Battle of Midway
MIDWAY
Hawaiian Is
OAHU
PEARL HARBOR
HAWAII
Dawn, 7 December 1941
Japanese carrier-borne aircraft attack Pearl Harbor
International date line (Monday) (Sunday)
PALMYRA
Line Islands
CHRISTMAS
JARVIS
MALDEN
Phoenix Is
NUMEA
Ellice Is
VICTORIA
Tokelau Is
Samoa Is
SUVOROV
Cook Is
Society Is
Tonga Is
RAROTONGA
KERMADEC IS
EW EALAND
©Richard Natkiel, 1982

Malaya and the Dutch East Indies

Admiral Yamamoto's prediction of early Japanese success in the war proved accurate. The British withdrawal from Malaya and the fall of the great naval base at Singapore were described by Churchill as the worst disasters in British military history. Allied forces lost 138,000 men; Japanese casualties were under 10,000. The whole campaign took only 70 days.

Japanese forces deployed included three divisions of General Yamashita's Twenty-fifth Army supported by some 200 tanks and 500 aircraft. Allied forces had a comparable number of troops, but almost no tanks or antitank weapons. RAF planes in Malaya – a mere 150 – were largely obsolete. Another critical Japanese advantage was in leadership and training. The British military in Malaya were beset by morale and administrative problems, under the erratic leadership of General A E Percival. They were also infected with an ill-judged sense of contempt for nonwhite forces – not only the Japanese, but their own Indian and Malayan soldiers. This attitude on the part of British officers could lead only to low morale and inefficiency among indigenous forces.

The British were prepared – if at all – for a European-style campaign that took no account of local conditions. There were only a few main roads suitable for supply and troop movement of the conventional kind. The Japanese, by contrast, traveled light, often by bicycle, making use of minor roads, tracks and several amphibious operations on the west coast. Superior Allied motor transport was of little use in the jungle. Thus it was easy for small Japanese units to outflank the British from secondary roads and create the impression that they were a much larger force. Where Allied units held strong positions, Japanese tanks came into play to force still another retreat. The British were harried all the way down the Malay Peninsula; at last, only Singapore remained in their hands.

By late January 1942 the fleet was already gone from the venerable British bastion. The battleships *Prince of Wales* and *Repulse* had been sent out to prevent the Japanese from attacking Singapore, only to be sunk with ease by enemy aircraft on 10 December. The Allies were left without a single battleship in the Pacific. Japanese landings on Singapore Island began in early February, and British forces surrendered almost without a fight on the 15th. It was a never-to-be-forgotten blow to European prestige in Southeast Asia.

The Dutch East Indies made another tempting target for the Japanese on account

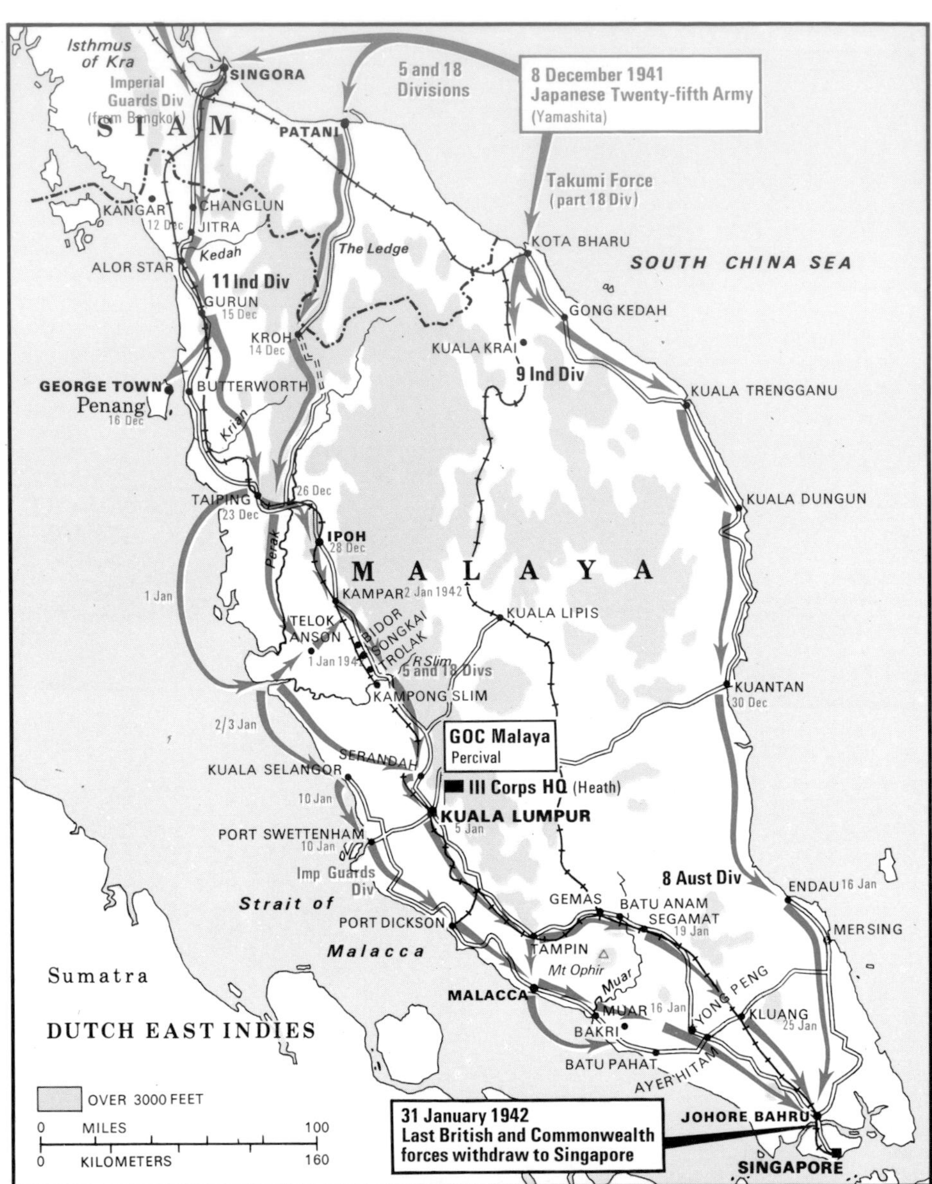

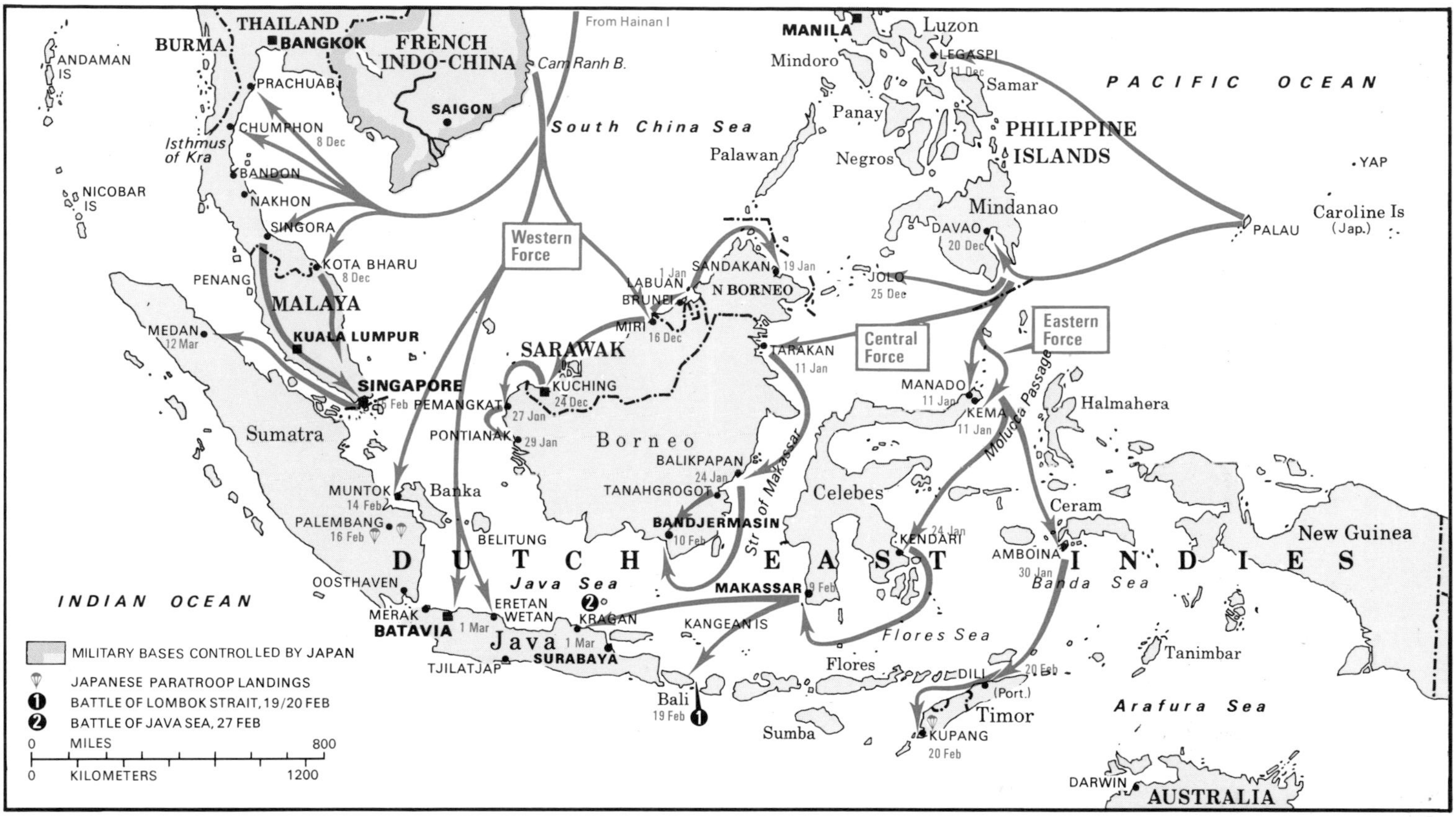

Left: The campaign in Malaya. Despite the popular belief to the contrary, the Japanese forces generally avoided any operations in the true Malayan jungle but were far more ready to use minor roads and tracks.
Below left: Japanese troops enter Kuala Lumpur.

Below: General Yamashita (seated) accepts the surrender of Singapore from General Percival (at right, back to the camera).

Above: The three-pronged Japanese attack on the Dutch East Indies. Japanese air and naval superiority left the outcome in little doubt.

of their important oil and other resources. Widely spaced garrisons there were easily overwhelmed by plane and by ship in February 1942. Three main lines of attack leap-frogged from airfields to more distant objectives, each new conquest providing a jumping-off place for the next. Outnumbered Allied ground and air forces acquitted themselves honorably, but only the naval units could really hope to stop the Japanese. Three progressively larger naval engagements culminated in the Battle of the Java Sea (27 February), in which the Allied cruiser and destroyer squadron was dispersed; two days later, it was almost obliterated. On 19 February Japanese carrier aircraft led a devastating raid on Darwin, northern Australia, confirming that nation's worst fears about the proximity of the new Japanese conquest. Allied forces on Java succumbed on 8 March, and a formal surrender was agreed four days later.

The Fall of the Philippines

Like other Allied enclaves in Asia and the Pacific, the Philippine Islands were ill-prepared for the war against Japan. General Douglas MacArthur had assumed joint command of US and indigenous forces there in July 1941, but their training and equipment were still inadequate. MacArthur had some 31,000 regular troops, 19,000 of them Americans and over 100,000 Filipino conscripts, to defend the whole archipelago. The largest force was on Luzon; others were widely scattered among the smaller islands.

Prewar US plans had called for strong ground and air forces on Luzon to defend the islands until the US Pacific Fleet could bring help. This hope was blasted with Pearl Harbor, and air strength was a second casualty of the surprise attack: fully half the 150 planes allocated to Philippine defense were destroyed on Oahu.

The Japanese made a series of early landings to seize strategic Philippine airfields, then launched their main attack on 22 December 1941. It was clear within 48 hours that MacArthur and all his forces would have to retreat to the Bataan Peninsula, which was accomplished in a week's time. Believing their campaign to be over, the Japanese withdrew their best infantry unit, the 48th Division, and most of their planes for use in the East Indies operation. Subsequent attacks by remaining Japanese units ended in a stalemate; by late January both sides were worn out.

By April, however, the Japanese had reinforced the Philippine units. New and determined attacks forced an American surrender on 9 April. Corregidor was overrun on 5–6 May, and General MacArthur, who had been evacuated in March under orders from President Franklin D Roosevelt, had already gone to Australia pledged to return. Surviving US forces under General Jonathan Wainwright were subjected to the infamous Death March from Bataan – a journey from which few returned.

Right: The Japanese attack on the Philippines with, inset, the Allied retreat to Bataan.
Below: MacArthur (right) and General Wainwright shortly before the outbreak of war.

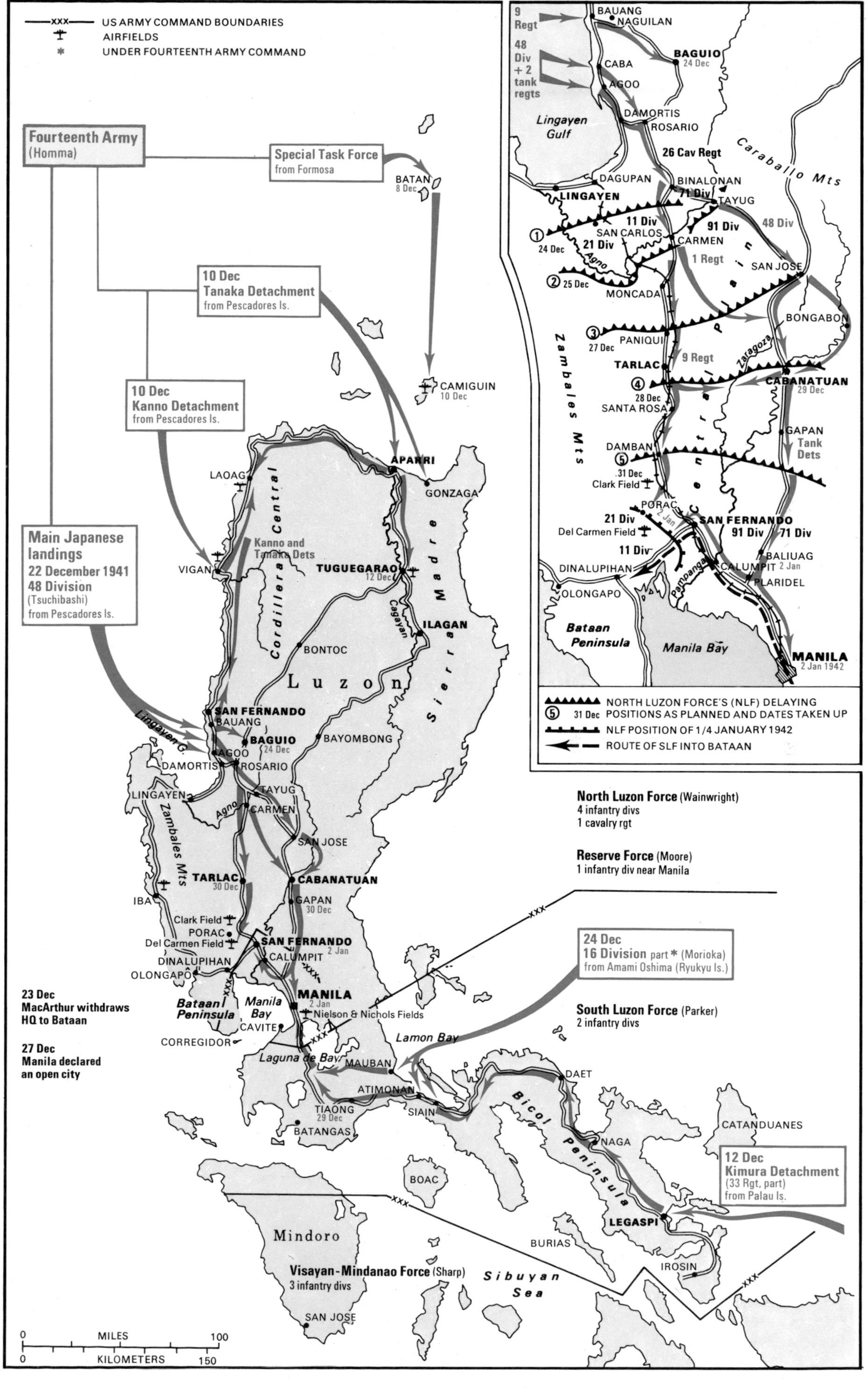

US ARMY COMMAND BOUNDARIES
AIRFIELDS
UNDER FOURTEENTH ARMY COMMAND
Fourteenth Army (Homma)
Special Task Force from Formosa
BATAN 8 Dec
10 Dec Tanaka Detachment from Pescadores Is.
10 Dec Kanno Detachment from Pescadores Is.
CAMIGUIN 10 Dec
Main Japanese landings 22 December 1941 48 Division (Tsuchibashi) from Pescadores Is.
APARRI
LAOAG
GONZAGA
Cordillera Central
Kanno and Tanaka Dets
VIGAN
TUGUEGARAO 12 Dec
Cagayan
ILAGAN
Sierra Madre
BONTOC
Luzon
SAN FERNANDO
BAUANG
BAGUIO 24 Dec
BAYOMBONG
Lingayen G.
AGOO
DAMORTIS
ROSARIO
LINGAYEN
TAYUG
Agno
CARMEN
Zambales Mts
SAN JOSE
TARLAC 30 Dec
CABANATUAN
IBA
GAPAN 30 Dec
Clark Field
PORAC
Del Carmen Field
SAN FERNANDO 2 Jan
CALUMPIT
DINALUPIHAN
OLONGAPO
MANILA 2 Jan
Bataan Peninsula
Manila Bay
Nielson & Nichols Fields
CAVITE
CORREGIDOR
Laguna de Bay
Lamon Bay
MAUBAN
ATIMONAN
TIAONG 29 Dec
SIAIN
BATANGAS
DAET
Bicol Peninsula
NAGA
CATANDUANES
BOAC
LEGASPI
BURIAS
IROSIN
Mindoro
Sibuyan Sea
SAN JOSE
23 Dec MacArthur withdraws HQ to Bataan
27 Dec Manila declared an open city
North Luzon Force (Wainwright) 4 infantry divs 1 cavalry rgt
Reserve Force (Moore) 1 infantry div near Manila
24 Dec 16 Division part * (Morioka) from Amami Oshima (Ryukyu Is.)
South Luzon Force (Parker) 2 infantry divs
12 Dec Kimura Detachment (33 Rgt. part) from Palau Is.
Visayan-Mindanao Force (Sharp) 3 infantry divs
MILES 0 100
KILOMETERS 0 150
9 Regt
48 Div + 2 tank regts
BAUANG
NAGUILAN
CABA
BAGUIO 24 Dec
AGOO
DAMORTIS
ROSARIO
Lingayen Gulf
26 Cav Regt
Caraballo Mts
DAGUPAN
BINALONAN
LINGAYEN
71 Div
TAYUG
11 Div
91 Div
48 Div
SAN CARLOS
24 Dec
21 Div
CARMEN
1 Regt
SAN JOSE
Agno
25 Dec
MONCADA
Central Plain
BONGABON
PANIQUI
27 Dec
Zaragoza
9 Regt
TARLAC
CABANATUAN 29 Dec
28 Dec
SANTA ROSA
Zambales Mts
GAPAN
Tank Dets
DAMBAN
31 Dec
Clark Field
PORAC 2 Jan
21 Div
SAN FERNANDO
Del Carmen Field
91 Div
71 Div
11 Div
BALIUAG
DINALUPIHAN
CALUMPIT 2 Jan
Pampanga
PLARIDEL
OLONGAPO
Bataan Peninsula
Manila Bay
MANILA 2 Jan 1942
NORTH LUZON FORCE'S (NLF) DELAYING
31 Dec POSITIONS AS PLANNED AND DATES TAKEN UP
NLF POSITION OF 1/4 JANUARY 1942
ROUTE OF SLF INTO BATAAN

The Invasion of Burma

Japanese success in Malaya confirmed the decision to attack the British in Burma. In mid-January 1942 British airfields at Victoria Point and Mergui were overrun, and days later most of the Japanese Fifteenth Army moved against Moulmein. A like number of British defenders faced it, but their disadvantages in training and equipment soon decided the outcome.

British defense plans hinged on protecting the port of Rangoon, whence flowed all supplies and reinforcements. Allied air forces in Burma had only one RAF squadron at the outset, plus a squadron of Major Claire Chennault's Flying Tigers, the able American volunteer group that flew the China run. This small force inflicted heavy losses on the 200 Japanese aircraft sent over Rangoon, but on 23 February the lone available bridge over the Sittang River was prematurely demolished before the 17th Indian Division had made its crossing. The error was disastrous; despite the appointment of General Harold Alexander and the arrival of the British 7th Armoured Brigade, Rangoon capitulated. With the capture of Malaya, the Japanese were able to reinforce themselves and advance in strength up the great river valleys.

Meanwhile, Chinese armies (each equal in strength to an American division) had arrived to join the Allied forces. General Joseph Stilwell, the American commander in the field, tried to weld them into an effective fighting force, but both they and the British were soon forced into rapid retreat. What remained of Allied forces in Burma struggled across the Indian frontier in mid-May, just as the monsoon season began.

Right: Japanese soldiers cross the Chindwin on an improvised raft.
Below: Japanese soldiers fighting among the oil installations at Yenangyaung.

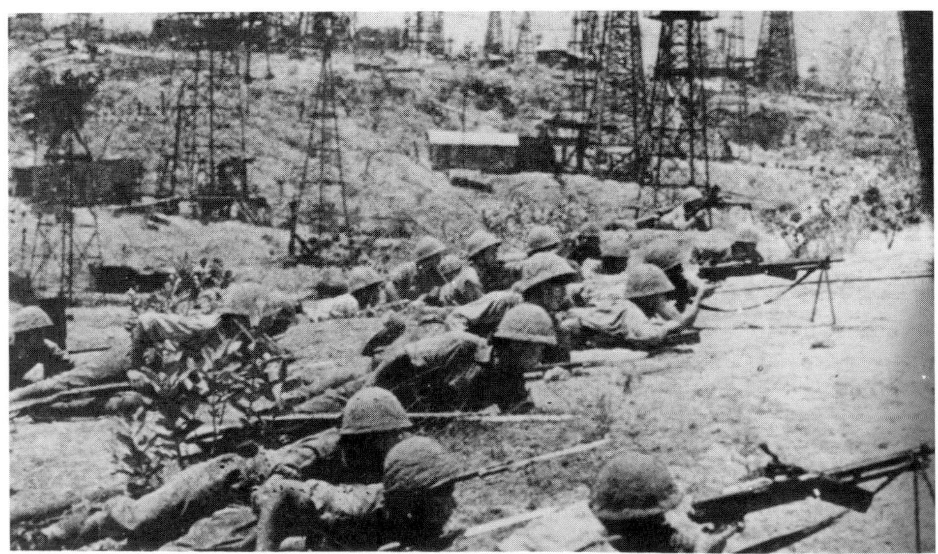

Right: The Burma campaign. British casualties in the campaign were about 30,000; no accurate estimate of Chinese losses can be made but the Japanese lost under 10,000.
Bottom: Bicycles and an improvised bridge help speed the Japanese advance in Burma.
Below: Japanese infantry rest during their advance up the Chindwin Valley.

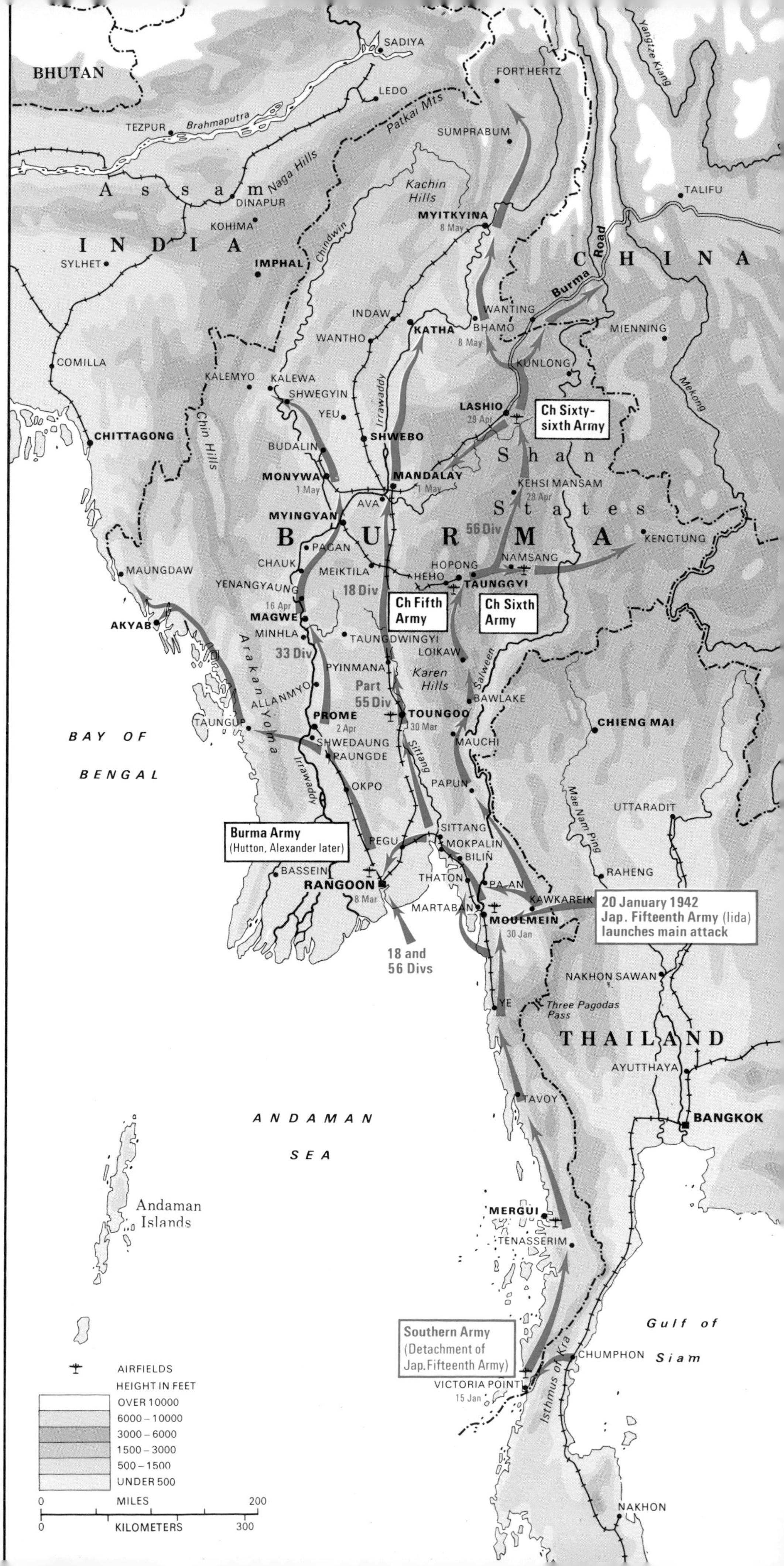

Coral Sea and Midway

On 18 April 1942 the Doolittle bombing raid on Tokyo shocked Japanese leaders into extending their defensive perimeter beyond their original plans. This entailed a move into southern Papua via an amphibious attack on Port Moresby, resulting in the Battle of the Coral Sea. This was the first engagement in naval history in which neither fleet ever sighted the other – the entire action was fought by carrier aircraft.

Forewarned by code-breaking information, the Americans sent in two carriers to face the Japanese attack. The Japanese had three carriers at the ready, including the powerful *Zuikaku* and *Shokaku*; the smallest carrier was deployed for close support of the invasion group. Action began on 4 May, when a Japanese seaplane base set up on Tulagi the previous day was attacked by planes from the USS *Yorktown*. The Americans then moved south to concentrate their forces and refuel, just as the main Japanese operation was getting underway. On 7 May warplanes bore down on a US tanker and destroyer and sent them to the bottom, but land-based attacks failed to damage the ships of TF 44, which had been sent to cut off the Japanese Invasion Group. American carrier aircraft then scored a notable victory by sinking the *Sholo*.

On 8 May a full-scale battle was fought in which American ships were heavily damaged and the *Lexington* was sunk. However, the Japanese lost so many planes that the invasion of Port Moresby had to be called off. The Japanese carriers withdrew, and American forces had clearly won a strategic victory despite their tactical losses.

A second battle soon developed around the Japanese High Command decision to extend its defensive perimeter: this was the decisive battle of Midway (3–6 June 1942). Here the Japanese lost their early initiative, which had swept them from victory to victory ever since Pearl Harbor. The course of this battle was deeply affected by the Coral Sea confrontation of the previous month.

The carriers *Zuikaku* and *Shokaku* were not yet seaworthy for the Battle of Midway, and the Japanese believed (erroneously) that the US carrier *Yorktown* was also too

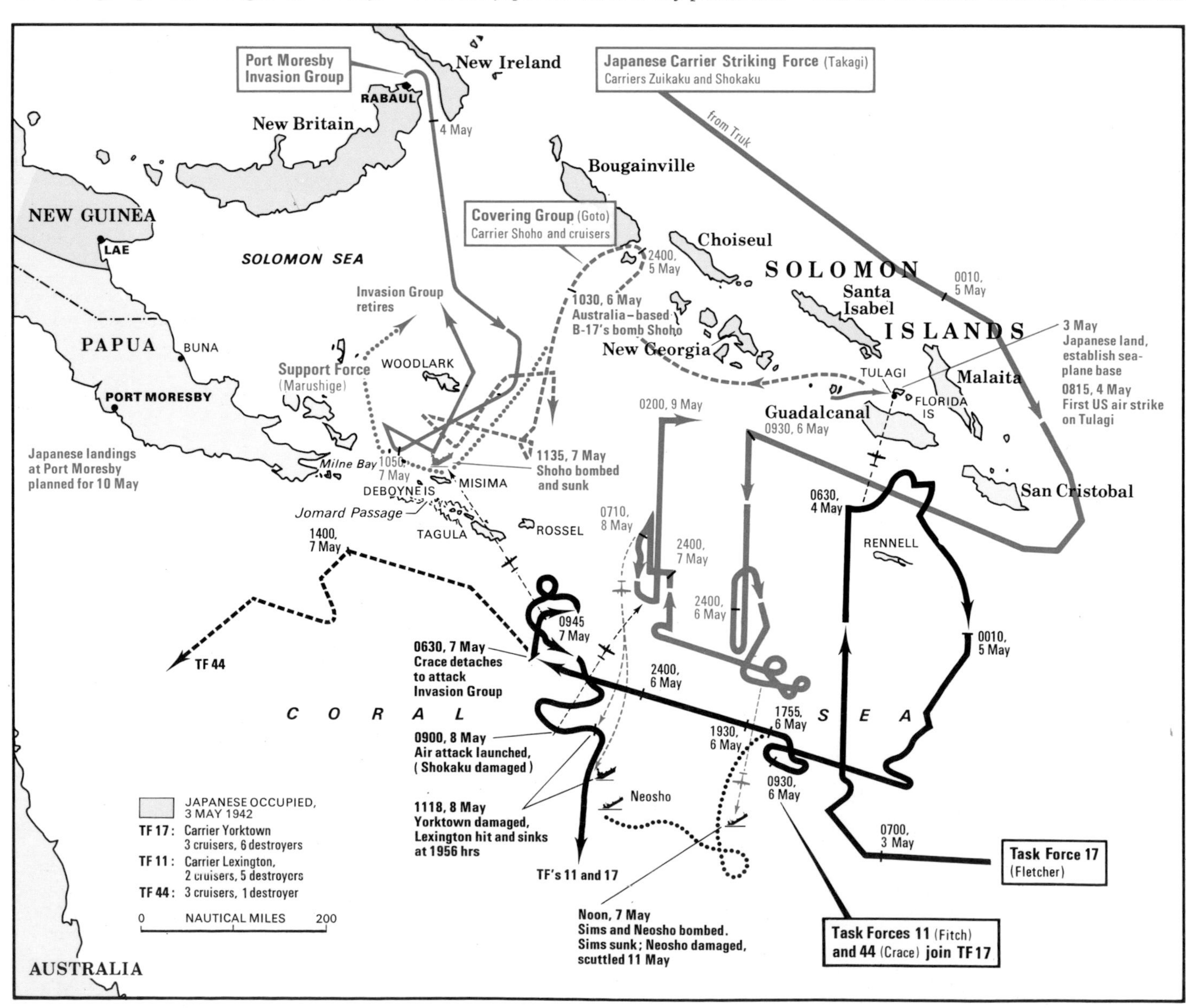

Below left: The Battle of the Coral Sea.
Bottom: The carrier *Lexington* burns furiously following the Japanese attacks. Many lessons were learned by the Americans from the loss of the *Lexington* and better damage-control procedures instituted.
Below right: The maneuverings of the carrier forces during the Battle of Midway.

severely damaged to join the fight. In fact, the *Yorktown* was patched up at Pearl Harbor in the incredibly short time of 48 hours. This was only one of several breakdowns in Japanese intelligence and communication that contributed to the American victory.

Admiral Yamamoto believed that the US *Enterprise* and *Hornet* were likely to be in the South Pacific; even if they were not, diversionary attacks on the Aleutian Islands were planned to distract the Americans from the landings on Midway. The strategy was to destroy US forces in all-out battle once the island was taken. A code-breaking coup by US intelligence put the whole plan into American hands and guaranteed that the attacks on the Aleutians would be disregarded in favor of concentrating on Midway.

The Japanese were sighted on 3 June, and the action began the following day. Japanese attacks on Midway-based planes were highly successful, but before the strike force had returned to its carriers, American aircraft appeared to launch an assault. Three of the four Japanese carriers were crippled and later sank; the fourth, the *Hiryu*, was put out of action after inflicting heavy damage on the *Yorktown*.

The Japanese tried to draw American commanders into a gunfight the following day, in the hope of overwhelming them by force of numbers, but they refused to be drawn. The whole operation was abandoned, with the loss of Japan's best pilots and crews. Japanese superiority in planes and carriers was largely offset by the lack of veteran pilots in subsequent Pacific operations.

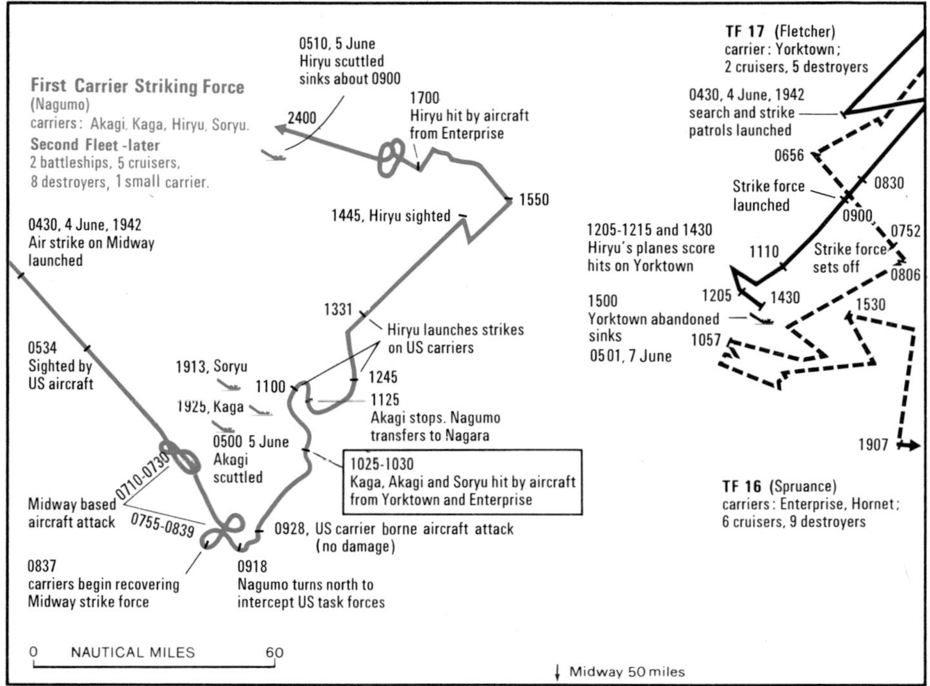

The Siege of Stalingrad

In early April 1942 orders came down from Hitler for a new offensive in Russia. Leningrad was the primary objective in the north; the center would essentially hold its position; the south was to overcome the Red Army at the River Don and open the way to Caucasian oilfields and the capture of Stalingrad. 'Stalin's City' was a vital rail and river center, and the site of tank and munitions factories. Its fall would have far-reaching effects on Russian morale as well as the war effort.

In preparation for the campaign, General Fritz von Manstein drove the Red Army from the Kerch Peninsula and captured the Crimea, including the naval base of Sevastopol. The main offensive by Army Group South was delayed for four weeks by a major Soviet attack at Kharkov, but it reached the Don by mid-July. It was stopped there by a Soviet counteroffensive at Varonezh, but to the south the Germans recaptured Rostov.

Hitler then issued new orders, against staff advice: priority was to shift from the Caucasus to Stalingrad, despite the viability of the Red Army. In the Caucasus, Army Group A made a rapid advance that stalled out, ironically, for lack of fuel at the outlying Maykop oilfield. Three hundred thousand troops were then allocated to the capture of Stalingrad. A simple frontal assault was the tactic of choice, since encirclement would have entailed crossing the Volga, which was commanded by Russian emplacements. The Soviets kept few troops in the city itself, relying on high morale and civic determination to fight the Germans every foot of the way. This is, in fact, what happened. Soviet soldiers and armed civilians gave little ground as the city was destroyed around them by German shells and bombs. Growing numbers of German units were drawn into the brutal struggle, as Soviet leaders pre-

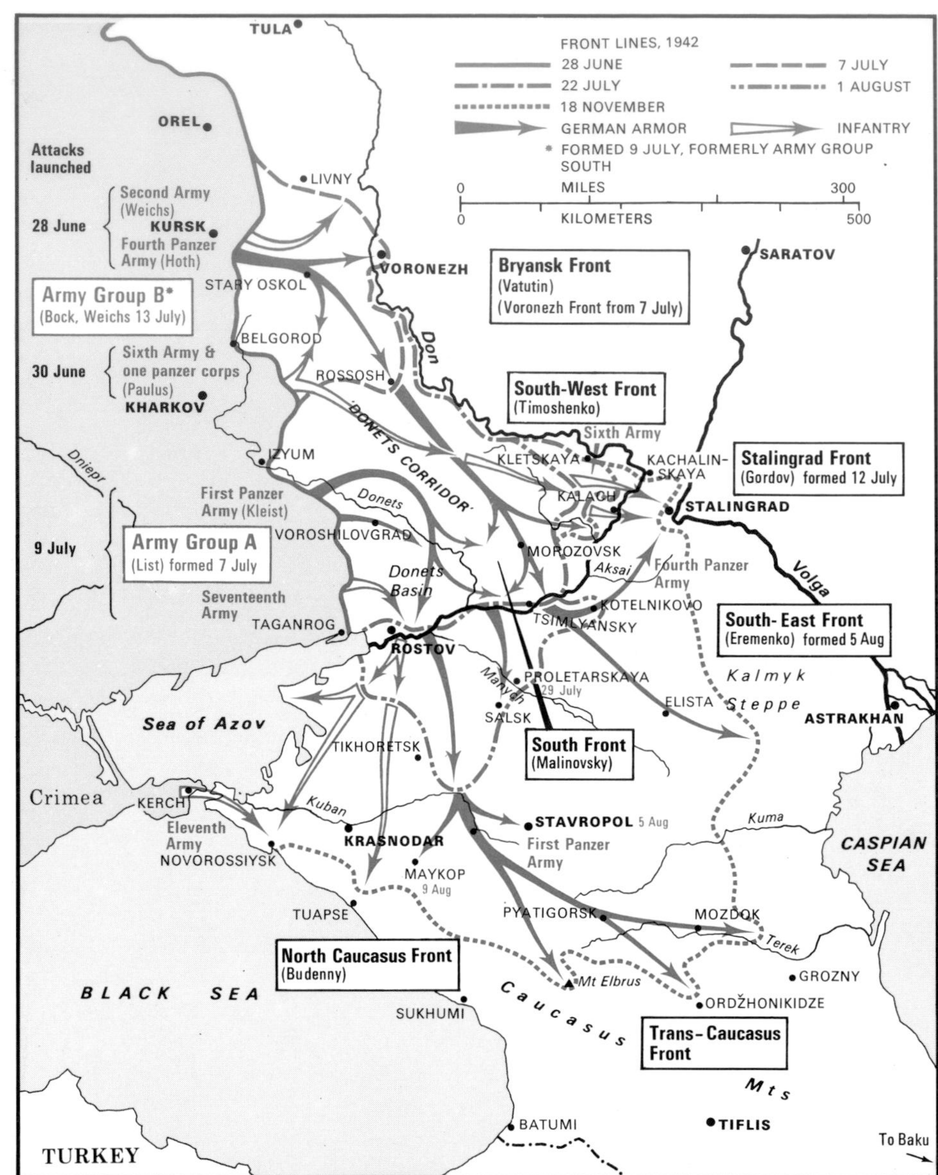

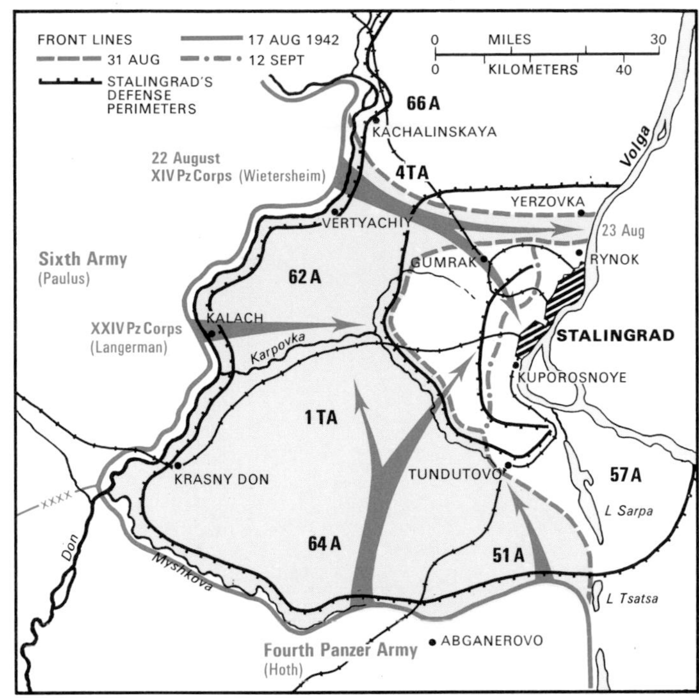

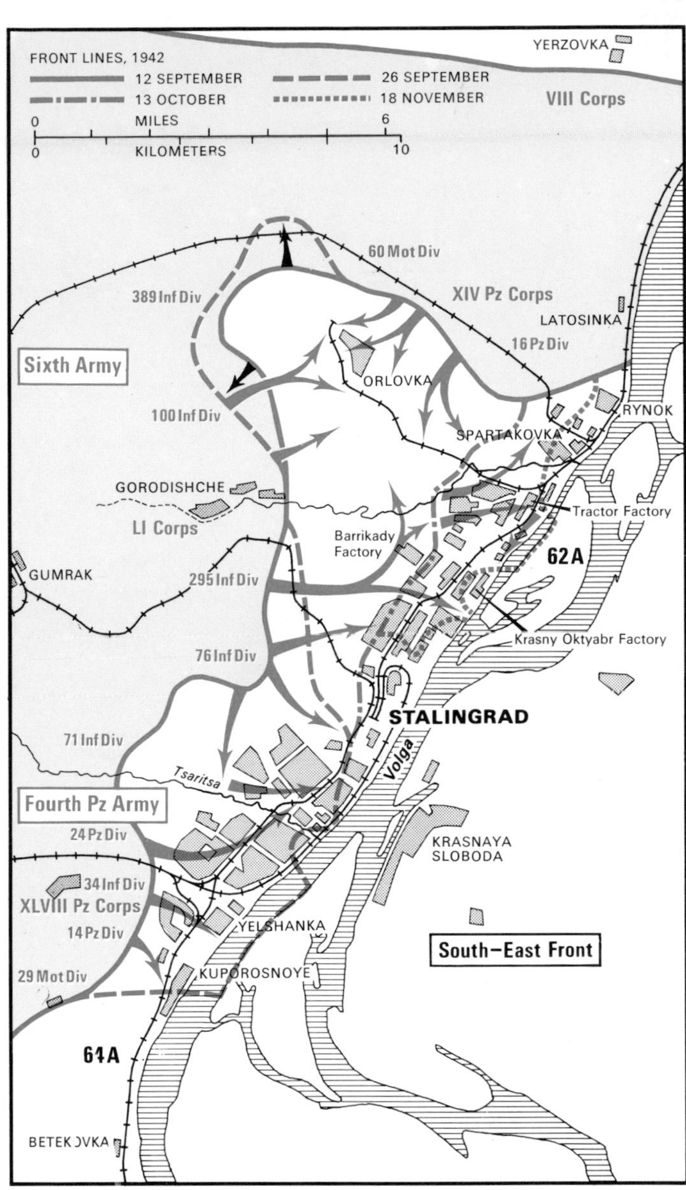

Maps, left to right: Despite the early successes of the German offensive, the focus of action was soon narrowed to include only Stalingrad. Right: General Chuikov who led the 62nd Army, the Stalingrad garrison. Below: Soviet artillery pound German positions at Stalingrad. Bottom left: The Ilyushin 2 'Shturmovik' ground attack aircraft, the most important weapon of the Soviet air forces.

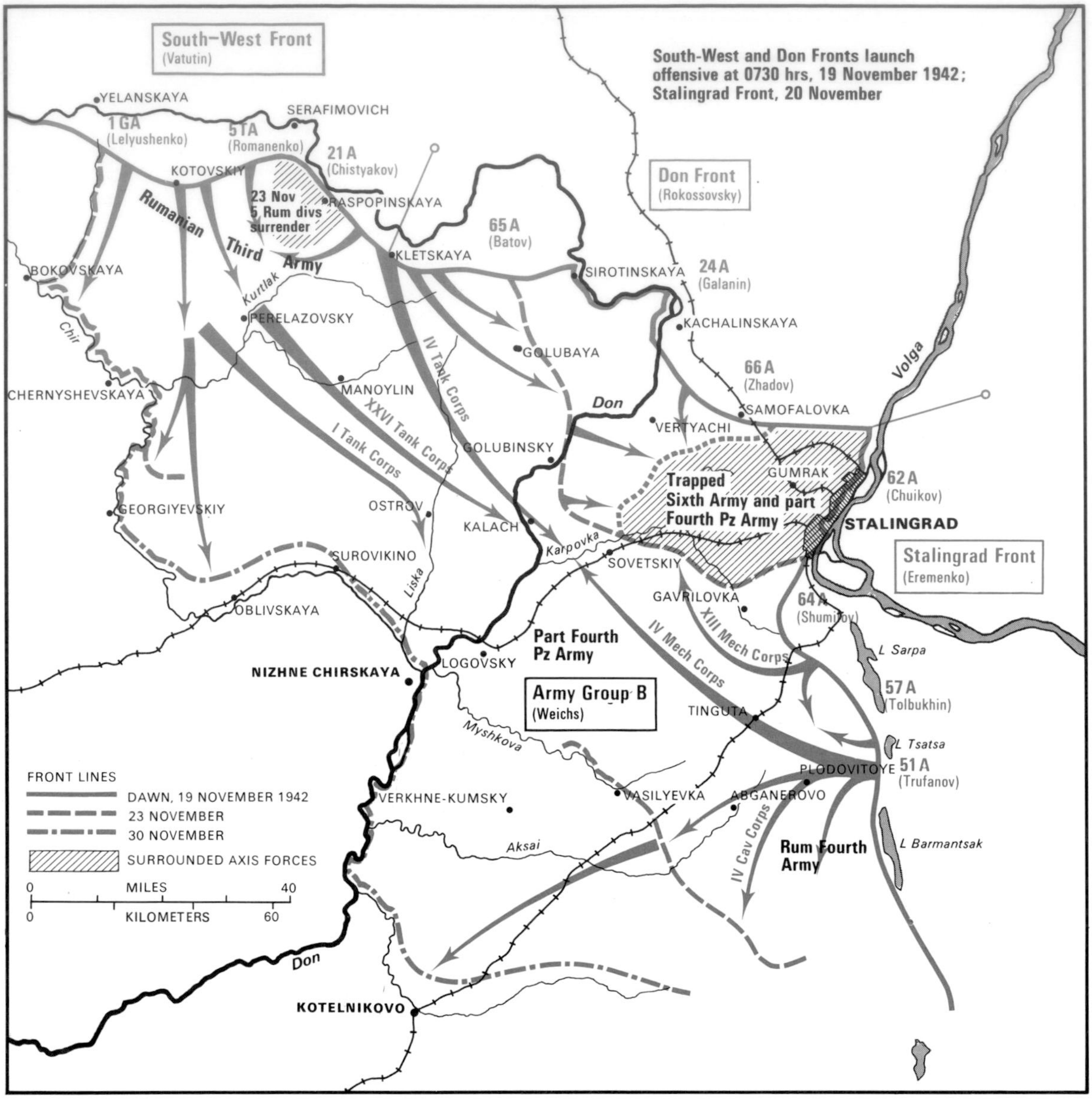

South-West Front
(Vatutin)

South-West and Don Fronts launch offensive at 0730 hrs, 19 November 1942; Stalingrad Front, 20 November

Don Front
(Rokossovsky)

Stalingrad Front
(Eremenko)

Army Group B
(Weichs)

YELANSKAYA
SERAFIMOVICH
1 GA
(Lelyushenko)
5 TA
(Romanenko)
21 A
(Chistyakov)
KOTOVSKIY
23 Nov
5 Rum divs
surrender
RASPOPINSKAYA
Rumanian Third Army
65 A
(Batov)
KLETSKAYA
BOKOVSKAYA
Kurtlak
SIROTINSKAYA
24 A
(Galanin)
KACHALINSKAYA
PERELAZOVSKY
Chir
GOLUBAYA
IV Tank Corps
66 A
(Zhadov)
CHERNYSHEVSKAYA
MANOYLIN
XXVI Tank Corps
Don
SAMOFALOVKA
I Tank Corps
VERTYACHI
Volga
GOLUBINSKY
GUMRAK
Trapped
Sixth Army and part
Fourth Pz Army
62 A
(Chuikov)
GEORGIYEVSKIY
OSTROV
KALACH
STALINGRAD
SUROVIKINO
Karpovka
SOVETSKIY
Liska
GAVRILOVKA
64 A
(Shumilov)
OBLIVSKAYA
XIII Mech Corps
IV Mech Corps
L Sarpa
Part Fourth
Pz Army
LOGOVSKY
NIZHNE CHIRSKAYA
57 A
(Tolbukhin)
TINGUTA
Myshkova
L Tsatsa
PLODOVITOYE
51 A
(Trufanov)
VASILYEVKA
ABGANEROVO
VERKHNE-KUMSKY
IV Cav Corps
Aksai
Rum Fourth
Army
L Barmantsak
Don
KOTELNIKOVO

FRONT LINES
DAWN, 19 NOVEMBER 1942
23 NOVEMBER
30 NOVEMBER
SURROUNDED AXIS FORCES
0 MILES 40
0 KILOMETERS 60

Left: The Soviet counteroffensive at Stalingrad. The German forces had been joined by substantial contingents from Germany's allies in the early part of 1942 but experience showed their fighting power was limited.

Right: The later stages of the Soviet offensive and the German counterattack which retook Kharkov and restabilized the front.

Below right: Italian troops retreat before the Russian advance in November 1942.

Below: German ski troops and a Dornier 17 bomber on a Russian airfield in late 1942.

pared for their counteroffensive.

German General Friedrich Paulus had some 300,000 men concentrated to the west of Stalingrad. His northwest flank was protected by Italian and Rumanian troops, with additional Rumanian units on the southern flank. On 19 November 1942 the Soviet counteroffensive was launched with the primary objective of relieving Stalingrad. Diversionary actions were launched on the central (Moscow) front to draw off German reinforcements. Marshal Georgi K Zhukov had three army groups (fronts), two of which attacked the non-German troops; they soon gave way, providing a link-up with the third or Stalingrad Front. Paulus was surrounded, but Göring assured Hitler that an airlift could keep the trapped troops supplied; thus the siege of Stalingrad went on. In mid-December General Manstein broke through the Russian lines on the west in an attempt to relieve Paulus, but the Soviets blocked his move. The Red Army turned back to the steady destruction of Paulus's Sixth Army, which would never receive the help that Göring had promised.

On 2 February German forces at Stalingrad – now little more than isolated detachments – surrendered. It was the first major defeat for the German Army, and the blow to morale was devastating. Hitler's generalship was revealed as incompetent by his refusal to allow Paulus to withdraw from the embattled city. The Russians had achieved a clear-cut moral victory by their unwavering defense. Thousands of German prisoners were taken among the smoldering ruins; most died in Russian camps, and of those who survived, many were held for years after the war was over.

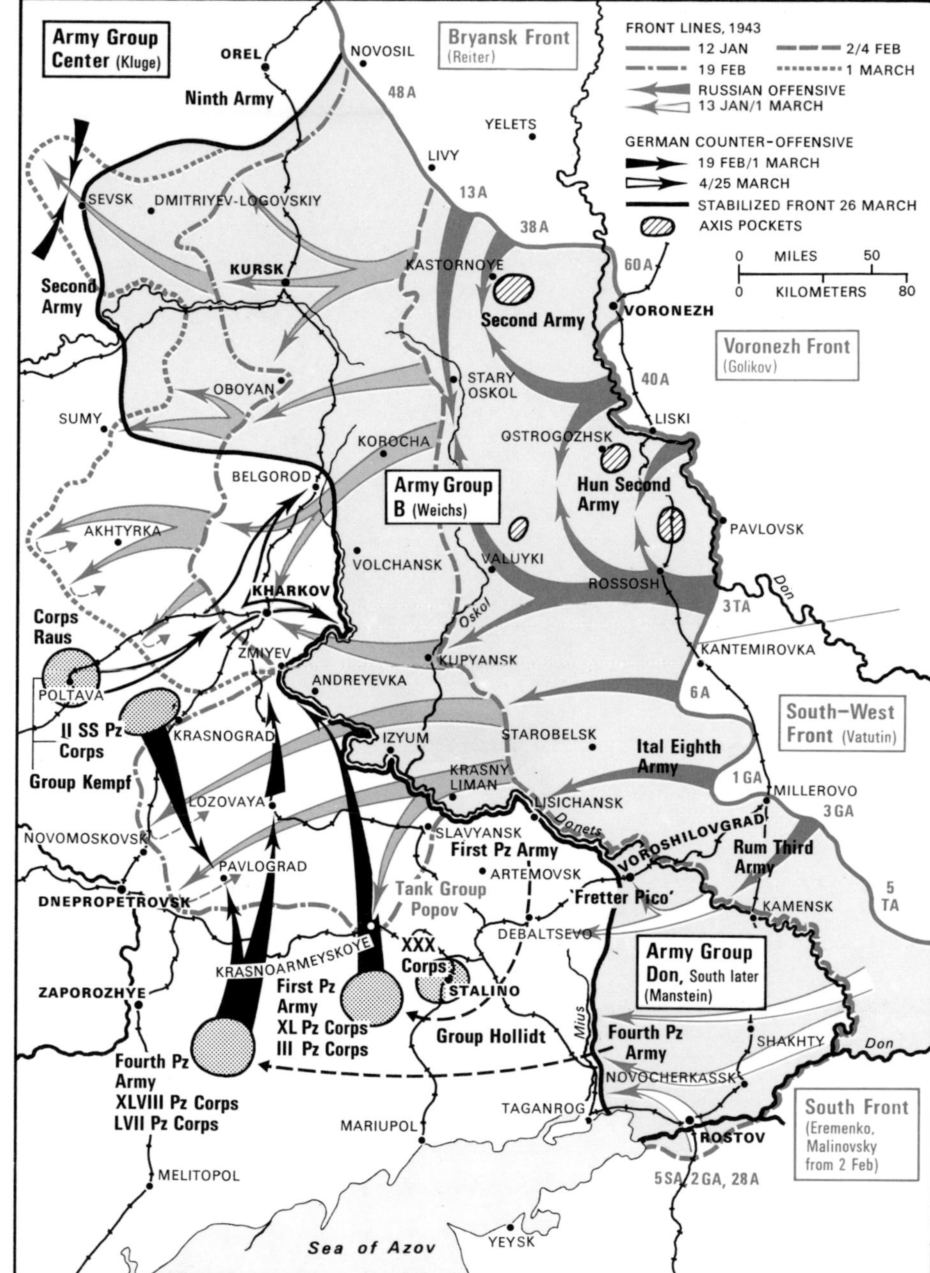

El Alamein

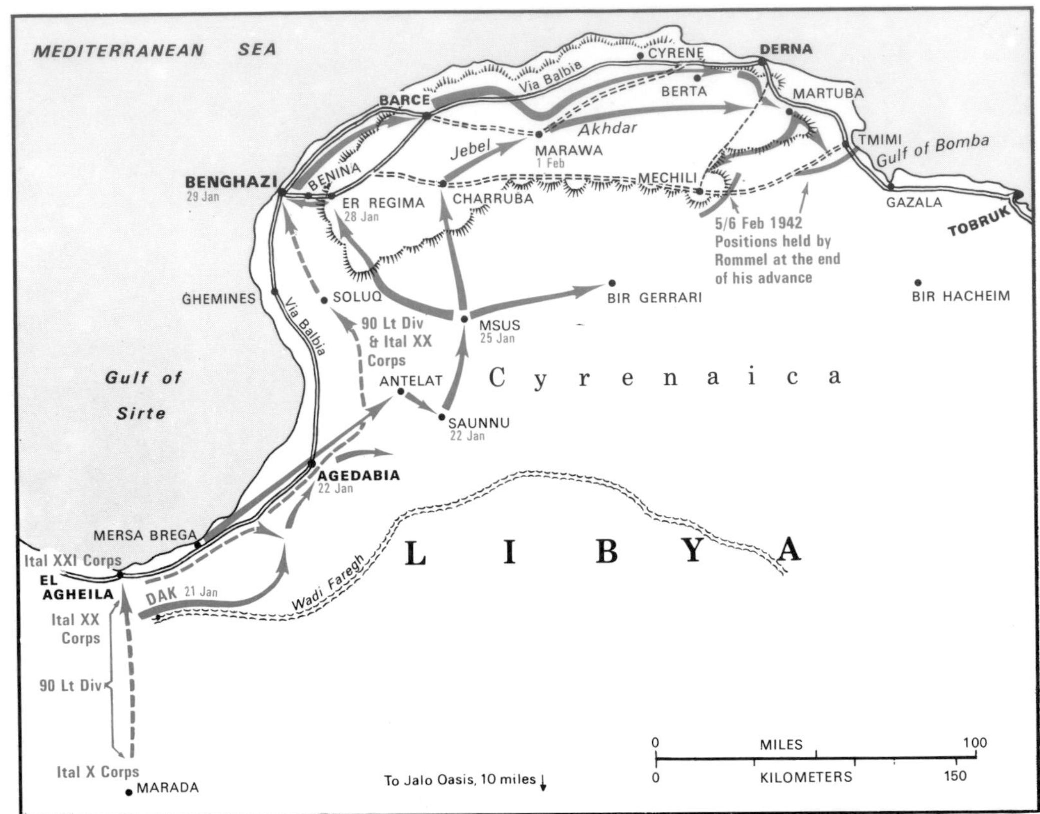

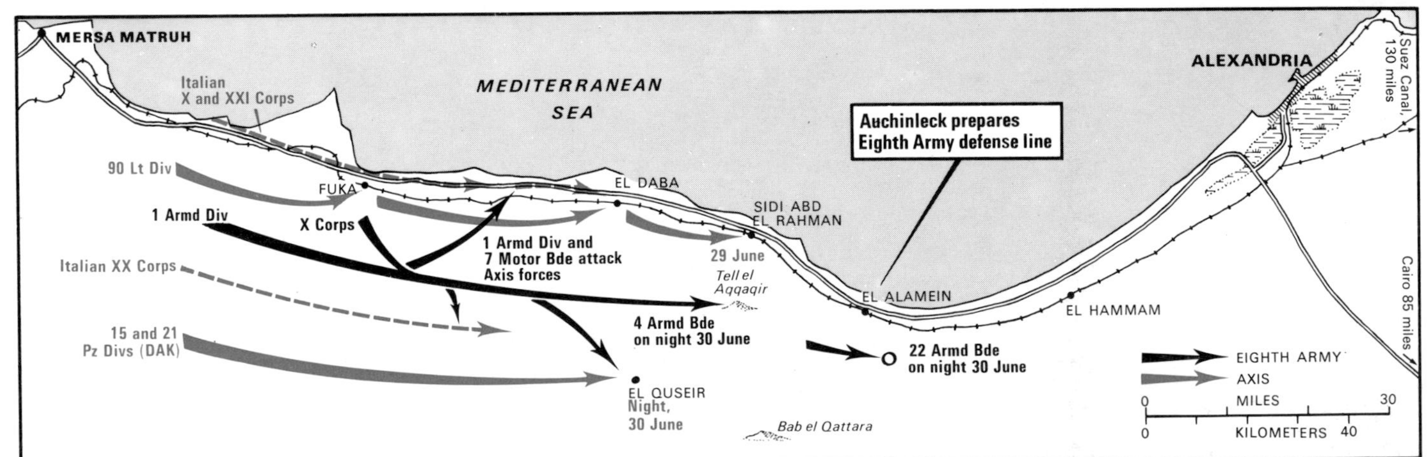

The war in North Africa was a see-saw struggle which raged across hundreds of miles of Libya and Egypt. After a brief Italian advance into Egypt in the fall of 1940 the British attacked and advanced west to El Agheila before German forces led by General Erwin Rommel intervened. The British were soon pushed back beyond Tobruk which was isolated and besieged. British attacks from November 1941 brought another spectacular advance but by the summer of 1942 the Germans had totally reversed the situation and were at the gates of Egypt.

In June 1942 the British attempt to halt Rommel at Mersa Matruh failed, and British troops fell back to the next defensible position, centered on a small rail station called El Alamein. The Eighth Army, under General Claude Auchinleck, Commander-in-Chief, Middle East, sought to prepare a position here in a narrow gap between the Qattara Depression and the sea, blocking the way to the Nile.

Combined German and Italian attacks were fought to a standstill on 2–4 July, thanks partly to improved co-ordination of Eighth Army artillery. Auchinleck attacked selected Italian formations one after another so that Rommel would be forced to use valuable fuel in coming to the rescue with his German units. Larger Allied efforts took place in the Ruweisat Ridge area, with both sides becoming worn out by late July. General Auchinleck finally declined to continue these attacks, which are known as the First Battle of El Alamein, and Churchill replaced him with Montgomery.

Several months later, Axis and Allied

Left: Rommel's advance in the early months of 1942. Below left: The drive into Egypt following the fall of Tobruk. Right: The First Battle of El Alamein.

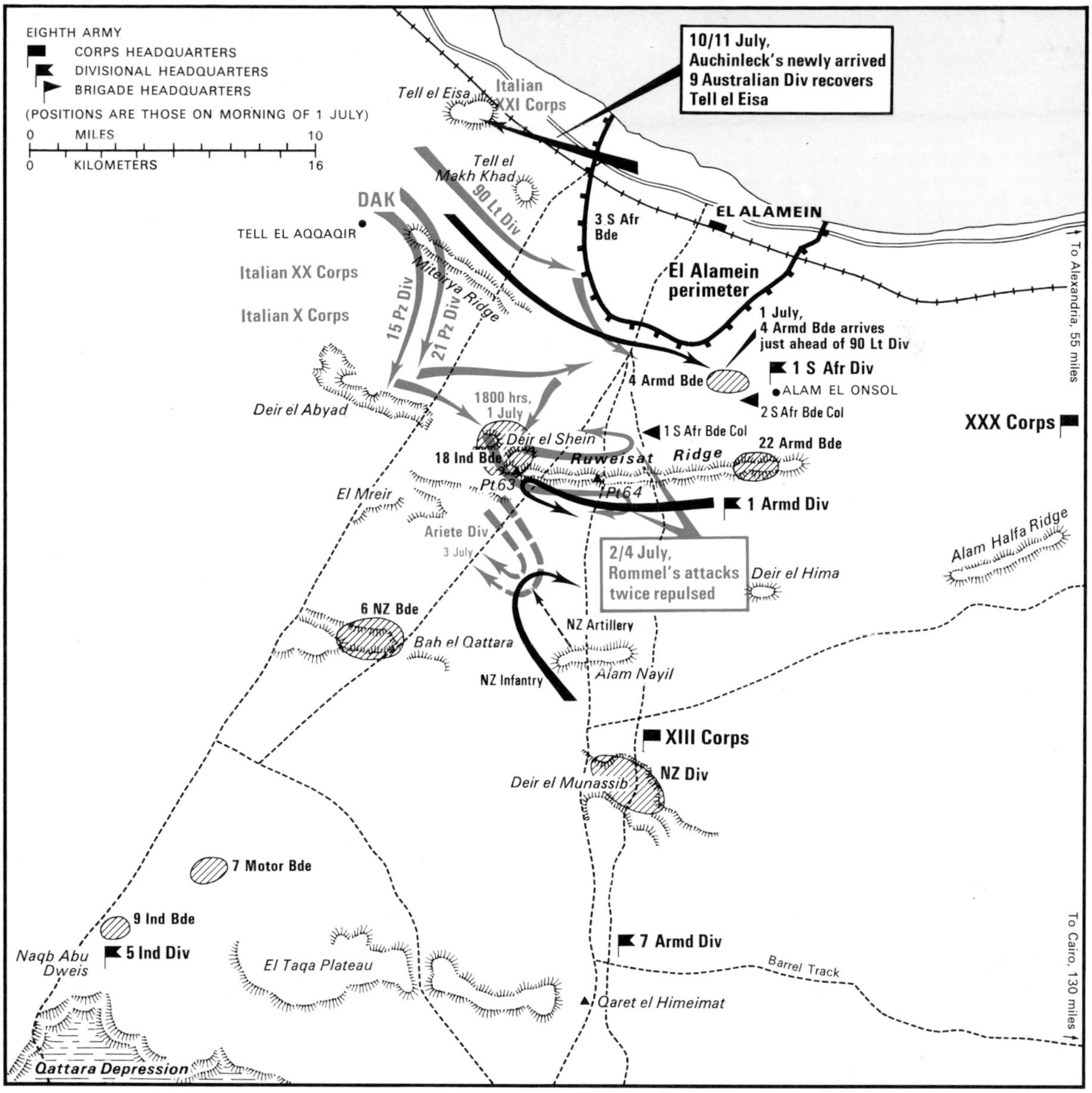

Above: Australian infantry on the advance in the desert. Below: German troops examine a knocked-out Matilda tank.

Right: The Battle of Alam Halfa finally halted Rommel's attempts to take Egypt.
Below: A German doctor tends British wounded.
Below right: An Italian antiaircraft position on the Alamein front.

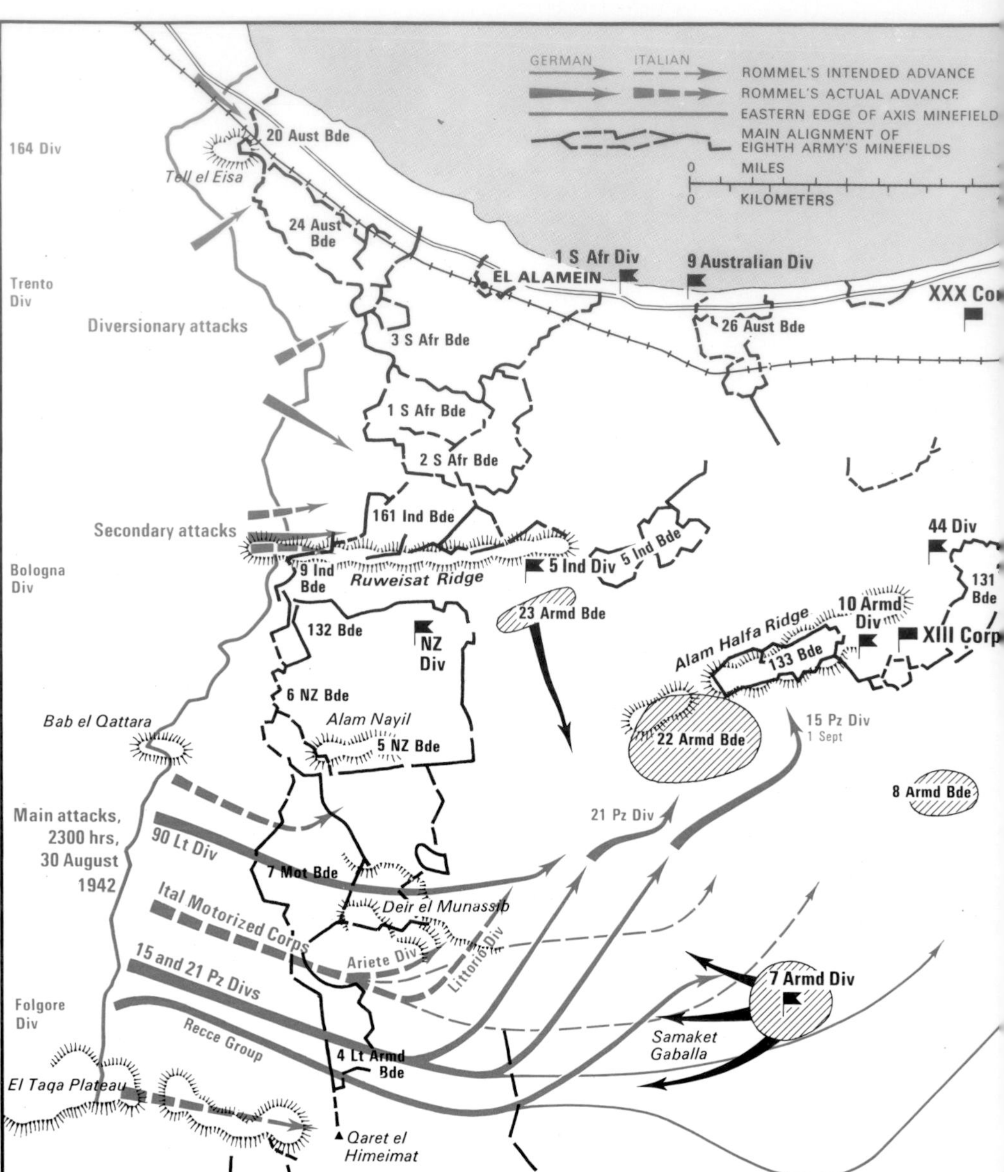

forces rejoined battle at El Alamein. Afrika Korps fuel shortages led to a splitting up of the armored reserve, so that at least part of it would be able to reach any threatened sector. General Rommel was in Germany on sick leave, and the German defense was led at first by General Stumme.

Montgomery's strategy called for infantry units of XXX Corps to win corridors through the Axis minefields; then X Corps tanks would pass through to destroy German armor on open ground. A powerful British artillery barrage got the infantry off to a good start, but it proved impossible to move the tanks forward as planned.

German defenders were shaken by the death of General Stumme from a heart attack during heavy fighting on 24 October (the day before Rommel returned from Germany). Diversionary efforts by XIII Corps kept the 21st Panzer Division out of the battle for several days. By the 26th British forces had to pause and regroup.

On the night of 1–2 November, Montgomery implemented his revised breakthrough plan – Operation Supercharge. By the end of the day, only 35 German tanks were still in action. Rommel signaled to Hitler that he must retreat, and received reluctant consent on 4 November. This Second Battle of El Alamein was the last major German effort in North Africa.

Right: Italian infantry under fire.
Below right: The Battle of El Alamein.
Below: Both sides used captured vehicles extensively. Clear recognition signs were therefore needed.

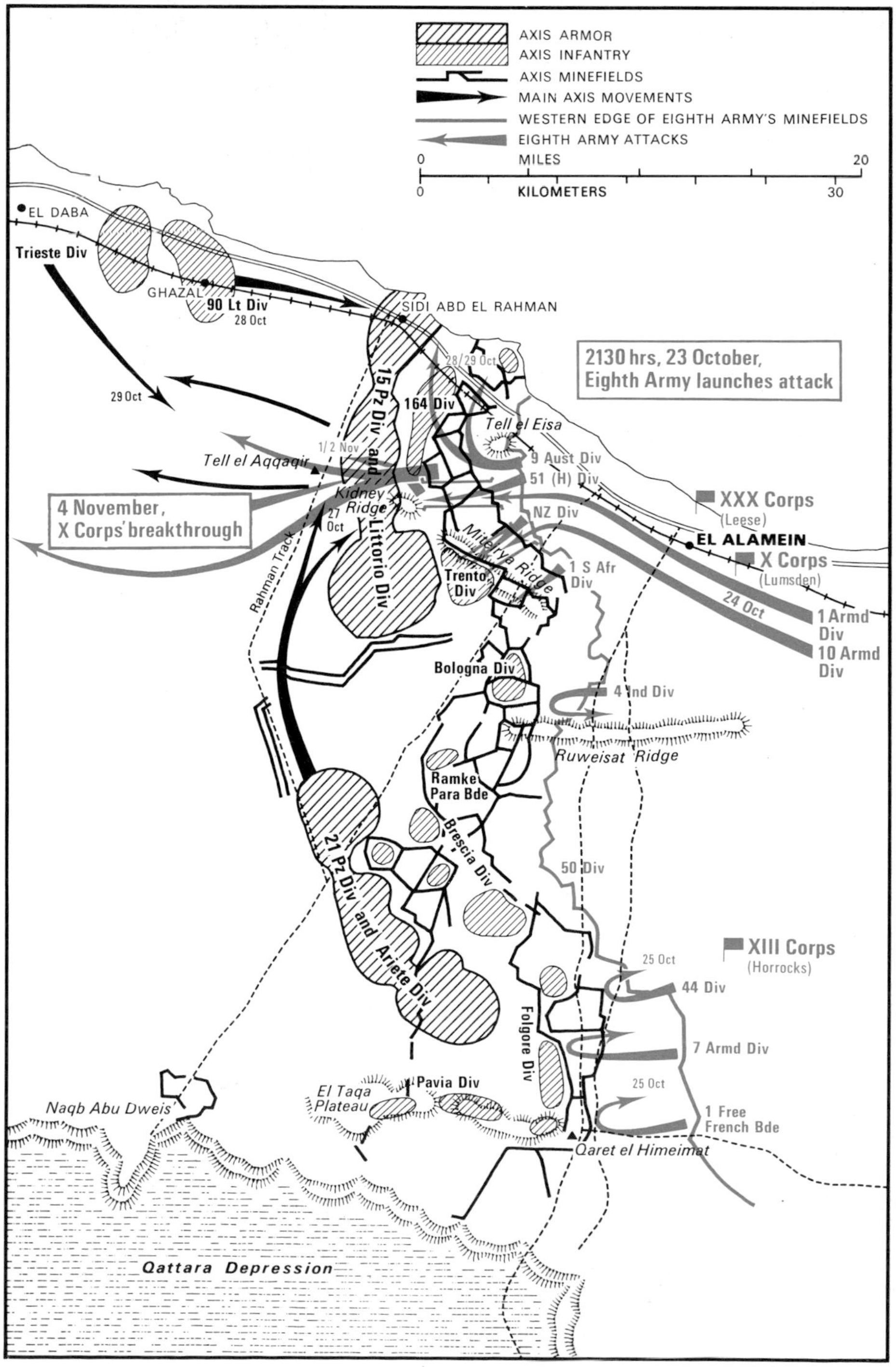

Operation Torch and Tunisia

Rommel's forces were retreating from Egypt when US and British troops began the series of landings code-named Operation Torch, on 8 November 1942. It was the first large-scale US ground-troop participation in the European war, but US Chiefs of Staff had objected to it as peripheral: their preferred strategy was the direct invasion of Western Europe. President Roosevelt had overruled their objections in the conviction that a US delay would lead to domestic political pressure for abandonment of the policy of defeating Germany first.

Secret talks with local French leaders had preceded the Torch landings, as strong Vichy forces in North Africa might well be prepared to resist the invasion. Anglo-French rivalry stemming from the events of 1940 made the US the logical mediator and led to an exaggerated emphasis on the American presence in the early days of the operation. In fact, the British contribution, especially on the naval side, was more substantial. Even so, Torch was the best co-ordinated Allied effort of the war to date: General Dwight D Eisenhower brought to his assignment as commander-in-chief the determination – and the ability – to weld the participants into an effective team.

There were three principal landing areas, and the landings themselves were largely successful, although hampered in most areas by anticipated resistance from scattered Vichy forces. The early capture of Admiral Jean Louis Darlan, an influential French leader, was instrumental in securing better co-operation with the Allied cause. But the logistical difficulties remained – how to push the large invasion force the 400 miles into Tunis with all possible speed. This problem was compounded by swift and decisive German reaction to the North African incursion: troops and aircraft

Right: The final Allied offensive in Tunisia.
Above: German Messerschmitt 323 transport plane in Tunisia. These planes were used extensively in the German buildup after Operation Torch, but were very vulnerable to attack.
Below: Operation Torch. Some Allied leaders had wanted to risk landing troops further east than Algiers and so forestall a German response but this plan was turned down.
Below right: German half-track on patrol in southern Tunisia early in 1943.

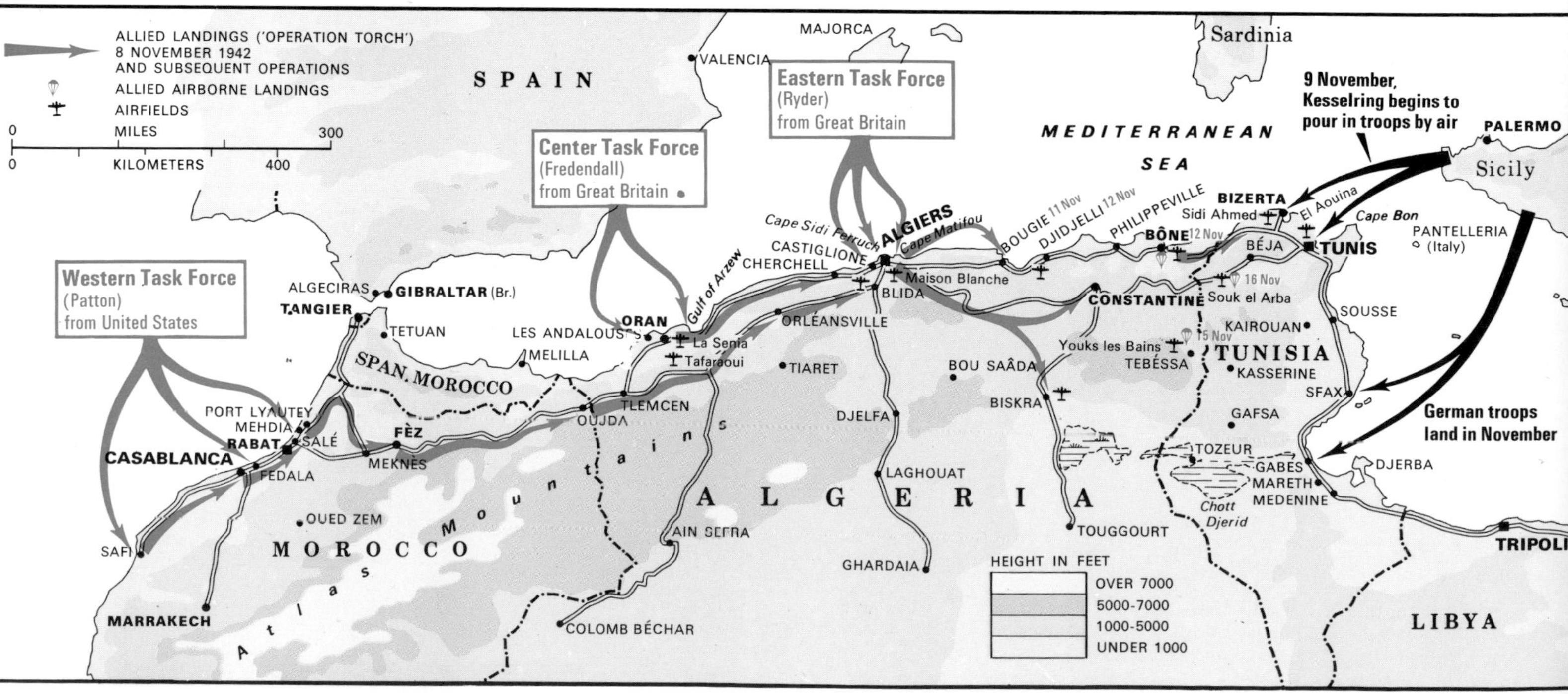

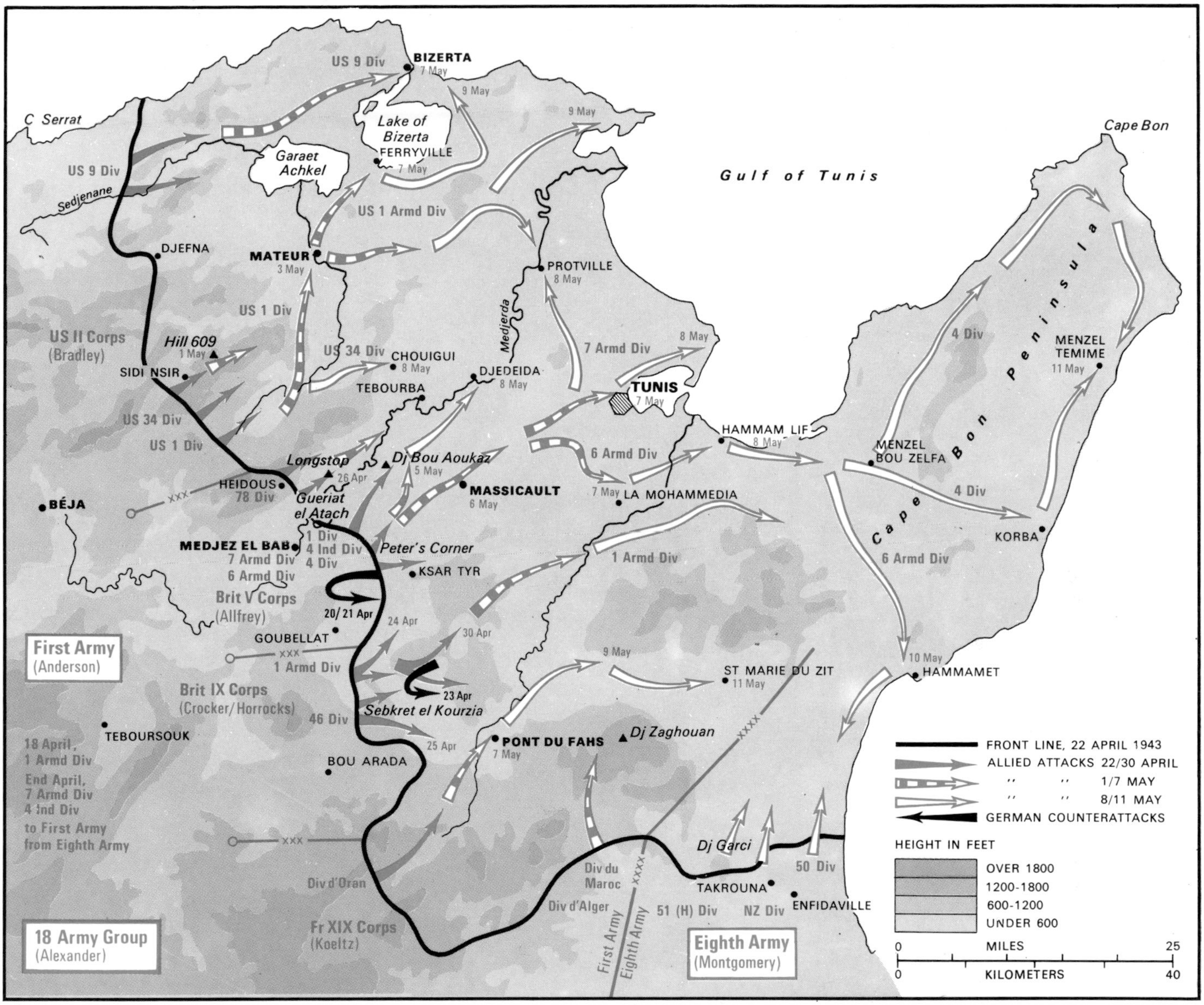

poured in to cut off the Allied advance. It was 14 April 1943 before combined German and Italian troops had been driven back to the last line of hills around Tunis and Bizerte.

Allied attacks on this line began a week later, concentrating in the sectors between Hill 609 and Peter's Corner. Only limited gains were made by US forces at Hill 609 and the nearby Mousetrap Valley and by British troops at Longstop Hill. General Harold Alexander decided to transfer seasoned British units from Eighth Army to V Corps, which helped create an Allied breakthrough on 5 May. A week later 250,000 enemy troops had surrendered.

Field Marshal Erwin Rommel had left North Africa on 9 March to urge that German and Italian forces be evacuated. Hitler refused, and thereby helped ensure both the success of the Allied invasion of Italy and the German defeat at Stalingrad: German troops and transport aircraft were tied up in North Africa to no purpose when they were desperately needed elsewhere.

The Battle of Kursk

No major offensive was planned in Russia for the summer of 1943; the German High Command needed time to re-equip and redeploy the troops on other fronts. However, a large, if limited, attack was aimed toward Kursk, where the Russians had ended their winter campaign of 1942–43. The large salient at Kursk seemed vulnerable to the kind of pincer movement that had been so successful for Germany in 1941. And a Russian defeat would reverse the morale advantage gained in the successful Soviet counteroffensive.

Having learned of German intentions through their intelligence sources, the Red Army constructed three lines of defense

Right: The German plan for the Kursk battle.
Far right: The limited success of the German attacks and the far more effective Soviet response.
Below: Soviet T34 tanks and infantry on the attack.
Bottom: Soviet antitank crew in training before the Kursk battle.

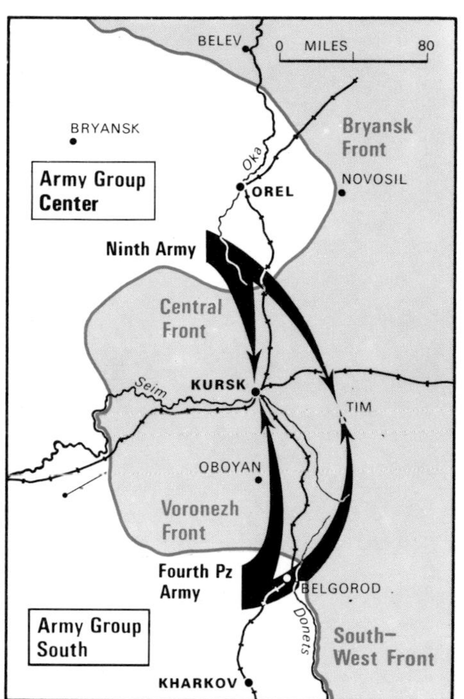

around the Kursk salient – elaborate trenchworks and antitank positions covered by artillery. The Germans began their advance on 5 July in the belief that they were making a surprise attack, but they were soon disabused of this notion. Soviet armor and aircraft had come of age since 1940: the T34 tank was strong and reliable and air command of the battlefield was ensured by overwhelming numbers of Soviet planes. Neither aircraft nor crews were yet up to the German standard, but this would make no difference to the outcome.

The attacking German tanks made small progress on the northern arm, and at a very high cost. The pincer's southern arm, led by General Fritz von Manstein, had better initial success. The Fourth Panzer Army overcame the Russian Sixth Army, only to be confronted by fresh Soviet armor units brought up from the rear. The largest tank battle of all time began on 12 July near Prokhorovka. In the next 48 hours both sides lost hundreds of tanks; early German success was offset by a Soviet offensive north of the salient toward Bryansk. After this the German effort slackened, but the battle raged on for five more days. Meanwhile, the Western Allies were landing in Sicily; many German tanks were disengaged from Kursk and sent straight to the Italian front. This abandonment of the German offensive left the Soviets free to advance on the entire front south of Moscow.

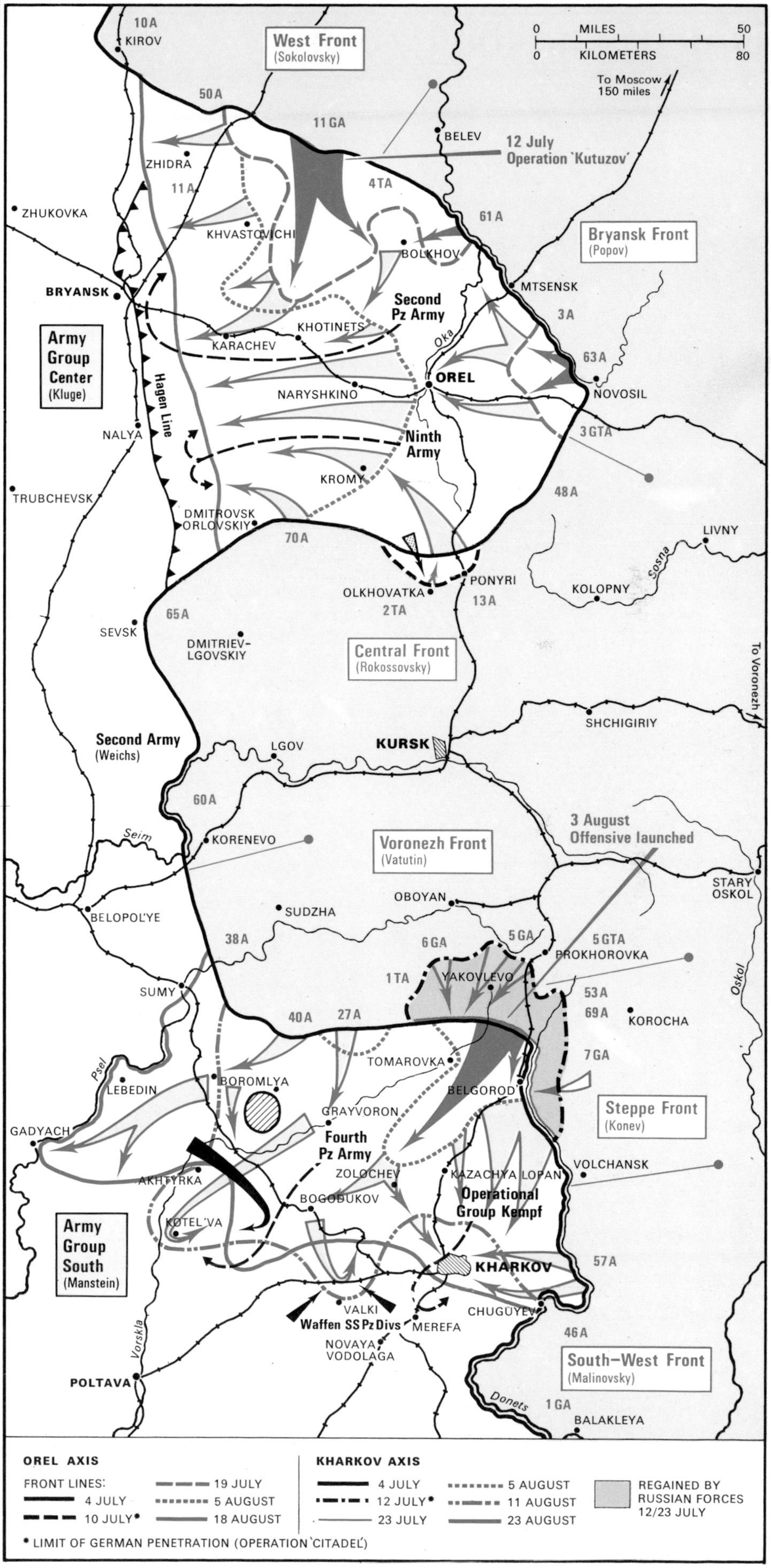

Dniepr and the Ukraine

Some five weeks after Hitler abandoned the Battle of Kursk, the Soviet front line had moved far to the west. German commanders in the field were handicapped by the loss of some of their best units, transferred to the Italian front. Their retreat did not become a rout, and they made optimum use of their geographical situation, but Soviet forces soon captured the two base areas used by the Germans for the movement on Kursk – Orel and its salient in the north, and Kharkov and environs in the south.

By the fall of 1943 Russian forces had taken Stalino, Taganrog and Smolensk. The next objectives were across the Dniepr River, on which the Germans had planned to form their defense lines for the winter. Early in October three Russian armies under Generals Rokossovsky, Vatutin and Konev forced crossings of the Dniepr and poured into Dnepropetrovsk and Melitopol. Manstein sought in vain to find forces for an attack with which to secure a winter position at the river's bend, but Russian force of numbers was overwhelming. The Germans were forced back.

Farther north Rokossovsky had crossed the Dniepr, taken Kiev and pushed on to cut the vital railroad link between Mogilev and Kazatim. At Zhitomir he encountered a German force that stopped him for the moment. It was only a breathing space for German forces in the Ukraine.

By the end of 1943 the Germans were under heavy attack around Krivoy Rog and Nikopol: Hitler insisted that they hold this salient because of the valuable mineral resources in the area. The renewed Soviet offensive began on Christmas Eve with attacks by Vatutin's First Ukraine Front which very soon reached into former Polish territory as well as the southwest. Konev's troops then advanced toward Kirovgrad, eliminated the Nikopol salient and trapped large German forces in a pocket around Korsun; only about half the German force was able to break out.

With the spring thaw came a sea of mud that made any kind of movement difficult, but the Soviets maintained their momentum. On 4 March the First and Second Ukraine Fronts led new attacks that sent large German forces into rapid retreat. Later that month the First Ukraine Front crossed the Dniestr and captured Chernovtsy, severing the last rail link between the Germans in Poland and those in the southern USSR. To the south Malinovsky's troops captured Odessa almost without a fight, and Tolbukhin took Perekop and freed the Crimea of German troops.

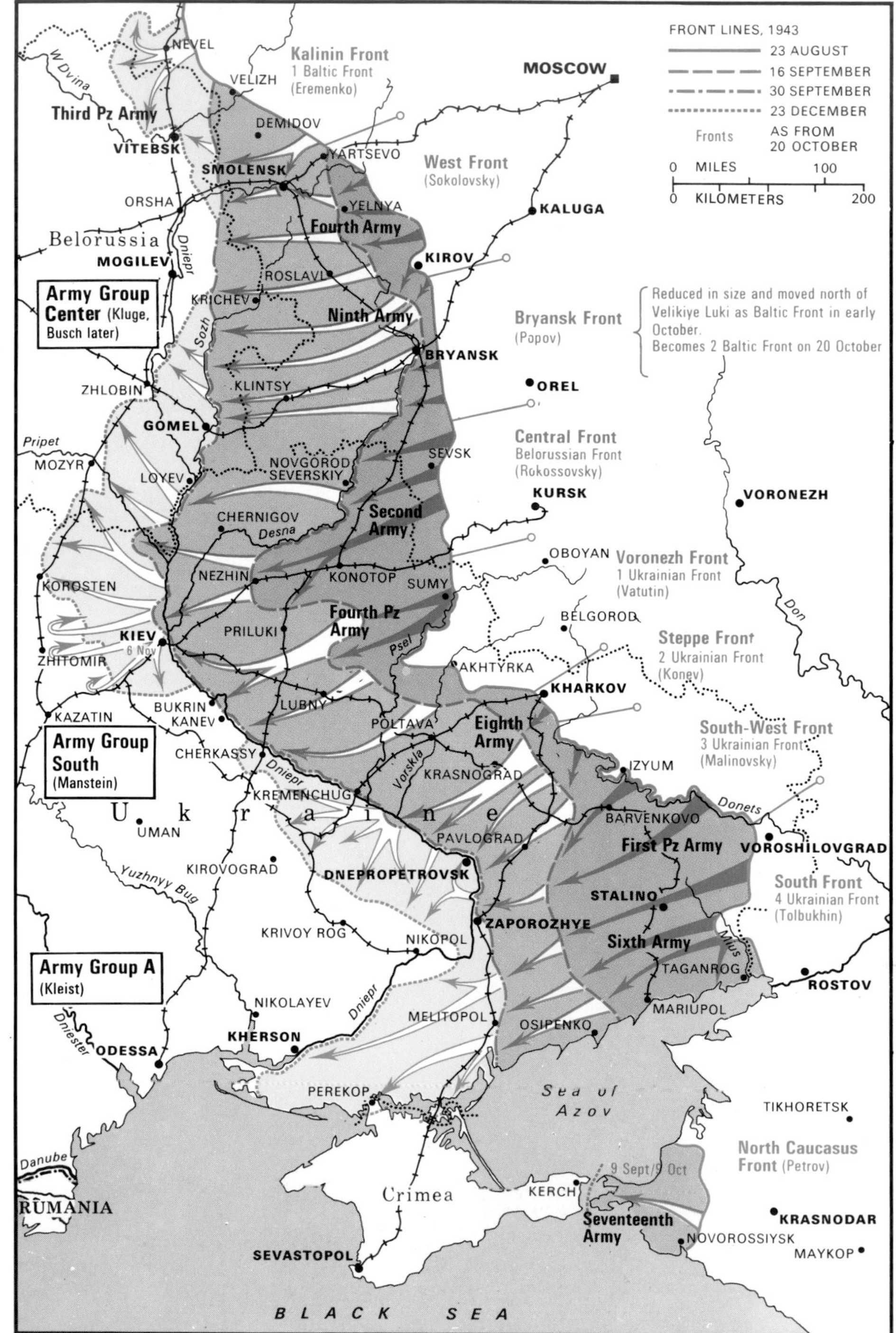

Left: The successful Russian attacks in the summer of 1943 marked a total reversal of fortunes on the Eastern Front. The German Air Force and the tank units were now outmatched.
Above right: The pattern of German losses continued virtually without pause despite the onset of winter.
Right: A long column of German prisoners captured during the encirclement of the Korsun-Shevchenovsky pocket by the 2nd Ukraine Front.

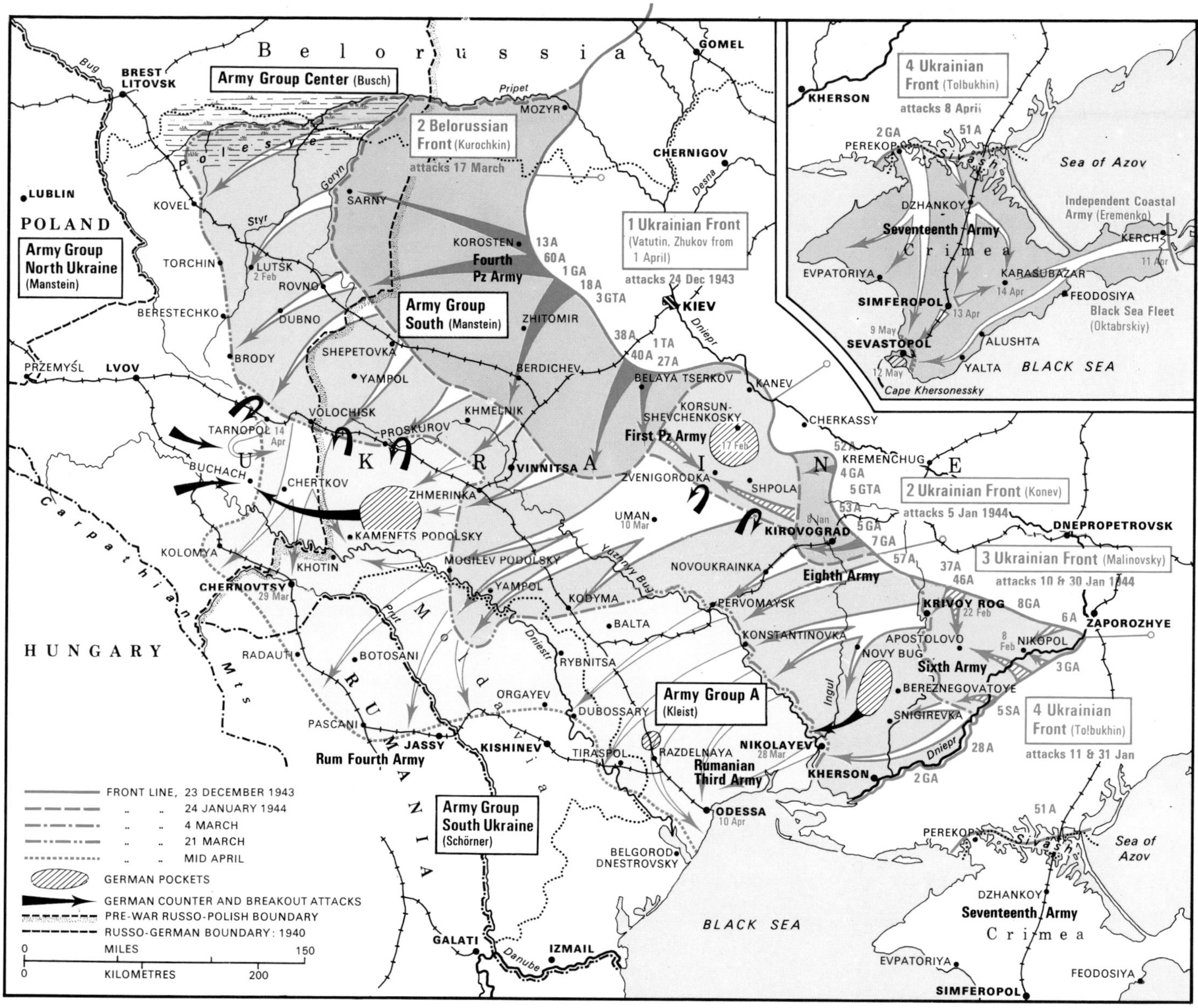

Belorussia
Army Group Center (Busch)
2 Belorussian Front (Kurochkin) attacks 17 March
1 Ukrainian Front (Vatutin, Zhukov from 1 April) attacks 24 Dec 1943
4 Ukrainian Front (Tolbukhin) attacks 8 April
Sea of Azov
Independent Coastal Army (Eremenko)
Seventeenth Army
Crimea
Black Sea Fleet (Oktabrskiy)
BLACK SEA
Cape Khersonessky
POLAND
Army Group North Ukraine (Manstein)
Fourth Pz Army
Army Group South (Manstein)
First Pz Army
UKRAINE
2 Ukrainian Front (Konev) attacks 5 Jan 1944
3 Ukrainian Front (Malinovsky) attacks 10 & 30 Jan 1944
Eighth Army
Sixth Army
4 Ukrainian Front (Tolbukhin) attacks 11 & 31 Jan
Army Group A (Kleist)
Rumanian Third Army
Rum Fourth Army
Army Group South Ukraine (Schörner)
HUNGARY
RUMANIA
Moldavia
Carpathian Mts
BLACK SEA
FRONT LINE, 23 DECEMBER 1943
24 JANUARY 1944
4 MARCH
21 MARCH
MID APRIL
GERMAN POCKETS
GERMAN COUNTER AND BREAKOUT ATTACKS
PRE-WAR RUSSO-POLISH BOUNDARY
RUSSO-GERMAN BOUNDARY: 1940
MILES 0 150
KILOMETRES 0 200

Battle of the Atlantic, 1943-45

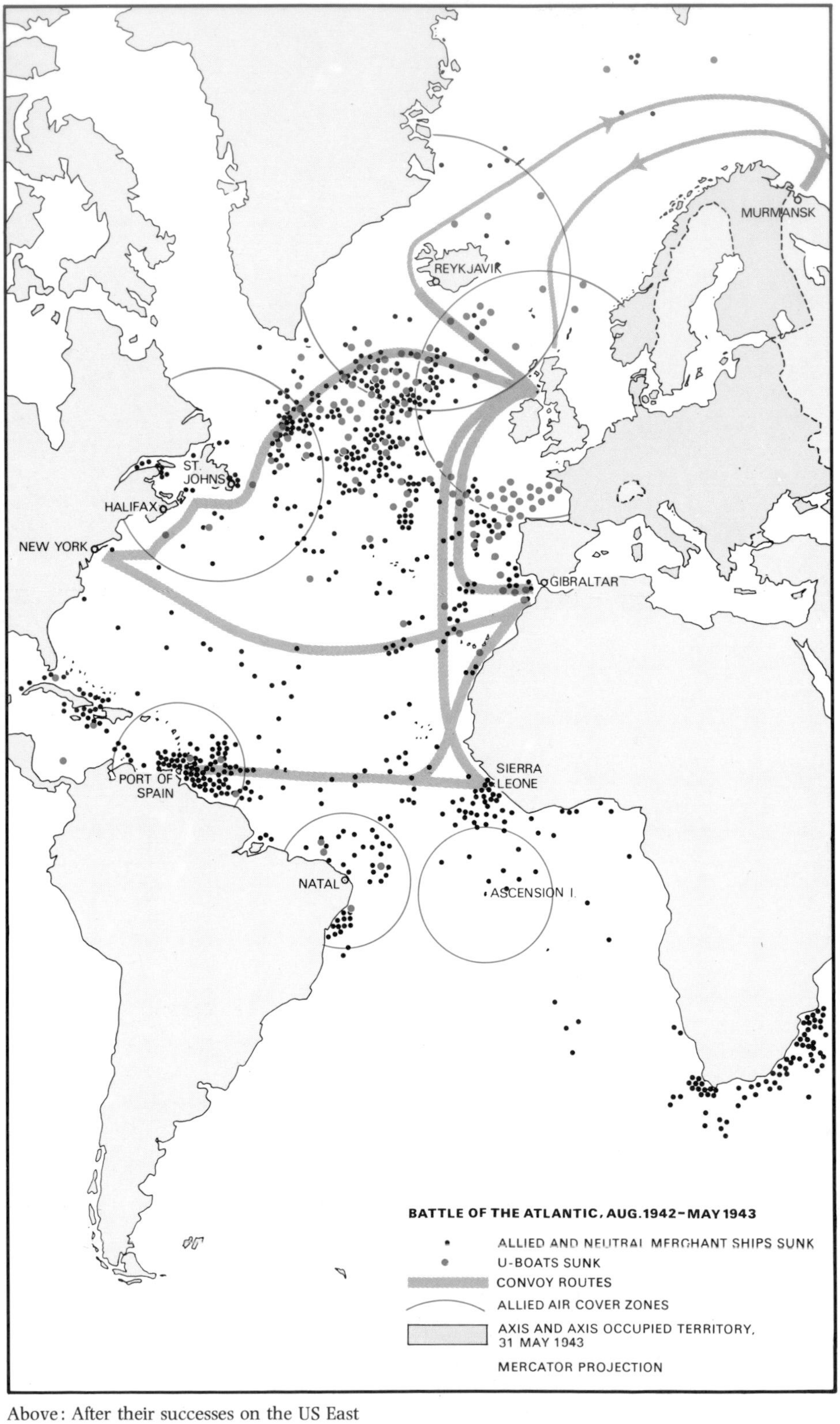

MURMANSK
REYKJAVIK
ST. JOHNS
HALIFAX
NEW YORK
GIBRALTAR
PORT OF SPAIN
SIERRA LEONE
NATAL
ASCENSION I.

BATTLE OF THE ATLANTIC, AUG.1942–MAY 1943

- ALLIED AND NEUTRAL MERCHANT SHIPS SUNK
- U-BOATS SUNK
- CONVOY ROUTES
- ALLIED AIR COVER ZONES
- AXIS AND AXIS OCCUPIED TERRITORY, 31 MAY 1943

MERCATOR PROJECTION

Above: After their successes on the US East Coast, the German U-boats returned to full-scale attacks on the Atlantic convoys in the second half of 1942.

The second half of 1942 saw the establishment of Allied Support Groups to deal with the German U-boat menace. These were specially trained groups of escort vessels deployed at need to help hard-pressed convoys or to patrol waters where U-boats were known to be on the prowl. Ideally, such a group would include a small aircraft carrier along with perhaps six or eight surface vessels. Another boost to the Allies came with a cryptographic breakthrough at the year's end. Code-breaking became more successful right through to the end of the war, while German intelligence efforts grew progressively more ineffectual after Allied code-system changes in mid-1943.

These improvements came not a moment too soon, for this was the critical Allied testing period in the Battle of the Atlantic. The Torch invasion of North Africa (Novem-

Opposite: The ineffective German efforts in the last two years of war.
Right: *U.101*, a German Type VII U-boat.

ber 1942) diverted the newly formed Support Groups to the Mediterranean, and North Atlantic shipping suffered accordingly through March of 1943. In that month alone 120 Allied ships were sunk (72 of them from Atlantic convoys); it seemed that the Germans were winning the years'-long battle. But this was to be the Allied nadir in the North Atlantic: by April losses were far less, and in May 41 U-boats were destroyed. Late that month the submarines were ordered to withdraw from the area because their losses had become insupportable. Several factors were probably involved, including stepped-up US production of escort carriers, redeployment of the Support Groups that had been in North Africa and refinements in radar and long-range reconnaissance planes.

Although the U-boat offensive continued until the war's end, it was never again a serious threat. A brief attempt to renew the convoy battles in the fall of 1943 resulted in the loss of 25 submarines; during this time, only nine merchantmen were sunk. March 1944 brought orders from Admiral Karl Dönitz that the U-boats were to abandon the 'wolf-pack' strategy and operate singly – a tacit admission of the effectiveness of Allied escort forces.

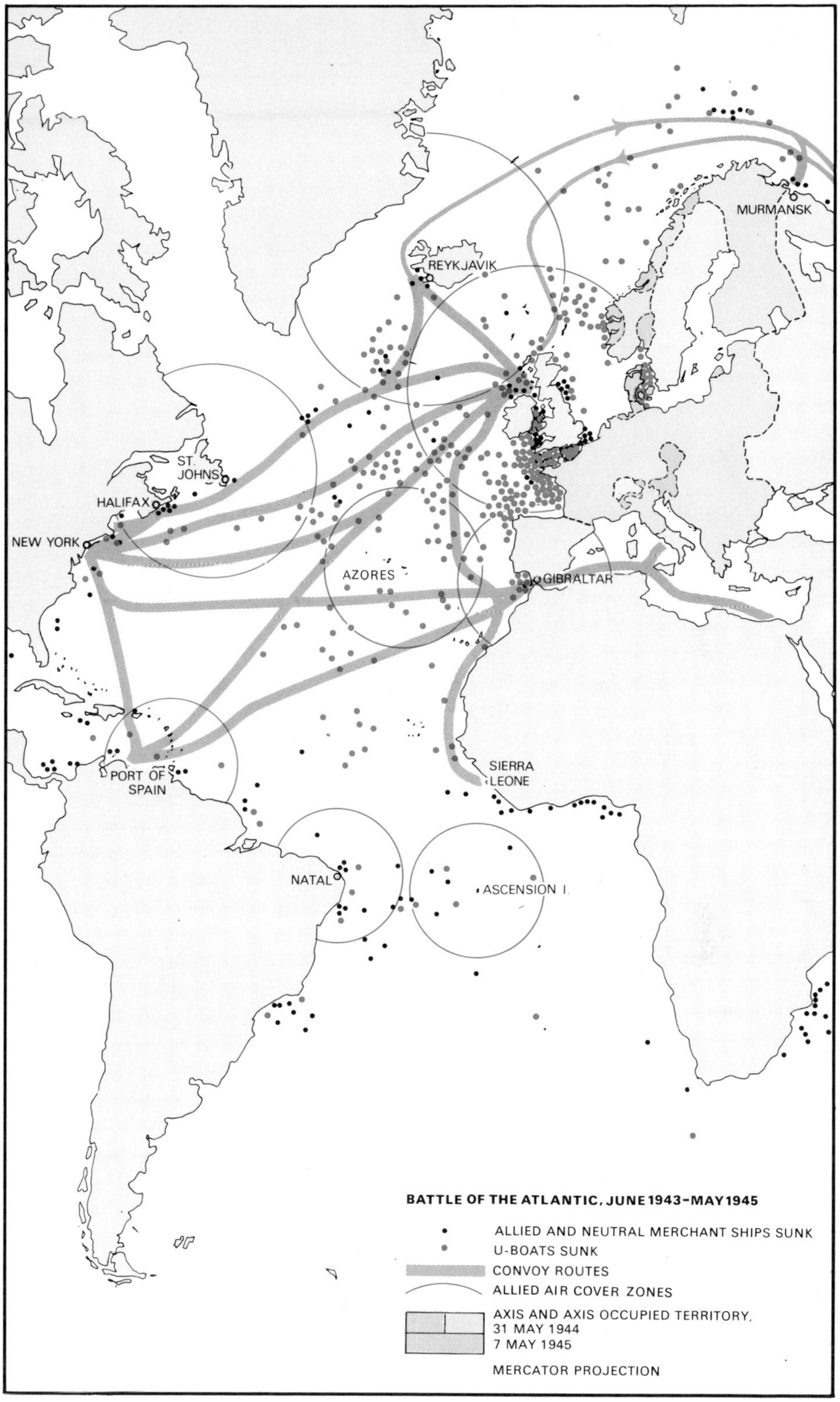

In the closing months of the war the U-boats operated primarily around the British Isles, where they achieved little despite the reinforcement of their fleet (up to 150 vessels in early 1945). Allied victory in the Battle of the Atlantic was largely the result of good co-ordination. Although German submarine research was ahead of the field, poor industrial and scientific management led to declining results. When the Third Reich was finally overthrown, the U-boats had become totally ineffective.

MURMANSK
REYKJAVIK
ST. JOHNS
HALIFAX
NEW YORK
AZORES
GIBRALTAR
PORT OF SPAIN
SIERRA LEONE
NATAL
ASCENSION I.

BATTLE OF THE ATLANTIC, JUNE 1943–MAY 1945

- ALLIED AND NEUTRAL MERCHANT SHIPS SUNK
- U-BOATS SUNK
- CONVOY ROUTES
- ALLIED AIR COVER ZONES
- AXIS AND AXIS OCCUPIED TERRITORY, 31 MAY 1944 / 7 MAY 1945

MERCATOR PROJECTION

The Allied Invasion of Italy

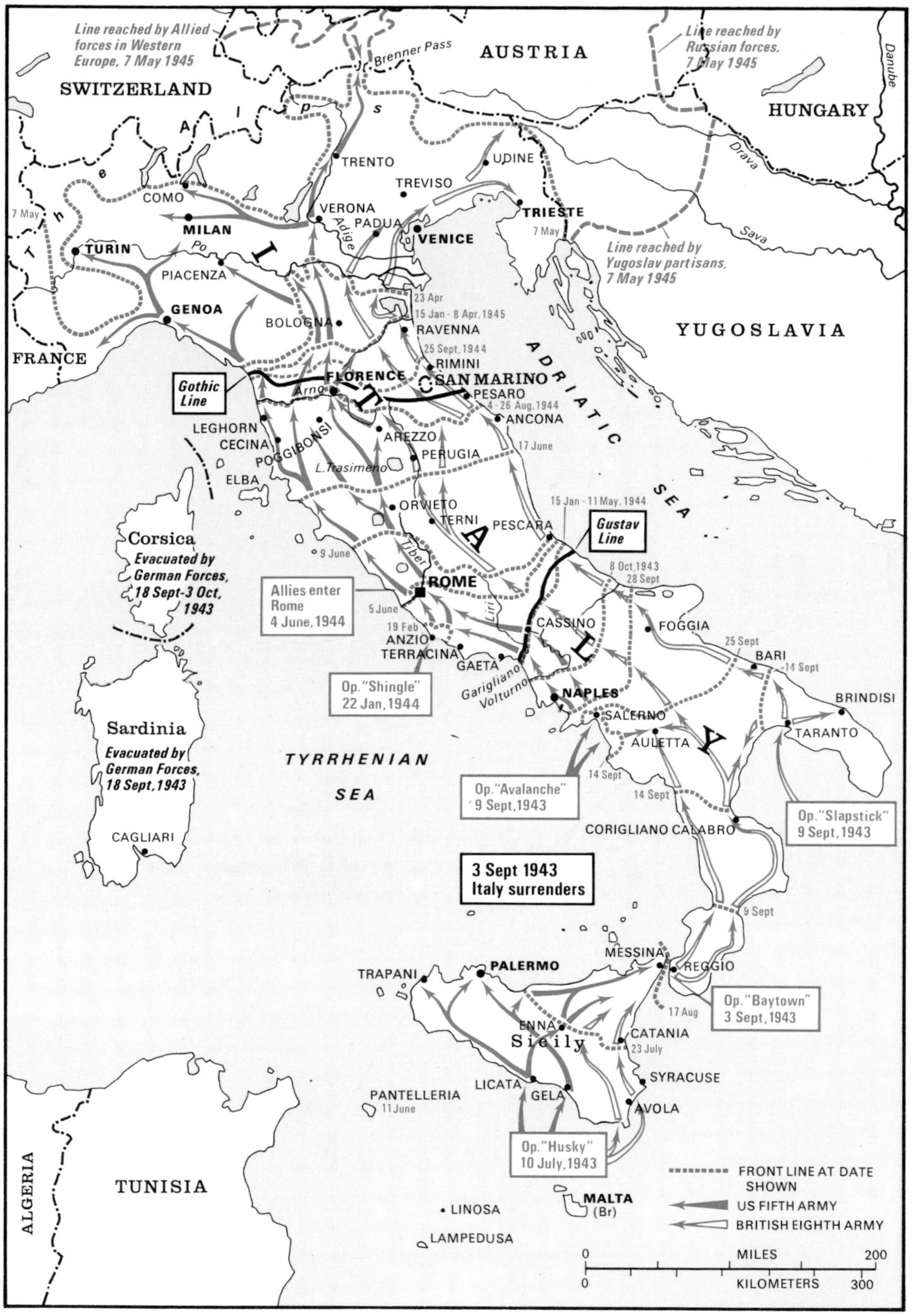

After the North African campaign it was clear to Allied leaders that they could not build up forces in Britain sufficiently to strike northwestern Europe in 1943. In January of that year it was agreed at the Casablanca Conference that Sicily would be the next objective when North Africa had been subdued. This would essentially free the Mediterranean sea lanes, but it seemed too limited an objective for the large concentration of Allied forces in the theater and the massive organizational base already in place. The British favored using Sicily as a jumping-off point for an invasion of mainland Italy, and the Americans came around to this view after the mid-summer collapse of Mussolini's government.

Allied landings on Sicily in July 1943 were quick and decisive, but the subsequent attack on mainland Italy was bitterly opposed. Hitler wanted to stop the Allies at Salerno; failing that, he wanted them held at the Gustav Line: German success in Italy could deter the Allies from a comparable effort in northwestern Europe. The Italian campaign saw some of the war's fiercest fighting, including the battle for Monte Cassino, which recapitulated the pattern of the whole campaign – successive river crossings dominated by German-fortified hills. The historic monastery at Monte Cassino became a warren of German positions that defied repeated Allied attacks in early 1944, after it was bombed and shelled into rubble.

Throughout the campaign, the British were far readier to press for reinforcements and to maintain an aggressive policy. The Americans continued to favor a more direct assault on Fortress Europe through France. Late in 1943 experienced troops and leaders were withdrawn from Italy and sent to England to prepare for D-Day. Six months later, after Rome was taken, large Allied forces were redeployed for the invasion of southern France. A long hiatus ensued, followed by renewed Allied attacks in April 1945. German forces in Italy finally surrendered the following month.

Above: The Italian campaign.
Above left: British troops at work improving landing areas on the first day of Operation Husky.
Left: Allied wounded are evacuated from Syracuse at the end of the fighting in Sicily.
Right: American troops enter Rome, 4 June 1944.

The Solomons and Guadalcanal

To thwart Japanese plans for the Solomons and New Guinea, Australian and American forces built an airstrip at Milne Bay, southern Papua, in 1942. Then they defied horrendous weather and ground conditions to advance over the Owen Stanley Range and capture Buna and Sananda.

The focal point of the Solomons campaign was the island of Guadalcanal, where land and sea battles comprised the first major steps in the Allied counteroffensive against Japan. American preparation was still incomplete when landings had to be improvised in response to news that the Japanese were building an airfield on the island. The 1st Marine Division went in with no reserves or reinforcements in sight.

The Japanese Navy had superior torpedo equipment and night-fighting techniques that asserted control of the waters around Guadalcanal by night and enabled them to make successive landings in strength. The Marines succeeded in capturing the airfield (renamed Henderson Field), and planes based there helped US forces gain command of the sea lanes by day. Two carrier battles – those of the Eastern Solomons and Santa Cruz – were fought to a draw, with heavy losses on both sides.

On land the Japanese mounted three major attacks, two of which (August/September 1942) were understrength due to miscalculation of the size of American forces. Even so, it took a fierce struggle to turn them back. The Marines were becoming increasingly fatigued by the long operation, and would not be relieved until December. The last major Japanese attack came on 23–26 October, but it was badly co-ordinated and soon repulsed.

During the fight for Guadalcanal US Navy night-fighting skills had improved and better use was being made of radar. Japanese night-supply operations (known as the Tokyo Express) remained a problem, but when fresh US troops arrived at year's end, the outcome was no longer in doubt. The Japanese High Command had completed withdrawal of its depleted forces by February 1943. The US would now pursue the familiar island-hopping campaign throughout the latter half of the Pacific War.

Japanese forces were kept guessing about US points of attack, and once ashore the Construction Battalions or Seabees quickly prepared airstrips for local defense and air support of the next attack. A typical case was that of Bougainville, where there were 60,000 Japanese defenders; only a few hundred of them were near the landing point at Empress Augusta Bay, and before a full-scale attack could be mounted four

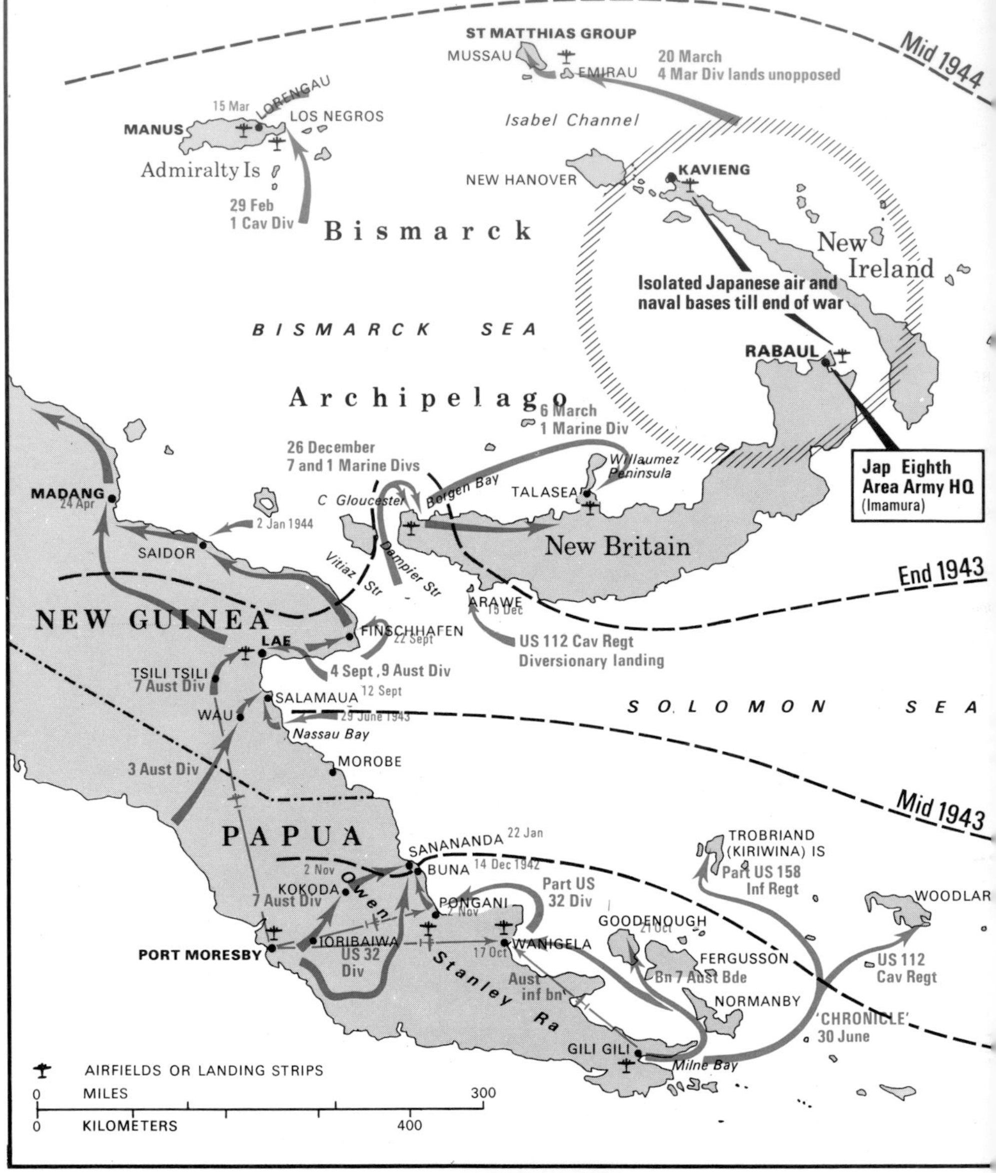

ST MATTHIAS GROUP
MUSSAU
EMIRAU
20 March
4 Mar Div lands unopposed
Mid 1944
MANUS
LORENGAU
15 Mar
LOS NEGROS
Admiralty Is
29 Feb
1 Cav Div
Isabel Channel
NEW HANOVER
KAVIENG
Bismarck
New Ireland
Isolated Japanese air and naval bases till end of war
BISMARCK SEA
RABAUL
Archipelago
6 March
1 Marine Div
26 December
7 and 1 Marine Divs
Willaumez Peninsula
Borgen Bay
TALASEA
Jap Eighth Area Army HQ (Imamura)
MADANG
24 Apr
C Gloucester
2 Jan 1944
New Britain
SAIDOR
Vitiaz Str
Dampier Str
ARAWE
15 Dec
End 1943
NEW GUINEA
LAE
FINSCHHAFEN
22 Sept
US 112 Cav Regt
Diversionary landing
TSILI TSILI
7 Aust Div
4 Sept, 9 Aust Div
SALAMAUA
12 Sept
SOLOMON SEA
WAU
29 June 1943
Nassau Bay
MOROBE
3 Aust Div
Mid 1943
PAPUA
SANANANDA 22 Jan
BUNA 14 Dec 1942
TROBRIAND (KIRIWINA) IS
Part US 158 Inf Regt
2 Nov
KOKODA
7 Aust Div
Owen Stanley Ra
Part US 32 Div
PONGANI
2 Nov
WOODLARK
GOODENOUGH
21 Oct
PORT MORESBY
IORIBAIWA
US 32 Div
17 Oct
WANIGELA
FERGUSSON
US 112 Cav Regt
Aust inf bn
Bn 7 Aust Bde
NORMANBY
'CHRONICLE'
30 June
GILI GILI
Milne Bay
AIRFIELDS OR LANDING STRIPS
MILES 0 300
KILOMETERS 0 400

Below: General map of the Solomons and New Guinea campaign.
Bottom left: An American air attack on a small Japanese island garrison.
Bottom: US Army men training on Guadalcanal after its capture.
Below right: Marines on jungle patrol on Bougainville.

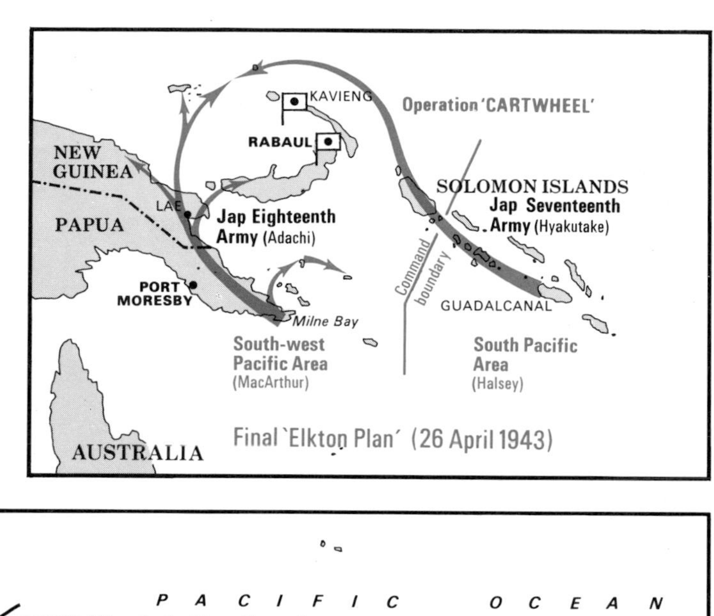

months later, the US beachhead was well defended.

During the Solomons campaign it was decided to bypass the main Japanese bases at Rabaul and Kavieng, originally seen as crucial objectives. By early 1944 both their harbors and their airfields were largely out of action, and the campaign was completed by landings in eastern New Britain and the Admiralty and St Matthias groups. Isolated Japanese garrisons remained in place until the end of the war, but there was little they could do to effect the outcome.

Poland and Warsaw, 1944

The Soviet summer offensive of 1944 was timed to coincide with Allied D-Day landings in Normandy, and it scored an early success in the north by forcing Finland out of the war. The main offensive opened later in June in the central sector, where four fronts advanced to encircle German army groups in the Minsk-Vitebsk-Rogachev triangle. Soviet air superiority and effective guerrilla activities against German supply routes helped open the way for the Red Army, but it crossed the Berezina at a heavy cost. Minsk was captured on 3 July, followed weeks later by Bialystok and Brest Litovsk. These two towns controlled the approach to Warsaw, and although German counter-attacks delayed Rokossovsky's drive, his advance troops were in the suburbs of the Polish capital by 15 August.

The Soviet approach to Warsaw was the signal for a long-planned rising by the Polish Home Army, a resistance group with strong ties with the exiled Polish Government in London. Polish patriots wanted to liberate their homeland themselves, rather than face 'deliverance' by the Russians – this would also put them in a stronger post-war bargaining position. But Rokossovsky confounded Polish expectations by stopping his advance in the eastern suburbs. He would later attribute this to the need to rest and regroup before crossing the river into the city proper. Critics would accuse him of deliberate delay that enabled the Germans to destroy the Polish Home Army and much of the city as well. Whatever the true explanation, Warsaw and her courageous defenders were undone by the fatal Russian pause.

FRONT LINES: 1944
BELORUSSIA: 22 JUNE; 4 JULY; 28 JULY; 29 AUGUST
UKRAINE: 13 JULY; 18 JULY; 28 JULY; 29 AUGUST
GERMAN COUNTERATTACKS
GERMAN POCKETS
PRE-WAR RUSSO-POLISH BOUNDARY
RUSSO-GERMAN BOUNDARY: 1940
MILES 0 150
KILOMETERS 0 250
*Friessner later, then Schörner † Model later, then Reinhardt

Above right: The Soviet summer offensive of 1944, described by some historians of the German Army as 'the destruction of Army Group Center.' 1944 is known in Soviet histories as 'the year of ten victories.'
Right: Soviet artillery in action in the streets of a German town.
Opposite, top: A Russian Tu-2 attack aircraft. Although this was a robust and effective design comparatively few aircraft of the type were produced.
Opposite, bottom: A Soviet Katyusha rocket battery fires a salvo.

D-Day : 6 June 1944

The Allied invasion of France by land, sea and air was the largest operation of its kind in the history of warfare. Supreme Commander General Dwight D Eisenhower had almost three million men and a massive array of equipment assembled for the invasion (code-named Operation Overlord). Months of planning had preceded it, including preparations for emplacement of two artificial ports (Mulberry Harbors), to be towed across the Channel and sunk or anchored off two of the target beaches – Omaha and Gold. Thus heavy supplies could land before the capture of a major port.

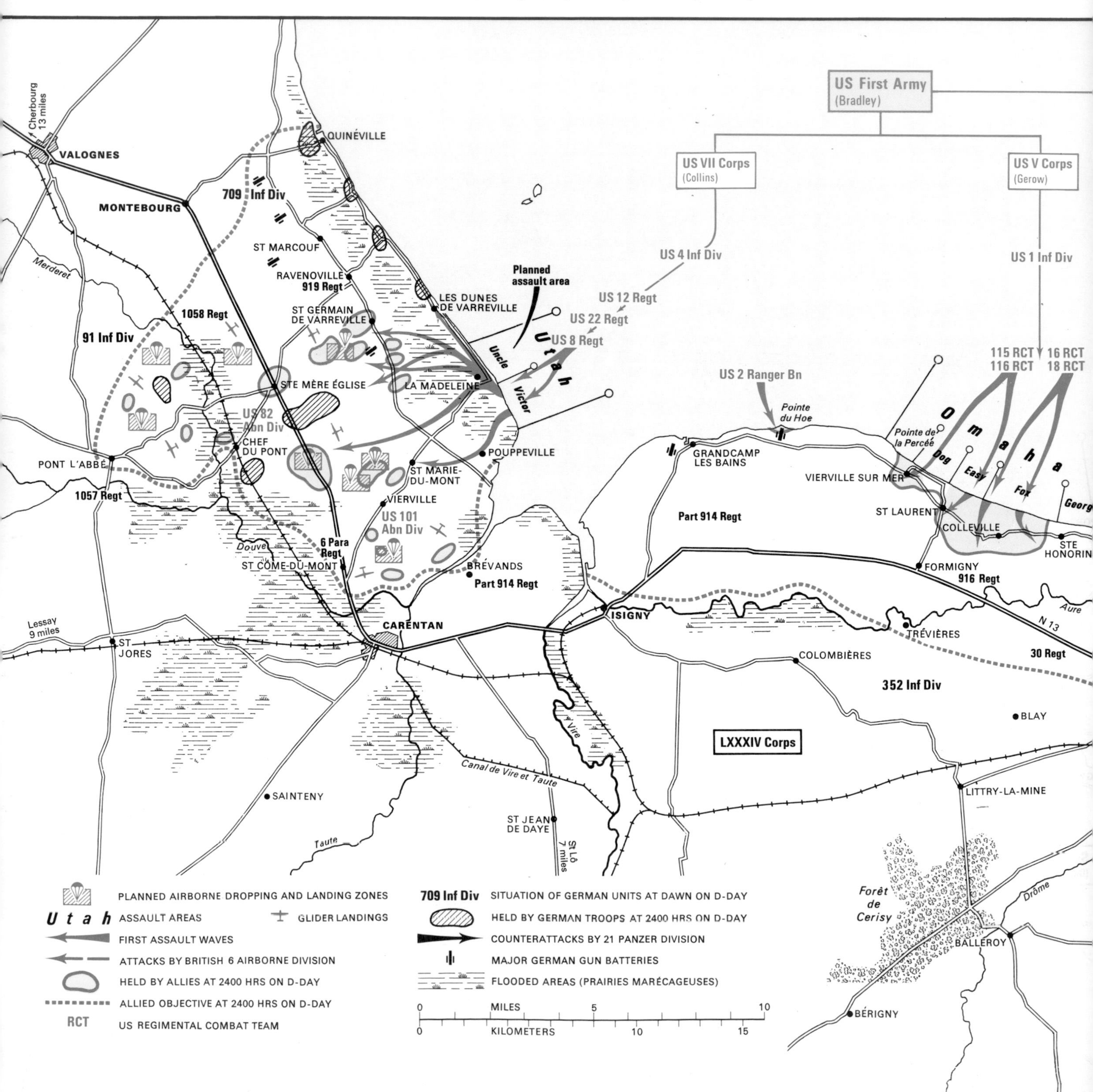

The Allied plan relied heavily on disinformation, deception and preparatory air attacks to prevent German conquest of limited ground forces in the early phase of the invasion. Allied fighting aircraft and warships were abundant, but there was a shortage of paratroop planes and naval landing craft. An elaborate deception was staged to suggest that the (non-existent) First US Army Group would cross the Channel at its narrowest point under General Patton, a ruse backed up by 'preparatory' air attacks. Most of these attacks were actually aimed at isolating Normandy from the rest of France, but they increased confusion

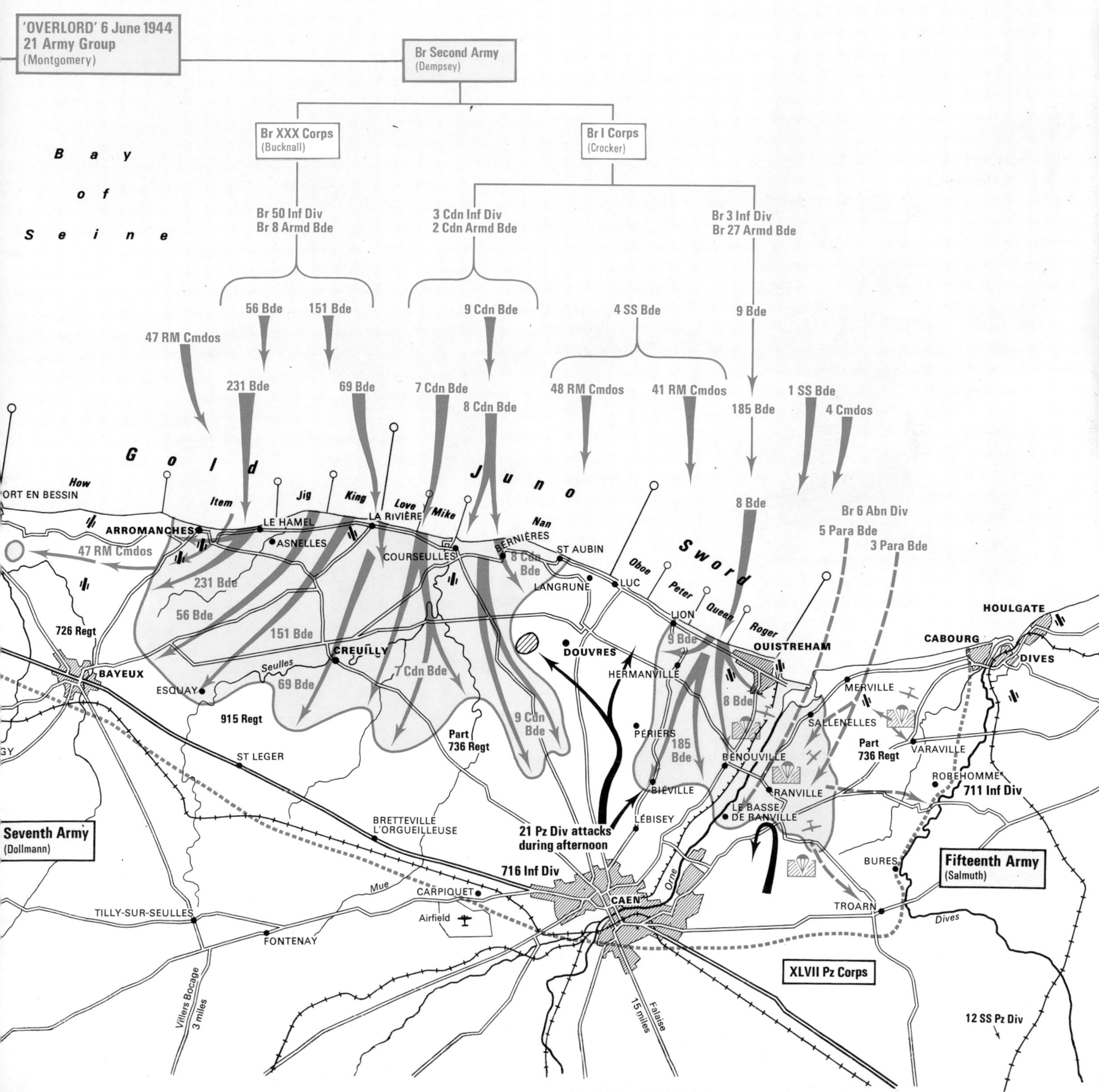

LCA

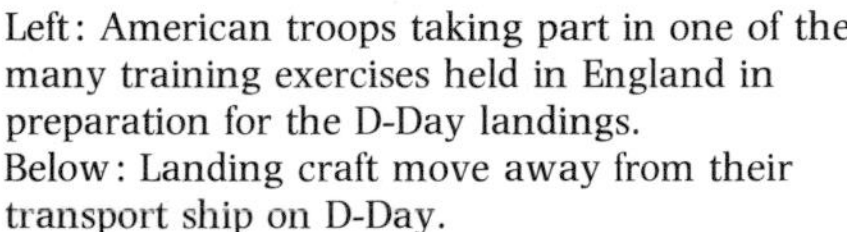

Left: American troops taking part in one of the many training exercises held in England in preparation for the D-Day landings.
Below: Landing craft move away from their transport ship on D-Day.

among the German High Command. Field Marshal Karl von Rundstedt, Commander-in-Chief, West, believed that a strong central reserve must be assembled to repel the invaders once their main objective was clear; General Erwin Rommel held out for defeating the Allies on the beaches before they could reach full strength. Hitler satisfied neither commander by insisting on personal control of Rundstedt's reserves and limiting Rommel's beach defence forces.

On D-Day Allied landings were made on five separate beaches, with paratroop support planned (but not always achieved) on either flank of all five units. There was hard fighting on the British and Canadian target beaches, but specially designed armored vehicles helped overrun the defense and progress inland began. The Americans met little opposition at Utah Beach, thanks to some lucky navigational errors that landed them in lightly defended areas. But at Omaha Beach, disaster was only narrowly averted: German defenses were strong, and early confusion among US troops compounded planning errors. Casualties at Omaha were high, but the landing force had gained a foothold before the day was out. Not all paratroops reached their initial targets, but most achieved some success in a series of hard-fought actions.

During D-Day almost 150,000 Allied troops were landed in Normandy (although they did not fully realize their objectives for Day One). Rommel's plan to win on the beaches – hamstrung by Hitler – had failed. It remained to be seen whether Allied air forces could slow the assembly of German reserves enough to complete the landing and supply of Allied armies.

The Normandy Campaign

In June and July 1944 the Allies extended their initial beachheads inland into Normandy. General Bernard Montgomery remained in control of ground forces, which fought the campaign largely on the guidelines he had laid down. The plan was to exert pressure on the strongest German forces on the Allied left so that the right could advance more rapidly. British and Canadian forces made up the left wing and American units the right. Montgomery was not well liked by some of the American leaders, and he did little to improve his public image through the press, but his leadership was widely respected.

The breakout began in late July, and newly arrived forces of Patton's Third Army began moving from Avranches into Brittany and east into central France. Other Allied armies pressed forward simultaneously. In response, Hitler ordered counterattacks around Mortain to cut off Patton's progress, but these were soon checked by Allied ground and air forces. The Germans found themselves trapped in an exposed salient west of Falaise and Argentan; many were killed or captured as a result. The German position deteriorated with Hitler's insistence on a no-retreat policy and his pervading distrust of his generals. (Field Marshal Gunther von Kluge had replaced both Rundstedt and Rommel in early July and was himself dismissed on 17 August.) German morale suffered accordingly.

Before the heavy fighting around the Falaise Gap was over, all the Allied armies joined the Third in the rapid advance to the Seine. Some historians have criticized Allied handling of the Falaise operations, but German forces defending Normandy were scarcely recognizable as a fighting force thereafter. Resistance groups began the fight to free Paris on 19 August, and the next day the Allies established their first bridgehead over the Seine. Rapid advances in early August made up time lost from the original schedule during June and July.

By late August Allied generals were arguing heatedly about the strategy that should carry them farther in their advance. Allied armies were still almost entirely

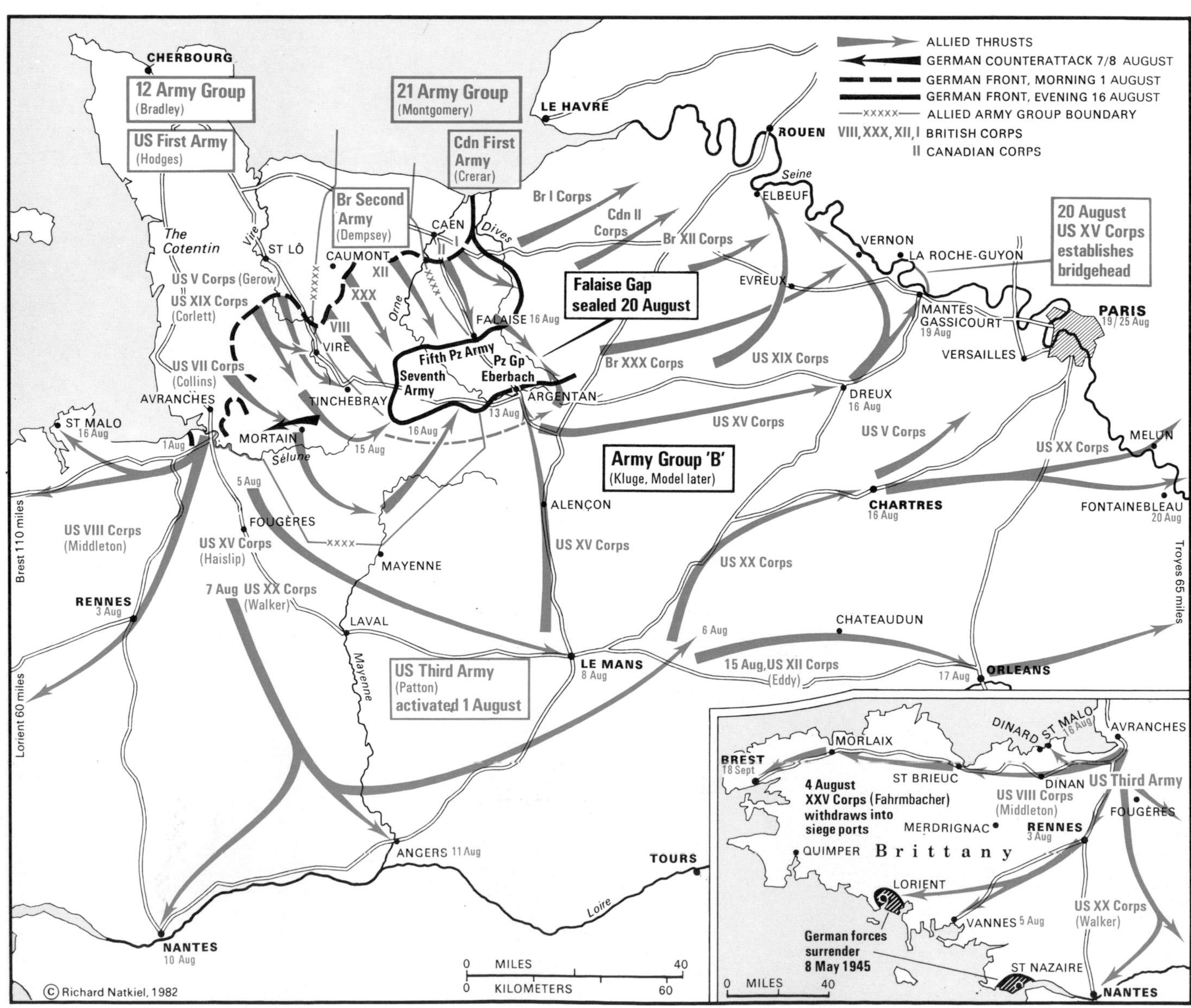

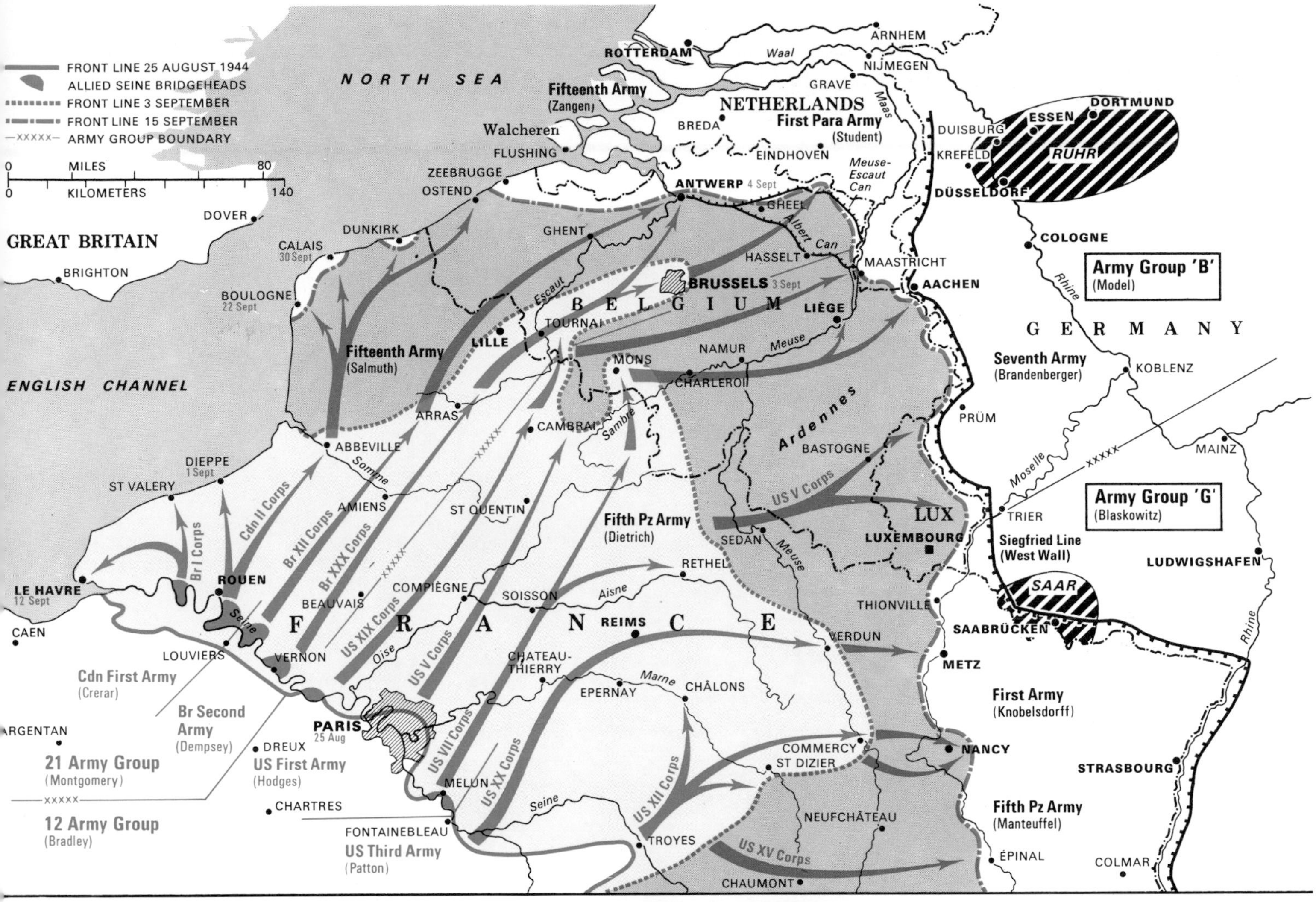

FRONT LINE 25 AUGUST 1944
ALLIED SEINE BRIDGEHEADS
FRONT LINE 3 SEPTEMBER
FRONT LINE 15 SEPTEMBER
ARMY GROUP BOUNDARY

Above: The liberation of northern France.
Left: Even in the late summer, Allied supplies still arrived over the Normandy beaches.
Opposite: The break out from Normandy and the battle for the Falaise pocket.

dependent on supplies landed over the Normandy beaches, ever farther from the front. These were no longer sufficient to keep every unit advancing at full strength and speed. Montgomery led the faction that favored taking advantage of German disorganization to send a priority Allied force on a narrow-front advance into Germany itself: thus the war could be ended within the year. General Eisenhower rejected this plan, insisting on a broad-front policy by which all Allied armies would have an equal share in the advance. This course offered little prospect of quick success, but far less risk of defeat.

If the supply problem could be alleviated, many other difficulties would resolve themselves. The Canadian First Army did take several of the French Channel ports in September, but they were not large enough to be of major help. On 4 September the important port of Antwerp was seized virtually intact, but its importance was not fully appreciated at first. A series of minor delays and errors allowed the Germans to consolidate their hold on the seaward approaches to the port.

Operation Market Garden and Advance to the Rhine

In an effort to capitalize on rapid Allied progress during August and early September 1944, General Montgomery devised a plan for paratroop landings to seize a series of important river and canal crossings that might block further advances. The projected approach through Arnhem had the advantage of bypassing the West Wall defenses of Germany (believed to be formidable) by going around their northern end. The necessity for rapid planning to keep pace with the Allied advance led to weaknesses that did not become apparent until after the fact.

The two US airborne divisions involved reached their objectives with the help of the British XXX Corps, but the third phase of the operation brought major problems. The British airborne division dropped at Arnhem was deliberately dropped some way from its objectives to allow time for organization before its attack. As a result, German forces (far stronger than Allied intelligence had believed) had ample time to prevent the paratroops from reaching their objectives in any strength. At the same time, German resistance to XXX Corps' advance increased, and the operation had to be abandoned after a fierce struggle, with most of the British paratroops taken prisoner.

Then British and Canadian troops began the long effort to clear the Germans from the Schelde Estuary so as to open the port of Antwerp. Minesweeping began on 4 November after elaborate amphibious attacks and hard fighting. The first cargoes were finally landed at Antwerp on 28 November, and from this time on there was dramatic improvement in the Allied supply situation.

Throughout this period US forces were pushing forward in a number of sectors, but German resistance had become better organized. The US First Army faced heavy opposition around Aachen, and Patton's Third Army fought a grueling action at Metz. It was clear that Allied hopes of finishing the war in 1944 would have to be abandoned.

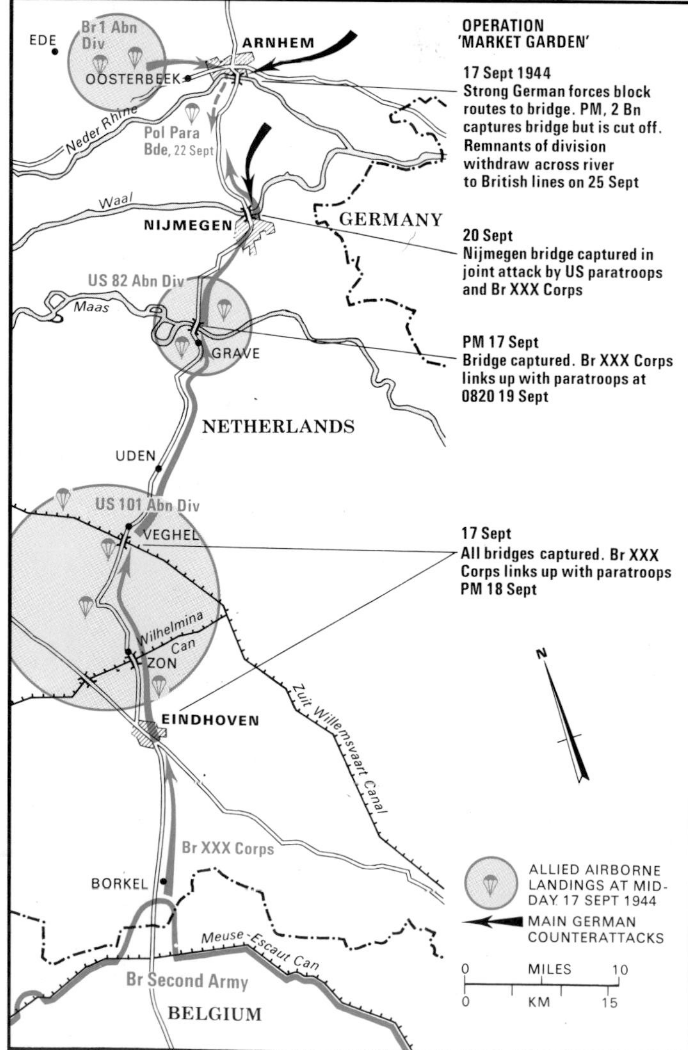

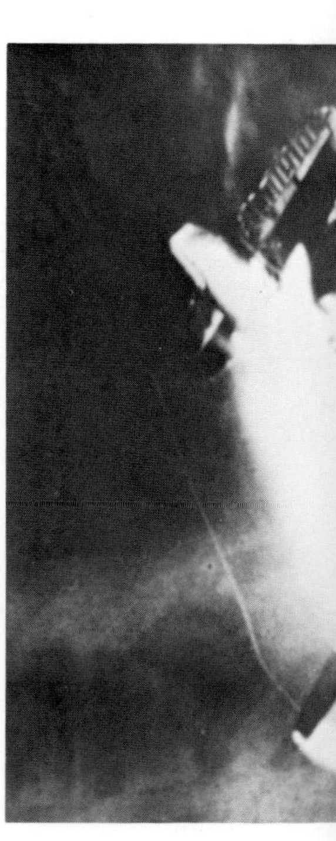

Above right: Generals Hodges, Montgomery, Bradley and Dempsey.
Right: Operation Market Garden – described as 'A Bridge Too Far.'
Second right: An American B-26 Marauder medium bomber plunges to earth after being hit by antiaircraft fire while on a mission in support of the US First Army.

Left: The Western Front in the fall of 1944. The British and Canadians trying to free the approaches to the port of Antwerp and the Americans bogged down in fighting around Aachen and Metz.
Below: US Army Shermans in a French village.
Bottom: British paratroops land near Arnhem.

The Battle of the Bulge

When the Germans launched their Ardennes offensive on 16 December 1944, they achieved complete surprise: the 24 German divisions involved were soon making gains at the expense of the six defending divisions of the US V and VIII Corps. There were 10 armored divisions in the German advance, and most of the infantry units were from the newly formed *Volksgrenadier*. Top-secret preparations were safeguarded from Allied reconnaissance planes, and radio interception was prevented by order distribution by land line or messenger.

Other factors contributed to the early German success in the Ardennes. Allied air support was almost grounded by bad weather. Special German units composed of English-speaking troops wearing US uniforms were sent through the front line on sabotage missions: they did little physical damage, but caused widespread confusion in the American line, which was formed largely of inexperienced recruits and tired veterans. However, the Allies soon rallied from the shock of the attack and hastened to counter it.

Patton's Third Army rushed forces north, while the US 82nd and 101st Airborne Divisions arrived from the main reserve – the first of many units. On 19 December Eisenhower gave Montgomery control of the British and American units north of the Bulge and put General Omar Bradley in charge of forces to the south.

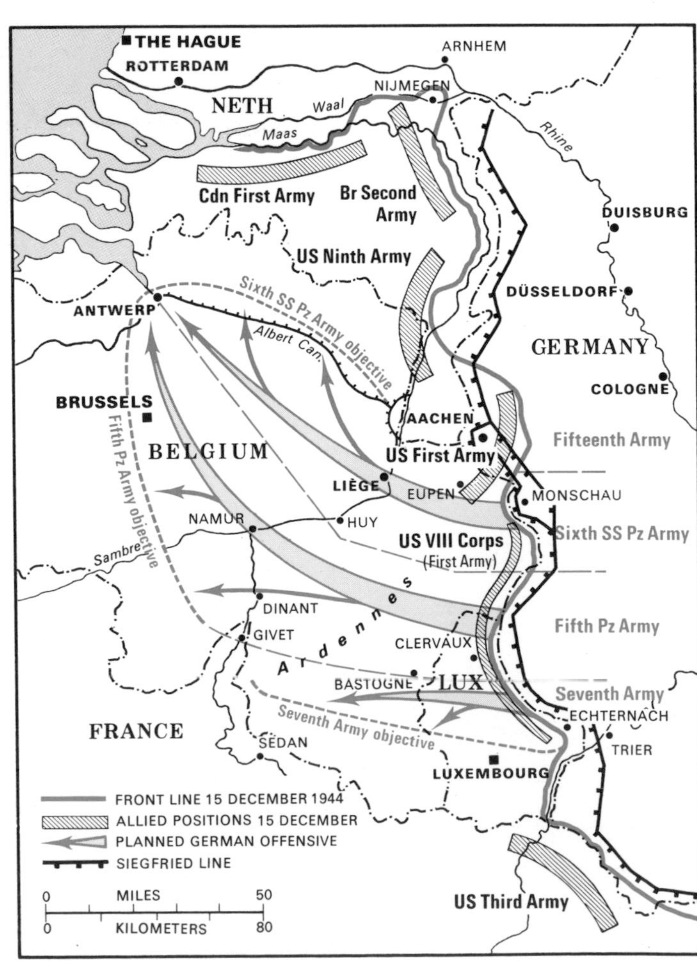

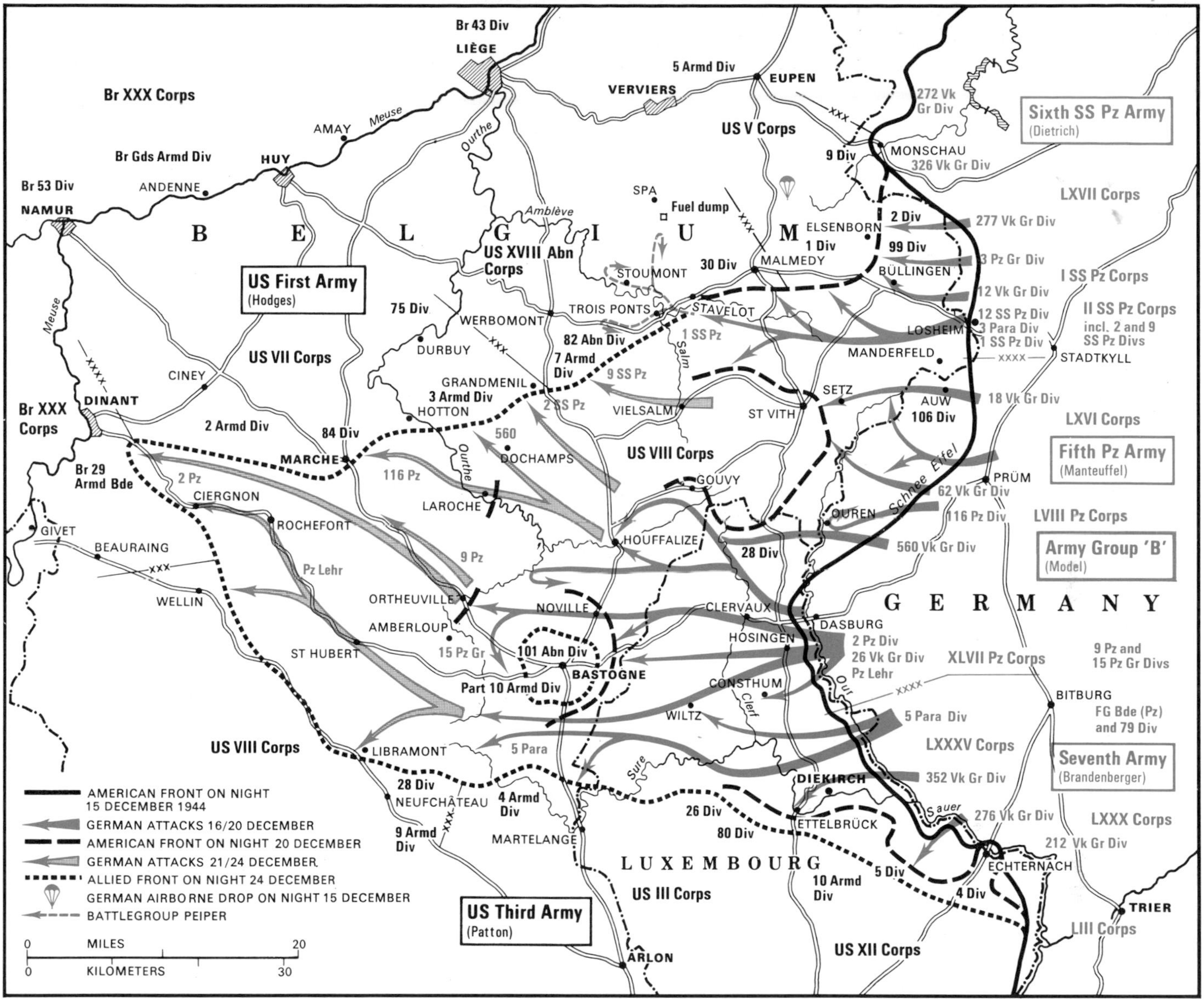

Br 43 Div
LIÈGE
5 Armd Div
EUPEN
Br XXX Corps
VERVIERS
272 Vk Gr Div
Sixth SS Pz Army (Dietrich)
AMAY
Meuse
US V Corps
Ourthe
9 Div
MONSCHAU
326 Vk Gr Div
Br Gds Armd Div
HUY
Br 53 Div
ANDENNE
SPA
Fuel dump
LXVII Corps
NAMUR
Amblève
2 Div
277 Vk Gr Div
B E L G I U M
ELSENBORN
1 Div
99 Div
US XVIII Abn Corps
3 Pz Gr Div
US First Army (Hodges)
STOUMONT
30 Div
MALMEDY
BÜLLINGEN
I SS Pz Corps
12 Vk Gr Div
75 Div
TROIS PONTS
STAVELOT
12 SS Pz Div
II SS Pz Corps incl. 2 and 9 SS Pz Divs
WERBOMONT
1 SS Pz
LOSHEIM
3 Para Div
1 SS Pz Div
82 Abn Div
Meuse
US VII Corps
DURBUY
7 Armd Div
Salm
MANDERFELD
STADTKYLL
CINEY
GRANDMENIL
9 SS Pz
SETZ
3 Armd Div
AUW
18 Vk Gr Div
Br XXX Corps
DINANT
HOTTON
2 SS Pz
VIELSALM
ST VITH
106 Div
LXVI Corps
2 Armd Div
84 Div
560
Fifth Pz Army (Manteuffel)
MARCHE
DOCHAMPS
US VIII Corps
Schnee Eifel
Br 29 Armd Bde
116 Pz
2 Pz
GOUVY
PRÜM
CIERGNON
Ourthe
62 Vk Gr Div
LAROCHE
OUREN
116 Pz Div
LVIII Pz Corps
GIVET
ROCHEFORT
BEAURAING
HOUFFALIZE
560 Vk Gr Div
Army Group 'B' (Model)
28 Div
9 Pz
Pz Lehr
WELLIN
ORTHEUVILLE
NOVILLE
CLERVAUX
G E R M A N Y
AMBERLOUP
DASBURG
HOSINGEN
2 Pz Div
26 Vk Gr Div
Pz Lehr
9 Pz and 15 Pz Gr Divs
ST HUBERT
15 Pz Gr
101 Abn Div
BASTOGNE
XLVII Pz Corps
Part 10 Armd Div
CONSTHUM
Our
BITBURG
Clerf
WILTZ
5 Para Div
FG Bde (Pz) and 79 Div
US VIII Corps
LIBRAMONT
5 Para
LXXXV Corps
Seventh Army (Brandenberger)
Sure
DIEKIRCH
352 Vk Gr Div
28 Div
NEUFCHÂTEAU
4 Armd Div
Sauer
276 Vk Gr Div
LXXX Corps
26 Div
9 Armd Div
80 Div
ETTELBRÜCK
MARTELANGE
212 Vk Gr Div
L U X E M B O U R G
5 Div
ECHTERNACH
10 Armd Div
US III Corps
4 Div
TRIER
US Third Army (Patton)
LIII Corps
ARLON
US XII Corps

AMERICAN FRONT ON NIGHT 15 DECEMBER 1944
GERMAN ATTACKS 16/20 DECEMBER
AMERICAN FRONT ON NIGHT 20 DECEMBER
GERMAN ATTACKS 21/24 DECEMBER
ALLIED FRONT ON NIGHT 24 DECEMBER
GERMAN AIRBORNE DROP ON NIGHT 15 DECEMBER
BATTLEGROUP PEIPER
0 MILES 20
0 KILOMETERS 30

Above: The Battle of the Bulge.
Above left: German prisoners in the Ardennes.
Far left: The plan for the German offensive.
Left: General McAuliffe, commander at Bastogne.
Right: A German assault gun emerges from a camouflaged position.

Road movement was restricted by the steep wooded terrain, and focal points of the battle were the junctions at St Vith and Bastogne. The 101st Airborne and 10th Armored Divisions under General A C McAuliffe waged an epic defense of Bastogne, and St Vith held out until 22 December. By that time the German advance had been so severely delayed that its commanders wanted to abandon the offensive. Hitler insisted that the attacks continue, but by Christmas Eve they had been stopped for good. Bastogne was relieved on 26 December, as Allied counterattacks were launched. Hard fighting prevailed throughout January, but by the end of the month all the German gains had been retaken. Overall, the operation was far costlier to Germany than to the Allies.

Western Breakthrough, 1945

The Western Allies had established major bridgeheads over the Rhine north and south of the Ruhr industrial area by March 1945. Supreme Commander General Eisenhower had originally planned to aim his main effort farther north: now he grew concerned by reports that the Germans were fortifying an Alpine stronghold in the south where they could make a last stand. Eisenhower decided to switch his main attacks farther south to forestall such a strategy.

Many British leaders were dismayed by the fact that Eisenhower signaled this decision directly to the Soviet High Command, without permission from his superiors in Washington and London. But the Allied advance continued as ordered – toward the Elbe. German forces had almost exhausted their fuel and ammunition, and many units offered only token resistance before surrender to the Allies – an alternative preferable to giving up to the Soviets. The rumored Alpine Redoubt turned out to be little more than one of Hitler's fantasies. Thus Eisenhower's decision to concentrate on defeating the German Army before crossing the Elbe appears conservative in retrospect; many would argue that the Western Allies could have profited by crossing the river and advancing farther into Czechoslovakia, even though Allied occupation zones had already been agreed.

The British and Americans accepted the surrender of German forces facing them on 4–5 May; formal documents were signed two days later. Fighting went on in Czechoslovakia for several more days, as Allied advances freed thousands of concentration camp inmates and other victims of Nazi persecution. Films and pictures from these liberations revealed to the world the full horror of the Third Reich regime.

Below: Soviet and American officers at the famous meeting of the armies on the Elbe.

DENMARK
BALTIC SEA
NORTH SEA
FLENSBURG
KIEL
Kiel Canal
RÜGEN
ROSTOCK
7 May
LÜBECK
WISMAR
SCHWERIN
HAMBURG
3 May
WILHELMSHAVEN
EMDEN
BREMERHAVEN
STETTIN
NEUSTRELITZ
STARGARD
GRONINGEN
OLDENBURG
BREMEN
26 Apr
18 Apr
Elbe
DÖMITZ
DANNENBERG
Lüneberg
ÜLZEN
WITTENBERG
Belsen
Heath
AMSTERDAM
Army Group 'H'
(Blaskowitz)
Oder
TANGERMÜNDE
BERLIN
KUSTRIN
NETHERLANDS
OSNABRÜCK
Weser
4 Apr
HANNOVER
10 Apr
US Ninth Army
Twenty-fifth Army
MINDEN
POTSDAM
FRANKFURT
ARNHEM
Teutoburger Wald
BRUNSWICK
HAMELN
MAGDEBURG
Twelfth Army
MÜNSTER
First Para Army
GERMANY
Cdn First Army
(Crerar)
Br Second Army
(Dempsey)
WESEL
PADERBORN
BARBY
Eleventh Army
ROSSLAU
Harz Mts
BLANKENBURG
Brocken Pk
DESSAU
24 Apr
HAMM
LIPPSTADT
US Ninth Army
(Simpson)
Leine
Saale
COTTBUS
ESSEN
DORTMUND
BOCHUM
GÖTTINGEN
US First Army
21 Army Group
(Montgomery)
Ruhr
NORDHAUSEN
HALLE
Neisse
DUISBURG
WUPPERTAL
KASSEL
4 Apr
Sauerland
DÜSSELDORF
MERSEBERG
LEIPZIG
Elbe
Fifteenth Army
Army Group 'B'
(Model)
Buchenwald
WEISSENFELS
GÖRLITZ
COLOGNE
ERFURT
WEIMAR
ZEITZ
COLDITZ
Fifth Pz Army
GOTHA
JENA
DRESDEN
LIEGE
BONN
Sieg
MARBURG
OHRDRUF
Dill
Mulde
CHEMNITZ
REMAGEN
US First Army
(Hodges)
US Third Army
BELGIUM
Rhine
GIESSEN
FULDA
2 Apr
USTÍ
Lahn
Seventh Army
Seventh Army
KOBLENZ
BAD ORB
Thüringian Forest
12 Army Group
(Bradley)
Erzgebirge
HOF
WIESBADEN
FRANKFURT
HANAU
Main
KARLOVY VARY
HAMMELBURG
Spessart Mts
Moselle
MAINZ
US Third Army
(Patton)
SCHWEINFURT
PRAGUE
LUX
BAYREUTH
OPPENHEIM
ASCHAFFENBURG
BAMBERG
LUXEMBOURG
TRIER
Odenwald
WÜRZBURG
CZECHOSLOVAKIA
KITZINGEN
5 Apr
WORMS
US Seventh Army
(Patch)
4 Apr
PILSEN
Bohemian Forest
THIONVILLE
MANNHEIM
NÜREMBERG
20 Apr
FÜRTH
Army Group 'G'
(Hausser)
Neckar
Jura
SAARBRÜCKEN
ANSBACH
6 Army Group
(Devers)
18 Apr
Vltava
First Army
HEILBRONN
Löwenstein Hills
7 May
KARLSRUHE
4 Apr
PFORZHEIM
8 Apr
REGENSBURG
26 Apr
Fr First Army
(de Lattre de Tassigny)
US Seventh Army
Franconian
CESKE BUDEJOVICE
NANCY
STUTTGART
Danube
KIRCHHEIM
INGOLSTADT
STRASBOURG
ESSLINGEN
DONAUWÖRTH
TÜBINGEN
Isar
LANDAU
FRANCE
DILLINGEN
First Army
LANDSHUT
30 Apr
PASSAU
Nineteenth Army
Schwarzwald
Swabian Highlands
ULM
23 Apr
AUGSBURG
EHINGEN
Dachau
Inn
LINZ
5 May
COLMAR
SIGMARINGEN
MUNICH
30 Apr
BRAUNAU
US Third Army
LANDSBERG
FREIBURG
Fr First Army
MEMMINGEN
Lake Constance
US Seventh Army
ROSENHEIM
SALZBURG
4 May
OBERAMMERGAU
BERCHTESGADEN
4 May
BASLE
FÜSSEN
Oberjoch Pass
GARMISCH-PARTENKIRCHEN
KUFSTEIN
Enns
SWITZERLAND
BREGENZ
Fern Pass
KITZBÜHEL
IMST
INNSBRUCK
AUSTRIA
Aarlberg Pass
Tyrol
LANDECK
ALPS
TAMSWEG
Brenner Pass
4 May
Resia Pass
KLAGENFURT
BOLZANO
ITALY
US Fifth Army
YUGOSLAVIA
OCCUPIED BY ALLIED FORCES, 28 MARCH 1945
BRITISH ATTACKS
US ATTACKS
FRENCH ATTACKS
GERMAN POCKETS
OCCUPIED BY RUSSIAN FORCES, 16 APRIL
CONCENTRATION CAMPS
0 MILES 120
0 KILOMETERS 200

Eastern Breakthrough, 1945

After a five-month delay outside Warsaw, the Red Army renewed its advance toward Berlin in January 1945. In the interim, major Soviet efforts were concentrated in the Balkans and the Baltic States. The long pause in the Warsaw sector enabled Russian forces there to rest and re-equip for the final advance of the war.

On 12 January an intense artillery bombardment enabled Marshal Georgi Zhukov to advance past German-occupied Warsaw, then turn north and threaten the capital from the west. The Germans were forced to evacuate, and Soviet forces entered the city two days later. Meanwhile, Konev had been advancing through southern Poland; his army took Krakow on 19 January. Rokossovsky crossed the Vistula, passed the site of the Battle of Tannenberg and reached the Baltic near Elbing. This cut off the Germans in East Prussia, who could be dealt with by Chernyakhovsky's forces. Victory was in sight for the Red Army, as German resistance collapsed on every front.

Konev's army was the first to cross the Oder River, the last obstacle between the Red Army and Berlin. Two bridgeheads were established north and south of Kustrin by Zhukov's troops, which had been joined by Rokossovsky's after the capture of Danzig. On 9 April Königsberg surrendered to the Soviets, bringing an end to German rule in East Prussia. The conquest of the Junker heartland was a heavy blow to German military morale.

Right: The Soviet advance to the Oder.
Below right: A German tank turret dug in as a pillbox but smashed by the Soviet attack.
Below: Soviet artillery in the streets of Danzig.

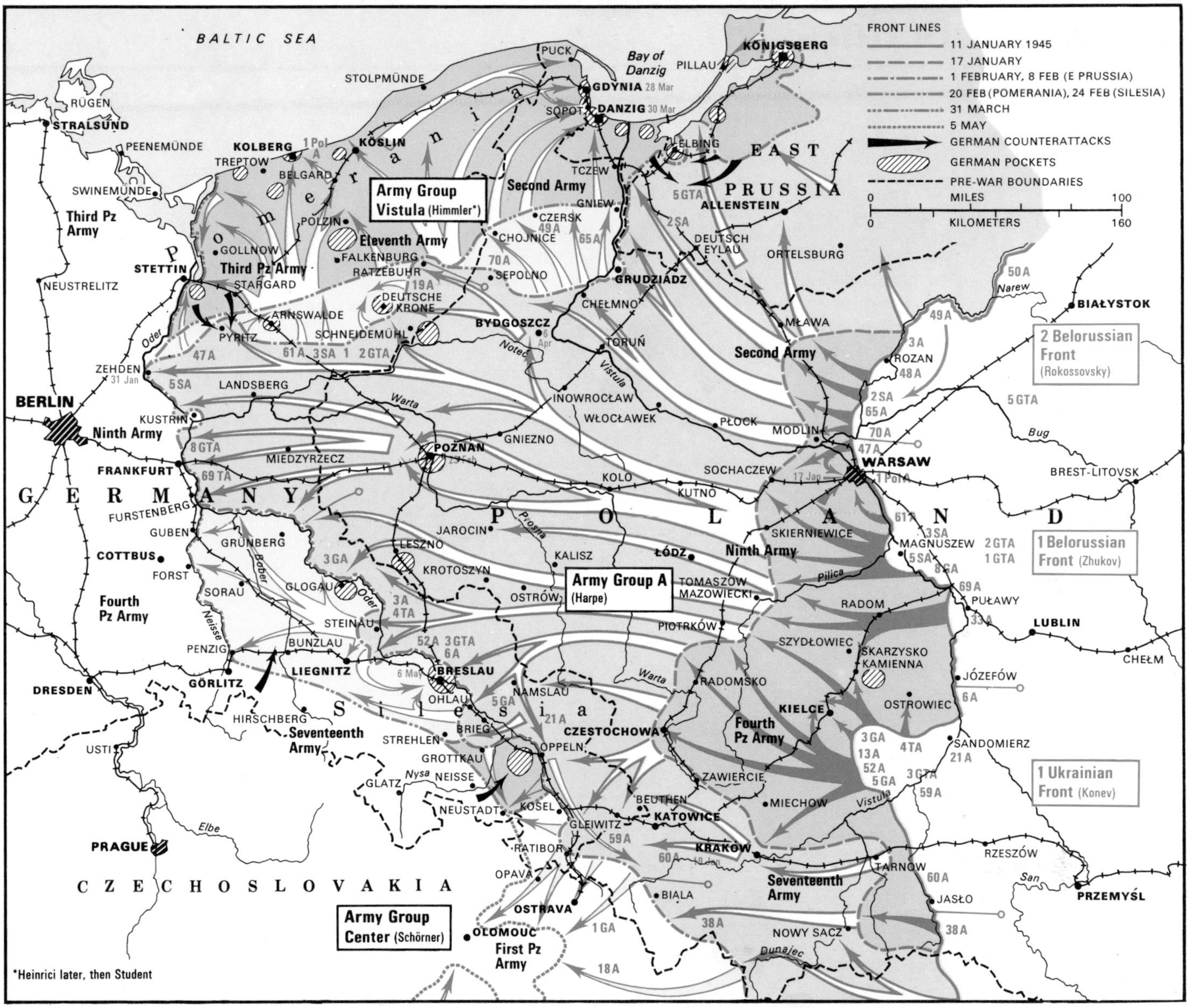

FRONT LINES
11 JANUARY 1945
17 JANUARY
1 FEBRUARY, 8 FEB (E PRUSSIA)
20 FEB (POMERANIA), 24 FEB (SILESIA)
31 MARCH
5 MAY
GERMAN COUNTERATTACKS
GERMAN POCKETS
PRE-WAR BOUNDARIES
MILES 0 100
KILOMETERS 0 160

BALTIC SEA
Bay of Danzig
RÜGEN
STRALSUND
PEENEMÜNDE
SWINEMÜNDE
STOLPMÜNDE
PUCK
GDYNIA 28 Mar
SOPOT
DANZIG 30 Mar
PILLAU
KÖNIGSBERG
ELBING
EAST PRUSSIA
KOLBERG
1 Pol A
KÖSLIN
TREPTOW
BELGARD
Pomerania
Army Group Vistula (Himmler*)
Second Army
TCZEW
GNIEW
CZERSK
5 GTA
ALLENSTEIN
2 SA
Third Pz Army
POLZIN
Eleventh Army
CHOJNICE
49 A
65 A
DEUTSCH EYLAU
ORTELSBURG
GOLLNOW
FALKENBURG
RATZEBUHR
70 A
SEPOLNO
GRUDZIADZ
STETTIN
Third Pz Army
NEUSTRELITZ
STARGARD
19 A
DEUTSCHE KRONE
CHEŁMNO
50 A
Narew
ARNSWALDE
BIAŁYSTOK
PYRITZ
SCHNEIDEMÜHL
BYDGOSZCZ
6 Apr
MŁAWA
49 A
Oder
Noteć
TORUŃ
2 Belorussian Front (Rokossovsky)
ZEHDEN 31 Jan
47 A
61 A
3 SA
1
2 GTA
Second Army
3 A
ROZAN
48 A
Vistula
5 SA
LANDSBERG
BERLIN
KUSTRIN
Warta
INOWROCŁAW
2 SA
65 A
5 GTA
Ninth Army
WŁOCŁAWEK
PŁOCK
MODLIN
70 A
Bug
8 GTA
MIEDZYRZECZ
POZNAŃ 23 Feb
GNIEZNO
47 A
WARSAW
FRANKFURT
69 TA
KOLO
SOCHACZEW
17 Jan
1 Pol A
BREST-LITOVSK
GERMANY
KUTNO
POLAND
FURSTENBERG
Prosna
JAROCIN
61 A
3 SA
SKIERNIEWICE
GUBEN
GRÜNBERG
LESZNO
KALISZ
ŁÓDŹ
Ninth Army
MAGNUSZEW
2 GTA
1 GTA
1 Belorussian Front (Zhukov)
COTTBUS
3 GA
KROTOSZYN
5 SA
8 GA
FORST
Bober
Army Group A (Harpe)
TOMASZÓW MAZOWIECKI
Pilica
69 A
PUŁAWY
Fourth Pz Army
SORAU
GLOGAU
Oder
3 A
4 TA
OSTRÓW
RADOM
LUBLIN
STEINAU
PIOTRKÓW
33 A
Neisse
52 A
3 GTA
6 A
SZYDŁOWIEC
SKARZYSKO KAMIENNA
CHEŁM
PENZIG
BUNZLAU
BRESLAU
6 May
Warta
JÓZEFÓW
DRESDEN
GÖRLITZ
LIEGNITZ
OHLAU
NAMSLAU
RADOMSKO
6 A
Silesia
5 GA
KIELCE
OSTROWIEC
HIRSCHBERG
21 A
Fourth Pz Army
Seventeenth Army
STREHLEN
BRIEG
CZESTOCHOWA
3 GA
13 A
52 A
5 GA
4 TA
SANDOMIERZ
21 A
USTI
GROTTKAU
OPPELN
1 Ukrainian Front (Konev)
Nysa
NEISSE
ZAWIERCIE
3 GTA
59 A
GLATZ
BEUTHEN
MIECHOW
Vistula
NEUSTADT
KOSEL
KATOWICE
Elbe
GLEIWITZ
59 A
PRAGUE
RATIBOR
KRAKOW
19 Jan
60 A
RZESZÓW
TARNOW
San
CZECHOSLOVAKIA
OPAVA
Seventeenth Army
60 A
PRZEMYŚL
BIALA
JASŁO
OSTRAVA
Army Group Center (Schörner)
38 A
NOWY SACZ
38 A
OLOMOUC
1 GA
First Pz Army
Dunajec
18 A

*Heinrici later, then Student

The Fall of Berlin

On 16 April 1945 the Red Army began its final drive on Berlin. Zhukov's army was the first to break through German defenses and move toward the city, with the ultimate objective of the Elbe River beyond it: this was the previously agreed meeting line for Anglo-American and Russian occupation zones. To the south, Konev used bridgeheads on the west bank of the Neisse to begin a two-part advance whose left flank would take Dresden while its right turned north to help surround Berlin. It was this army that would link up with the American advance at Torgau on 25 April.

In a week's time Zhukov's First Belorussian Front reached the autobahn that ringed Berlin and moved along it to Spandau, completing encirclement of the German capital. There two million civilians and some 30,000 defenders awaited the Soviet attack, while outside the city proper almost a million German troops prepared for a last-ditch defense. Although many of these soldiers were poorly trained, debilitated, or underage, they could be expected to fight desperately for the collapsing Reich. Hitler and his closest advisers took to a bunker beneath the city. The approaching forces numbered about two and one-half million well-trained and well-equipped men, with the additional advantage of strong air support.

In the final assault Zhukov's army attacked from the north and Konev's from the south. After two days of fierce fighting, Zhukov's tanks reached the northern outskirts (28 April) and Konev's forces the Tiergarten, close to Berlin center. Thus the two Russian armies were only a mile apart. Still it took four days of house-to-house fighting to enable them to join forces. During this time Hitler killed himself, and the senior surviving German officer, General Hans Krebs, went out to meet the Russian demand for unconditional surrender. By 2 May resistance had ended; the Red Flag flew from the German chancellery.

Right: The Soviet advance to the Elbe and the capture of Berlin. Stalin refused to give priority for the advance to Berlin to either Zhukov or Konev preferring instead that the two most successful Soviet commanders of the war should compete in a race for the prestige of capturing the city.

Below: Dejected German soldiers pass in front of a Soviet heavy assault gun amid the ruins of Berlin after its capture.

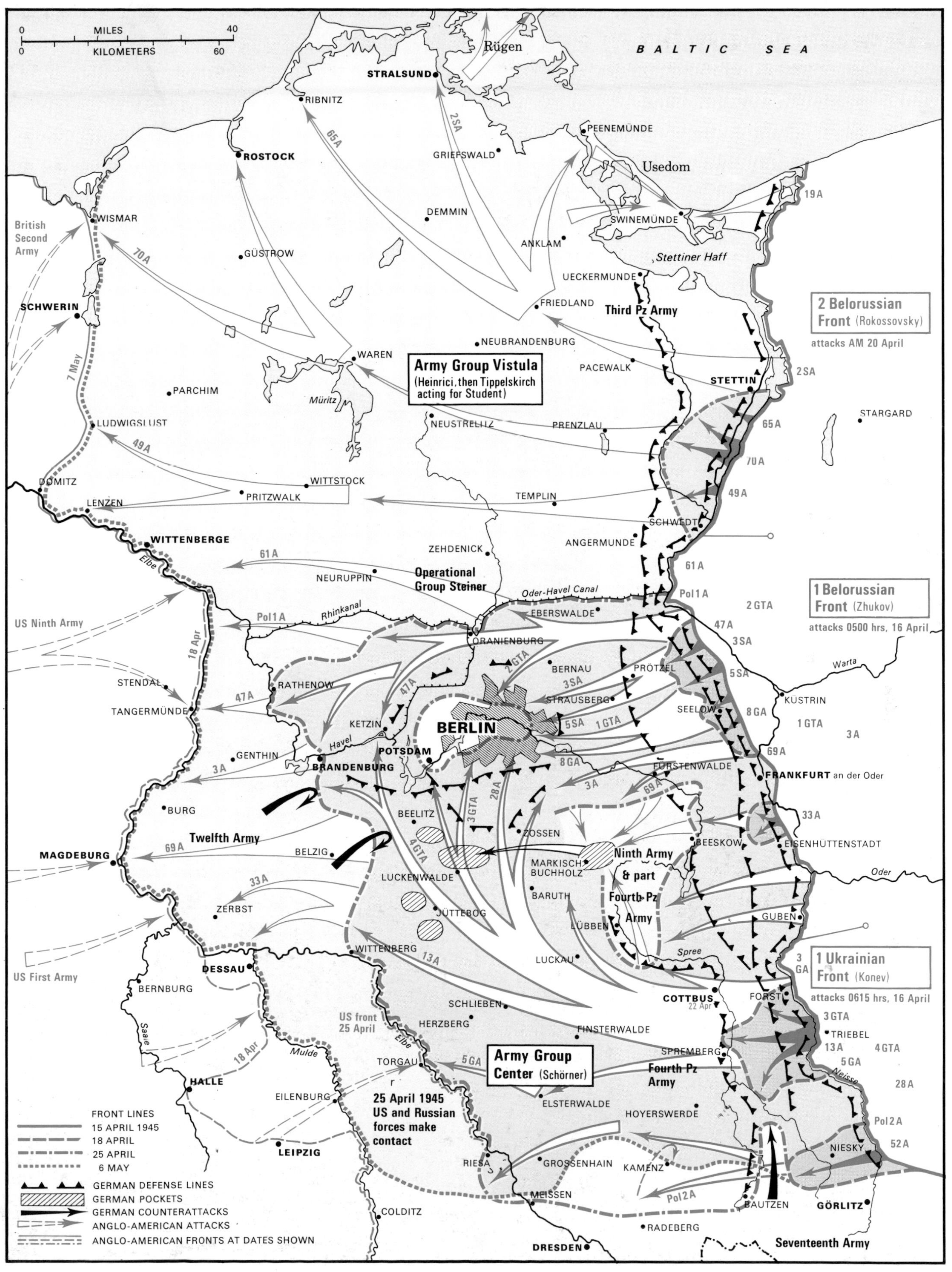
0 MILES 40
0 KILOMETERS 60
BALTIC SEA
Rügen
STRALSUND
RIBNITZ
ROSTOCK
GRIEFSWALD
PEENEMÜNDE
Usedom
19A
SWINEMÜNDE
DEMMIN
WISMAR
British Second Army
GÜSTROW
ANKLAM
Stettiner Haff
UECKERMUNDE
SCHWERIN
FRIEDLAND
Third Pz Army
2 Belorussian Front (Rokossovsky)
attacks AM 20 April
NEUBRANDENBURG
WAREN
Army Group Vistula
(Heinrici, then Tippelskirch acting for Student)
PACEWALK
STETTIN
2SA
7 May
PARCHIM
Müritz
STARGARD
65A
LUDWIGSLUST
NEUSTRELITZ
PRENZLAU
70A
49A
DOMITZ
WITTSTOCK
PRITZWALK
LENZEN
TEMPLIN
SCHWEDT
WITTENBERGE
ANGERMUNDE
Elbe
61A
ZEHDENICK
NEURUPPIN
Operational Group Steiner
Oder-Havel Canal
Pol1A
1 Belorussian Front (Zhukov)
attacks 0500 hrs, 16 April
2GTA
Rhinkanal
US Ninth Army
EBERSWALDE
47A
3SA
ORANIENBURG
18 Apr
Warta
BERNAU
PRÖTZEL
5SA
STENDAL
RATHENOW
3SA
STRAUSBERG
KÜSTRIN
TANGERMÜNDE
SEELOW
8GA
KETZIN
BERLIN
5SA
1GTA
3A
GENTHIN
Havel
POTSDAM
69A
BRANDENBURG
8GA
FÜRSTENWALDE
FRANKFURT an der Oder
3A
28A
BURG
BEELITZ
3GTA
33A
ZOSSEN
BEESKOW
EISENHÜTTENSTADT
MAGDEBURG
Twelfth Army
BELZIG
4GTA
MARKISCH BUCHHOLZ
Ninth Army & part Fourth Pz Army
Oder
LUCKENWALDE
BARUTH
ZERBST
JÜTTEBOG
GUBEN
LÜBBEN
WITTENBERG
13A
Spree
LUCKAU
US First Army
DESSAU
3 GA
1 Ukrainian Front (Konev)
attacks 0615 hrs, 16 April
BERNBURG
SCHLIEBEN
COTTBUS
22 Apr
FORST
US front 25 April
HERZBERG
3GTA
TRIEBEL
FINSTERWALDE
13A
4GTA
Saale
18 Apr
Mulde
5GA
Army Group Center (Schörner)
SPREMBERG
5GA
Neisse
TORGAU
Fourth Pz Army
28A
HALLE
EILENBURG
25 April 1945 US and Russian forces make contact
ELSTERWALDE
HOYERSWERDE
Pol2A
NIESKY
52A
LEIPZIG
RIESA
GROSSENHAIN
KAMENZ
MEISSEN
Pol2A
BAUTZEN
GÖRLITZ
COLDITZ
RADEBERG
DRESDEN
Seventeenth Army
FRONT LINES
15 APRIL 1945
18 APRIL
25 APRIL
6 MAY
GERMAN DEFENSE LINES
GERMAN POCKETS
GERMAN COUNTERATTACKS
ANGLO-AMERICAN ATTACKS
ANGLO-AMERICAN FRONTS AT DATES SHOWN

The Leyte Landings and the Battle of Leyte Gulf

In 1944 the Allied High Command made plans to reconquer the Philippines with initial landings on Leyte Island. The combined forces of General Douglas MacArthur's South West Pacific Command and Admiral Chester Nimitz's Seventh Fleet would undertake the operation. Japanese troops on Leyte numbered some 20,000 at the outset, and reinforcements came under heavy US air attack, often arriving with few rations or artillery. Nevertheless, the number of Japanese troops involved tripled over the course of the action. The US Sixth Army landed about 130,000 men (of 200,000) on the first day of the land campaign – 20 October 1944.

At sea the Japanese brought a major fleet to bear in the three-part Battle of Leyte Gulf. The Japanese naval air arm had lost so many pilots and planes in previous operations that their aircraft carriers were more useful as a decoy than as a fighting force. Japanese hopes rested on their substantial battleship and cruiser units, of which Force A – the strongest – was to reach the American invasion area via the San Bernardino Strait.

Force A was detected en route and came under heavy attack by US submarines and carrier planes from the main (TF 38) formation. In turning away from these attacks, the Japanese force led the Americans to believe they were making a permanent withdrawal; US carriers sped north to fall upon Admiral Jisaburo Ozawa's decoy fleet. Force B was largely destroyed by the Seventh Fleet, and American carriers sank many of Ozawa's ships, including the *Zuikaku*, the last veteran of Pearl Harbor.

Admiral Takeo Kurita of the third Japanese force gave battle to part of the Seventh Fleet on 25 October, but withdrew after limited success. The Battle of Leyte Gulf was the last major Japanese naval effort of the war, and the first in which suicidal Kamikaze attacks were deliberately launched – a measure of Japanese desperation.

Above right: The US cruiser *Portland* fires her 8-inch guns in support of the Leyte landings.
Right: Unloading stores from US Coast Guard-manned landing ships at Leyte.
Opposite, top: The Battle of Leyte Gulf.
Opposite, right: MacArthur fulfills his promise of 1942, 'I shall return,' as he comes ashore at Leyte.
Opposite, center: MacArthur and his staff in conversation with Filipino leader, Sergio Osmena.

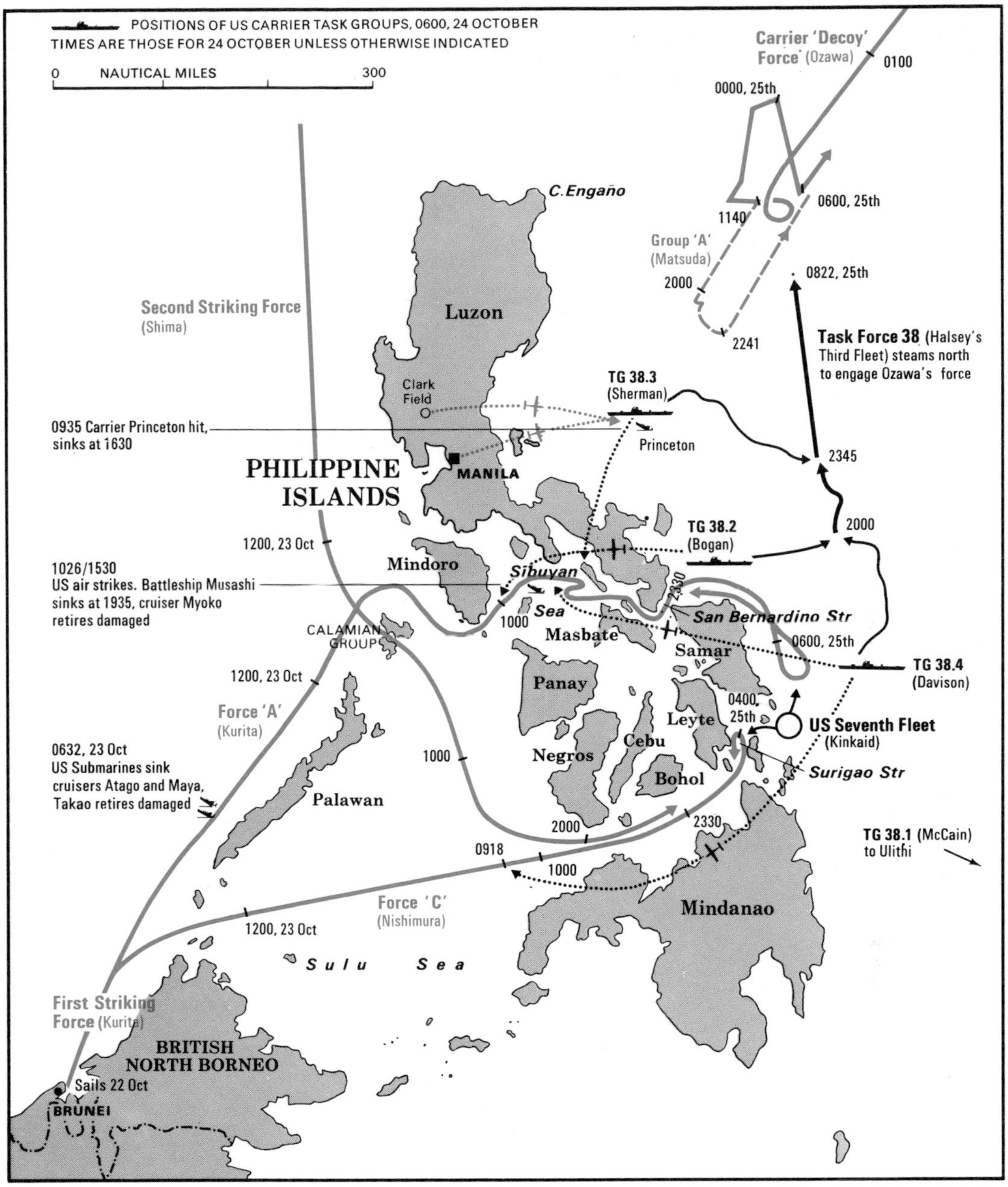

POSITIONS OF US CARRIER TASK GROUPS, 0600, 24 OCTOBER
TIMES ARE THOSE FOR 24 OCTOBER UNLESS OTHERWISE INDICATED
0 NAUTICAL MILES 300

Carrier 'Decoy' Force (Ozawa)
0100
0000, 25th
C. Engaño
1140
0600, 25th
Group 'A' (Matsuda)
2000
0822, 25th
2241
Second Striking Force (Shima)
Luzon
Task Force 38 (Halsey's Third Fleet) steams north to engage Ozawa's force
Clark Field
TG 38.3 (Sherman)
0935 Carrier Princeton hit, sinks at 1630
Princeton
2345
PHILIPPINE ISLANDS
MANILA
2000
1200, 23 Oct
TG 38.2 (Bogan)
1026/1530 US air strikes. Battleship Musashi sinks at 1935, cruiser Myoko retires damaged
Mindoro
Sibuyan Sea
2330
San Bernardino Str
1000
CALAMIAN GROUP
Masbate
0600, 25th
Samar
TG 38.4 (Davison)
1200, 23 Oct
Panay
0400, 25th
Force 'A' (Kurita)
Leyte
US Seventh Fleet (Kinkaid)
0632, 23 Oct US Submarines sink cruisers Atago and Maya, Takao retires damaged
1000
Negros
Cebu
Bohol
Surigao Str
Palawan
2000
2330
0918
1000
TG 38.1 (McCain) to Ulithi
Force 'C' (Nishimura)
Mindanao
1200, 23 Oct
Sulu Sea
First Striking Force (Kurita)
BRITISH NORTH BORNEO
Sails 22 Oct
BRUNEI

The Capture of Luzon

The Japanese commander in the Philippines, General Yamashita, doubted that he could repel US landings on Luzon after his losses at Leyte. As a result, the beaches were lightly defended; Japanese strategy focused on making a stand in mountainous inland areas so as to tie up large American forces as long as possible. The fighting on the principal Philippine Island largely followed this course, especially in the north.

Baguio, where Yamashita had had his headquarters, was not taken until 27 April, four months after the US landings began. The Clark Field airbase was hotly contested, and the defenders of Manila, the Philippine capital died almost to a man. US Navy PT-Boats came under heavy attack from Japanese bombers as they took part in successive landings the length of the island.

The Japanese defenders of Luzon were numerous, if poorly armed and supplied. When Yamashita's Shobo Group finally surrendered at the end of the war, it still comprised 50,000 men.

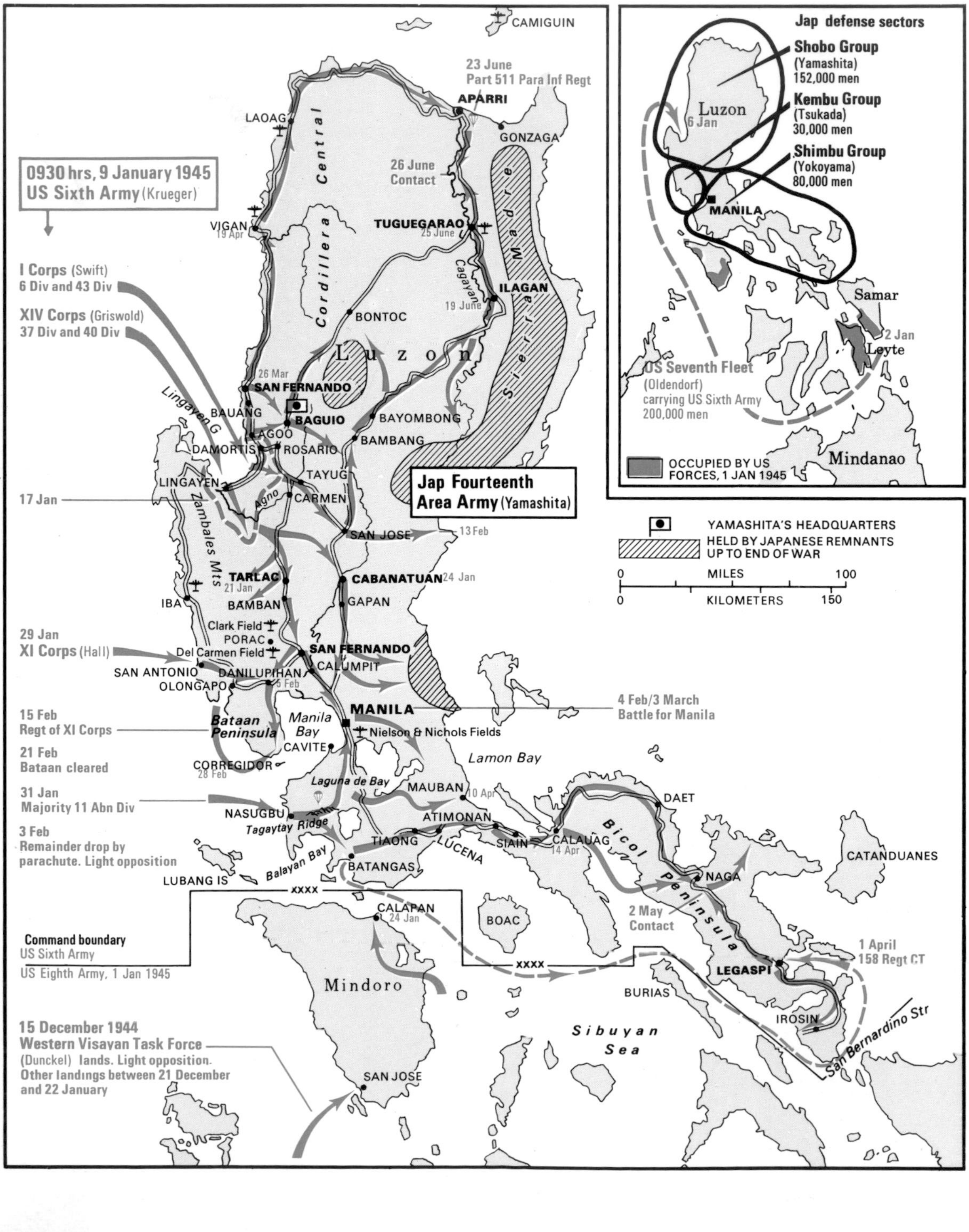

Left: The liberation of Luzon.
Right: The Allied recapture of Burma, 1944–5.
Below: Allied troops wait to be flown to Burma.

The Burma Campaign

British and American leaders disagreed on strategy in the Burma Theater, which was a kind of stepchild in World War II. The Americans saw Burma primarily as a means of reopening a land route by which to assist Chinese Nationalist forces against the Japanese Army in China. British leaders were far less sanguine about Chiang Kai-shek's value as an ally: they saw the Burmese effort in terms of possible recovery of imperial territories lost to the Japanese in their initial victorious sweep through the area.

It took many months to rebuild the shattered Allied force that had retreated to the Indian border in the spring of 1942. The first new offensive, in the Arakan in early 1943, was swiftly defeated by Japanese infiltration tactics. After this, the newly appointed British commander, General William Slim, introduced tactics more appropriate to jungle warfare. A new reliance on air supply made it possible to form units designed to operate behind Japanese lines. These groups (the Chindits and the Marauders) contributed to Allied morale even where their military success was limited – they proved that the Japanese could be beaten at their own game.

Surrounded Allied formations began to hold their ground instead of retreating, with the help of air supply: thus major victories were achieved at Imphal and Kohima. Late in 1944, when the monsoon ended, the Allies resumed their advances on all fronts; the Japanese were defeated again at key battles around Meiktila and Mandalay. By May 1945 virtually all enemy forces had been driven from the country, and Rangoon had been recaptured.

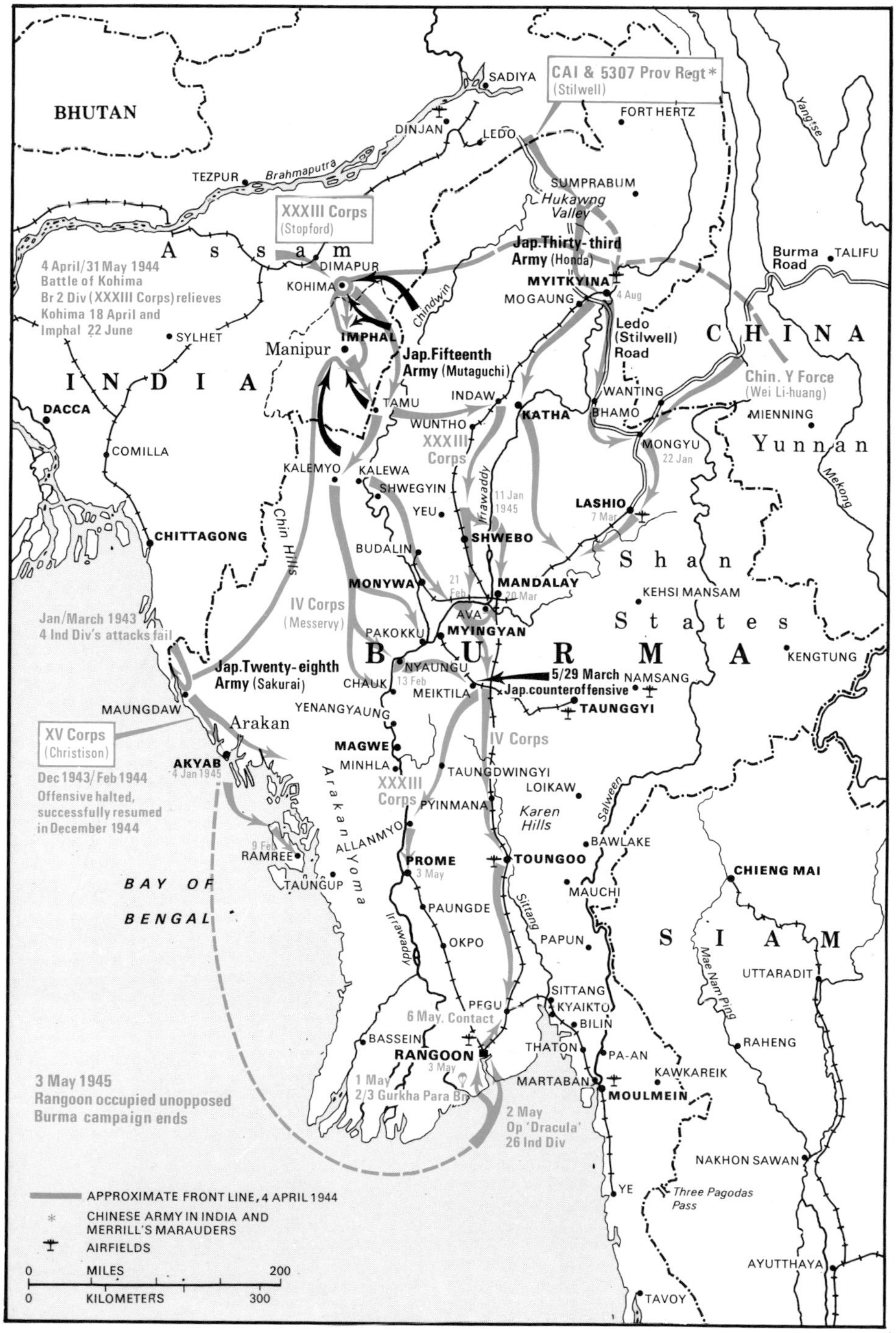

CAI & 5307 Prov Regt* (Stilwell)

XXXIII Corps (Stopford)

4 April/31 May 1944 Battle of Kohima Br 2 Div (XXXIII Corps) relieves Kohima 18 April and Imphal 22 June

Jap.Thirty-third Army (Honda)

Jap.Fifteenth Army (Mutaguchi)

Ledo (Stilwell) Road

Chin. Y Force (Wei Li-huang)

IV Corps (Messervy)

Jan/March 1943 4 Ind Div's attacks fail

Jap.Twenty-eighth Army (Sakurai)

5/29 March Jap.counteroffensive

XV Corps (Christison)

Dec 1943/Feb 1944 Offensive halted, successfully resumed in December 1944

6 May. Contact

1 May 2/3 Gurkha Para Bn

2 May Op 'Dracula' 26 Ind Div

3 May 1945 Rangoon occupied unopposed Burma campaign ends

APPROXIMATE FRONT LINE, 4 APRIL 1944

* CHINESE ARMY IN INDIA AND MERRILL'S MARAUDERS

AIRFIELDS

0 MILES 200

0 KILOMETERS 300

Iwo Jima and Okinawa

The conquest of Iwo Jima offered US forces the prospect of a base near Japan that could provide fighter support and emergency-landing facilities for Marianas-based aircraft on bombing runs to Tokyo. Its proximity to the Japanese home islands would make its capture both a moral and a strategic victory. By the same token, Iwo Jima could be expected to offer fierce resistance to any US incursion.

The island was garrisoned by 21,000 Japanese under the command of General Kuribayashi, who prepared an astonishingly elaborate and flexible defense system that largely survived preliminary US air and naval bombardments, heavy though they were. Japanese strategy faltered, however, when 30,000 Marines began their landings on 19 February 1945. The Japanese plan was to open fire after the landings began, but the defenders waited too long before showing their hand, and the Marines fought their way off the beaches despite heavy losses. US superiority in numbers virtually guaranteed the outcome from this point on, but it would take weeks of savage fighting to overcome the embattled Japanese. From 23 February, when the US flag was raised on Mount Suribachi, to 26 March, when Japanese resistance ended, over 6000 Americans were killed on Iwo Jima. Another 20,000 were wounded in the campaign.

The subsequent attack on Okinawa was planned as the last major landing before the invasion of Japan: the island was to provide harbor and air-base facilities for the projected attack on the home islands. The new British Pacific Fleet took part in preliminary bombardments and gave support throughout the operation, in which American landings began on 1 April.

Defending the island was the Japanese Thirty-second Army under General Ushijima, who concentrated his 130,000-man force behind the strong Shuri Line at the southern end of Okinawa. There was no serious effort to defend the beaches, and the American invasion was virtually unopposed until it came up against the Shuri Line. It would be late May before resistance there was overcome.

In nearby waters the Japanese Kamikaze attacks reached their highest level of the war – several thousand pilots immolated themselves against US and British ships, of which 36 were sunk and 368 damaged. The renowned battleship *Yamato* was dispatched to Okinawa without enough fuel for a return journey, with orders to inflict as much damage as possible before it was destroyed. This bizarre suicide mission was aborted by US carrier planes on 7 April, long before the *Yamato* reached the target area.

The Okinawa campaign was the first in which a significant number of Japanese prisoners – over 7000 – was taken. Civilian casualties on the relatively populous island were high, and many suicides resulted from Japanese indoctrination on the brutality of American conquerors. US casualties totaled 12,500 dead and 35,000 wounded – alarming statistics that supported the case for bringing the war to an end by means other than the invasion of Japan itself.

Right: The battle for Iwo Jima. The harsh volcanic terrain on the island provided ideal assistance for the determined Japanese defenders.
Below: The Okinawa campaign.
Opposite, top: Scenes of devastation on the landing beach at Iwo Jima on the second day of the fighting.
Opposite, lower: Marines close in on a Japanese defensive position on Okinawa.

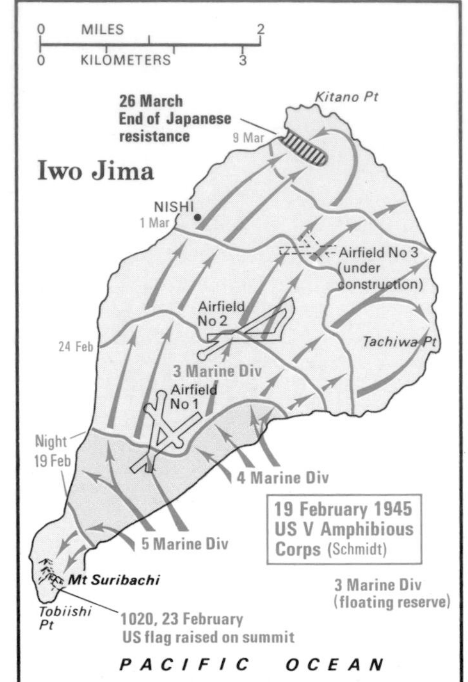

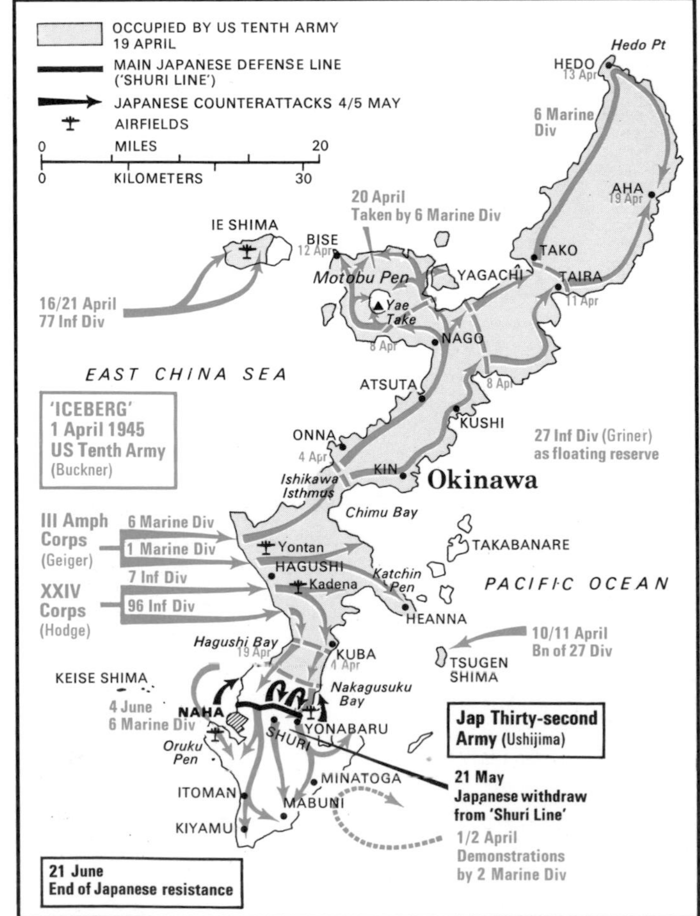

The Korean War

After Japan's surrender in 1945 the Red Army occupied the northern part of Korea and the US Army the southern. The 38th Parallel was the line of demarcation, and there was a loose understanding that North and South Korea would be reunited and elections held in the near future. US/Soviet disagreement on what constituted a free election, however, resulted in elections being held only in the South, whose new government was recognized by the United Nations. In the North the Russians established a Communist Government, backed up by a numerous and well-equipped army.

In 1949, when the Republic of Korea (ROK) seemed secure, US forces left the country. The following year the North Korean Army invaded South Korea (25 June 1950). US troops were sent in from Japan to assist ROK divisions, but they were soon forced to retreat to a small area that included the port of Pusan. Other American troops entered the fray under United Nations auspices, and were soon joined by units from other member nations, including many from Britain. Douglas MacArthur, US Commander-in-Chief, defied the advice of most colleagues and launched a successful amphibious assault at Inchon, near the 38th Parallel. This attack threatened North Korean supply lines, and Communist Forces began to withdraw. US and ROK forces then recaptured the South Korean capital of Seoul.

By now there were 50,000 US troops in Korea and more were on the way. MacArthur faced the decision of whether or not to pursue the invaders across the 38th Parallel in the face of Communist Chinese threats to intervene if UN forces approached any closer to the Yalu River – the Chinese-Korean frontier. With authorization from Washington, MacArthur moved across the parallel on 27 September and captured the North Korean capital of Pyongyang. On 26 October ROK forces reached the Yalu, but major Chinese forces crossed the river and repelled them. The Chinese then pursued UN forces south along high ground, attacking them from flank and rear. By the end of the year, UN units had retreated behind the 38th Parallel, and Seoul was lost.

Early in 1951 UN counteroffensives, bolstered by strong US air support, began to turn the tide. Seoul was recaptured in March, and the Chinese fought a costly action at the Imjin River. Long-drawn-out armistice negotiations began in July 1951 and lasted until July 1953, when an armistice was finally signed. In the interim, sporadic hostilities continued along defensive lines laid out early in the conflict. After the armistice, the two Koreas pursued their former course of separate development shaped by mutual distrust.

Bottom: The initial Communist offensives.
Right: The Inchon landings.
Below: British Marines on a coastal raid.
Bottom right: British troops relieve an American unit, Naktong River area, September 1950.

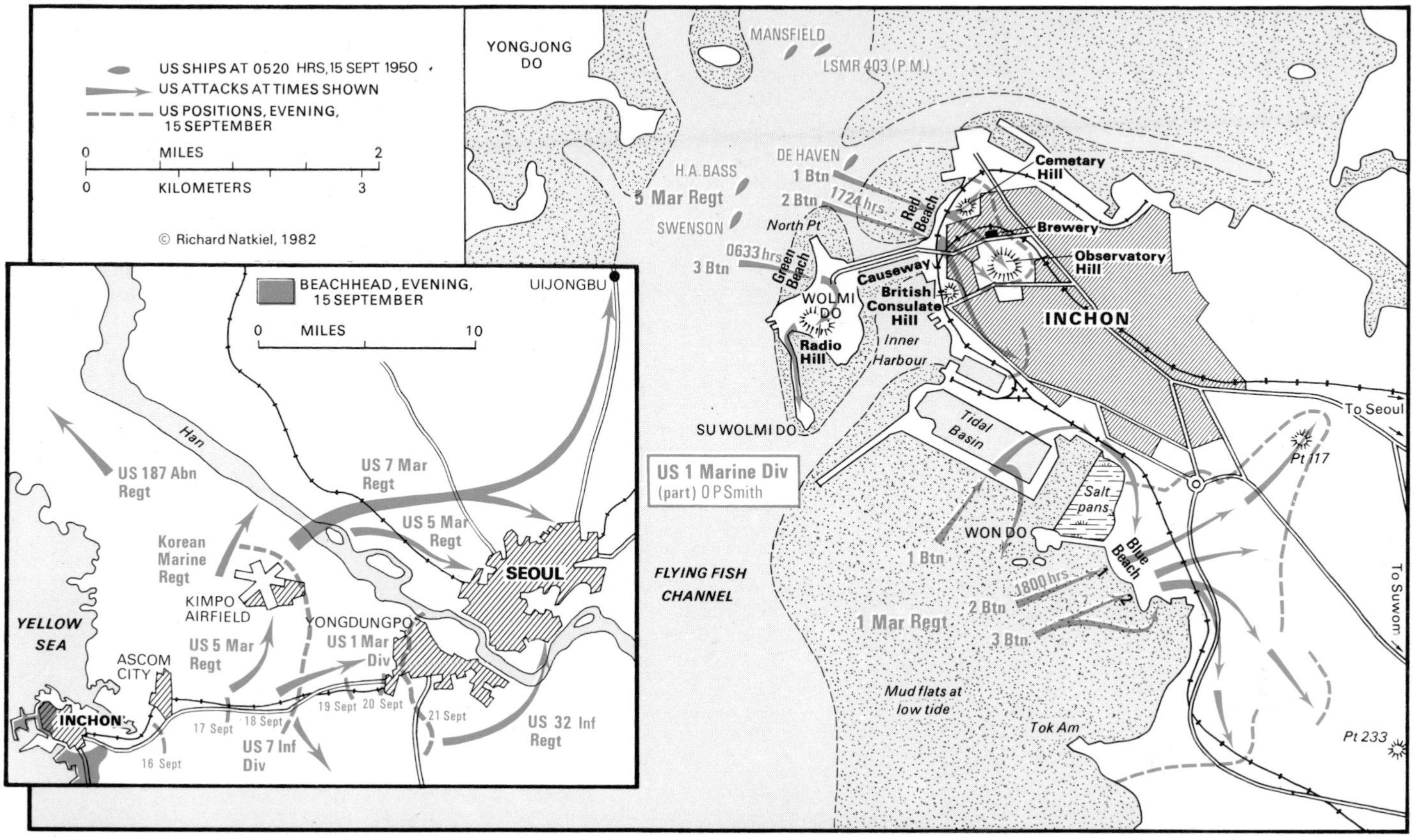
US SHIPS AT 0520 HRS, 15 SEPT 1950
US ATTACKS AT TIMES SHOWN
US POSITIONS, EVENING, 15 SEPTEMBER
0 MILES 2
0 KILOMETERS 3
© Richard Natkiel, 1982
BEACHHEAD, EVENING, 15 SEPTEMBER
0 MILES 10
UIJONGBU
Han
US 187 Abn Regt
US 7 Mar Regt
US 5 Mar Regt
Korean Marine Regt
KIMPO AIRFIELD
SEOUL
YELLOW SEA
YONGDUNGPO
US 5 Mar Regt
US 1 Mar Div
ASCOM CITY
INCHON
16 Sept
17 Sept
18 Sept
19 Sept
20 Sept
21 Sept
US 7 Inf Div
US 32 Inf Regt
YONGJONG DO
MANSFIELD
LSMR 403 (P.M.)
DE HAVEN
H.A. BASS
1 Btn
2 Btn
5 Mar Regt
1724 hrs
SWENSON
North Pt
0633 hrs
3 Btn
Green Beach
Red Beach
Cemetary Hill
Brewery
Observatory Hill
Causeway
WOLMI DO
British Consulate Hill
Radio Hill
Inner Harbour
INCHON
SU WOLMI DO
Tidal Basin
To Seoul
Pt 117
US 1 Marine Div
(part) O P Smith
Salt pans
WON DO
1 Btn
Blue Beach
FLYING FISH CHANNEL
1800 hrs
2 Btn
1 Mar Regt
3 Btn
To Suwon
Mud flats at low tide
Tok Am
Pt 233

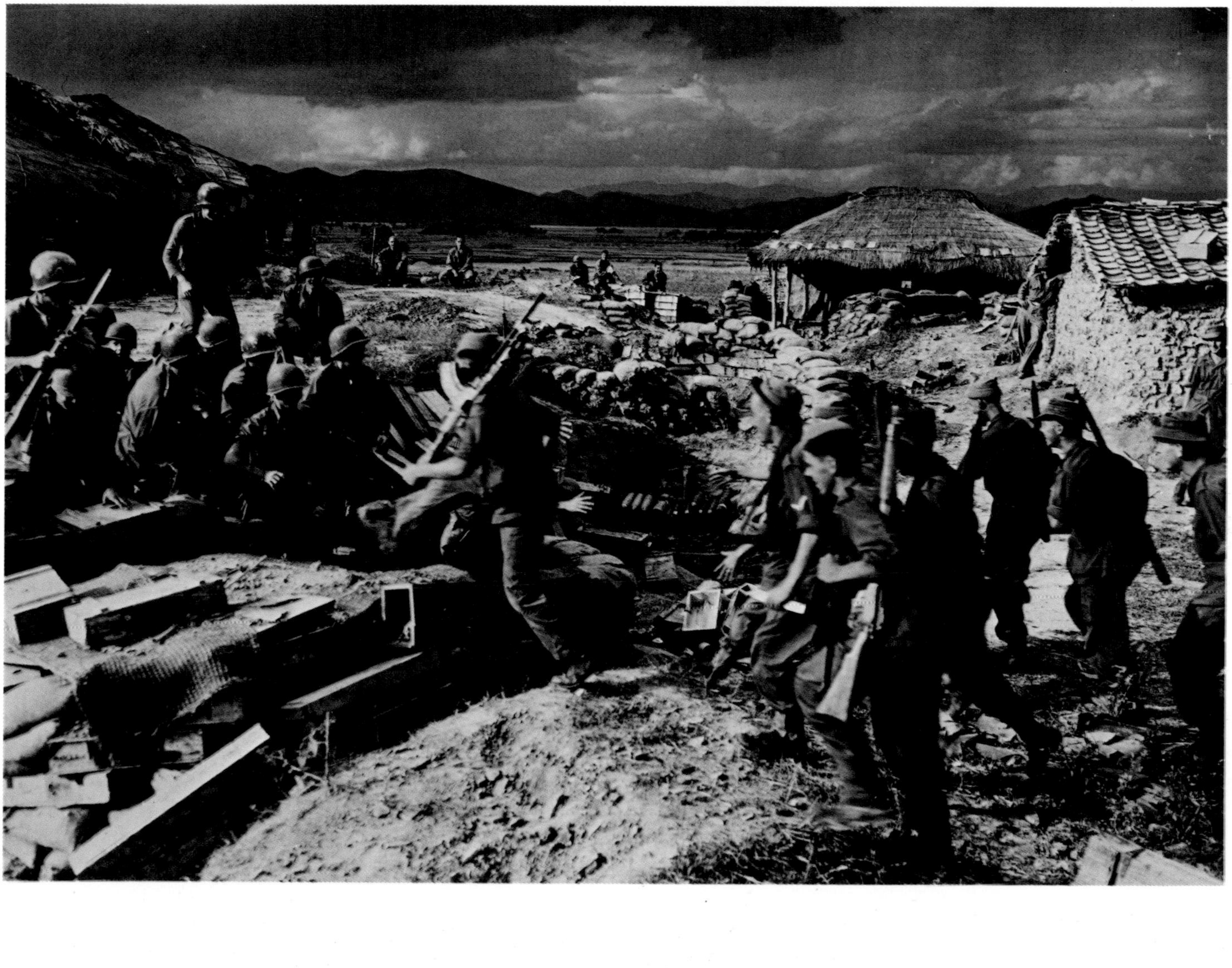

FRONT LINES
23 OCT, 1950
6 NOV
24 NOV
UN ATTACKS
AND SORTIES
—xxxx— UN COMMAND BOUNDARY
CHINESE ARMY IS EQUIVALENT TO UN CORPS
0 MILES 50
0 KILOMETERS 80

C H I N A
N O R T H K O R E A
Ch 9th Army Group
Ch 13th Army Group
Ch XXVII Army
Ch XXVI Army
Ch XX Army
Ch XXXVIII Army
Ch XXXIX Army
Ch XL Army
Ch LXVI Army
Ch XLII Army
Ch L Army
CHUCHANGGANGGU
HYSANJIN
MANPOJIN
KANGGYE
CHOSAN
PYOKTONG
KOJONG
MUPYONG
HAGARU
KOTO
HUICHON
ONJONG
UNSAN
SINUIJU
CHONGJU
KUNU-RI
TOKCHON
YONGWON
ANJU
SINANJU
SUKCHON
SUNCHON
YANGDOK
PYONGYANG
WONSAN
HAMHUNG
HUNGNAM
IWON
PUNGSAN
SONGJIN
KILCHU
YONGBAN
Yalu
Changjin
Choshin Res
Fusen Res
Chongchon
Kuryong
Taedong
26 Oct
ROK 6 Div
ROK 8 Div
ROK 3 Div
ROK Cap Div
7 Div
1 Marine Div
24 Div
IX Corps
ROK II Corps
I Corps
X Corps (Almond)
Eighth Army (Walker)
29 Oct 7 Div lands,
1 Marine Div lands, 26 Oct
SEA OF JAPAN
YELLOW SEA

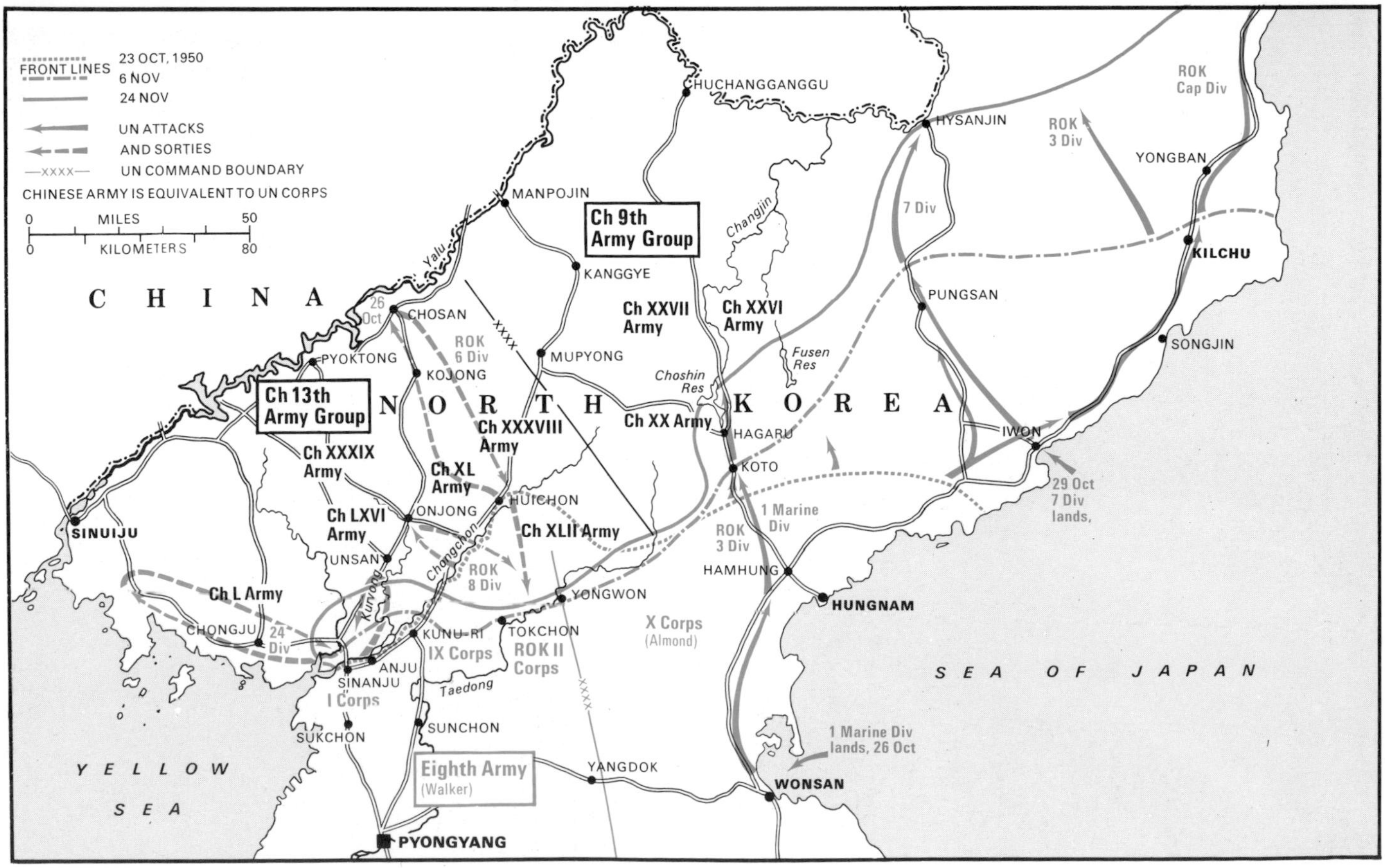

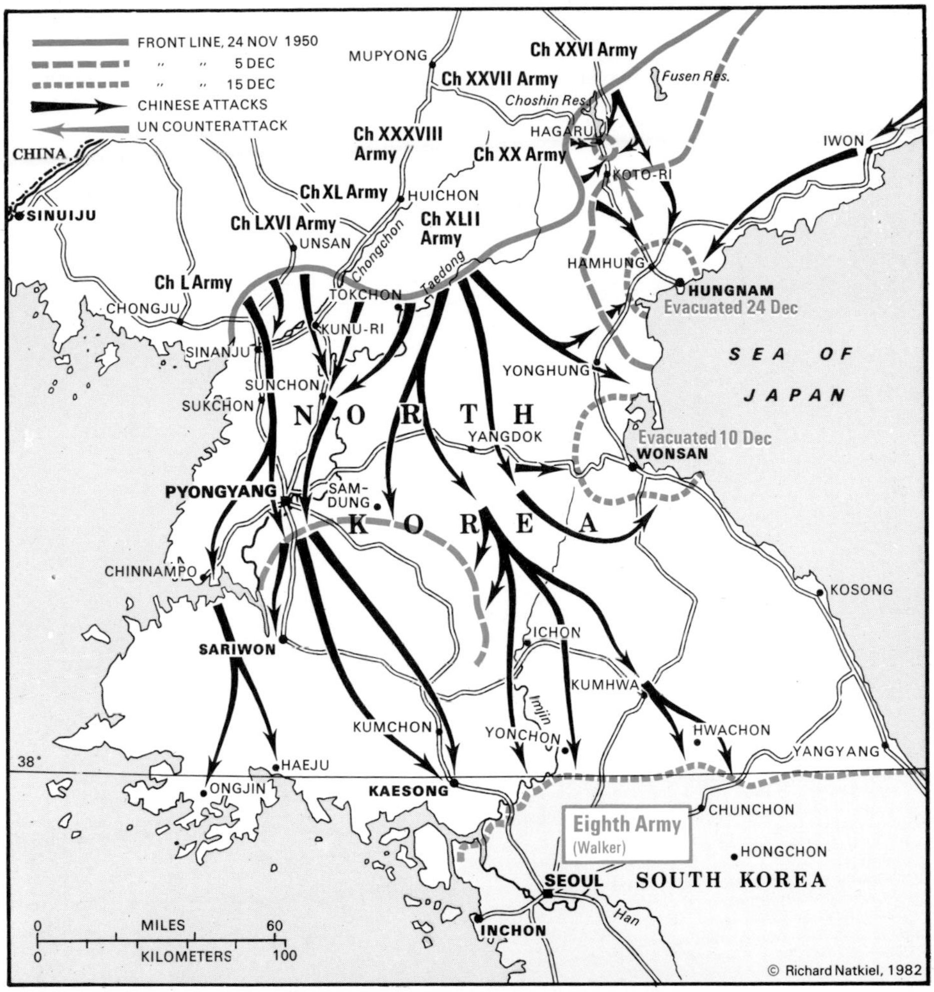

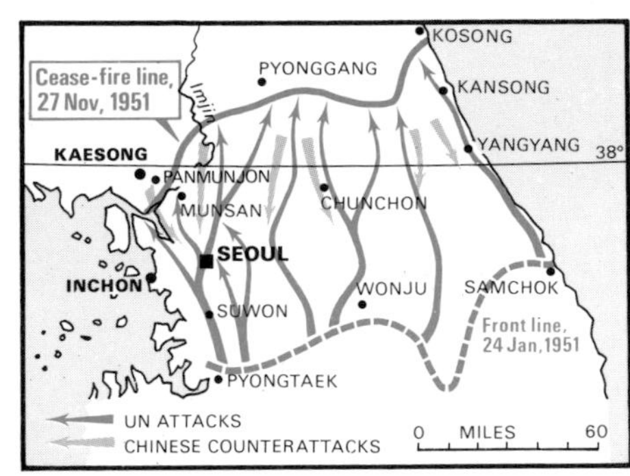

Opposite, top: Men of the US 35 Infantry watch an air attack on Communist positions in February 1951.
Opposite, bottom: The Allied advance into the North after the Inchon landings and the breakout from the Pusan perimeter.
Left: The Chinese retaliation.
Above: The final major changes on the front.
Below: British troops man an outpost overlooking the Imjin River early in 1952.

Dien Bien Phu

The long struggle between the French and the Communist-led Viet Minh in French Indochina took a new turn in 1953 when General Giap's forces invaded a new French territory adjacent to Vietnam – Laos. Having made his point by drawing in a host of French troops, Giap withdrew, but the French expected his early return. The settlement of Dien Bien Phu was selected as a strongpoint, fortified in a rudimentary way and garrisoned with French troops. When the Viet Minh did renew their attack (March 1954), there were about 18,000 defenders at Dien Bien Phu, of whom some

Right: Discussions on the repatriation of French prisoners of war.
Opposite, top left: The areas of Communist activity during the war with the French.
Opposite, right: The Battle of Dien Bien Phu.
Opposite, bottom: A French representative announces the fall of Dien Bien Phu to a press conference in Geneva. The Viet Minh success made the outcome of the Geneva peace conference certain.
Below: French prisoners captured at Dien Bien Phu.

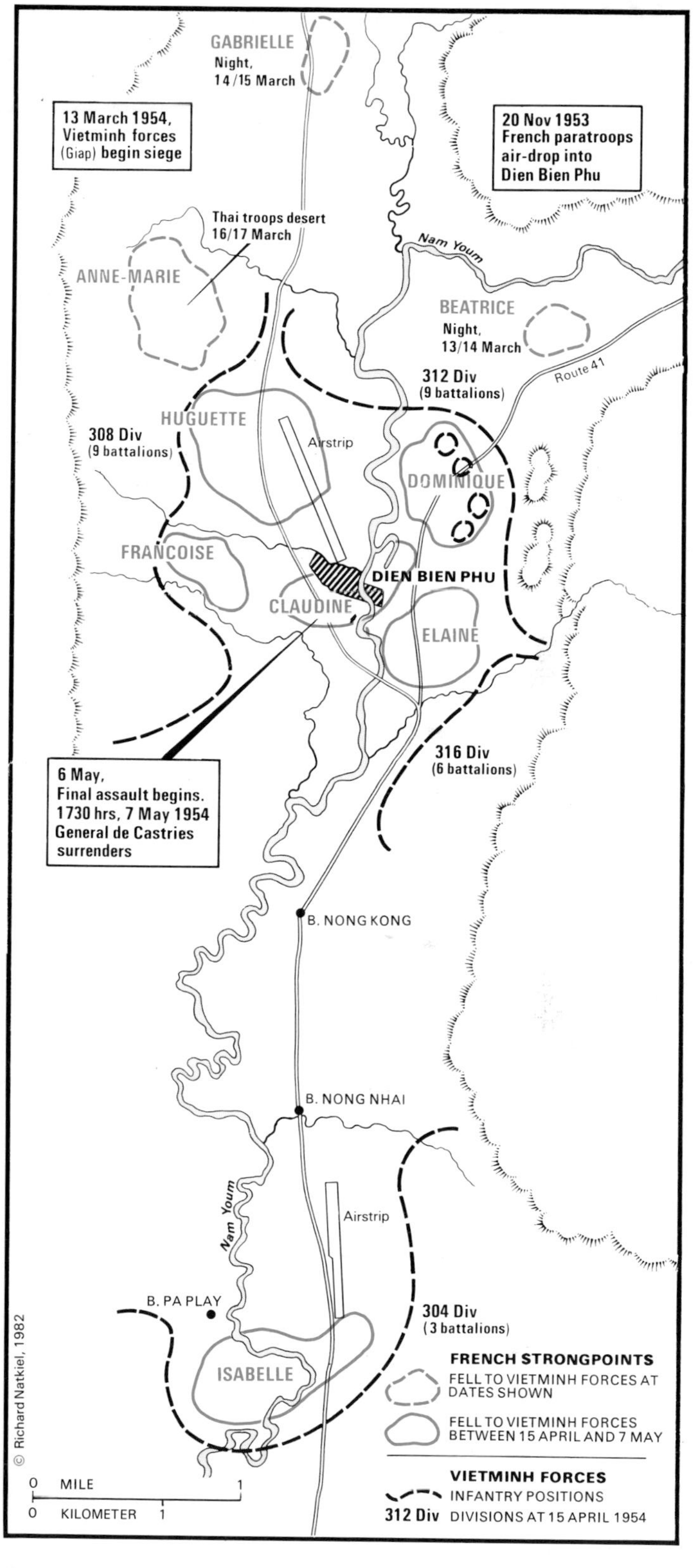

3000 were of the French Foreign Legion and the balance colonial troops.

The Viet Minh had an overwhelming advantage in numbers and in artillery, supplied in part by the Chinese. Once Dien Bien Phu was surrounded, its airstrip became unusable on account of Communist antiaircraft emplacements. Supplies could come in only by parachute, at considerable risk of their loss or destruction, and the wounded could not be evacuated. The fortress was commanded by several nearby hills, which the Communists captured and used to good advantage in bombarding the area and launching successive attacks. The defense was heroic, but defeat was inevitable: the Viet Minh broke in on 7 May and General de Castries surrendered.

By this time the Geneva Conference to end the war in Indochina was already in progress. The French agreed to provisional formation of a Viet Minh North Vietnam and a French-oriented South Vietnam; internationally supervised elections were to be held in both areas within two years (a prospect that never materialized). Cambodia and Laos were recognized as independent of French rule, and the stage was set for continuing conflict that smolders on to the present day.

Suez, 1956

After the Arab-Israeli War of 1948–49, border battles, guerrilla activity and terrorism continued. In 1955 Egypt's President Nasser, having secured by agreement the evacuation of British troops from the Suez Canal Zone, announced that the canal would be closed to Israeli commerce. This was followed by Egypt's declaration that ships using the Israeli port of Eilat might be shelled by guns commanding the Tiran Strait; soon after, a British steamer was hit. The Israeli Government decided on a counterstroke.

Right: Israeli Chief of Staff, Moshe Dayan, inspects troops after the capture of Sharm el Sheikh.
Opposite, top: The Anglo-French and Israeli attacks.
Opposite, bottom: Israeli troops in the Sinai.
Below: Israeli Sherman tank in the Sinai, 2 November 1956.

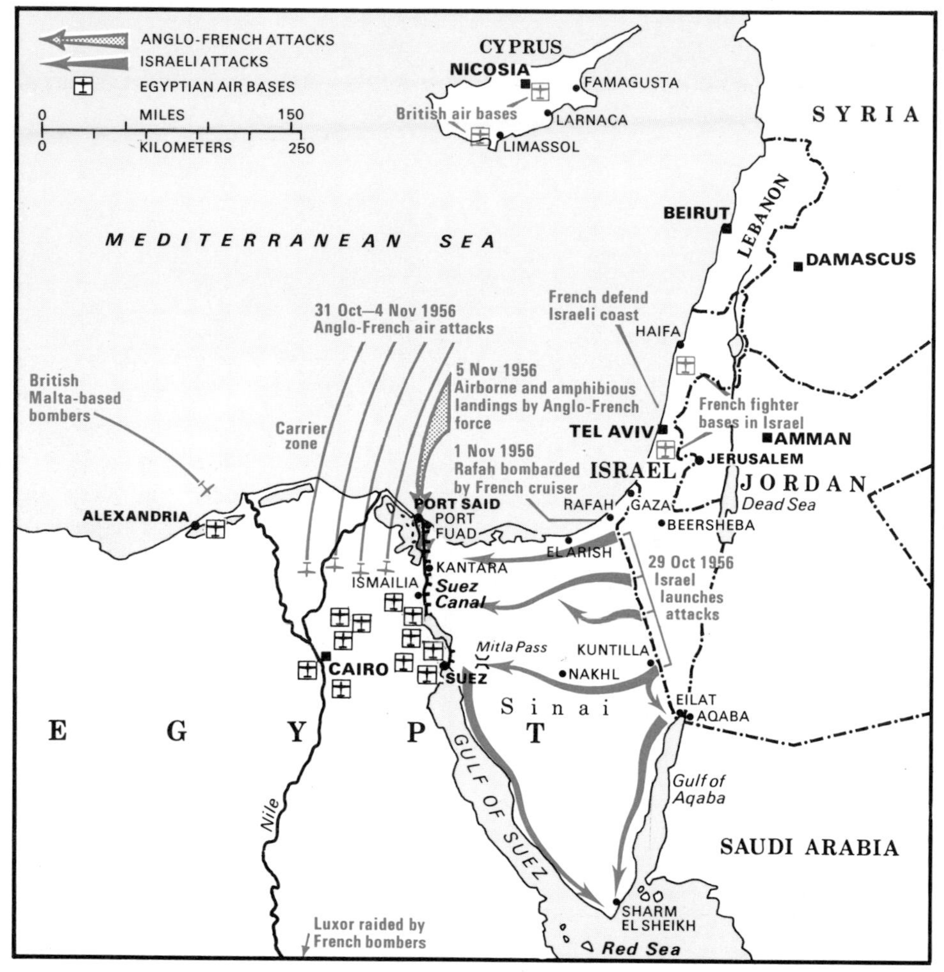

Meanwhile, Nasser turned for armaments to the Eastern bloc when the US and Britain refused to supply them. As a result, the two Western powers withdrew their offer of help to Egypt for the Aswan Dam project. In retaliation Nasser announced the nationalization of the Suez Canal. This action was seen as a threat to international commerce, and was a body blow to France and Britain, the principal shareholders. They evolved, with Israel, a plan for the invasion of Sinai and the Canal Zone.

Israel began hostilities on 29 October 1956, upon which Britain and France announced that they would forcibly occupy the Canal Zone to preserve it from possible damage in the course of the Israeli-Egyptian conflict. Anglo-French forces had little difficulty in getting ashore near Port Said and advancing down the Canal: Egyptian forces were already demoralized by Israeli victories in the Sinai Desert. However, the US, which had taken a dim view of the Anglo-French invasion throughout, prevailed upon the United Nations to intervene: Britain and France were pressured into stopping their advance and then into withdrawing (December 1956). Meanwhile, the Suez Canal had been blocked by sunken ships and was out of operation for several months. More lasting was the damage inflicted on British and French prestige in the Middle East.

The Six Day War, 1967

Israel's strategic position did not improve after the short-lived Suez War despite her successes in Sinai (subsequently occupied by a United Nations peacekeeping force). A new regime in Iraq dropped out of the Western-sponsored Baghdad Pact in 1959 to ally itself with Egypt. Other Arab countries besides Egypt were now receiving both armaments and diplomatic support from the Soviet Union. The Suez Canal had remained shut to Israeli commerce, and Egyptian artillery covered the Gulf of Aqaba. Palestinian refugees remained unsettled and presented a threat to Israel's security, especially along the Syrian border where the Golan Heights served as a position for frequent Syrian bombardment of Israeli settlements.

In May 1967 Egypt deployed its army on the frontier with Israel and at Sharm el Sheikh, with the claim that Israel was about

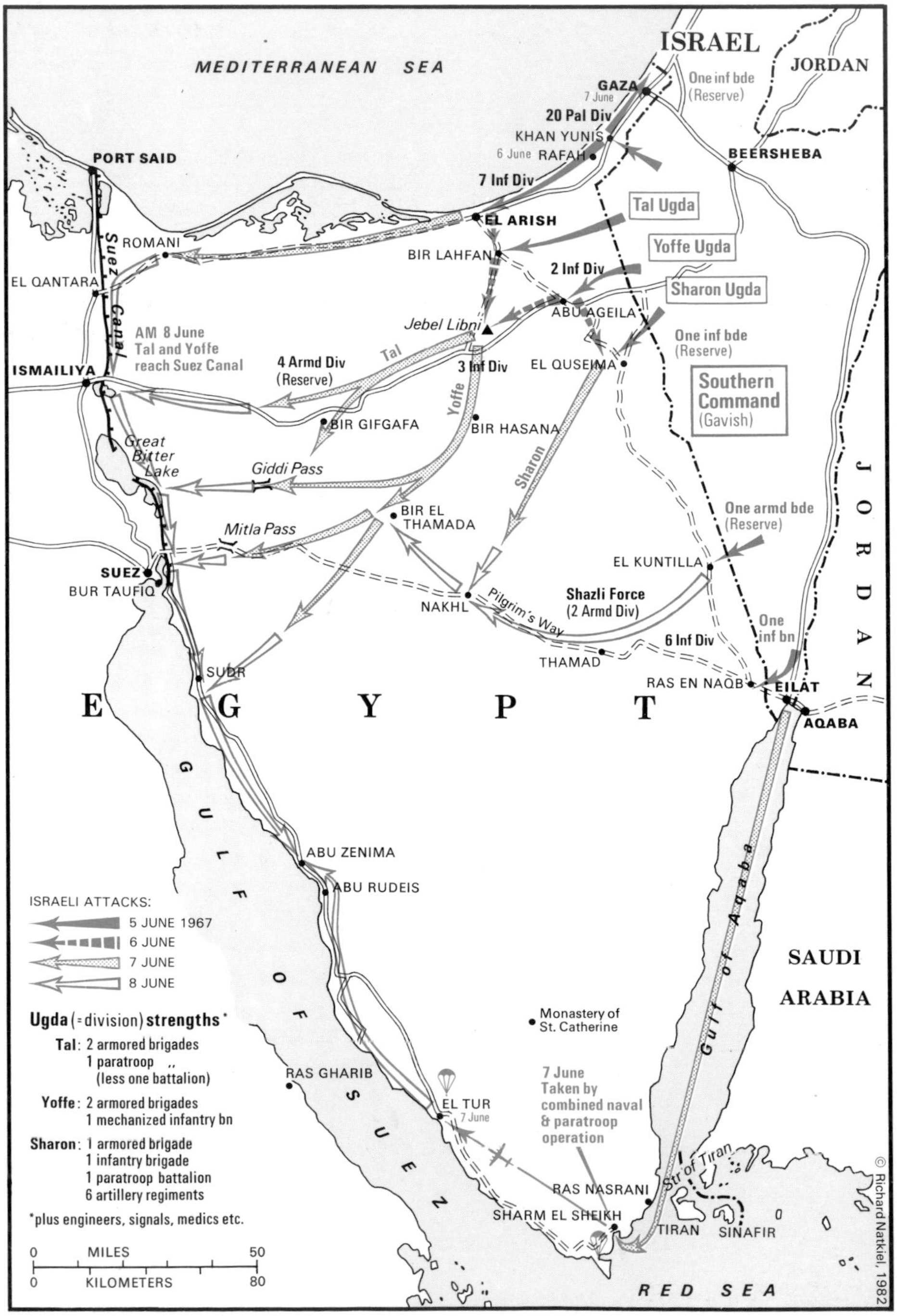

Below left: As well as having complete air superiority, the Israeli ground forces were much better trained which, in the ideal tank country of the Sinai, ensured their rapid victory.
Below: A Syrian tank knocked out in the fighting in the Golan Heights.

Below: Although the Jordanian forces fought rather more effectively than many of their allies, the Israeli victory was equally quick here.
Bottom left: Israeli tanks going into action near Rafah, in the Sinai.

to take reprisals against Syria. The United Nations was asked to remove its 3000-man peacekeeping force from Sinai, and consented to do so. Egypt's Nasser and other Arab leaders appeared to be collaborating on an imminent attack against Israel, which appealed to the United Nations and other powers to no avail: reassurances were not forthcoming. Before the month was out, Iraq, Jordan, Syria and Saudi Arabia had deployed their forces along Israeli frontiers and Egypt had closed the Strait of Tiran to Israeli shipping.

At the beginning of June the surrounded nation saw itself outnumbered on the frontiers by three to one and launched a pre-emptive attack (5 June) that destroyed Egyptian air bases as far afield as Cairo and Luxor. Having seized immediate command of the air, Israeli forces routed the Egyptian army in Sinai in three days' time. On 9 June the Syrian Golan Heights were assaulted

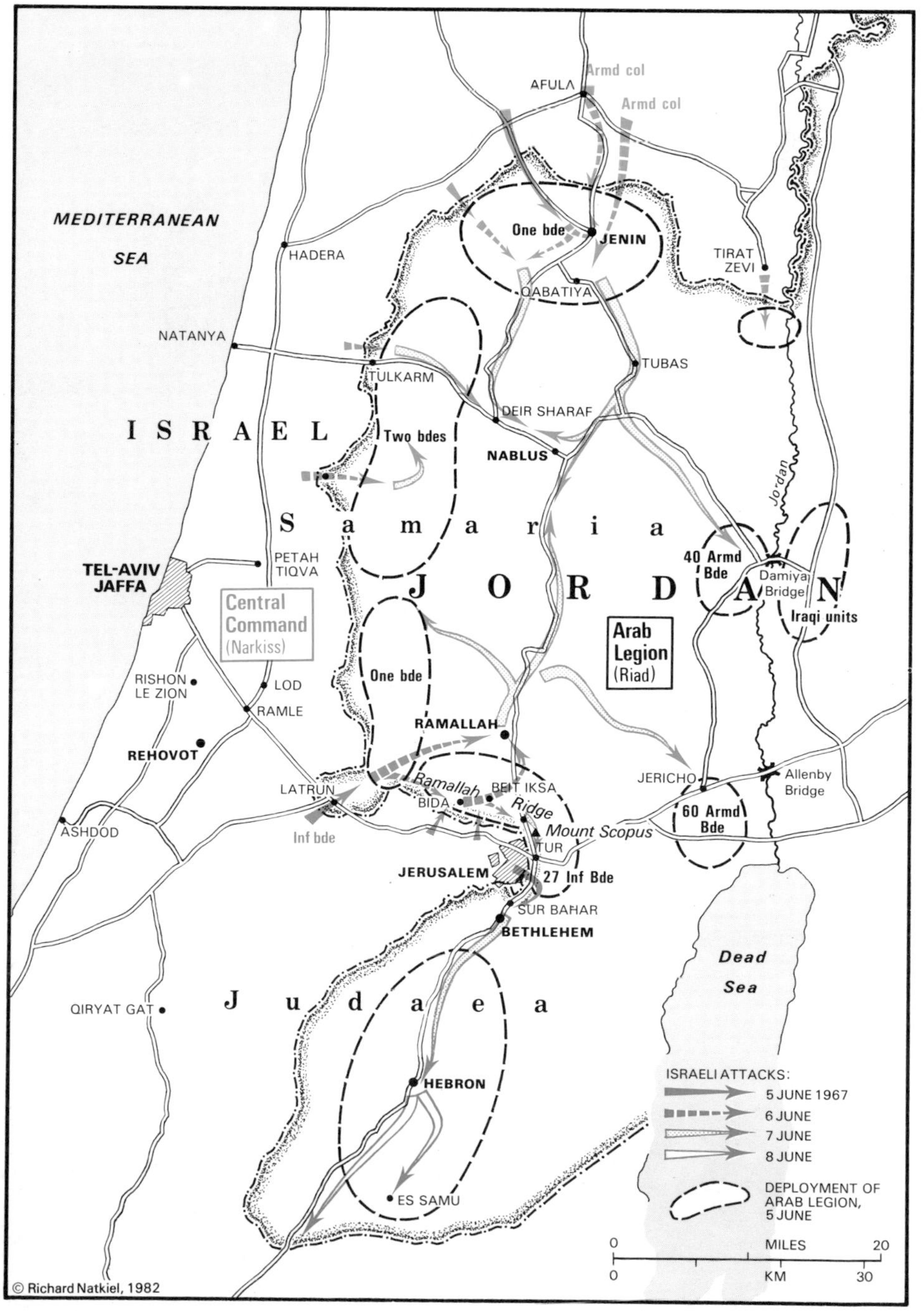

MEDITERRANEAN SEA
AFULA
Armd col
Armd col
One bde
JENIN
TIRAT ZEVI
HADERA
QABATIYA
NATANYA
TUBAS
TULKARM
DEIR SHARAF
ISRAEL
Two bdes
NABLUS
Samaria
Jordan
JORDAN
40 Armd Bde
Damiya Bridge
Iraqi units
TEL-AVIV JAFFA
PETAH TIQVA
Central Command (Narkiss)
Arab Legion (Riad)
One bde
RISHON LE ZION
LOD
RAMLE
RAMALLAH
REHOVOT
LATRUN
BEIT IKSA
Ramallah Ridge
BIDA
JERICHO
Allenby Bridge
60 Armd Bde
Mount Scopus
TUR
ASHDOD
Inf bde
JERUSALEM
27 Inf Bde
SUR BAHAR
BETHLEHEM
Dead Sea
QIRYAT GAT
Judaea
HEBRON
ES SAMU
ISRAELI ATTACKS:
5 JUNE 1967
6 JUNE
7 JUNE
8 JUNE
DEPLOYMENT OF ARAB LEGION, 5 JUNE
0 MILES 20
0 KM 30
© Richard Natkiel, 1982

and soon captured; the Jordanians were thrown back from west of the Jordan and in Jerusalem. Cease-fire agreements were concluded within a week of the 5 June surprise attack, leaving all of Sinai in Israeli hands, along with the West Bank of the Jordan and the Golan Heights. The confident and well-trained Israeli forces had performed brilliantly but no political settlement was in sight.

Right: Israeli troops on the east bank of the Suez canal near Ismailia in July 1967 shortly after their victory in the Six Day War.
Below: The Israeli successes in the Golan Heights sector in 1967.

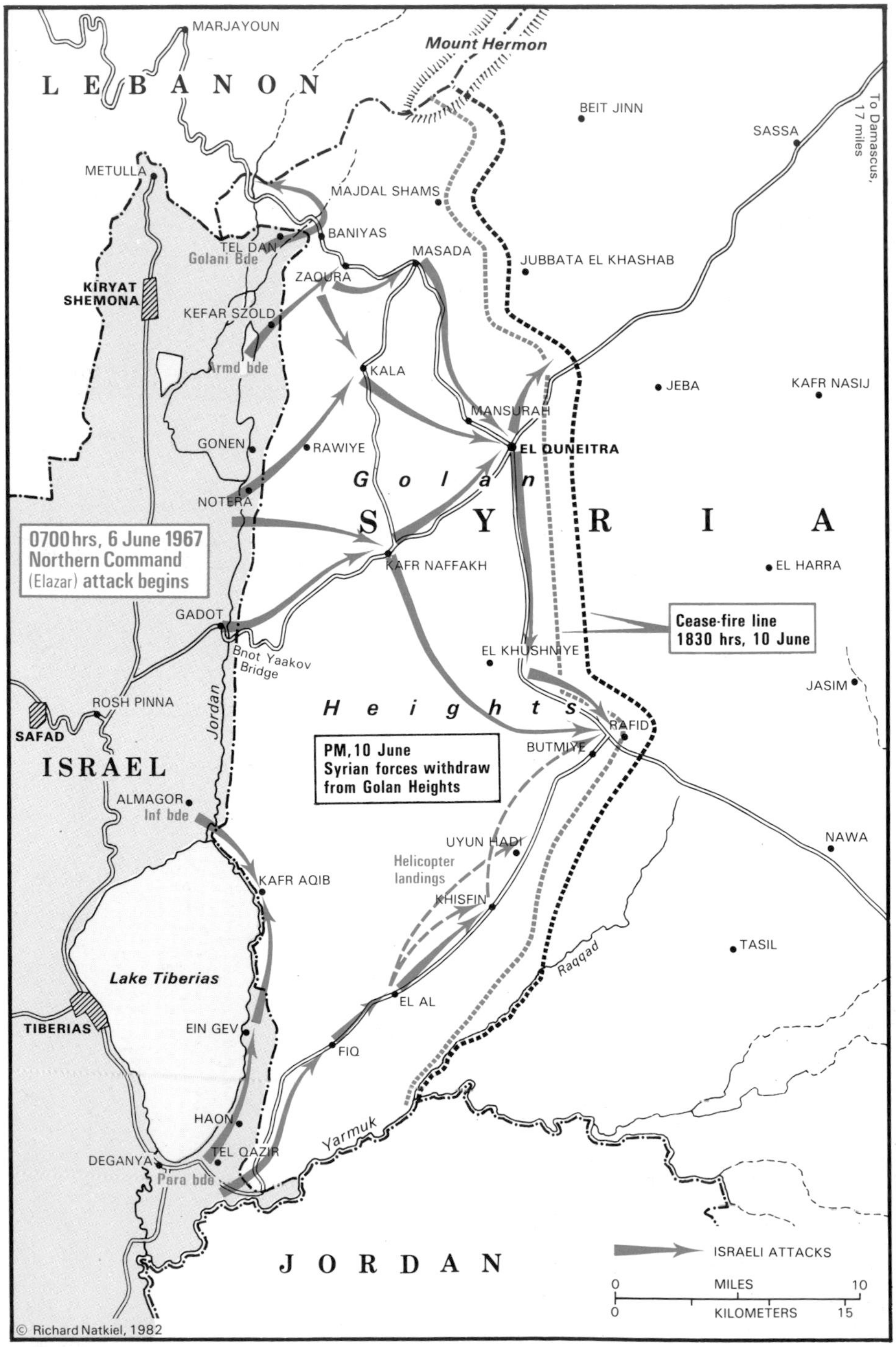

LEBANON
SYRIA
ISRAEL
JORDAN
Golan Heights
Mount Hermon
MARJAYOUN
METULLA
TEL DAN
Golani Bde
BANIYAS
MAJDAL SHAMS
BEIT JINN
SASSA
To Damascus, 17 miles
KIRYAT SHEMONA
KEFAR SZOLD
ZAOURA
MASADA
JUBBATA EL KHASHAB
Armd bde
KALA
MANSURAH
JEBA
KAFR NASIJ
GONEN
RAWIYE
EL QUNEITRA
NOTERA
0700hrs, 6 June 1967
Northern Command
(Elazar) attack begins
KAFR NAFFAKH
EL HARRA
GADOT
Bnot Yaakov Bridge
Cease-fire line
1830 hrs, 10 June
EL KHUSHNIYE
JASIM
ROSH PINNA
SAFAD
Jordan
RAFID
BUTMIYE
PM, 10 June
Syrian forces withdraw
from Golan Heights
ALMAGOR
Inf bde
UYUN HADI
NAWA
KAFR AQIB
Helicopter landings
KHISFIN
TASIL
Raqqad
Lake Tiberias
EL AL
TIBERIAS
EIN GEV
FIQ
HAON
Yarmuk
DEGANYA
TEL QAZIR
Para bde
ISRAELI ATTACKS
0 MILES 10
0 KILOMETERS 15

The Vietnam War

The Vietnam War lasted for 30 years. The French involvement lasted for 10, and the American for 20 more. After World War II the French attempted to re-establish the position they had held before the war, but the independence movement under the Communist leader Ho Chi Minh held sway among many of the peasants, particularly in the northern part of the country. While holding on to all the major cities, factories, mines and most of the rich agricultural land, the hills belonged to the Viet Minh, who dominated some of the peasant villages at night. Several attempts to crush this indigenous guerrilla force were made half-heartedly by the French Government, whose main efforts were concentrated on rebuilding the metropole from the ravages of war and occupation. The French will to retain their former colony collapsed when the Foreign Legion lost the Battle of Dien Bien Phu in 1954 to the guerrillas of Vo Nguyen Giap, commander-in-chief of the Viet Minh. The Geneva Conference of 1954 divided French Indo-China into four parts. The French agreed to withdraw from their strongholds in the north, Hanoi and Haiphong, and their allies, once led by the retired Emperor of Annam, Bao Dai, regrouped in the south. The northern section became the Democratic Republic of Vietnam, backed initially by China and the Soviet Union, led by Ho Chi Minh. It was separated from the south by the 17th parallel, below which the Republic of Vietnam was created, under its new president, Ngo Dinh Diem. The other two parts were the Kingdom of Laos and the Principality of Cambodia, later to become a republic under its former Prince, Norodom Sihanouk. The King of Laos ruled but did not reign, and Prince Souvanna Phouma became sometime-Premier throughout the period following 1954.

The South Vietnamese seemed fairly secure under the vague umbrella of the Southeast Asia Treaty Organization (SEATO), but the United States was its principal supporter. North Vietnam took time to absorb its newly gained territory, but incursions into South Vietnam began as early as the mid-1950s. By 1961 their penetration of the south via the Ho Chi Minh Trail, a series of routes through the mountains of Laos and Cambodia along the South Vietnamese border, became severe enough for President Kennedy to order military 'advisers' in from the United States to aid the Republic. These advisory groups often led South Vietnamese troops into battle, and by the time Diem and Kennedy were killed, both in the fall of 1963, some 16,000 American troops were in the south.

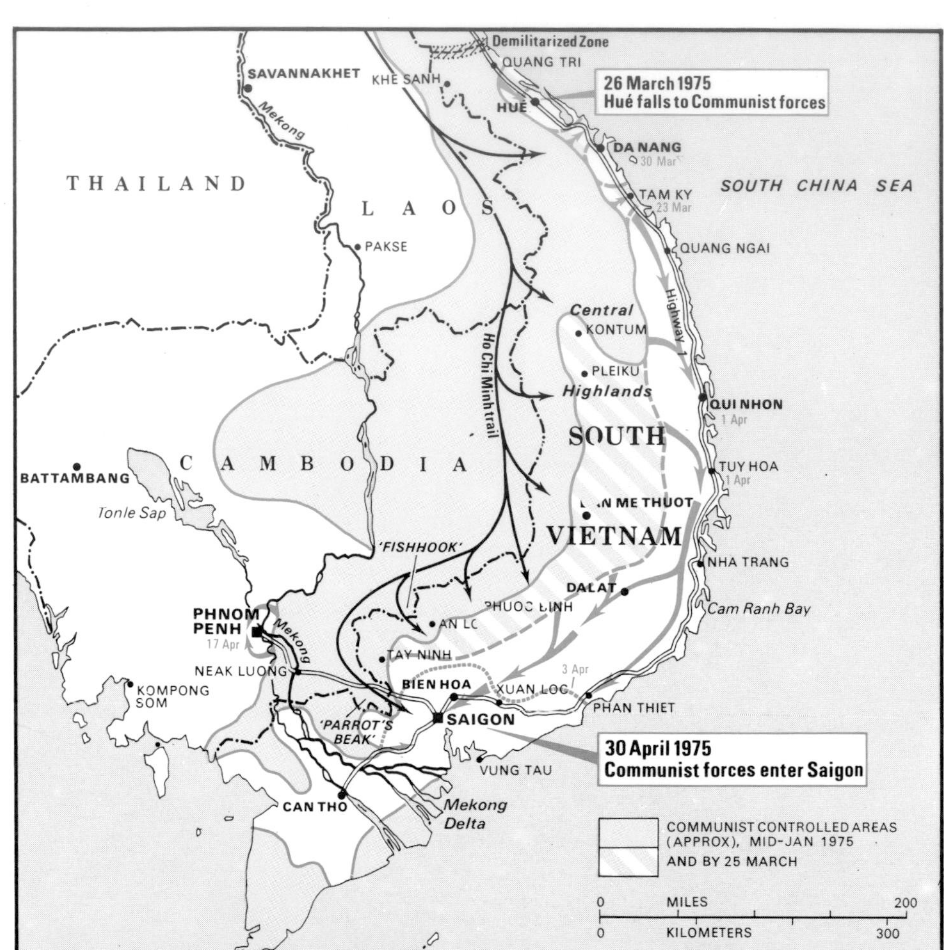

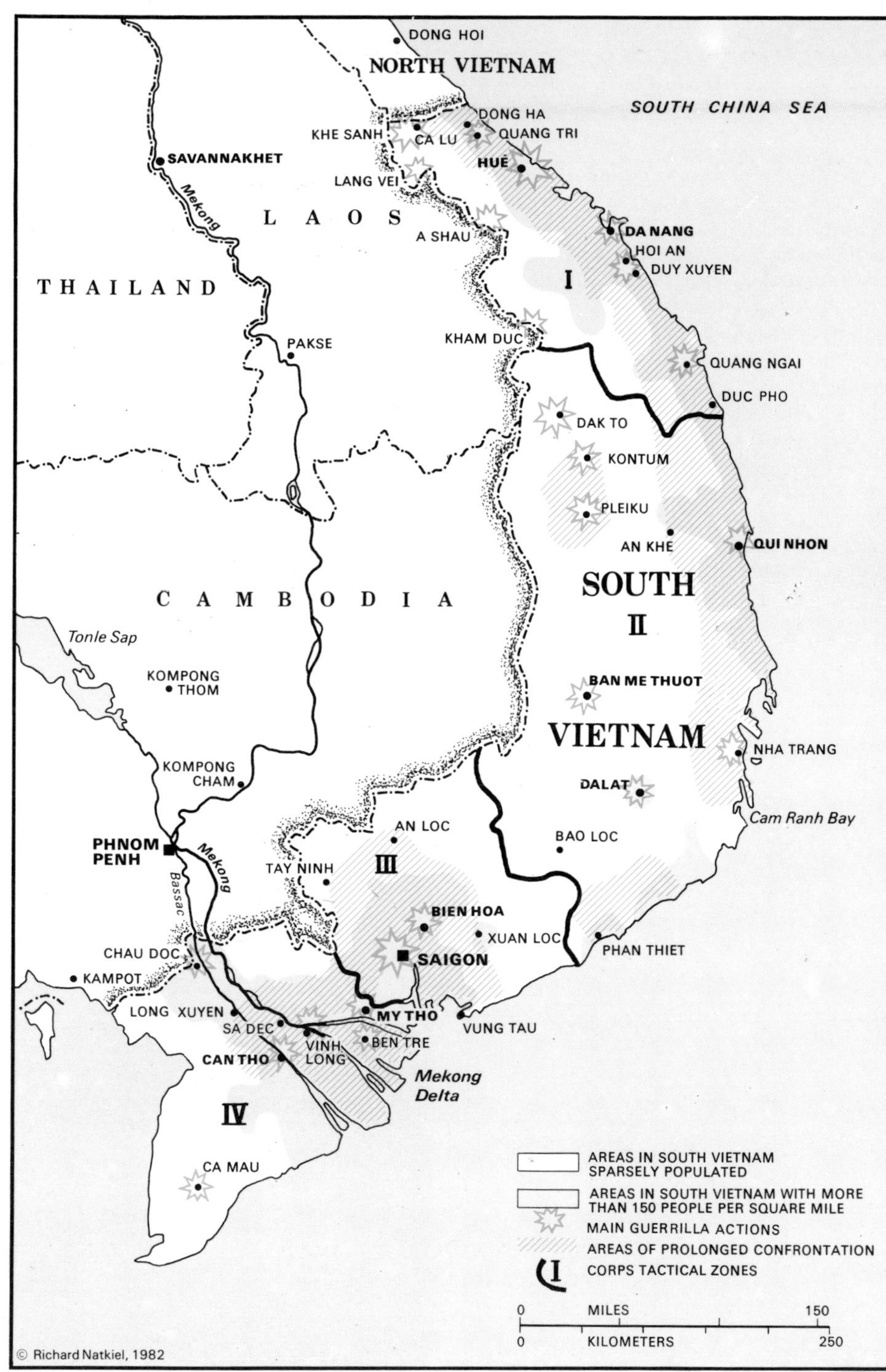

Above left: The final Communist offensives which overran South Vietnam and led to the humiliating evacuation of American personnel and sympathizers from Saigon.
Left: An American patrol boat at work in the Mekong Delta area in 1969.
Above: The situation during the American involvement.

President Johnson opted to escalate the American role, so that, by 1968, over a half million Americans were stationed in South Vietnam and had taken over the bulk of the fighting.

During the Asian New Year's holiday of Tet, in late January 1968, the Viet Cong, as they were now styled, launched the Tet Offensive against all American positions in Vietnam. The embassy in Saigon was attacked, as were most of the American airfields. Saigon almost fell to the Viet Cong, and Hué did fall. The Americans fought valiantly to regain lost territory, and retook Hué after a long and bloody fight. The Viet Cong sacrificed tens of thousands of men and most of their arms, suffering a defeat which threw back their advance for years. But the American people saw the Tet Offensive as a symbol of their frustration at not winning the war quickly and totally.

President Johnson was obliged not to run again for president, and his successor in office, Richard Nixon, had the wholehearted support of the American people in 'Vietnamizing' the war, which meant a gradual American withdrawal from the territory while strengthening the weak South Vietnamese armed forces. By 1973 most Americans had left Vietnam, but the Viet Cong had increased its hold over much of the countryside of South Vietnam. When the Watergate crisis brought down the Nixon presidency in August 1974, the American Congress refused to vote further assistance to the South Vietnamese. When it became clear to North Vietnam that there would be no further American resistance, they launched a major offensive which brought about the fall of the whole of South Vietnam in late April 1975. The United States suffered a severe international humiliation, and Vietnam was united under the Communists.

In the following months Cambodia and Laos both fell to the Communists. In the case of Laos, a regime which was a mere puppet of Hanoi took power. In Cambodia a Chinese-backed Communist regime took over and millions of Cambodians were slaughtered. By this time Communist Vietnam was a client state of the Soviet Union. Even as it tried to rebuild its shattered cities and villages, which had been bombarded for years by American aircraft, North Vietnam began guerrilla incursions into Thailand, which still go on unabated. Pockets of resistance to the Communists continue to function in South Vietnam and Laos, playing a role similar to that which the Viet Cong and Viet Minh had held previously.

The Vietnam War was one of the longest and most bloody wars of the 20th century. American hegemony in the world was broken by the conflict, and the American public's willingness to support foreign adventures waned considerably. The results affected the American position throughout the world. SEATO collapsed, NATO was considerably weakened, and Soviet incursions by their surrogate, Cuba, in Angola, Grenada, Nicaragua and elsewhere, as well as a direct Soviet invasion of Afghanistan, went ahead without much difficulty. From the fall of Saigon in 1975 to the American invasion of Grenada in 1983, the Americans were, in effect, impotent internationally, as the hostage crisis in Iran in 1980–81 amply proved. The Vietnam War will be seen by future historians as a watershed in American history, as significant in the 1960s and 1970s as the Boer War was to the British Empire at the turn of the 20th century.

The October War, 1973

Six years of tension succeeded the Six-Day War in the Middle East. Both Arabs and Israelis resorted to terrorist attacks and counterattacks punctuated by an occasional air battle over the disputed frontiers. By 1973 Egypt's President Anwar Sadat had strengthened his army at Soviet expense, then invited Soviet military advisers to leave the country so as to have a free hand for his military ambitions.

On 6 October 1973 (Yom Kippur, the Jewish Day of Atonement), Egyptian and Syrian forces launched a surprise attack on Israel to regain the 1967 frontiers. The advantage of surprise enabled the Egyptians to cross the Suez Canal and throw Israeli forces in Sinai into confusion. The Israelis were also thrown back in the north, where they lost much of the Golan Heights. Egypt and Syria were soon reinforced by Iraq, Jordan, Kuwait, Saudi Arabia, Morocco and Algeria. Meanwhile, the US airlifted military supplies to Israel, which was again outnumbered by about three to one. The Soviet Union was sending supplies to Egypt and Syria.

By 10 October the Israelis had gained

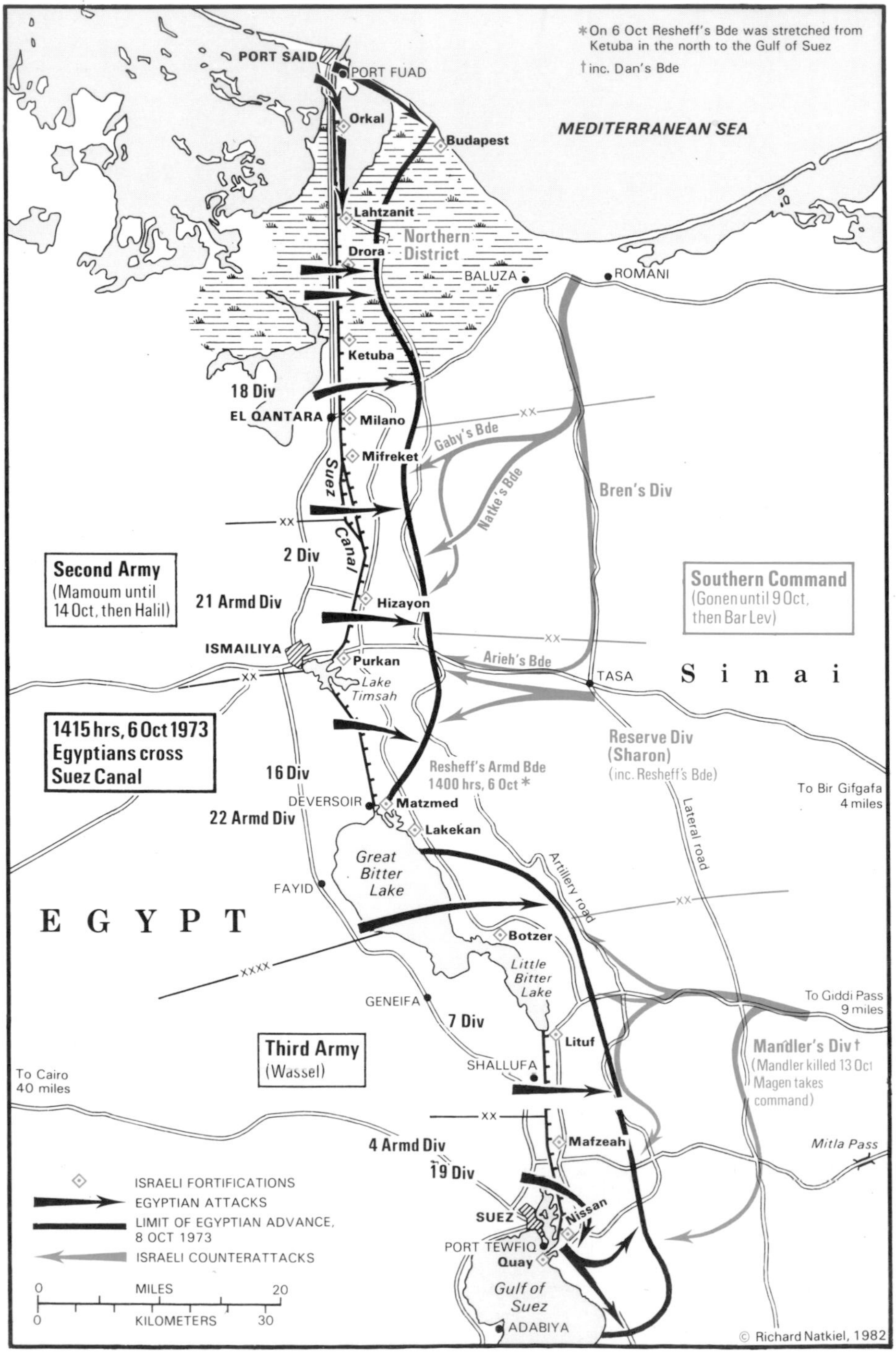

Right: Israeli tanks advance, Sinai, 9 October 1973.
Below left: The initial Egyptian attacks in the October War. One of the factors in the early Egyptian success was their effective use of anti-aircraft missiles of new types to prevent air attacks by the superior Israeli air force. The Israelis soon modified their equipment and tactics however.
Below: Knocked-out Syrian T62 tanks on the Golan front.
Below right: The Israeli counteroffensive across the Suez Canal.

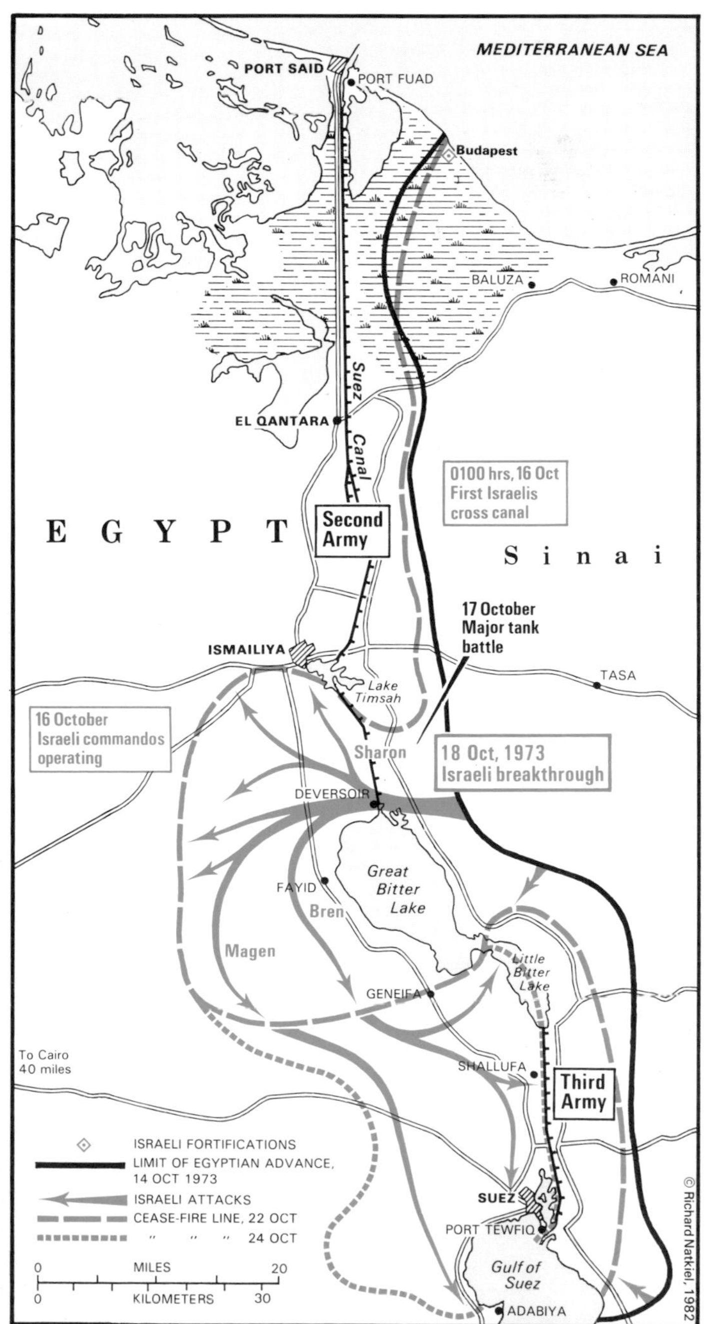

ground against the Syrians in the north and were holding their own in Sinai. A counter-offensive against the Syrians pushed back their defense line but avoided a threat to Damascus; it was feared this would bring the Soviet Union actively into the war on behalf of her protégé Syria. On the Suez Front, Egyptian tanks were baffled in their attempt to push eastward toward the Mitla Pass and were soon in rapid retreat from Israeli armor and aircraft.

This victory encouraged Israeli generals to aim a counterblow across the Suez Canal in the Great Bitter Lake region. A bridgehead was established there despite stiff Egyptian resistance, and subsequently enlarged until the Egyptian Third Army was effectively isolated. A USSR delegation to Cairo realized that Egypt faced total defeat, and with US and Soviet help the United Nations Security Council arranged a cease-fire as of 24 October.

UN forces returned to Sinai in their peace-keeping role, as Israeli troops withdrew east of the passes. The Egyptians remained on the right bank of the Suez Canal, but the UN buffer zone ensured both sides of early warning against a new surprise attack.

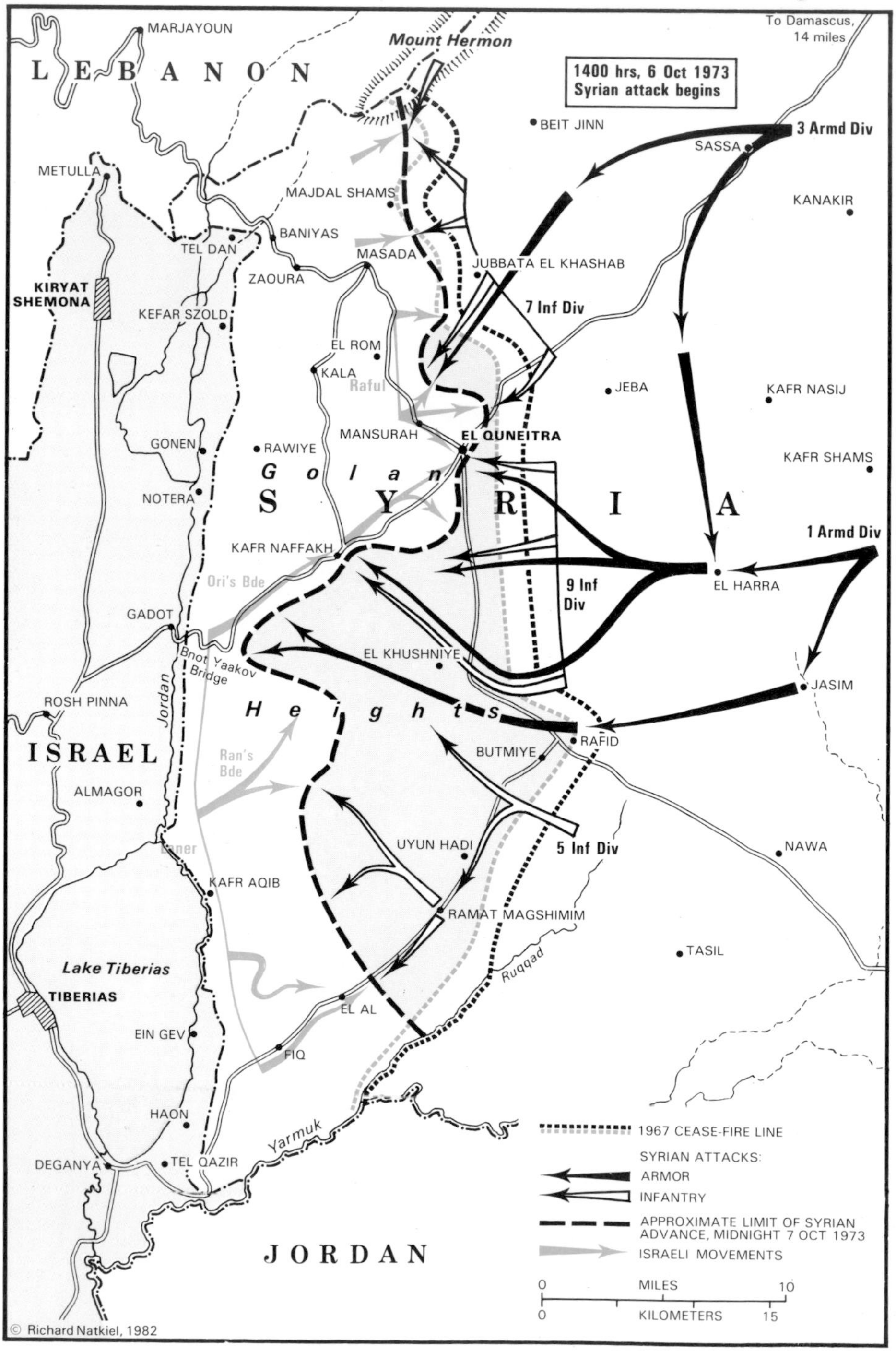

1400 hrs, 6 Oct 1973
Syrian attack begins

LEBANON
MARJAYOUN
Mount Hermon
To Damascus, 14 miles
BEIT JINN
SASSA
3 Armd Div
METULLA
MAJDAL SHAMS
KANAKIR
BANIYAS
TEL DAN
MASADA
ZAOURA
JUBBATA EL KHASHAB
KIRYAT SHEMONA
KEFAR SZOLD
7 Inf Div
EL ROM
KALA
Raful
JEBA
KAFR NASIJ
MANSURAH
EL QUNEITRA
GONEN
RAWIYE
KAFR SHAMS
Golan
SYRIA
NOTERA
1 Armd Div
KAFR NAFFAKH
EL HARRA
Ori's Bde
9 Inf Div
GADOT
EL KHUSHNIYE
Bnot Yaakov Bridge
JASIM
ROSH PINNA
Jordan
Heights
RAFID
ISRAEL
BUTMIYE
Ran's Bde
ALMAGOR
UYUN HADI
5 Inf Div
NAWA
KAFR AQIB
RAMAT MAGSHIMIM
TASIL
Lake Tiberias
TIBERIAS
Ruqqad
EL AL
EIN GEV
FIQ
HAON
Yarmuk
DEGANYA
TEL QAZIR
JORDAN

1967 CEASE-FIRE LINE
SYRIAN ATTACKS:
ARMOR
INFANTRY
APPROXIMATE LIMIT OF SYRIAN ADVANCE, MIDNIGHT 7 OCT 1973
ISRAELI MOVEMENTS
MILES 0 10
KILOMETERS 0 15

Far left: The initial stages of the fighting in the Golan.
Below: Moshe Dayan tours Israeli positions in the Golan shortly after the ceasefire.
Bottom: Israeli paratroopers on the Cairo-Suez road – west of the Suez Canal.
Right: The Israeli counterattacks against the Syrians and their allies.
Bottom right: A downed Egyptian pilot comes to earth near an Israeli armored unit.

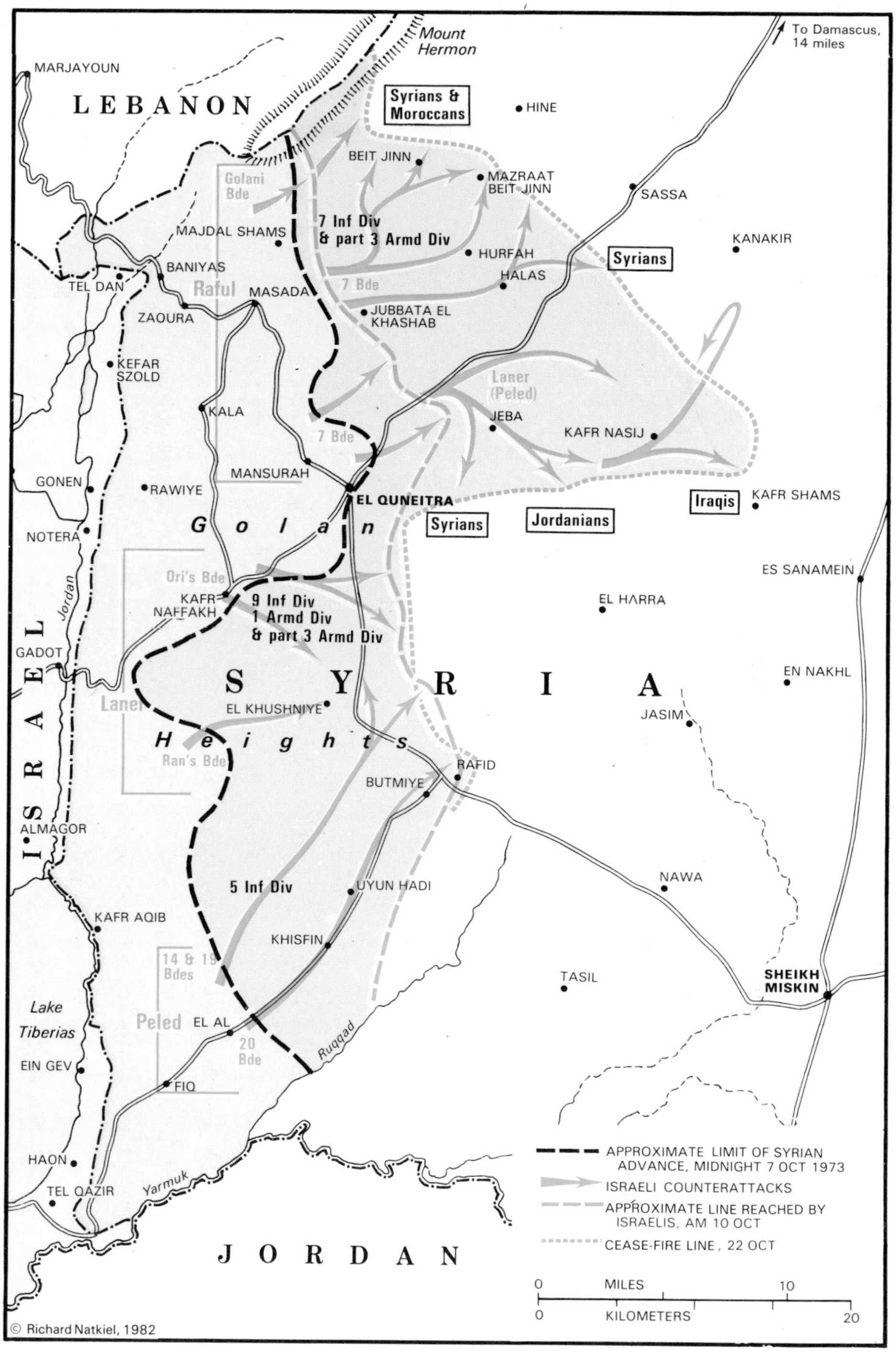

The Soviet Invasion of Afghanistan

In 1973 the King of Afghanistan was overthrown by Mohammed Daoud, who accepted Soviet military and financial assistance to back up Afghan claims to territory on the Pakistan side of the nation's frontier. Daoud was the victim of a Marxist coup in 1978, and Afghanistan's new leaders were largely Soviet-trained army officers who played on antipathies between the country's hard-line progressive and conservative factions. In 1979 Prime Minister Amin came to power and aggressively pushed a reform program that was widely resisted by rebels who clung to traditional feudal practices. Amin called on Soviet-armed helicopters to bombard villages rumored to be harboring rebels, and the smoldering ideological conflict blazed into open warfare.

The USSR soon staged a coup that replaced Amin with Babrak Karmal, regarded by the Soviets as a reliable Communist who would tread more softly than his predecessor. But peace did not follow, and by the summer of 1980 Red Army and Air Force units were operating in Afghanistan in growing numbers. The Afghan Army had become demoralized, and rebels dominated the countryside, subdued only briefly by punitive Soviet expeditions.

Soviet forces numbering up to 100,000 used helicopters and armored vehicles, but were handicapped by the lack of roads. Raids by helicopter gunships and ground-support aircraft on rebellious villages had little effect, even though the rebels had no way of opposing them. Almost a million refugees poured over the frontiers into neighboring Pakistan. Another half million went to Iran. By 1981 one in every seven Afghans had fled his country.

In 1982–84 the military situation remained at a stalemate, with Soviet troops making the cities safe for the regime but having little lasting sovereignty over the countryside. The Karmal Government persisted in its attempts to introduce social reforms based on Marxist principles in the teeth of popular resistance.

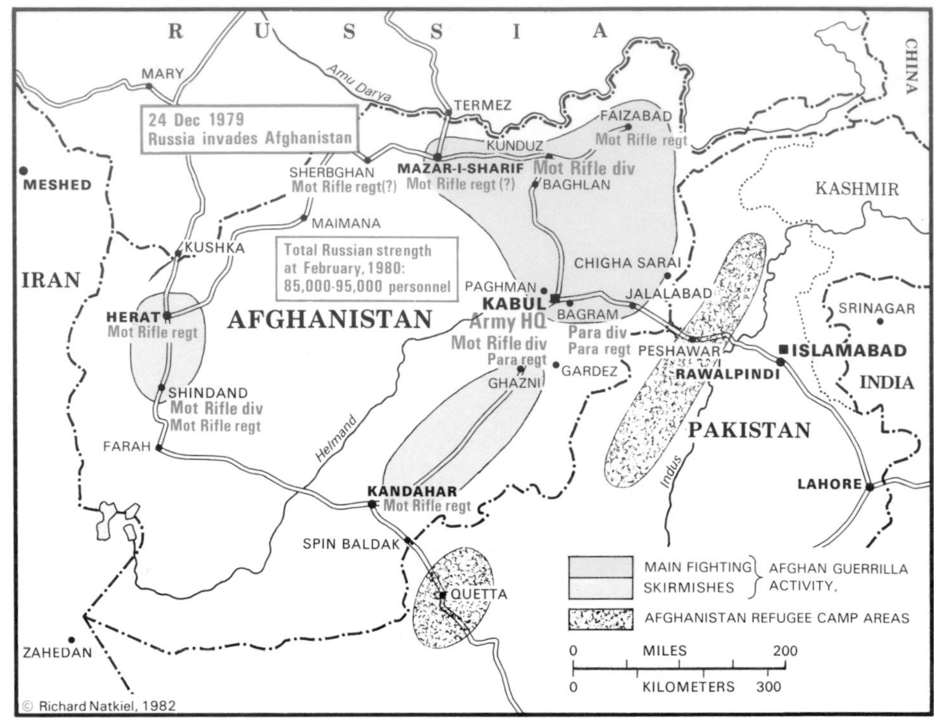

Above: The Soviet deployment in Afghanistan. Below: A BTR-60PB armored personnel carrier leads a column of Soviet vehicles through the streets of Kabul.

Right: A group of Afghan guerrillas pose with a typical assortment of weapons including, left, an AK-47 Kalashnikov assault rifle.

The Falklands Crisis

The Argentine invasion of the Falkland Islands on 2 April 1982 came as a shock not only to Britain but to the world; however, the status of the islands had been a source of dispute between Britain and Argentina for many years. The Argentines, who call the islands the Malvinas, still consider them a part of their country, but the islanders themselves insist on their allegiance to Britain. It had been suggested in negotiations over the years that sovereignty over the islands be transferred to Argentina, with Britain administering them on a 'lease-back' arrangement similar to that of Hong Kong vis-à-vis China. Britain had been unwilling to enforce this kind of policy over the objections of the islands' inhabitants.

Negotiations in early 1982 brought no progress, and the surprise invasion of the Falkland Islands and South Georgia by Argentine forces ensued. One possible motive was the Argentine military junta's desire to distract the nation's people from overwhelming economic problems. In any event, Argentina was dismayed by the speed and decisiveness of the British response. Britain mobilized extensive diplomatic support in the UN and among EEC partners who joined in imposing economic sanctions against the South American aggressor. The US remained neutral at first, then condemned Argentina's action. Diplomatic efforts to resolve the dispute were still under way when a British task force set sail for the South Atlantic.

The British Government requisitioned a number of merchant vessels, including luxury liners, to carry troops and supplies and serve as hospital ships. Two small carriers with Harrier aircraft seemed insufficient to hold off the Argentine Air Force, even with missile support from the ships, but they proved equal to their role in carrying out the British operation. The Argentine Navy played only a small part and suffered an early deterrence in the sinking of the cruiser *General Belgrano* by a British nuclear submarine.

South Georgia was easily recaptured by British forces, and the main landings at San Carlos soon followed. The first British formation to land was made up of elite Royal Marine and Parachute Regiment troops. Goose Green was captured after

TOTAL MARITIME EXCLUSION ZONES
BRITISH FROM 12 APRIL
ARGENTINE LATER
ARGENTINE AIR BASES

SOUTH ATLANTIC OCEAN

TRELEW
ARGENTINA
COMODORO RIVADAVIA
CHILE
RIO GALLEGOS
PUNTA ARENAS
RIO GRANDE
USHUAIA
FALKLAND IS.
STANLEY
SOUTH GEORGIA
SOUTH SANDWICH ISLANDS
S Thule Is

7 May
Britain extends exclusion zone (to Argentine shipping) outside 12 miles from coast

3 May
Argentine patrol boat sunk

Vulcan bombers from Ascension Is (3400 miles)

4 May
HMS Sheffield* struck by air-launched missile and sunk

25-26 April
South Georgia recaptured by British assault force. Argentine submarine badly damaged

Vulcan bomber and Sea Harrier strikes on airfields. Stanley airport bombed and bombarded

2 May
General Belgrano† torpedoed and sunk

*Destroyer
†Cruiser

0 MILES 500
0 KILOMETERS 800

SETTLEMENTS
ROADS
TRACKS
0 MILES 20
0 KILOMETERS 30

25 May
Atlantic Conveyor sunk (Container ship)

Dawn, 21 May
Beach-heads established by 3 Para, 42 and 45 Mar Cmdo Btns (North) 2 Para, 40 Mar Cmdo Btns (South). Diversionary landings elsewhere (C-in-C land forces J. Moore)

Night, 15 May
Commando raid destroys aircraft, ammunition and fuel dumps

C-in-C Argentine forces (Falklands), M. Menendez

PEBBLE ISLAND
Foul Bay
Middle Bay
SALADOR
DOUGLAS
PORT SAN CARLOS
3 Para Btn
RINCON GRANDE
JOHNSONS HARBOUR
PORT LOUIS
San Carlos Water
SAN CARLOS
Airstrip
TEAL INLET
27 May
GREEN PATCH
PORT HOWARD
Falkland Sound
2 Para Btn
Patrolling by 1/7 Gurkha Btn
AIRPORT
Mt Kent
31 May
STANLEY
Grantham Sound

Evening, 28 May
Argentine garrison surrenders after 12-hour battle

British ships sunk by Argentine aircraft in San Carlos area -
21 May: Ardent
24 " : Antelope } Frigates
25 " : Coventry (Destroyer)
Port Fitzroy
8 June: Sir Galahad (Landing ship)

DARWIN
GOOSE GREEN
Airstrip
FITZROY
BLUFF COVE
Choiseul Sound

4/8 June
British reinforcements landed.
8 June, landing ships Sir Galahad and Sir Tristram destroyed

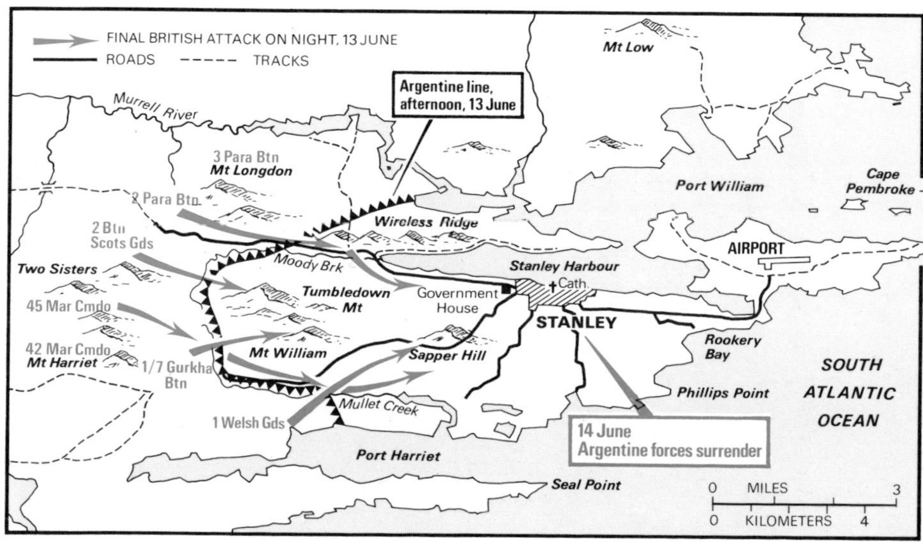

heavy fighting, and the British, reinforced by Ghurka and Guards units, pushed forward to surround and capture Port Stanley. Argentine forces were at least as numerous as British, but far from equal in training and morale.

President Galtieri of Argentina was forced to resign after the surrender, but British determination to hold the Falkland Islands, as shown on the battlefield, made it seem unlikely that the dispute had been resolved for good.

Left: The maps show the successive stages in the British reconquest of the Falklands. The Argentinian forces were taken by surprise by the British decision to land at San Carlos rather than make a more direct attack on Stanley, the islands' capital and principal settlement.
Bottom, far left: An Argentinian fighter-bomber passes low over a British support ship unloading supplies in San Carlos Water.
Below: A British Marine operating a Blowpipe antiaircraft missile. These weapons were relatively ineffectual against the major Argentinian aircraft but useful against helicopters and light attack planes.

Lebanon

Although Lebanon had managed to avoid being involved in earlier Arab-Israeli wars there had been repeated Israeli and Syrian interventions in the country from 1975 on. Dissensions had arisen between the Moslem and Christian elements in the population and the Israelis were angered by the presence of many supporters of the Palestine Liberation Organisation in the refugee camps. A United Nations force (UNIFIL) had attempted to keep the peace but in June 1982 the Israelis invaded once more with the aim of settling with the Palestinians once and for all.

The Israeli forces were soon fighting in Beirut but in August 1982 an agreement negotiated by US envoy Philip Habib called for Israeli withdrawal. An international peacekeeping force was to come into the area for a limited time. The Lebanese Government formally requested troops for such a force from the US, France and Italy, and 800 US Marines were assigned to Lebanon. Their orders were to assume a 'carefully limited non-combat role' that was to last for only 30 days.

The Marines joined French and Italian troops in Beirut on 25 August, and a week later all the Palestinians and their Syrian supporters were officially gone from the city. On 10 September the Marines returned to their ships offshore.

Three days later the newly elected president, Bashir Gemayel, was assassinated. The Israelis moved back into Beirut to control the violence that was expected to ensue, but their ill-judged admission of Christian-Phalangists into Palestinian refugee camps resulted in a vengeful massacre that shocked the world. President Ronald Reagan agreed to send back American troops, and on 29 September US Marines were assigned to guard the Beirut International Airport.

Less than four weeks later (23 October), a yellow Mercedes truck pulled into the Marine compound and drove straight into the entryway, where it exploded with terrific force, killing or trapping most of the 300 Marines inside. A similar attack killed almost 60 French troops. More US Marines died in this terrorist attack than in any single action of the Vietnam War. Popular sentiment in the US turned increasingly toward withdrawal from Beirut. Gradually the Lebanese government came to play a less and less effective role and in the spring of 1984 the peacekeeping troops were withdrawn, the last of them leaving in April.

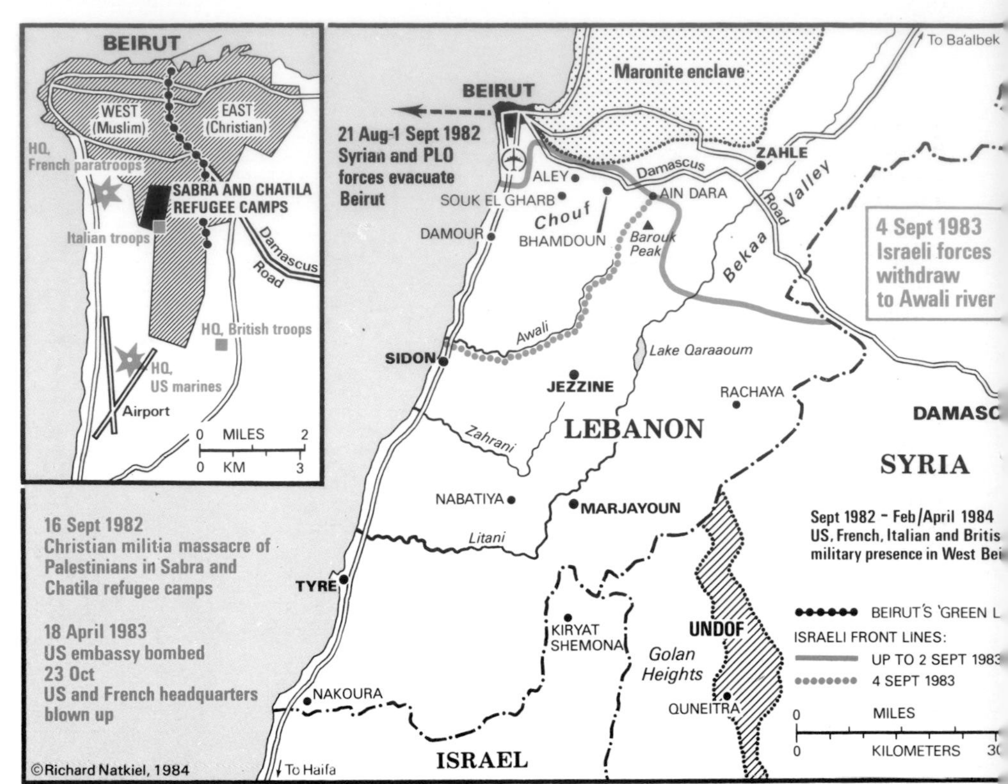

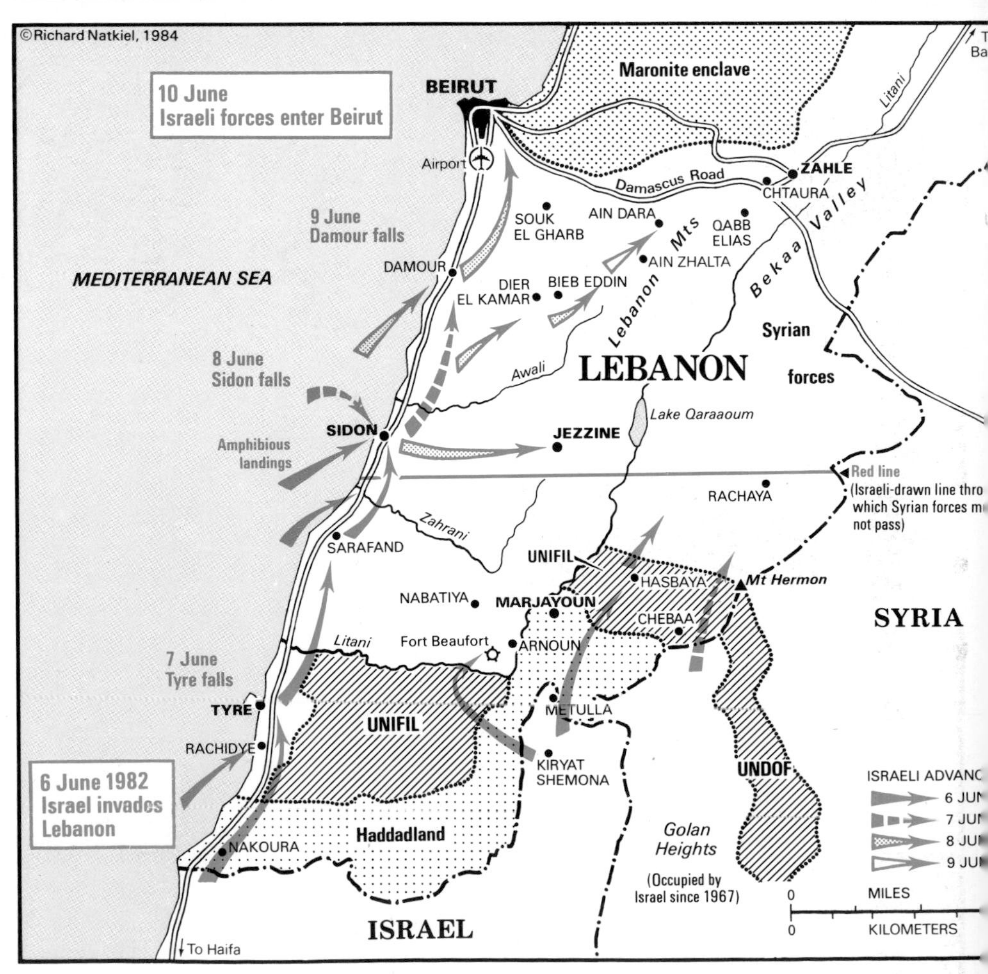

Grenada, 1983

For some time before its October 1983 intervention in Grenada, the US had been concerned about developments on the tiny Caribbean island. Its Marxist Prime Minister, Maurice Bishop, had invited Cuban workers and technicians to help construct a 10,000-foot airstrip (obviously built with Russian support) that he claimed would enhance tourism by making the island accessible to large planes. US observers believed it was designed to allow Soviet planes to 'service' Caribbean nations.

On 19 October a surprise coup by leftists more radical than the Marxists killed Bishop and about 100 other Grenadians; the insurgents took nominal control of the island. A round-the-clock curfew was imposed, but no clear leader emerged, and Grenada seemed headed for anarchy. The fact that there were ome 1000 Americans in residence there – ost of them students at St George's niversity School of Medicine – roused US pprehensions of another hostage crisis comparable to the Iranian experience. Requests for US intervention from six neighboring Caribbean nations were an additional factor in President Ronald Reagan's decision to send in troops.

Initial landings on 25 October were accomplished in secrecy by a small group of US Navy 'Seals' assigned to rescue the Governor-General, Sir Paul Scoon, who had been placed under house arrest by coup leaders. On the opposite side of the island, some 400 Marines in troop helicopters from the amphibious assault ship *Guam* landed at Pearls Airport. They were soon joined by hundreds of special-force Army Rangers who parachuted onto the new airstrip at Point Salines. The Marines secured their objective within two hours, but the Rangers faced heavy resistance, apparently originating in the area occupied by the Cuban workers. The Cubans were heavily armed – antiaircraft weapons included – and it took all day to clear the airstrip so that C-130s could land.

That afternoon the *Guam* sent ashore 13 amphibious vehicles, with 250 Marines and five tanks, to take Fort Frederick and its Richmond Hill prison outside St George, the capital. By the following day most organized resistance was at an end. Marines went to the rescue of the Navy Seals, who had been trapped at the Governor-General's mansion, and relieved the medical school campus, where hundreds of American students had been cut off by the revolutionaries. On 27 October the Atlantic Fleet Commander reported that 'All major military objectives on the island are secured.'

Total forces involved included some 500 Marines, 500 Rangers, 5000 paratroops of the 82nd Airborne Division and perhaps 400 members of the six-nation Caribbean force that had feared establishment of a Soviet regime on Grenada. Total American casualties were 18 dead and 67 wounded.

it: The competing factions and the fighting in e Lebanon.
ight: US plane and Cuban prisoners at Point alines airfield.
Below: US troops in Grenada.
Bottom: Maps of the Grenada action.

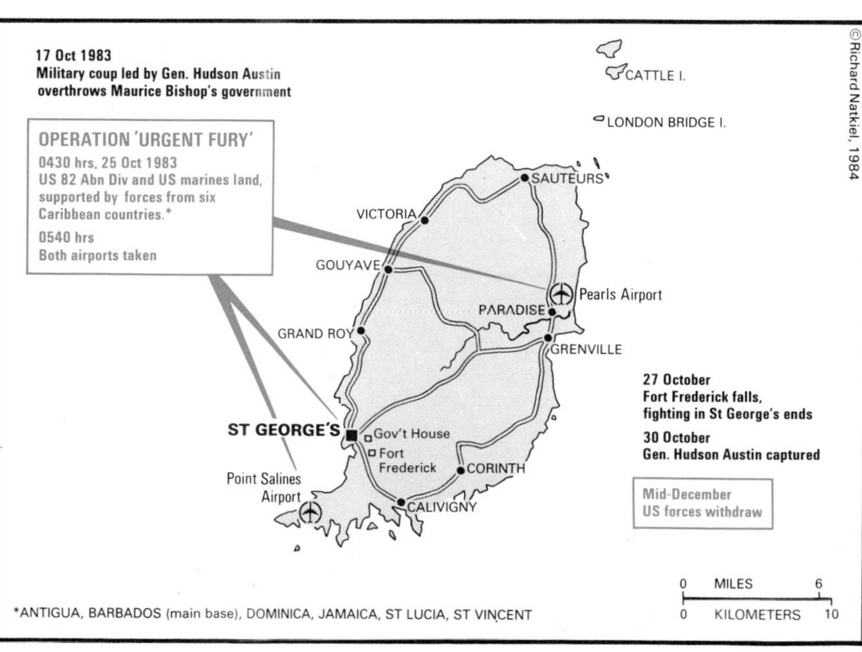

ACKNOWLEDGMENTS

The publishers would like to thank Adrian Hodgkins who designed this book. The following agencies and individuals kindly supplied the illustrations.

AP: p 141
Bison Picture Library: pp 62-63, 109
Bundesarchiv: pp 57 top, 58 both, 66, 80-81 both, 94, 98, 99 three
Crown Copyright, Royal Navy Fleet Photographic Unit: pp 156, 157
Fox Photos: p 61 bottom left
Paul Huldermann Collection: p 53 both
Robert Hunt Library: pp 29 top, 30 lower, 31, 34 both, 35, 41 both, 48 top, 57 bottom, 61 right, 84, 88-89 four 95, 137, 140 both
Imperial War Museum, London: pp 2, 21, 27, 30 top, 32-33 both, 39 both, 40, 67, 68, 85, 96-97 top, 108 both, 120 top, 132-133, 136, 139
Israeli Government Press Office: pp 4-5, 142 both, 143, 144-145 both, 147, 150-151 both, 152-153 three
Library of Congress: pp 10-11
National Maritime Museum, UK: pp 29 bottom, 78-79
Novosti Press Agency: pp 1, 8 bottom, 15-16, 24, 50 bottom right, 60, 72-73 both, 74, 92, 93 both, 102 both, 105, 112, 113 both, 124, 126, 127, 128
Ramplee-Smith Collection: 50-51 except 50 bottom right
Rijksinstitut voor Oorlogsdocumentatie, Amsterdam: p 65
Roger-Viollet: pp 54-55 both, 56
US Air Force: pp 37 top, 120-121 bottom two
US Army: pp 86, 111 bottom, 116-117, 119, 121 top, 122 both, 131 both, 138
US Department of Defense: p 159 both
US Marine Corps: pp 111 right, 135 both
US Navy: pp 117, 148
US National Archives: pp 7-8 top, 37 bottom, 43 bottom, 44, 45, 47, 71 both, 83 both, 91, 110, 130 both
Wide World Photos: pp 154, 155